ACADEMIC LEADERSHIP AND GOVERNANCE OF HIGHER EDUCATION

ACADEMIC LEADERSHIP AND GOVERNANCE OF HIGHER EDUCATION

A Guide for Trustees, Leaders, and Aspiring
Leaders of Two- and Four-Year Institutions

*Robert M. Hendrickson, Jason E. Lane,
James T. Harris, and Richard H. Dorman*

Foreword by Stanley O. Ikenberry

STERLING, VIRGINIA

Sty/us

COPYRIGHT © 2013 BY
STYLUS PUBLISHING, LLC.

Published by Stylus Publishing, LLC
22883 Quicksilver Drive
Sterling, Virginia 20166-2102

Library of Congress Cataloging-in-Publication Data
Hendrickson, Robert M.
  Academic leadership and governance of higher
education : a guide for trustees, leaders, and aspiring leaders
of two- and four-year institutions / Robert M. Hendrickson,
Jason E. Lane, James T. Harris, and Richard H. Dorman ;
Foreword by Stanley O. Ikenberry.—First Edition.
    pages   cm
Includes bibliographical references and index.
ISBN 978-1-57922-481-3 (cloth : alk. paper)
ISBN (invalid) 978-1-57922-880-4 (library networkable
e-edition)
ISBN (invalid) 978-1-57922-881-1 (consumer e-edition)
1. Universities and colleges—United
States—Administration—Handbooks, manuals, etc.
2. College administrators—United States—Handbooks,
manuals, etc.   3. Eduational leadership—United States—
Handbooks, manuals, etc.   I. Lane, Jason E.   II. Harris,
James T., 1958–   III. Dorman, Richard H.   IV. Title.
LB2341.H433   2013
378.1'01—dc23   2012018900

13-digit ISBN: 978-1-57922-481-3 (cloth)
13-digit ISBN: 978-1-57922-880-4 (library networkable
e-edition)
13-digit ISBN: 978-1-57922-881-1 (consumer e-edition)

Printed in the United States of America

All first editions printed on acid-free paper
that meets the American National Standards Institute
Z39-48 Standard.

Bulk Purchases

Quantity discounts are available for use
in workshops and for staff
development.
Call 1-800-232-0223

First Edition, 2013

10   9   8   7   6   5   4   3   2

To our wives,
Linda, Kari, Mary, and Bev
and
For the Glory of Old State

CONTENTS

ACKNOWLEDGMENTS

This book has been a labor of love. All four authors contributed equally to the formulation and writing of this book. Each of us, as a scholar and an education leader, has had a long-standing interest in understanding and improving the administration, management, and leadership of academic organizations. Collectively we have worked for numerous private and public colleges and universities, serving as faculty members, directors, deans, vice presidents, and presidents. In addition, we have served on and staffed boards of trustees and worked for a state-level department of higher education. Through all these experiences, we recognized that very limited resources exist to help academic leaders, external stakeholders, and lay board members understand the complexities of the academic organization and how it interacts with various aspects of society.

The initial idea for this book came from Robert M. Hendrickson, who for three decades has taught a graduate course titled Administration in Higher Education. The outline of this book resembles the outline of that course. Since each of the areas covered in this book has a vast literature, it is impossible for busy administrators to delve into this literature while meeting their administrative responsibilities and keeping current in their area of expertise. What was needed was a book that pulled together this knowledge and made it accessible and understandable to busy academic leaders, external stakeholders, and lay board members.

Three colleagues—Jason E. Lane, associate professor of educational administration and policy and director of education studies at the Nelson A. Rockefeller Institute of Government, State University of New York at Albany; James T. Harris, president of Widener University; and Richard H. Dorman, president of Westminster College in Pennsylvania—were intrigued by the idea of creating a book for academic administrators and joined Bob Hendrickson in developing the concept for this book.

This book is the culmination of dozens of years of practice and study. In conceiving and writing this volume, we spent countless hours debating various issues. While we underestimated the amount of work involved in this project, the discussions and debates that occurred during all-day meetings and many conference calls have greatly enriched our own understanding of the academy and, we believe, have enriched the volume. Our relationship as friends and colleagues has been strengthened, and we are thankful for the skills, talents, and understandings that each of us brought to this endeavor. Looking back we all agree that we had fun taking on this task and working together to complete it.

We owe a great debt of gratitude to many individuals who helped us in this process. As with any project such as this, our thinking has been influenced by a wide array of students, colleagues, mentors, and friends. There is no way to thank all who have in some small or large way helped with the development of this book or our own understanding of academic leadership.

Specifically, without the editorial work of Sarah Fuller Klyberg, doctoral candidate in higher education at Pennsylvania State University, this book would have never reached the publisher. Sarah took the writings of four authors with disparate perspectives and created a volume that provides a unity of voice. Her knowledge of higher education as a field of study, attention to detail, and sense of organization and flow of writing resulted in a publication that fosters the reader's acquisition of knowledge and understanding. She was gracious with criticism and was a pleasure to work with. Sarah and the authors experienced enriching conversations and acquired a deeper understanding of the field of higher education.

Ezekiel W. Kimball, doctoral candidate at Penn State in higher education, served in a consultative role from the very beginning of this project. His command of the literature in higher education and his advice contributed to its completion.

The research contributions of Erik S. Wessel and Rachel Frick-Cardelle, graduate students at Penn State, and Taya L. Owens, a graduate student at the University at Albany–SUNY, were critical for capturing the vast literature covered in this volume.

We would like to thank John von Knorring and the staff at Stylus Publishing. From the very beginning when we floated the idea to John, he felt a book on academic leadership would clearly fill a gap in the higher education literature and encouraged us to pursue this project.

Finally, we wish to thank our friend and valued colleague Stanley O. Ikenberry for his foreword to this volume. Few people in U.S. higher education have the richness of experience and the universal respect of so many in the academy as Ikenberry. His opening remarks provide the reader with a useful context and broad framework for understanding the myriad issues and challenges that appear throughout the book.

It is our hope that this volume will provide a useful guide and reference for many people who seek answers to complex questions concerning U.S. higher education. The book is intended for a wide audience of seasoned professionals in the field and laypeople alike. Regardless of the role one may have in relation to the administration and management of higher education, better decision making begins with better understanding. We hope that we have provided that for you here.

Robert M. Hendrickson
Jason E. Lane
James T. Harris
Richard H. Dorman

Academic Leadership and Its Consequences

I f academic institutions functioned in a stable environment, the demands for leadership would be modest. Vision, mission, programs, and policies could simply be put on automatic pilot. For colleges and universities, however, automatic pilots don't work. The environment is in continual flux, and the implications and consequences of these changes for the future of colleges and universities are often profound. Sound, authentic, creative, empowering leadership is indispensable, and it spells the difference between healthy, productive, sustainable academic institutions and programs and those that are in continual crisis, vulnerable, and failing.

One need only reflect on the change that has come about in higher education over the last century. The very mission and scale of colleges and universities have been transformed. Institutions are altering the ways and means of teaching and learning. New directions in research and service to society are evolving. The costs and benefits of the academic enterprise are in continual fluctuation and open to challenge. The roles of faculty are different, as are campus cultures. The very definition of precisely who is served and touched by academic institutions is in transition. Amid this whirlwind, the authors of this handbook on academic leadership make a conscious effort to think afresh about the challenges and opportunities of leadership. The main themes of the book are grounded in the argument that successful higher education institutions embrace three essential principles:

1. Sound institutional decisions must be based on a clearly articulated mission and set of core values.
2. Successful institutional adaptation to a changed environment must be grounded and aligned with the fundamental mission and core values.
3. Successful academic leaders must be able to create and foster partnerships, bringing diverse individuals and interests together around a shared vision and mission based on common values.

Each of these three themes surfaces throughout the book, and for good reason. Every decision and the very definition of each issue and problem is based on and defined by core values. The issue of access, for example, is embedded in fundamental human values that touch on equality of opportunity, notions of fairness, human rights, and our aspirations for our democracy and society. The issue of college costs must be understood as a never ending contest among competing interests and values, including the tensions between costs and quality, costs and vested interests, and costs and opportunity. The very meaning of quality itself can only be grasped in the context of a clearly understood and widely shared sense of mission and purpose. Defining, articulating, testing, promulgating, and applying these core values and a sense of mission is the most fundamental job of any academic leader.

Leading and managing change is clearly the most difficult and taxing challenge faced by academic leaders. Occupying a position of leadership and exercising the role of leader are entirely different. The first requires only a title. Too many positions of academic leadership are filled by those who occupy the chair and carry the title but fail to lead academic institutions in ways that enable them to adapt to a demanding environment, optimize their mission, align with values, and produce a lasting contribution to society. This handbook does not speak to the position of leadership, to title, or to mere survival skills; rather it speaks to the creative act, the behavior, the hard work and courage, and the art and skill of academic leadership.

The third theme that appears here and in the life of every effective academic leader is the notion of teamwork, collaboration, empowerment of others, and the art of coalition and team building. This is the essence of academic leadership and is indispensable to bringing about successful and enduring institutional change. Leadership is a team sport. It involves working with and inspiring other people. It involves effective and authentic communication based on the integrity of core values and clarity of mission.

Too often we think of the leader as reaching down to empower and bring along the followers, forgetting that communication and team building are a two-way street in which leaders almost always learn and receive more from the team than they give. Thinking of leadership as reaching down also fails to recognize that effective academic leaders reach out and reach up. Team building and collaboration doesn't begin and end in a department, a program, or an institution. It involves reaching out and building coalitions across departments, programs, and institutional boundaries. And truly creative leadership involves reaching up, building coalitions, and aligning with the larger forces of the institution's operation, and ultimately society itself.

Sound academic leadership is more important than ever before. At many higher education institutions mission is no longer obvious. Core values are no longer so obvious that they are self-executing. Change—in whatever form—is viewed as threatening. Regaining a clear vision and crafting consensus around core values is not easy when the larger environment is in a whirl, and individual interests and programs are threatened. Strengthening academic quality and performance while containing and reducing costs is a trick few administrators of institutions have mastered, and yet it is precisely the challenge facing all of U.S. higher education.

This book addresses the basic building blocks of 21st-century higher education. There is no easy three-step cookbook recipe, nor are there any pat answers to be found in the back of the book. Academic leadership is difficult. Almost always the way forward is ambiguous. Still, asking honest questions, defining and prioritizing the options, and gathering, valuing, and using evidence in decision making are the qualities that served successful leaders in the past, and those same habits will sustain those who lead in the future.

One fundamental fact merits repetition: Colleges and universities touch more lives more profoundly than any social institution in society. The strength of America's democracy, economic competitiveness, and quality of life, and the health of our communities, our culture, and the arts—all of this and more—rests on the quality and performance of academic institutions. U.S. higher education will be profoundly different in the 21st century. Bringing about change and understanding and managing the consequences will be the overriding challenges of academic leaders going forward. How well American higher education responds and performs will turn on the quality of leadership it receives.

Stanley O. Ikenberry

INTRODUCTION

O ver the past decade a significant transformation has occurred in the operating environment of higher education institutions. The United States has been engaged in two wars, the world economy has experienced the worst recession in 80 years, democratic reform movements have swept across the globe, and information technology has changed forever the way people communicate and share information. While adapting to change has always been a challenge for higher education, in recent years the pace of change has accelerated so rapidly that academic leaders face new and unprecedented demands, making it difficult to manage these challenges and adapt to new realities. In this environment, academic leaders must understand not only how to manage but also how to lead their institutions.

To be successful, academic leaders need to develop a broad understanding of how their college or university is structured and functions, and simultaneously understand the loci of decision making on institutional issues. They must also learn to cultivate relationships with myriad stakeholders including faculty, students, alumni, and parents by taking advantage of new communication tools such as social media. New environmental forces, such as changing demographics, increased competition, additional government regulations, and reduced state and federal funding for education, make leading these institutions more difficult than ever. In this environment, academic leaders who acquire new knowledge and skills on how to adapt will enhance their ability to thrive rather than simply survive in tough times. In other words, academic leaders must be more knowledgeable than ever about the effects of external pressures on their institutions and develop strategies to adapt to these influences.

A vast literature exists on administration, management, and leadership in higher education, but it tends to focus on the impact the environment, external forces, and internal issues have on research universities. The hallmark of higher education in the United States, however, is the diversity of institution types, each of which is affected differently by external and internal influences. To address this void in the literature, this book uses specific institutional examples to provide background and knowledge of the environment, organization, and management of U.S. colleges and universities.

Moreover, instead of focusing only on one level of academic leadership, this book addresses the management and leadership issues facing board members, presidents, provosts, vice presidents, deans, and department chairs, placing those issues in organizational and environmental contexts.

Three Essential Principles

The authors believe that colleges and universities have the potential to be the most influential institutions in society. Higher education's civic purpose, societal role, and extraordinary possibility for promoting the common good provide it with a unique opportunity to contribute powerfully to meaningful change in a global society. We suggest that the administrators of the institutions that have been most successful in the past in advancing the academy, as well as society as a whole, have embraced three common principles that have distinguished those institutions in the marketplace and helped them navigate tough times. We believe these same three elements will characterize successful colleges and universities in the 21st century:

1. Institutional decisions are made based on a core mission and set of values.
2. Institutional adaptation to environmental change is in alignment with the mission and core values.
3. Institutional leaders seek to create and foster democratic partnerships with myriad constituents.

It is important to note that administrators of institutions that have flourished over time have practiced all three principles, because no one element guarantees success on its own.

While higher education institutions today are diverse, global, and ever changing, the sheer sustainability of colleges and universities compared to other organizations over time is remarkable. As Kerr (1987) noted,

> About 85 institutions in the western world established by 1520 still exist in recognizable forms, with similar functions and with unbroken histories, including the Catholic church, the Parliaments of the Isle of Man, of Iceland and of Great Britain, several Swiss cantons and seventy universities. (p. 184)

Moreover, in the United States none of the original 30 industries listed on the Dow Jones Industrial Average in 1928 are on the list today, and many no longer exist at all, yet all 30 of the top universities in the country in 1928 still exist, and most of them would still be considered among the best (Geiger, 2004).

This record is important because a plethora of business articles suggest to the average reader that those in business and industry understand their missions as well or better than college and university administrators do because the primary mission of a business is to bring value to its shareholders. This focus on shareholder value makes the mission of these organizations seem simple and easy to understand. However, a simple focus on shareholder value does not appear to be enough to guarantee success over time. Similarly, engagement in teaching, research, and service does not guarantee a college's or university's success, as is evidenced by the hundreds of higher education institutions that have closed over the centuries. Rather, it is the combination of focusing on a specific mission, adapting to a changing milieu while maintaining a mission, and promoting democratic partnerships that has allowed institutions of higher learning to become arguably the most respected organizations in society today.

Organization of This Book

This book is intended to serve as a reference for scholars as well as a useful guide for professionals in the field of higher education. To make the subject matter more accessible, the book is divided into five parts. The first part introduces the reader to the scholarly field of higher education and establishes the contextual framework for the rest of the book. The second part investigates the multifaceted and often complex relationships that exist between institutions of higher learning and the external constituencies they encounter. The third unit focuses on how college and university presidents and their boards of trustees keep an institutional mission focused while adapting to changes in the environment, and the fourth unit analyzes how colleges and universities fulfill their core mission through shared democratic partnerships. The fifth part describes how effective academic leaders implement their institution's academic mission. We first discuss student learning and development through the curriculum and cocurriculum, after which we address issues of resource management, strategic planning, and the integration of external forces and internal constituencies.

We recommend that all readers review Part 1 before reading the rest of the book, as it sets the stage for the remaining chapters. The chapters in Parts

2 through 5 do not have to be read in successive order. They are designed as self-contained modules to provide the reader with a greater understanding of specific topics. Throughout the book, examples of certain colleges and universities and their leaders are cited as models of the application of theory to practice.

Moreover, we should note that this book draws specifically on the context of higher education in the United States. Institutions around the world, in developing and developed countries, could benefit from learning about and adopting our three themes: being mission driven, being adaptable, and being based on democratic partnerships. However, the contexts in which higher education institutions operate vary by country and state. Not embedding a book such as this in a specific context risks creating a volume so general in nature that it provides very little value to those reading it. As much as possible, however, we have sought to structure this book in such a way that those in other national contexts can distill lessons for their own work. Throughout the book, we use the terms *U.S.* and *American* interchangeably to refer to the U.S. context and not to the broader continental contexts of North and South America.

Note

Study questions for each chapter can be found at http://www.styluspub.com/resrcs/other/ALGHEQUESTIONS.pdf.

References

Geiger, R. L. (2004). *Knowledge & money: Research universities and the paradox of the marketplace*. Palo Alto, CA: Stanford University Press.

Kerr, C. (1987). A critical age in the university world: Accumulated heritage versus modern imperatives. *European Journal of Education, 22*(2), 183–193.

PART ONE

HISTORY, POLITICS, GLOBALIZATION, AND ORGANIZATIONAL THEORY IN HIGHER EDUCATION

Part One contains three chapters that introduce the reader to the scholarly field of higher education and provide tools for understanding the nuances of these complex organizations. While the focus of this book is on postsecondary education in the United States, its themes—understanding core mission, adapting to environmental change, and promoting democratic partnerships—can serve as a model for institutions across the globe.

In chapter 1 the basic premise of this book is outlined. We elaborate on the three essential principles that guide successful colleges and universities and provide a theoretical framework for understanding them. We also propose that leaders of institutions who wish to succeed in the 21st century will be wise to consider these three principles as they plan for the future.

Chapter 2 provides the reader with foundational information about the structure of organizations, the characteristics of academic institutions, and tools for understanding how to lead and manage colleges and universities. It develops contextual frameworks through environmental, historical, and political perspectives to understand colleges and universities as complex organizations. We also introduce readers to several leading organizational theories to help them understand the contemporary role of colleges and universities, as well as to help them navigate the complicated relationships within higher education institutions and with their myriad stakeholders.

Chapter 3 provides a framework for understanding the impact of globalization on postsecondary institutions. The chapter introduces readers to many of the current trends in globalization, including policy developments in other regions that may affect the work of U.S. institutions. It also provides practical administrative advice to maximize the benefits and minimize the negative effects of such trends. We also provide the readers with a checklist of items to consider when deciding whether to engage in multinational operations (e.g., joint degrees, twinning relationships, international branch campuses).

PRINCIPLES OF
ACADEMIC LEADERSHIP

I n the summer of 1994 a group of new college and university presidents
from around the world gathered at Harvard University to discuss their
roles as academic leaders. During that meeting, a small group of those
presidents (one of the authors was among them) had the opportunity to
meet with distinguished American sociologist the late David Riesman. The
purpose of the meeting was to expose these recently hired presidents to some
of the research Riesman and his colleagues at Harvard had been conducting
on successful academic institutions and the people who lead them.

After a brief presentation of the data he collected and the conclusions
he had drawn from his research, Riesman asked if there were any questions.
At first there was silence, but then one president raised his hand and asked
if there was any one thing he could do as the leader of his university to
guarantee he would be successful in his new role. Riesman paused, looked
directly at the man, and said, "Become the living embodiment of the mission
of the institution you serve." He went on to describe how a successful institution, and the people who lead it, understand the institution's basic purpose
or mission and make decisions in alignment with that specific mission. Riesman added that while there were no guarantees, institutions and leaders that
were mission driven and democratic in nature were more likely to weather
tough times successfully and adjust to challenges than those with less clear
direction and purpose.

In many ways, Riesman's advice to the new president seems obvious and
logical. It makes sense that leaders of institutions with a clear sense of purpose and direction would make better decisions about how to use scarce
resources and face changes in the environment with greater resiliency. Or
does it?

Conflicting Goals, Ambiguous Aims

Many scholars would have us believe that the basic purpose or mission of any institution of higher education could be described as having three basic components: teaching, research, and service. In *How Colleges Work*, Birnbaum (1988) stated that these three elements are interrelated, mutually reinforcing, and to some extent broadly describe the work of individual faculty members and the primary goal of the academy as a whole. Furthermore, he noted that as institutions of higher learning have become more diverse and complex, missions have not become clearer. Rather, they become more complex and create greater tensions between competing constituencies. These tensions may be best characterized by the decades-old conflict between teaching and research, that is, which one is the most prized activity within the academy.

Other scholars (Gross & Grambsch, 1974) have proposed similar ideas, mainly that the problem is not that college and university officials are unable to identify their goals and direction, but rather that they embrace too many conflicting goals, which causes more tension and leads to confusion about an institution's mission. Cohen and March (1974) were more direct when they stated that institutions of higher learning, specifically American universities, were really "organized anarchies" (p. 2) with ill-defined goals, ambiguous organizational processes, and ever changing boundaries.

Because of the increased complexity of higher education in the second half of the twentieth century, one may be led to believe that focusing on institutional mission is not as important as identifying and clarifying the roles and responsibilities of various constituents within the academy—primarily the board, administration, and faculty. Much has been written on the subject, and several major higher education accrediting bodies and associations, including the Association of Governing Boards of Universities and Colleges (1996) and the American Association of University Professors (n.d.), have issued statements on the importance and predominance of shared governance in the successful management of the academy. These statements speak to the difficulty of managing a complex organization and subscribe to the notion that good governance, however it may be applied at any particular institution, is the key to success in higher education—and is perhaps even a viable substitute for being mission driven. Indeed, with the predominance of literature on the importance of academic governance models, one could almost be led to believe that a good organizational structure is at the heart of institutional success, regardless of whether an organization is producing something that is desirable to the marketplace or related to its mission.

The notion that since institutions of higher learning are too complex to lead the best we can do is hope for collaboration and effective power sharing within wisely devised governance structures is myopic and one dimensional. A highly effective shared governance model is as much the product of an institution whose administrators understand its purpose or mission as healthy enrollments, strategic planning, and clear budgeting and management. In other words, leaders of healthy, thriving institutions understand their purpose and niche in the broader higher education community, and because of this knowledge, their institutions are better governed and positioned to succeed in tough times.

Importance of Being Mission Driven

What exactly does it mean to be mission driven? The literature is full of examples of the importance of a clear purpose or a set of core values that drives decision making at an institution. Welzenbach (1982) described mission as the "broad, overall, long term purpose of the institution" (p. 15). That broad purpose may be based on religious or philosophical tenets or may be driven by an institution's relationship to the state or federal government (Davies, 1986; Dewey, 1916; Kerr, 1964). Handy (1997) proposed that because of the growing complexity of life in a virtual world, organizations are not necessarily tied in tangible ways to a campus with buildings or a specific location. Under these conditions, the work of the academic leader is to help people in the institution understand how their work contributes to the mission regardless of the location, time, or place in which it is fulfilling its educational purpose. That task requires the college or university to have a distinctive mission, one that helps it to distinguish it from others.

Institutional leaders who clearly identify their mission and articulate in unequivocal terms what matters most to them have a greater opportunity to claim a distinctive position in the marketplace and to have the greatest impact on society. In his book on strategic planning, Keller (1983) emphasized the importance of an organizational charter in developing a clear mission for an organization that would help drive decision making at all levels. Maurrasse (2001) believed an institution's mission should address the overall reason for its existence and establish a set of norms and expectations of a "way of doing business" (p. 6).

For this book, the word *mission* refers to the purpose, philosophy, and educational aspirations of a college or university. A college's or university's educational philosophy or mission statement should direct an institution and its leaders. It should provide a rationale for the way a college or university administrator approaches decisions about every aspect of the academy, from whom the board selects to lead to what the curriculum should be to how resources should be distributed. In the end, it should provide the focus or glue that binds the organization together as well as offer the core values that guide the institution's decision making. In other words, a mission statement should help organization administrators determine not only what the institution will do but, equally importantly, what it will not do. As was pointed out earlier, the lack of a clear and distinguishing mission can diminish an institution's focus and lead to unclear goals and objectives, which in turn can create problems internally and externally.

BoardSource's (2010) authors outlined 12 principles of governance they believe powers exceptional boards. Among the 12 recommendations for board members are remaining strategic in their thinking, creating an ethos of transparency, and being results oriented. Most important, however, is the underlining theme that all decisions—from selecting new leadership to budgeting—must "ensure the congruence between decisions and core values" (p. 23). That is, exceptional board members recognize that their primary role is to mold and uphold the mission of the institution they serve.

The value of mission statements is exemplified by the fact that all major accrediting bodies require that an institution demonstrate that its mission is appropriate and achievable in some reasonable manner. For example, the authors of *Characteristics of Excellence in Higher Education* (Middle States Commission on Higher Education, 2008) require that institutions seeking accreditation or reaffirmation be compliant with a specific set of standards and that each standard be "interpreted and applied in the context of the institution's mission and situation" (p. viii). The authors explained that an institution's mission "defines the institution, delineates the scope of the institution, explains the institution's character and individuality, and articulates values as appropriate" (p. 1). Furthermore, they argued that the main purpose of governance is to realize fully the stated mission of the college or university.

The mission of an institution has long been believed to be important in the creation of the academic curriculum and the promotion of democratic ideals. For example, in 1977 the Carnegie Foundation for the Advancement of Teaching published a report in which it asserted that "governing boards have a responsibility for making the institutional mission an explicit instrument of educational policy" (p. 258). In 1987 Boyer wrote a report on the state of undergraduate education in which he noted that several things reduce its quality. In his opinion the main problem was a lack of a clear understanding of the goals and purposes of higher education. In other words, he discovered that while some colleges and universities do reasonably well in helping students understand and even become competent in specific fields, most higher education institutions lack a clear sense of direction or purpose, which ultimately diminishes an undergraduate's education. The implication is clear: Institution administrators who understand their institution's core purpose and tie it to their educational outcomes provide the richest learning environments for their students.

In this book we make the case that one of the core purposes of all colleges and universities is to promote democratic ideals. In fact, evidence suggests that the broad support American colleges and universities have enjoyed over the centuries is because of an implicit understanding that higher education exists in part to help our democracy flourish. It is not enough, however, for administrators, faculty, and staff of colleges and universities to encourage students to develop into responsible citizens equipped to work collaboratively in a global society. Rather, they must model the same behavior. Institutions can best exemplify this aspect of their mission through the creation of reciprocal, democratic alliances locally and globally.

In their discussion on civic education, Colby, Ehrlich, Beaumont, and Stephens (2003) argue that the schools that are most successful in promoting a democratic agenda have a core institutional commitment that is "intentional and holistic" (p. 9) and shapes most, if not all, aspects of a student's experience while in school. In describing the more successful models of civic education, Colby and associates reaffirm that the mission of an institution is the starting point for the creation of a unique learning environment.

Having a clear sense of mission not only improves a college's or university's ability to obtain important accreditations, has a positive impact on student learning outcomes, and promotes civic education. It also helps institutions' trustees to assess leadership. In an essay by Colgan and de Russy (2006), sponsored by the Institute for Effective Governance in Higher Education, the authors argue that it is imperative for trustees to tie the assessment of a president to the institution's three most critical documents: its mission statement, strategic plan, and corresponding budget.

Adjusting to an Ever-Changing Environment

Being mission driven is no guarantee that an institution will enjoy success, however. In fact, Chait, Ryan, and Taylor (2005) suggest institutions will suffer if their board members assume that being mission driven insulates them from threats from outside the academy. Their research shows that administrators who have chosen to ignore environmental factors such as changes in technology or enrollment trends because they believe they are mission driven have done so at their peril. Therefore, boards and institutions that have found ways to engage continually in boundary-spanning assessment and planning are better able to adjust to the ever changing environment and ensure that the mission of the institution remains relevant.

Being mission driven does not mean that an organization cannot adapt to change. Instead, being mission driven allows an institution to use its mission as a lens to interpret changes in the environment and connect institutional aspirations with what is happening in the world. For example, most early colonial liberal arts colleges emphasized the classics for all students, which included language training in Greek, Latin, and Hebrew. As Rudolph (1962) stated in his history of American higher education, these languages served as "tools with which teacher and student found their way" (p. 25) through ancient texts. Today those languages, while still offered at some institutions, are not required because of the broad access everyone has to translations of those texts. Although core language requirements may have changed in response to a major environmental shift, no one would suggest that those institutions are not fulfilling their mission as liberal arts colleges because they no longer require those texts to be taught in their original languages.

The ability of academic leaders to understand and adjust to changes in the external environment while remaining in alignment with the core values of their college or university requires the discipline to interpret change through the lens of their institution's mission. For example, when developing a strategic plan, leaders must scan the external landscape as well as the internal workings of their institution to ensure that the future direction of their institution will be in alignment with its core values. This discipline is easy to ignore, however, when colleges and universities face environmental threats, and such disregard has led many administrators of higher education organizations to neglect their core mission in favor of becoming more like institutions they believe are more prestigious or ranked more highly.

A risk of emulating other colleges and universities in the hope of acquiring resources and prestige is *mission creep* (Lane, 2005). A particular problem with mission creep is not that schools have added new programs or services to enhance their mission, but rather that the additions make them more closely resemble other institutions in the marketplace. In a 2001 letter to the

California legislature, Clark Kerr described mission creep as "a phenomenon in which one segment of higher education redefines its mission to include the responsibility already being performed by another" (as cited in Lane, pp. 4–5). Beyond diminishing the diversity of higher education institutions, this mimicking of another mission to attain additional resources or prestige rarely results in a sustainable model of education and often moves an institution away from its original purpose.

The practice of imitation as a means to advance a college's or university's reputation differs significantly from the historical tradition of major shifts through which new institution types emerged. For example, the Morrill Act of 1862 facilitated the development of land-grant institutions, which advanced the American priority of agricultural and industrial education. The emergence of the German research university in the late 19th century had a tremendous impact on higher education in Europe as well as in the United States, and the creation of community college systems in the 20th century expanded access to higher education to many more Americans. Over the years, individual states have expanded the missions of particular higher education sectors to meet societal demands, but in these cases expansion of mission did not mean copying other institutions. Rather, through these reforms new institutions with distinct missions were developed.

Administrators of colleges and universities that are mission driven yet responsive to societal change do not allow their institutions to creep into an area that is incongruent with what they are or what they aspire to be. Rather they only add programs, services, or responsibilities that advance their basic purpose and are in harmony with their core values. Deciding what to add (or eliminate) is best completed through a rigorous, systematic, and ongoing planning and assessment process that leads to institutional renewal. Such a process is a sign of institutional vigor and sustainability and typically leads to better decision making and resource allocations. Institutional renewal in alignment with the mission is enhanced when the process has transparent aims and is inclusive of myriad constituents. In other words, the process of institutional renewal and growth is imbued with and guided by basic democratic decision-making principles that view participants as partners in the process.

Importance of Democratic Partnerships in Advancing the Academy

So far we have made the case that alignment with mission is paramount in all decision making in higher education. Moreover, we have argued that institutional renewal and change should be tied to a systematic assessment process in harmony with the core values of the organization. The remaining element of effective academic administration is ensuring that all decision making is congruent with democratic principles commonly associated with effective shared governance.

It is important to recognize that ultimate responsibility for any institution of higher learning rests with its governing board. Governing boards are required to have authority over all matters pertaining to the operation of the organization including academic, administrative, financial, and compliance issues. Although they retain ultimate authority, governing boards delegate their responsibilities through a shared governance model that is tied to the mission, history, and traditions of their institutions. While all shared governance models have unique characteristics, it is not the model that matters, but whether the institution has developed a democratic way to share governance.

Colleges and universities that are mission driven and have developed a process for institutional renewal also need to develop ways to engage their diverse constituencies. Such engagement requires time for appropriate discourse, is respectful of the distinctive role of each constituent group, and fosters an environment of mutual understanding and respect. To accomplish these goals, administrators of an organization must view each constituent as a partner in the shared governance process and adhere to basic democratic principles such as transparency, inclusiveness, and accountability. Adhering to these principles does not mean that everything is open to debate and a vote. Rather, it ensures that there is a mechanism for civil and rational discourse to occur, and that in the end the appropriate people in the governance structure are held accountable for the decisions that are made.

For many, this matter of accountability is the sticking point in governance. Board members have fiduciary and legal responsibilities that make them personally liable for damages, and presidents' and other senior administrators' jobs are on the line for their decisions. In contrast, faculty members have neither fiduciary responsibility nor career accountability for the decisions in which a typical governance structure allows them to participate. When tenure is considered, the lack of accountability within the faculty is almost ironclad. Fortunately, at most colleges and universities the majority of faculty members involved in governance understand these issues and participate with the best interests of the institution at heart.

Abraham Flexner (1930), an early 20th-century educator, described colleges and universities as organisms, and Kerr (1964) believed the various components of those organisms are "inextricably bound" (p. 20). If an institution of higher learning is an organism, to remain robust and healthy, the various components within it must discover ways to function in unison and recognize that no single element is predominant. In real terms, this realization requires a balance among and between an institution's various constituencies. While the ultimate responsibility for an institution rests with its governing board, it would be unrealistic to think that any board could manage every aspect of an organization as complex as a college or university. Institutions that create democratic processes to share this management fare better over time.

Unfortunately, shared democratic governance often is thought of only as an internal mechanism for ensuring that an institution can continue to function effectively. In highly effective institutions, however, the same principles and practices used inside the academy also apply to dealings with external groups and issues. Colby et al. (2003) assert that commitment to reasoned and honest discourse and respect for others are two basic values all colleges and universities should uphold, and those same values should guide decision making when dealing with issues outside the academy. The very notion that what is considered good democratic practice within the institutional governance structure is what should be modeled when dealing with people and organizations outside it is an idea that has been part of the lexicon of higher education for centuries but only recently has reemerged as a leading indicator of institutional strength and rigor. No longer can the members of colleges and universities remain inside their ivory towers and expect to be relevant to the outside world. The events of the second half of the 20th century coupled with the globalization of higher education has rendered such a quaint idea obsolete in the 21st century.

If the academy desires to maintain its exalted place in democratic society, the sharing of authority through thoughtfully designed and institutionally appropriate democratic processes cannot simply be an ideal practiced by college and university administrators within their own walls; it must be an imperative in their work outside the academy as well. Moreover, if institutions of higher learning do not engage their students in democratic and responsible ways, how can leaders of colleges and universities expect their students to behave as responsible members of society once they graduate? Over the past decade, many school officials have decided that one way to demonstrate their commitment to acting in a democratic and responsible way is by incorporating these principles into the learning environment. The rapid growth of service-learning, community-based learning, and other forms of experiential learning—in which faculty lead students in the "active construction of knowledge" (Colby et al., 2003, p. 2) requires the teacher and the student to consider the impact of their work on others and engage in democratic practices that advance democratic partnerships, scholarship, and learning.

In this book, we assert that higher education institutions that have committed to three essential principles—being mission driven, practicing adaptability in alignment with that mission, and perpetuating democratic partnerships—have consistently fared better than those institutions that have not adhered to these ideas. Therefore, administrators of institutions should consider them as key building blocks for success in the future. In the chapters that follow, these three principles are applied to the study and practice of effective academic administration and provide a framework for the reader to comprehend the nuances of the complex organizations that are colleges and universities.

References

American Association of University Professors. (n.d.). *1940 statement on principles of academic freedom and tenure.* Retrieved from http://www.aaup.org/AAUP/pub sres/policydocs/contents/1940statement.htm

Association of Governing Boards of Universities and Colleges. (1996). *Renewing the academic presidency: Stronger leadership for tougher times.* Washington, DC: Author.

Birnbaum, R. (1988). *How colleges work: The cybernetics of academic organization and leadership.* San Francisco, CA: Jossey-Bass.

BoardSource. (2010). *The handbook of nonprofit governance.* San Francisco, CA: Jossey-Bass.

Boyer, E. L. (1987). *College: The undergraduate experience in America.* New York, NY: HarperCollins.

Carnegie Foundation for the Advancement of Teaching. (1977). *Missions of the college curriculum: A contemporary review with suggestions.* San Francisco, CA: Jossey-Bass.

Chait, R., Ryan, W. P., & Taylor, B. E. (2005). *Governance as leadership: Reframing the work of nonprofit boards.* Hoboken, NJ: Wiley.

Cohen, M. D., & March, J. G. (1974). *Leadership and ambiguity: The American college president.* New York, NY: McGraw-Hill.

Colby, A., Ehrlich, T., Beaumont, E., & Stephens, J. (2003). *Educating citizens: Preparing America's undergraduates for lives of moral and civic responsibility.* San Francisco, CA: Jossey-Bass.

Colgan, C., & de Russy, C. (2006). *Essays in perspective: Assessing the university president*. Washington, DC: Institute for Effective Governance in Higher Education.

Davies, G. K. (1986). The importance of being general: Philosophy, politics, and institutional mission statements. In J. C. Smart (Ed.), *Higher education: Handbook of theory and research* (Vol. 2, pp. 85–102). New York, NY: Agathon Press.

Dewey, J. (1916). *Democracy and education: An introduction to the philosophy of education*. New York, NY: Free Press.

Flexner, A. (1930). *Universities: American, English, German*. New York, NY: Oxford University Press.

Gross, E., & Grambsch, P. V. (1974). *Changes in university organization, 1964–1971*. New York, NY: McGraw-Hill.

Handy, C. (1997). Unimagined futures. In F. Hesselbein, M. Goldsmith, & R. Beckhard (Eds.), *The organization of the future* (pp. 377–383). San Francisco, CA: Jossey-Bass.

Keller, G. (1983). *Academic strategy: The management revolution in American higher education*. Baltimore, MD: Johns Hopkins University Press.

Kerr, C. (1963). *The uses of the university*. Cambridge, MA: Harvard University Press.

Lane, J. E. (2005, November). *Politics of mission creep: A framework for understanding the phenomena*. Paper presented at the annual meeting of the Association for the Study of Higher Education, Philadelphia, PA.

Maurrasse, D. J. (2001). *Beyond the campus: How colleges and universities form partnerships with their communities*. New York, NY: Routledge.

Middle States Commission on Higher Education. (2008). *Characteristics of excellence in higher education* (12th ed.). Philadelphia, PA: Author.

Morrill Act of 1862, 7 U.S.C. 301 et seq. (1862).

Rudolph, F. (1962). *The American college and university: A history*. New York, NY: Random House.

Welzenbach, L. F. (Ed.). (1982). *College and university business administration*. Washington, DC: National Association for College and University Business Officers.

2

UNDERSTANDING ACADEMIC
ORGANIZATIONS

Among the most notable features of U.S. higher education are the rich diversity of institution types and the inherent complexity that accompanies their administration and management. This diversity has arisen not from any purposeful design but through a centuries-long evolutionary process that reflects the educational aspirations of myriad religious, individual, social, and governmental entities seeking independently to express their higher education ideals within a democratic society that permitted and encouraged organizational individuality and creativity.

The consequence of this historical evolution of higher education is the enormous diversity of choice available to those seeking to attend a college or university. According to the Almanac of Higher Education (2011), there are 4,495 accredited institutions of higher learning in the United States. Of these, 1,672 are public, 1,624 are independent nonprofit, and 1,199 are for profit, with nearly two thirds of all institutions offering degrees at the bachelor's level or above. Excluded from this vast number of postsecondary institutions are those organizations offering career and technical programs of less than two years and continuing education programs.

Given this rich organizational diversity, how can the subject of administration and management be approached to account for the vast differences that exist? Leadership and decision making by academic administrators, regardless of institution type, become more informed when they are first accompanied by a basic understanding of the uniqueness of academic organizations on several levels: typological, organizational, and contextual. The degree of nuanced understanding of each of these levels increases as one progresses through this conceptual hierarchy toward each individual institutional level within it.

Typological differences among higher education organizations are largely a function of historical development and institutional mission. Organizationally, colleges and universities share certain internal normative behaviors and processes that differentiate them from nonacademic organizations. However, each college or university must be understood within its own institutional context. Every institution of higher learning in the United States is idiosyncratic. Each possesses a unique history and organizational culture resulting from etiological circumstances determined by its founding; mission; level and source of resources; structure; and, most significantly, the institution's organizational ethos, which characterizes how the stakeholders have come to interact and behave collectively.

This chapter is meant to provide the reader with a broad overview of the academic organization and its internal operations. It addresses several important questions: How and why are academic organizations different from other organization types? What are the central characteristics and defining features of all academic organizations? Through what perspectives can the academic organization best be understood? What theories of leadership help us understand these complex organizations? What decision-making models are effective in achieving institutional goals? A fundamental understanding of the challenges inherent in the administration and management of higher education organizations can best be achieved by addressing these key questions.

To address these questions, the chapter is divided into three parts. Part One starts with a broad overview of academic institutions as special organizational entities. Within this section we examine the nature of organizations in general and the characteristics of colleges and universities specifically by applying key theories that help us understand their complexity and structures and processes as different from those of other organizational types. A short historical perspective begins the section to provide a useful context for the reader. Part Two examines the operating structure of academic organizations, first describing the different types of functions within colleges and universities and then presenting three models of academic governance. Finally, Part Three focuses on decision making and academic leadership, and selected theories that can help academic leaders better understand how to administer the complex decision environments in which they work.

Part One
Academic Institutions as Organizations: History, Typology, and Characteristics

An important theme of this book is that effective administration and management of higher education institutions are best achieved when individuals occupying administrative roles throughout the organization understand and embrace in a shared fashion the unique culture of the institution they serve. The emergence and evolution of colleges and universities in America since the early 17th century is largely a study of the American spirit itself, for few social institutions so harmoniously reflect the ideals, aspirations, beliefs, and competitive spirit of the United States and its people as the growth and development of its higher education organizations. Today's panoply of over 4,400 institutions include, but are not limited to, two-year community colleges, traditional four-year small liberal arts colleges, regional and state universities, large research universities, universities devoted only to professional preparation (such as medical or engineering schools), proprietary institutions, seminaries and rabbinical colleges, and a host of universities providing education exclusively through online means.

This impressive number and array of institutions and the institution types they represent have been a particular problem when attempting to analyze the work performed and the outcomes produced by them in terms of their individual institutional effectiveness and the shaping of public policy relating to the overall efficacy of U.S. postsecondary education. In 1970 the Carnegie Foundation for the Advancement of Teaching (2012) adopted an institutional classification coding structure in an attempt to provide researchers and policy makers with a useful matrix institutions could be compared and contrasted with between and among their many different types. Popularly known today as the Carnegie Classification, it has assumed a singular and essential role as the definitive source of categorizing and organizing colleges and universities into specific institution types for the purpose of research and public policy development. In addition, various publications for the general public have used these classifications as a sorting mechanism when attempting to rate institutions on a host of different measures.

Responding to the rise of new institution types, such as the for-profit sector, and the broadening of institutional missions to serve nontraditional student populations, the Carnegie Foundation has altered the classification structure numerous times to reflect a more layered and complex higher education system. The current classification system seeks to compare and contrast similarities and differences among and between institutions using data provided by institutions themselves through the Integrated Postsecondary Education Data System compiled by the National Center for Education Statistics. The Carnegie Foundation notes that the greater level of specificity now seen in the classification system is based upon answers to three general questions: What is taught? To whom? In what setting? In addition to yielding a more definitive and descriptive richness of the U.S. higher education landscape, the latest classification system seeks to lessen tendencies by some observers to ascribe qualitative and hierarchical judgments between different types of institutions. The resulting typological matrix employed today involves scores of classifications and subclassifications that are impressive in their diversity and daunting in their comprehensiveness.

An understanding and appreciation of these organizational differences is beneficial to the effective operation of the academic enterprise. This chapter reviews important historical and organizational factors that distinguish higher education organizations from other organizational types, giving special focus to the concept of democratic ideals and shared governance principles that have come to characterize the manner in which the academy's stakeholders interact to fulfill their individual roles in the organization's management and operation.

Historical Development of the Academic Institution

Today's colleges and universities were born from an organizational and evolutionary lineage that ranks among the most enduring of humanity's intellectual and social creations. In addition to its longevity, when compared with corporate organizations as mentioned in chapter 1, the modern academy continues to enjoy high regard by the public at large and is viewed as one of the United States' most important social institutions. These institutions' status and longevity are all the more noteworthy since over the centuries colleges and universities have taken a plethora of forms, and complex decision-making structures have emerged within them to accommodate the various internal and external constituencies competing for authority and legitimacy. Three main factors have contributed to this impressive state of permanence: (a) historical antecedents that established strong intellectual traditions, (b) the application of democratic principles that has encouraged individualism in the expression of educational ideals, and (c) the richness of diversity among those who claim legitimacy in the execution of the organizations' missions. An appreciation of these three factors is important to render more informed management and administration of higher education organizations, which is why they are deserving of mention here.

The longevity of higher education organizations rests in part on the many historical traditions that have followed their development. In his narrative on the history of U.S. higher education, Lucas (2006) noted that the precursors of the modern college and university essentially began in the medieval period, between the 11th and 15th centuries. Individuals with shared common interests in learning about specific disciplines collectivized into guilds governed by representatives elected from within the organizations. Often, those elected into oversight responsibilities were reluctant to assume such managerial duties because of the friction it caused among and between them and their peers. Vestiges of those early frictions continue to exist today among contemporary faculties. As organized entities, these shared social relationships developed into intellectual collectives exhibiting an organizational autonomy legitimized through the unique knowledge possessed by the organizations' members. Lucas notes that the strongest resemblance between the medieval university and the academic institution of today rests "in the sense of corporate, institutional identity, together with an elaborate system of rights, privileges, prerogatives, and special forms of academic authority" (p. 68). This authority was exercised even in the earliest centuries of higher education, when "once securely established, universities did not hesitate to intervene in public affairs, to air grievances before kings and popes alike, to offer advice, and to pass upon a variety of important legal and religious questions" (p. 69).

The relative autonomy enjoyed by the medieval guilds provided a historical foundation for new forms of higher education to emerge in the earliest years of the United States. Though the earliest American colleges barely resemble any of the higher education organizations of today, the European model of individual and independent guilds provided a historical template for creativity and individuality that permitted highly varied organizational interpretations on what higher education should look like in the development of a learned society.

As a new U.S. society itself was emerging, these fledgling institutions responded to a variety of environmental influences to help shape and sustain them. They were able to do so in part because of their independence and the ability to adapt through that independence. In his history of U.S. higher education, Thelin (2004) noted that the richness of diversity in U.S. higher education emerged as much from influences of local, state, and regional factors as from any national trends that mirrored the development of America from the time of the founding of Harvard College in 1636. Much like the rise of entrepreneurism that characterized the new American spirit, higher education became, according to Thelin, America's "cottage industry" (p. 41). Especially during 1785–1860, Thelin argued, higher education witnessed

> a period of extreme innovation and consumerism, with virtually no government accountability or regulation. Yet, it was not a period of chaos for higher education, because the college displayed a pattern of both initiation and response that was very much in tune with the nation's changing geographic, demographic, and economic character. (p. 41)

The factors of historical and intellectual autonomy born of a rich and embedded European medieval tradition, coupled with creative adaptation demanded by the necessities of adjusting to the societal needs of an emergent nation, produced a level of higher education organizational diversity that would later become the hallmark of U.S. higher education.

Geiger (2005) chronicled 10 generations of development in the historical evolution of the United States' colleges and universities, each lasting about 30 years from the founding of Harvard College in 1636 to the present. He charted these generations from two perspectives: (a) student origins that traced the diversity of students and (b) destinations that defined the outcomes sought for those students as a result of their education. This origins and destinations perspective is particularly useful when examining the diversity and uniqueness of academic organizations because it speaks to the multiple forces of individuals, religious bodies, governments, and foundations, among others, that exercised significant influence in the formation of today's wide array of institution types. Speaking to the democratic principles that guided this evolutionary process, Geiger stated, "Underlying the fortunes of individual institutions . . . lay fundamental questions stemming in large measure from the . . . putative republican model: Who owned the colleges? What was their mission? What should students be taught? And how could they be controlled" (p. 45). As the societal needs of a growing United States expanded and matured, new institutions of higher education emerged throughout this generational progression, but, just as important, existing institutions adapted to a changing environment in a fashion typical of the entrepreneurial spirit of the nation. A noteworthy irony about U.S. higher education has been its ability to adapt and conform to the external influences that created and shaped it over the centuries while possessing an organizational DNA often steeped in inflexible tradition and a codified set of fixed rights and organizational privileges that hearken to its earliest European roots.

The implications of these historical and developmental factors for the manner that colleges and universities should ultimately be managed and administered are significant. Basic to any managerial function within the academy is a firm understanding of the particular mission of one's institution, which emanates from the societal and historical traditions it was founded on. "The key to being effective and the ability to make change begins first with an accurate assessment of the type of organization in which you work" (Julius, Baldridge, & Pfeffer, 1999, p. 114).

The Nature of Organizations

Before we explore the unique characteristics of academic organizations, it is important to describe the nature of organizations. According to Scott and Davis (2007), "Most analysts have conceived of organizations as *social structures created by individuals to support the collaborative pursuit of specified goals*" (p. 11). Indeed, we live in a world of organizations. Businesses, civic groups, churches, and other charitable entities are all organizations. Because of the ubiquity of organizations, for more than a century, scholars have been trying to answer the question: "How does an organization go about doing what it does and with what consequence for its people, processes, products, and persistence?" (Weick, 1976, p. 1).

The study of organizations is at the core of much of higher education study and research, and serves as a foundation for much of this book, as it focuses on the production of knowledge relevant to problem solving or decision making within organizations (see, for example, Kast & Rosenzweig, 1970). While this book is intended to be understood by readers without an advanced knowledge of this subject, we feel it is important to provide a broad overview of the field. Attempts to understand and characterize organizations, academic and otherwise, focus on common elements: environment, strategy and goals, work and technology, formal and informal structures, and people (Scott & Davis, 2007). Understanding the essence of an organization requires looking at all its various aspects.

Environment. One cannot fully understand an organization without also recognizing the environment in which it operates. "No organization is self-sufficient; all depend for survival on the types of relations they establish with the larger systems of which they are a part" (Scott & Davis, 2007, p. 19). The environment is generally composed of the actors, organizations, and other entities an organization interacts with to survive and accomplish its goals. For colleges and universities, the environment significantly affects how they operate. Whether an institution is located in Albany, New York, or Los Angeles, California, the location will affect whom it serves, how it serves, and the types of services and academic programs it offers. Moreover, how and where resources are obtained will have an impact on the ways the organization structures itself (Pfeffer & Salancik, 1978). For example, whether an institution's budget is derived from tuition, state appropriations, or donations will affect the emphasis the organization places on such functions as student recruitment, lobbying, and fund-raising. Regardless of where an institution is located, its operations will be affected by such entities in the environment as local high schools, the city council, state government, nonprofit organizations, other higher education institutions, and so forth.

Strategy and goals. This second element of organizations determines what an organization intends to accomplish and how it goes about achieving it. At their core, organizations are entities designed to accomplish certain goals. However, most organizations must deal with goal complexity. That is, there is often a difference between the stated goals of an organization and the real goals that motivate individuals. In addition, there are support goals, which are necessary for maintaining the organization (Perrow, 1970). More than just setting goals, organizations also develop strategies to achieve those goals. Leaders make decisions about where they will operate, the type of product or service they will produce, and whom they will hire to perform the work. Most educational institutions, particularly those in the public sector, are often constrained in that they do not always have control over their budgets and have limited flexibility in terms of adjusting their workforce because of tenure and union rules. Yet within whatever constraints that may exist, organization officials must determine how best to achieve their goals. In fact, the constraints can themselves drive strategy. For example, some public colleges and universities have begun to offer courses in other states, as it is easier to expand outside their home state because of fewer regulatory constraints elsewhere (Lane, Kinser, & Knox, in press). Being able to operate in the midst of goal complexity and strategize within constraints is a key characteristic of successful academic administrators.

Work and technology. The process for achieving goals and implementing strategies is the *work and technology* of the organization. "*Work* describes the tasks that the organization needs to accomplish in order to achieve the goals that it has set for itself" (Scott & Davis, 2007, p. 21). Analysis of work looks at a variety of different factors, including the amount of interdependence among different parts of the organization, which affects how the work is accomplished and how actors interact. For example, units in academic affairs tend to be much more independent of each other than units in student affairs (this phenomenon, *coupling*, is discussed later in the chapter), often resulting in a higher degree of interaction among student affairs administrators in different departments than among faculty members in different units. Work analysis also looks at such things as the flow of work and the necessary skills and knowledge of participants. For a faculty member in a college of arts and science of a large university, for example, the dean is much less likely to have direct knowledge of his or her disciplinary expertise than if the faculty member worked in a college of education. Departments in a college of education tend to have greater affinity with each other than do those in arts and science colleges, which include a range of departments from English to chemistry. The result is that a dean of arts and science will have to rely more on the advice of others to assess faculty member performance than would a dean of education.

Technology is the way the organization transforms inputs into outputs. In this case, we are not specifically focusing on items such as computers, smartphones, and electronic tablets, although they are increasingly important components of how institutions achieve their mission. Colleges and universities have multiple outputs, but for our purpose here, we focus on the education of students. In this case, an analysis of a college's technology would look at how an institution transforms a newly admitted student into a graduate. The focus would be mostly on curriculum design, or on what courses and requirements a student has to meet to earn a degree. How that process occurs varies by academic program and by institution. Understanding the work and technology of academic institutions is a core component of this book.

Formal and informal structures. All organizations are made up of formal and informal structures. The *formal structures* of organizations are usually represented on organizational charts and in job descriptions. They are a combination of the official hierarchy, in terms of reporting lines, job responsibilities, and the rules and regulations that guide the work of the organization. Organizations are also replete with informal structures, which can sometimes prove to be more important or influential than the formal structures. The *informal structures* of an organization include culture and climate, unofficial power structures, external social networks, and internal friendship circles. These informal aspects influence the effectiveness of the formal structures and are often part of the organization's work processes.

People. At their core, organizations are composed of people. This detail is no less true for academic organizations that comprise students, faculty, staff, administrators, and alumni. However, one of the difficulties in understanding this aspect of the academic organization is identifying which people are part of the organization and which are not. Students are not employees, but it is difficult to imagine an educational institution without students. Alumni are neither employees nor students, but many are often active on alumni councils, provide substantial resources to the organization, and sometimes exercise influence over institutional decision making. Beyond understanding who is involved, it is also important to know what induces people to participate in the organization (see Barnard, 1938; Simon, 1945/1997). In addition, age, gender, race, knowledge, and skills can affect how people interact with each other and perform on behalf of the organization.

Organizational Boundaries and Systems

There are numerous schools of thought in the study of organizational theory, but one of the most relevant to understanding the operation of colleges and universities is systems theory, which asserts that organizations are made up of different components, and the relationship between those components varies based on the system. "Organizations we must consider as something in which there is an interdependence between the several organized parts but in which this interdependence has degrees" (Wiener, 1954, p. 322). This notion of degrees of interdependence led to the concept of organizational coupling, which describes how tightly or loosely connected two components are (see p. 31 for a discussion of coupling). However, systems theorists did not only explore the relationship between internal components.

Open systems theorists have studied the extent to which organizations operate in conjunction with their environment.[1] In open systems the stability of the organization is dependent on its ability to obtain adequate resources from its external environment (Buckley, 1967). As discussed previously, no organization can be self-sufficient. Organizations need, for example, employees, consumers, and suppliers. Most times these individuals are found in the environment. Indeed, engagement with multiple stakeholders can sometimes blur the boundary of the organization. As Scott and Davis (2007) explain,

> This is not to say that open systems do not have boundaries. They do, of course, and must expend energy in boundary maintenance. But it is of equal importance that energies be devoted to activities that span and, more recently, redraw boundaries. Because of the openness of organizations, determining their boundaries is always difficult and sometimes appears to be a quite arbitrary decision. Does a university include its students within

its boundary? Its alumni? Faculty during the summer? The spouses of students in university housing? (p. 95)

While boundaries do exist, identifying their exact location can be quite difficult. A useful approach put forth by Pfeffer and Salancik (1978) is to consider individuals not as unitary actors who have to be on one side of the boundary or the other. Rather, it is a certain subset of their actions that exist within the organizational boundary. However, while this approach is helpful, it does not provide total clarity. As Scott and Davis (2007) go on to note, some actions can affect more than one system. For example, a student departing one institution may be viewed as a newly admitted student at the school he or she is transferring to, or a graduating undergraduate may matriculate in a different graduate school.

Another important aspect of systems is that they usually comprise multiple subsystems and are often themselves part of larger systems (Scott & Davis, 2007). For example, the University at Albany in New York is composed of several different colleges and schools, each of which represents a different subsystem within the organization. Moreover, the University at Albany is one of 64 different campuses (or subsystems) within the State University of New York; each of these campuses has its own organizational identity and operating norms but is connected as part of the State University of New York system.

Finally, Scott and Davis (2007) argue that the complexity of their environments fosters the creation of great colleges and universities. Their assertion is based on the law of limited variety put forth by Pondy and Mitroff (1979): "A system will exhibit no more variety than the variety to which it has been exposed in its environment" (p. 7). The idea here is that organizations that develop strong boundaries to buffer themselves against the complexities of the environment fail to evolve and grow. "Great universities do not arise in deserts or other sparsely inhabited areas" (Scott & Davis, p. 97). We concur. We believe that great universities arise from dealing with complex social and scientific issues.

The Study of Academic Organizations

What is a college or university? A deceptively simple question, with no clear answer, it has been discussed by a wide array of scholars and education professionals. Still, no common answer exists. Great thinkers such as Adam Smith (1776/1991), John Henry Newman (1852/1990), and Thorstein Veblen (1918) have all contributed to the discussion, debating the role of teaching, research, curriculum, knowledge creation, and knowledge dissemination. The scholarly study of colleges and universities as unique organizations began in the early 1960s and has rapidly developed since that time. In a 1974 review of the literature, Peterson found that fewer than 200 research-based articles dealing with the subject had been published at the time. Since then hundreds of studies have surfaced in academic journals, books, book chapters, reports, dissertations, and conference papers. In sum, the discussion about the nature of higher education is quite expansive, and many different terms have been used to describe academic organizations. There is no way to provide a complete overview of the study of higher education institutions as organizations. Next, we describe three of the most popular theories on the topic and then discuss common characteristics of academic organizations.

Theories About Academic Organizations

Three of the most classic theories pertaining to academic organizations are organized anarchies, loosely coupled systems, and professional bureaucracies, which are only briefly described in this section. There are many more, some of which are discussed throughout this book.[2] These three provide a base for much of what is discussed throughout this volume.

Organized anarchy. Since the seminal study by Cohen, March, and Olsen (1972), academic organizations have been labeled as *organized anarchies.* Such organizations contain three common characteristics, the first of which is a high degree of goal ambiguity. While participants in the organization may have a general idea about the purpose of the organization, specific goals are often in dispute. Administrators of each department and each faculty member may have a different idea about the purpose of the college or university and their role in it. This is in large part because of the multiple functions performed by the academic organization and the high level of professional autonomy experienced by faculty. Second, decision-making processes are not clear. While the system of decision making may be familiar, the exact nature of the process changes based on the nature of the problem to be solved, the solutions available at any one time, and the individuals involved in the process. Third, participation in the decision-making process is fluid. People continually join and leave academic organizations, and their membership in decision-making groups varies over time, depending on when they choose to be involved or show up.

Loosely coupled systems. Coupling describes the extent to which departments in an organization are aligned (Glassman, 1973). Coupling can be tight or loose or some gradient in between. Loose coupling simply connotes things, "anythings," that may be tied together either weakly or infrequently or slowly or with minimal independence (Weick, 1976, p. 5). With tight coupling, the anythings are highly connected, with a high degree of dependence. Academic organizations are made up of tightly and loosely coupled systems. Departments in administrative and support divisions tend to be more tightly coupled than those in academic affairs. In most colleges and universities, academic affairs is a confederation of loosely aligned academic departments that have minimal interaction with each other, and decisions by department heads have little impact on other units. In many ways, they move separately from each other and can even pursue competing goals. For example, the faculty in one department may try to improve its rankings by increasing selectivity and reducing the number of students it accepts. Faculty in a different department may try to increase revenue production by accepting more students into its progam. It is likely that neither decision will affect the other department. Of course, some academic departments are more tightly coupled than others. Some decisions made by the faculty in departments that provide support courses such as English and science may affect other departments that rely on those courses. Departments that offer joint degree programs or interdisciplinary courses will be more tightly coupled than those that do not. Academic administrators need to be aware of the coupling that exists within their divisions.

Professional bureaucracy/adhocracy. Mintzberg (1979) identified five basic components of organizations. The operating core is the employees who are primarily involved in providing the core services (e.g., faculty). Those in the strategic apex, presidents and vice presidents, are responsible for the overall operation of the organization. The middle line consists of department chairs, deans, and directors who connect those in the strategic apex to the operating core. In addition, those in the technostructure, such as the human relations office and the institutional research staff, are responsible for setting operating procedures and standardizing the work efforts. Finally, the support staff, such as the facilities management team and dining services, provide services that are not directly aligned with the production of the main product. Each of these components has a tendency to pull the organization in a different direction. Academic organizations have been commonly considered to be professional bureaucracies because of the dominance of the operating core in which faculty members are hired because of their professional knowledge and given a high degree of autonomy to perform their work. This tendency causes academic organizations to contrast with other organizations that attempt to implement internally a high degree of standardization among the workers they hire.

Professional bureaucracies are most common in environments that are complex but stable. As our environments become increasingly unstable and dynamic, some colleges and universities may come to resemble adhocracies. Adhocracies, like professional bureaucracies, rely on professional staff, but the structure used to organize employees becomes more fluid (Mintzberg, 1979). Employees with different specialties are grouped together to deal with specific problems that arise in the environment. For example, the rise of interdisciplinary faculty teams to address complex social or environmental problems may be viewed as a move toward the adhocracy, where departmental structures become less important than the problems the organization chooses to address.

Characteristics of Academic Organizations

As organizations tend to have common components, academic organizations also have common characteristics. The theories described in the preceding section provide different lenses an academic administrator can use to evaluate the operations of an academic organization. We know that academic organizations are characterized by high levels of goal ambiguity, client-focused missions, highly professionalized staff, unclear decision-making processes, and environmental vulnerability. These characteristics, first described by Baldridge, Curtis, Ecker, and Riley (1978), will be found in most public and private nonprofit organizations. However, while some of these characteristics may be found among for-profit institutions, they are not likely to be as universal as in other sectors because of their different business models. Some of these characteristics are derived from the previously discussed theories.

Goal ambiguity. Whereas most bureaucratic organizations operate with high degrees of organizational rationality—that is, they are focused on the attainment of a specific goal or goals—academic organizations possess significant goal ambiguity. Do these organizations exist to teach or to perform research and create new knowledge? Do they provide services to the community, the state, or the nation? What goals are ascribed to the organization by its administration, faculty, trustees, alumni, students, parents, and community? Because of the diverse expectations that different constituencies place upon colleges and universities, higher education institutions are susceptible to myriad purposes that may be consigned to them by organizational stakeholders. Not only do they often try to be all things to all people but they rarely have a single mission; because their preferences are unclear, they also find it hard to decline additional goals (Baldridge et al., 1978).

Client-focused missions. As organizations designed for and intended as agencies of social transformation, academic organizations are client serving in their purpose. Academic organizations serve a cadre of clients, such as students, governments, foundations, businesses, and local community organizations. It may also be argued that they serve parents, alumni, and donors. Because of the focus on multiple clients, academic organizations are often pulled in multiple directions, and services provided are often complicated and require highly professionalized staff. For example, the educational process is highly complex, based upon the nature of the content to be taught, the pedagogical skills of the teacher, the learning styles of the student, and how that learning can be empirically assessed. Unlike manufacturing organizations, which employ static processes and machinery to yield a given product, colleges and universities grapple with problem-posing technologies in attempting to derive their educational products (i.e., a graduated student). The plethora of programs and approaches to improve teaching and learning that have been attempted at the local, state, and federal levels for decades have still not yielded a consistent and broadly accepted teaching template suitable for application in all educational circumstances. "Serving clients is difficult to accomplish, to evaluate, and show short-term successes. Considering the entire person is a holistic task that cannot be easily separated into small, routine technical segments" (Baldridge et al., 1978, p. 22).

Highly professionalized staff. Professionalism is perhaps the most important of the five distinct characteristics of colleges and universities. Baldridge et al. (1978) list four aspects of professionalism that affect the interpersonal dynamics in academic organizations: (a) a demand for work autonomy, (b) the tendency to have divided loyalties between one's discipline and the organizations he or she works for, (c) the strong tension between professional values and bureaucratic expectations, and (d) the expectation of professionals to be evaluated by their peers (p. 22). Of these components, the inherent friction between formalization and professionalism provides the most consistent flash point between administration and faculty. As Hall (1977) recounts, "All the studies . . . have concluded that professionalization and formalization are incompatible. The more professionalized the work force, the more likely that formalization will lead to conflict and alienation" (p. 110).

Unclear decision-making processes. The fourth area of departure between academic organizations and other organizational types rests with the technologies used to produce outcomes. The many variables that account for differences in students and how they learn translate into equally challenging ways to teach them. Students access and absorb information differently according to learning style, and methods of instruction may vary within and between disciplines. The process of education is highly fluid and must be modified according to a host of factors associated with the student, the content taught, and the institution providing the education. Assessing success in meeting educational goals is highly elusive for this very reason.

Environmental vulnerability. The fifth distinguishing characteristic is the academic organization's environmental vulnerability. Hall (1977) noted that organizations vary in the extent to which they are vulnerable to environmental pressures, and the level of environmental influence is correlated to an organization's dependency upon external resources. This relationship has important implications for the manner in which an organization is managed since its structure and processes will be required to conform to the expectations and resource opportunities placed upon it by the environment. This arrangement is especially true in the case of academic organizations, which can vary in their susceptibility to environmental pressures depending upon their reliance on external factors:

> When professional organizations are well insulated from the pressures of the outside environment, then professional values, norms, and work definitions play a dominant role in shaping the character of the organization. On the other hand, when strong external pressure is applied to colleges and universities, the operating autonomy of the academic professionals is seriously reduced. (Riley & Baldridge, 1977, p. 6)

Higher education institutions are now buffeted by pressures from a wide range of environmental actors, greatly limiting operating autonomy. For example, in many parts of the United States, the number of high school graduates is shrinking, creating greater competition among the institutions for traditionally aged college students. Nontraditional students often need to balance family and work life in addition to their studies and expect the institution to be more flexible and accessible. The availability of financial resources provided by states and private donors affects an institution's operating ability and staffing levels. Moreover, institutions are expected to be engaged civic partners and good neighbors. All these expectations, and others, work to confine and define the work of the institution.

The five distinguishing characteristics of academic organizations discussed in this section provide a useful, but still incomplete, inventory of features of these unique organizations. Informed management and administration require an understanding of additional factors endemic to the interaction between and among the various stakeholders in the academy. No discussion of the organizational context of colleges and universities, when examining how these organizations differ from other organizational types, is complete without also exploring the cultural determinants of difference that exist as well. These cultural factors relate in part to the roles assumed by various incumbents throughout an organization, not only as they may affect the relationship between administration and faculty as earlier discussed, but also in the interaction among faculty members themselves, where tensions and organizational conflict often present themselves in bold fashion.

Organizational Culture and Climate in Higher Education

Academic organizations possess a distinct culture compared to other organizational types. Though the higher education literature on administration and management tends to focus heavily on the role of institutional leadership in shaping and directing an organization—especially as it pertains to the role of the president—the distinctive cultural aspects of academic organizations rest primarily in the value system of the faculty, which evolved over many centuries. While academic organizations tend to share common cultural characteristics, the culture and climate of a specific college or university often are a function of the relationship between its faculty and administration, for which there is an inherent natural tension flowing from the incompatibility of professionalization and formalization. Moreover, campus culture is also heavily influenced by the characteristics of the student body. For example, whether an institution primarily enrolls mostly full-time traditional students or part-time nontraditional students can have a significant influence on the campus culture.

Culture is different from climate, and we employ the definitions of both provided by Austin (1994) to distinguish between the two: "Whereas culture pertains to the embedded and stable beliefs, values and norms of a group, climate refers to members' assessment, views, perceptions, and attitudes toward various aspects of organizational life" (p. 52). Austin underscored the need for those serving in academic administrative roles to understand fully the notion of institutional culture but, as importantly, to recognize that organizational culture is not monolithic but fragmented, as subcultures exist within and beyond the academy at multiple levels. In discussing the various cultures related to faculty, Austin noted,

> faculty cultures include the culture of the academic profession, the culture of the academy as an organization, the cultures of particular disciplines, the cultures of institutional types, and the culture of the particular department or unit where the faculty member has a position. Deans, department chairpersons, and institutional researchers seeking to support the work of department and college leaders must understand the values of each of these cultures. (p. 48)

By understanding faculty culture, institutional leaders can understand their own faculty better, and faculty members can better understand one another. Sensitivity to faculty cultures by administrators yields a more informed and astute leader capable of better decision making since one can more accurately project the consequences of future decisions based upon the values and norms already embedded in the organization. "The key to being effective and the ability to make change begins first with an accurate assessment of the type of organization in which you work" (Julius et al, 1999, p. 114).

But how does one assess culturally the type of organization one helps to lead? It is first important to distinguish between the culture of the academy and the culture of the institution, because each operates at different levels and exhibits different characteristics. The culture of the academy is present throughout U.S. higher education and is based on a concept we shall call *collective individualism*, whereby the values of personal independence and professional autonomy—held by individual faculty members, legitimized and protected through the doctrine of academic freedom—are juxtaposed with a broader social and institutional value of shared intellectual collegiality, forming an academic community that exhibits a socially cohesive body in appearance but in actuality is a loosely aligned confederation of independent scholars. The concept of faculty as an amalgamation of independent contractors is not an inaccurate depiction when one considers variations in remuneration patterns among faculty members even at the same institution based on such variables as scholarly discipline, academic rank, course load, overloads to the normal teaching load, additional compensation for nonteaching duties needed outside the normal teaching load, ability to attract external grant sources, and a variety of other factors all negotiated through individual contractual relationships or collective bargaining agreements. Understanding the concept of collective individualism requires higher education administrators to balance the group identity of the faculty with the individual professional values held by each member of that body. This tension between individualism of faculty members and the collective interests of the faculty as a group was highlighted by Gumport (2000), who noted the "chasm" that exists between faculty self-interest and a broader concern for the common good, and that "at the most basic operating level, the tension appears when faculty members try to get what they can from their institutions rather than puzzling over how best to serve them" (p. 9).

The culture of the institution is specific to the organization itself and is reflective of the idiosyncratic nature of each and every college or university. It is the ethos or personality of an organization, built from a sense of shared accomplishment and distinctive purpose. This topic was addressed by Clark (1972), who examined the psychosocial determinants of a group's collective embracement of its organization's history and achievements as an institution's saga. He defined *saga* as "a collective understanding of a unique accomplishment based on historical exploits of a formal organization, offering strong normative bonds within and outside the organization" (p. 178). Central to Clark's definition of saga are the themes of history, uniqueness of the organization itself, and the shared value placed upon that uniqueness by the organization's members.

While the concept of saga is useful in understanding the uniqueness of individual academic organizations, other factors affect the culture of an institution. One of them is the collective personality of the institution's faculty. The existence of tenure and its role as a protector of academic freedom is an important factor in shaping that personality. Though the merits of tenure are increasingly debated as financial pressures and a need for more institutional fiscal flexibility rise, the presence of tenure has provided continuity and stability to an institution's faculty and thus has contributed to the emergence of a particular group dynamic unique to that institution. This phenomenon is widely overlooked in debates over the benefits or challenges of tenure. Imagine how the culture of an institution would change if all its faculty members were free agents, unbound by tenure and institutional loyalties, to ply their intellectual skills competitively in an open market. Such a scenario would result in a significant loss of institutional memory and contribute to a fluid, rather than stable, organizational personality.

To assess institutional culture, a new higher education administrator will benefit from early, strong communication between and among constituents to conduct an expansive inventory of the attitudes and perceptions of the organization by those within their oversight. This process will allow the administrator to determine not only the issues or concerns most important to the group but the overall collective mind-set as well. Such a dialogue should include a thorough understanding of the organization's history, its norms, and the nature of its influential relationships and power structures. If constituent compliance to decision-making actions is to occur effectively, leaders must be perceived by others as having a prior working understanding of the organization, its history, and its constituents beyond the administrative issues at hand. The concept of *institutional fit* is appropriate to this discussion. Many failures in academic leadership occur when the incumbent is unable or unwilling to incorporate, adapt to, or, at a minimum, understand an academic or institutional culture that has been shaped over decades or even centuries.

Having examined the typological, organizational, and contextual differences that exist in higher education organizations, and having given added attention to cultural factors that influence administrative decision making, we can now examine the theoretical models that have emerged to characterize colleges and universities as unique organizational types. Specific to this examination are issues of legitimacy and authority in matters of institutional governance and decision making, as various stakeholders, internal and external to the institution, stake claims to their spheres of influence.

Part Two
Operating Structures of Colleges and Universities: Administrative Units and Governance Models

This book focuses specifically on the academic affairs of colleges and universities, but these functions do not take place in isolation from other aspects of the institution. According to Kerr (1963), the 20th century witnessed the birth of the "multiversity," a conglomeration of the following:

> the community of the undergraduate and the community of the graduate; the community of the humanist, the community of the social scientist, and the community of the scientist; the communities of the professional schools; the community of all the nonacademic personnel; the community of the administrators. (p. 14)

These communities then connect with other communities of elected officials, foundations, nonprofit organizations, industries, alumni, and local officials. Throughout this book, we describe various external communities and those internal communities that directly relate to academic affairs. However, many colleges and universities are complex organizations with hundreds or thousands of support staff members who are responsible for everything, from making sure the sidewalks are clear of snow to overseeing the student judicial office. Many of these functions are mentioned throughout the book, and although they are not our focus here, they are important and in some cases vital to the performance of the institution.

Administrative Units

In this section we describe some of the more common functions in the academic organization. Each college and university organizes these units in different ways. For example, in some institutions the director of athletics reports to the president, whereas in others he or she may report to the vice president for student affairs. Institutions also use different labels for similar roles. Those responsible for the cocurricular functions of the institution may report to a vice president of student affairs, student services, or student success. Our purpose here is to provide readers with a basic understanding of the most common units in a college or university.

Moreover, studying an institution's organizational chart can yield insights about the importance the institution places on particular units and its philosophy about different functions. Designating the athletic department as a direct report to the president may suggest the importance the unit has in the organization. Similarly, whether the office of residence life reports to the vice president of finance or the vice president of student affairs may suggest whether the institution places greater value on the revenue-producing aspect of residence halls or the student development role they play for their residents.

Academic affairs. This unit is at the core of the organization. It is usually structured around academic disciplines and fields of study. Faculty members are generally organized into academic departments. In larger institutions, several departments are grouped into schools or colleges, which are led by academic deans. The academic deans then report to a chief academic officer, usually referred to as a provost or vice president of academic affairs. In some smaller institutions, department chairs report directly to the institution's chief academic officer. Divisions of academic affairs may also have separate units that oversee research and graduate education. In some larger institutions with expansive research and development enterprises, vice presidents of research report directly to the president. Also, in response to concerns about the lack of attention paid to undergraduate education, medium and large institutions have developed support structures for academic advising and support outside the traditional academic departmental structure. These academic advising and support units may be placed in the student affairs division. The functions of academic affairs are widely explored throughout this volume.

Athletics. College and university athletics is a phenomenon that is somewhat unique to U.S. higher education. Since the latter part of the 19th century athletics has been a significant part of collegiate culture. Institutions now provide an array of athletic opportunities for their students, and consequently athletics has emerged as a significant administrative function for many colleges and universities. Most college students only participate in intramural competitions often organized by an office of recreational sports, usually affiliated with the institution's recreation center, or an athletic or physical education department. Most attention, however, is given to intercollegiate athletics, wherein teams from different campuses compete against each other. An athletic director serves as chief athletics officer for an institution and oversees coaches, compliance with athletic rules, and marketing of teams. In addition to the coaching staff, larger athletic departments may also comprise academic support staff, athletic trainers, compliance officers, and marketing personnel.

The major governing body of intercollegiate athletics is the National Collegiate Athletic Association, a private nonprofit organization led by a president who reports to a governing board made up of college and university presidents from across the country. The association is divided into three separate divisions (DI, DII, DIII); DI is subdivided. The largest number of schools participates in DIII, where student-athletes are treated no differently than the rest of the general student population in that they receive no special living accommodations, facilities, or scholarships. In contrast, the other two divisions offer varying amounts of athletic scholarships and special treatment for student-athletes, depending on the school, league, or division. Institutions across all three divisions offer a wide range of athletic opportunities for men and women, but it is DI men's football and basketball that often draw the most attention and controversy, primarily because of the expense of these programs as compared to expenditures on academic programs at the institution as well as the revenue produced from athletic contests that comes from ticket sales, television network rights, and sponsorships from corporations and individuals associated with the schools.

Auxiliary services. Colleges and universities often operate several revenue-producing activities, commonly referred to as auxiliary services. These operations are not core to the academic enterprise, but they provide important support functions. Examples of such operations include bookstores, dining halls and other eating facilities, residence halls, and so forth. They generate money for the institution through charging fees such as for staying in a residence hall or through selling merchandise such as food at the dining hall or a sweatshirt at the bookstore. A common trend now is for institutions to outsource these services to an external provider. It is not uncommon to see a Barnes & Noble bookstore sandwiched between Wendy's and Dunkin' Donuts in the student union. In most cases, the institution benefits by having the provider pay a service fee to set up shop, as well as mandating that the provider make certain capital improvements to the facilities. Also, some institutions have begun to outsource the care and maintenance of their residence halls to outside vendors. Rather than hiring and maintaining its own staff, the college or university will pay a fee for these services to be provided by an external entity.

Finance and administration. Colleges and universities are employers that must manage hundreds or thousands of employees. This requires administering payroll, health care, and retirement benefits, in addition to managing the revolving door of student workers and part-time faculty and staff. They are also service providers that charge tuition and fees for those services. The institution must track student accounts and handle their payments and facilitate a vast array of financial aid from the federal and state government as well as from private sources. These functions usually are managed by a large number of human resource experts, professionals highly knowledgeable in student aid, and other administrative personnel.

Facilities management. Colleges and universities are often cities within cities. Their campuses usually contain dozens of buildings that house a variety of different structures from classrooms to auditoriums to ice hockey arenas. In addition to the buildings, they own and are responsible for roads, sidewalks, parking lots, gardens, fountains, and all of the rest of the campus grounds. Moreover, some parts most people do not see, including the thousands of feet of steam tunnels, vents, and wires required to keep buildings warm and the lights on. All of this requires a vast army of electricians, plumbers, architects, engineers, landscapers, and many others to maintain the facilities and grounds.

Institutional development. In an era of tightening budgets, the functions of institutional development divisions have become even more important.

Academic organizations usually maintain communications and marketing staff to help promote the institution as well as manage media inquiries and public relations problems. Public and private institutions are increasingly focused on raising funds from private donors and commit resources to maintaining strong relationships with alumni and building relationships with potential donors. Most public colleges and universities (and large private institutions) now maintain (or share) lobbyists at either (or both) the state and federal levels as a means of influencing education policy and funding decisions. Because of the connection between institutional reputation and resource acquisition, we are increasingly seeing the functions of fund-raising, lobbying, alumni relations, and publications/communications offices merged to better integrate the institution's external messages. Such merged functions are often referred to as *institutional advancement*, an activity that has grown in stature and visibility because of the heightened competition among colleges and universities for students as well as for public and private resources.

Student affairs. While academic affairs are at the core of the enterprise, the cocurricular experience is also a meaningful component of college life, particularly for traditional undergraduate students. A growing number of nontraditional students, however, are also taking advantage of student activities and support that are often part of student affairs divisions. When considering student affairs divisions, what usually comes to mind are student organizations, campus activities, and the like, but such divisions are much more diverse, offering students an array of support functions, such as counseling, mentoring, and peer support; community service engagements; and leadership opportunities as part of student government and programming councils. These units provide resources for students with disabilities as well as students united through race, culture, or sexual orientation. Other offices generally overseen in this division are judicial affairs, career services, and recreational sports.

Other units. There is no way to capture all the different types of enterprises a college or university may be engaged in, and the following are just some examples of these activities. Some institutions have broken into the travel industry, managing airports and hotels. Those with medical schools often have responsibility for a hospital as well. To aid students and staff with young children, they provide day care facilities on campus. As an extension of their academic mission, several institutions also support academic presses, which publish scholarly books and journals. In addition, a growing trend is for colleges and universities to host research parks and small-business incubators for facilitating the development of patentable and profitable research products.

Models of Academic Governance

Organizational theory attempts to provide insight into the structure and process of organizations. Given the various differentiating and unique features of academic organizations previously described, a major challenge for higher education theorists over the decades has been how to adequately characterize these features in prevailing theoretical models of governance. Older models of organizational understanding largely rooted in traditional bureaucratic theories were deemed inadequate for application to higher education. The highly complex structure and process of academic organizations, with their multiple centers of decision-making authority, prompted the creation of new models.

Three theoretical models of governance now predominate in the literature. These distinct perspectives view authority and decision making in the academy through structural (bureaucratic), relational (collegial), and legislative (political) frameworks. These governance models provide a useful perspective in understanding the interrelationship between and among the organizational participants based on such factors as power, persuasion, or legislative influence. In reality, considerations of all three models are appropriate and helpful when attempting to understand the administration and management of colleges and universities.

The bureaucratic model. In his seminal book on bureaucratic theory, Weber (1947) described an organization as a system of hierarchical roles and formal chains of command acting in concert toward the realization of a set of defined goals. Central to Weberian bureaucratic theory is the linear and vertical relationship among decision makers based on role and rank in the organization and the formalization of rules and policies those organizational players follow. In an early attempt to apply existing bureaucratic theory to higher education, Stroup (1966) sought to characterize academic organizations against these bureaucratic features. To do so was understandable since the bureaucratic paradigm appropriately conforms to many of the processes and structures found in colleges and universities.

It is not surprising one would attribute traditional bureaucratic descriptors to contemporary higher education organizations given their enormous complexity. During remarks at a meeting of independent college presidents and foundation directors, Carnegie Foundation for the Advancement of Teaching's president, Vartan Gregorian (2008), illustrated this trend, noting that today's colleges and universities have become mini city-states, complete with hotels (residence halls), police departments (security departments), restaurants (dining halls), hospitals (health centers), and other operational functions that have grown in complexity and costliness over the years.

Yet for all the applicability of the bureaucratic model to academic organizations, significant weaknesses exist. According to Riley and Baldridge (1977), the bureaucratic model focuses more on formal power and the hierarchical structures that define it than the informal power relationships that often exist in organizations and that often change over time depending on the issue or policy being debated. Another weakness in the bureaucratic model can be its preoccupation with policy execution over policy formulation. The model also tends to minimize the role of multiple interest groups and political struggles that exist among them in campus settings.

The collegial model. A second way academic organizations may be viewed is as a community. This thesis was first introduced by Millett (1962), who believed that the application of hierarchical principles to colleges and universities failed to account for the internal decision-making pluralism that exists in higher education organizations. Millett argued that a focus on hierarchy emphasized the role that absolute authority played within an organization since the concept of bureaucracy implies formal power structures and a system of superior and subordinate relationships:

> In terms of their own internal organization our colleges and universities have sought arrangements which would equally reflect [a] concern to avoid absolute authority. In this endeavor the colleges and universities have built up a practice of community as the fundamental basis of organization. (p. 61)

In his book, Millett highlighted the various institutional constituencies that participate to varying degrees in institutional decision-making processes, citing the roles that students, alumni, and faculty all play in academic governance. As president of Miami University of Ohio when he published his book, Millet likely was reflecting on the administrative challenge of accommodating multiple interests in a spirit of group accommodation.

One central theme of the collegial model is the values that members of the faculty share as they relate to the academic profession itself and their role within the decision-making structure of the institution. Implied in the model is a strong sense of collegiality within the professoriate. In her discussion of the culture of the academic profession, Austin (1994) noted how faculty members share a commitment to intellectual honesty and fairness, as well as a commitment to the concept of a community of scholars whose collegiality guides their interactions and their involvement in institutional decision making. "However, these values are expressed in different ways depending on institutional and disciplinary contexts" (p. 49).

While the collegial model accurately portrays an organization's having to accommodate multiple constituencies in a harmonious—we hope—fashion, the weakness of the model rests in its failure to account adequately for the decision processes themselves as multiple constituencies compete within the decision-making environment. Decision making is a consequence of authority, and the collegial model is largely silent on the issue of which constituencies hold primacy over certain issues in the governance of colleges and universities. This weakness was later addressed in research that explored the authority structures of the academic enterprise and how competing interest groups influence organizational decision making through the exercise of political influence. This line of inquiry produced the following third model of academic governance.

The political model. The paradigm of viewing academic governance as a political process and colleges and universities as independent political systems was first proposed by Baldridge (1971). In this model, the campus is made up of a set of competing interest groups whose participation in the decision-making process is fluid, depending on the nature of a particular issue confronting a constituency at any given time. Policy formation serves as a focal point since the creation and adoption of policy is directly related to institutional mission and direction and the various operational decisions that flow from it. As a consequence, conflict among organizational interest groups is inherent. Such interest groups are not limited to those constituencies in the institution itself but extend to external parties that may hold vested interests in the organization as well.

Colleges' and universities' fragmented and complex decision-making processes lend the political model much credibility in the study of academic governance. The reality of academic governance is that decisions most often are not made unilaterally by a central authority but follow prescribed systems of review and consultation with a variety of individuals or entities, depending on the nature of the decision to be made:

> When the very life of the organization clusters around expertise, decision-making is likely to be diffuse, segmentalized, and decentralized. A complex network of committees, councils and advisory bodies grows to handle the task of assembling the expertise necessary for reasonable decisions. Decision-making by the individual bureaucrat is replaced with decision-making by committee, council, and cabinet. Centralized decision-making is replaced with diffuse decision-making. The process becomes a far-flung network for gathering expertise from every corner of the organization and translating it into policy. (Baldridge, 1971, p. 190)

The involvement of different interest groups in academic decision making by virtue of their role and expertise provides the legitimacy for the concept of shared governance developed by Mortimer and McConnell (1978). We include shared governance in our discussion of the political model because decision making in a shared governance environment is performed through the exercise of influence rather than formal position. Matters of shared governance are largely an issue between faculty and administration (and to a lesser extent trustees and students) because of the tensions identified in earlier organizational models between professional authority (the faculty) and formal authority (the administration). The notion of shared governance involves the acceptance of the authoritative rights possessed by certain constituencies based on their expertise or formal position. A central question in the discussion of shared authority is, How is authority distributed in recognition of the legitimate expertise ascribed to a particular incumbent or group? According to Mortimer and McConnell,

> A full account of governance should cover four basic questions: (1) *What* issue is to be decided? (2) *Who*—what persons or groups—should be involved in the decision? (3) *When* (at what stage of the decision-making process) and *how* should such involvement occur? (4) *Where*—at what level in the organizational structure—should such involvement occur? (p. 13, emphasis added)

The political model has several weaknesses. First, the model was developed in an era predating the creation of the growing for-profit education sector and of institutions specializing in online learning modalities. The mission of some for profits and the online campuses without walls often bear little resemblance to their more traditional academic counterparts in their structure and relationship among faculty, employees, and management. Second, the rise of collective bargaining and the role of faculty unions have significantly altered the decision-making process on campuses where unions exist, thereby substituting functional authority by virtue of expertise with formal authority that is legislatively and legally derived. Finally, the political model focuses predominantly on the internal organizational relationship between faculty and administration but fails to account sufficiently for the rise in external environmental factors that are substantially affecting college and university governance today. Diminishing federal and state resources designated for higher education, coupled with governmental efforts to exact greater accountability on the part of colleges and universities, are resulting in greater encroachment by governmental entities on how precious resources should be expended and what society should expect in the way of outcomes from those investments.

In an evaluation of the future challenges facing higher education governance, Kezar and Eckel (2004) provided a thorough review of 40 years of research. They concluded that the primary models of academic governance we have described focus on structural and political theories of governance but provide a limited explanation of how academic governance could actually be improved. An important theme they highlight is that the structural and political models that have guided the understanding of governance in recent decades will be inadequate to understanding and accommodating rapid organizational change in the coming years as colleges and universities must adapt to new internal and external constraints. The authors cite three factors that have emerged in the last decade that will make governance more of a problem: (a) an increase in imposed accountability and competition from an increasingly challenging external environment, (b) the changing nature of the faculty with significant retirements and a more diverse faculty replacing them, and (c) a need to expedite decision making to accommodate rapid change (p. 371). Efficiency, effectiveness, participation, leadership, and environmental responsiveness are the five key challenges to future governance cited by Kezar and Eckel.

Now that we have reviewed how academic organizations significantly differ from other organizational types and how different theoretical models have been employed to describe academic governance, let us turn our attention to the theoretical and practical aspects of leadership and decision making.

Part Three
Decision Making and Academic Leadership

Higher education organizations are arguably among the most difficult organizations to administer and manage for the reasons outlined in this chapter. In addition to the organizational variables discussed in this chapter, a vast array of practical challenges face academic leaders: Internal constituencies lay claim to authority over operational domains of the enterprise based on the legitimacy of their administrative or professional roles; boards of trustees hold fiduciary responsibility over the entire organization and can exercise that responsibility in ways that are supportive or detrimental to the institution; alumni, parents, and students increasingly exert influence as a result of rising consumerism, which translates into greater feelings of entitlement over how tuition or philanthropic dollars are applied; and legislatures and government agencies demand greater institutional accountability through efforts to ensure legislatively mandated educational outcomes. Academic leadership at all levels, therefore, requires a special set of skills, knowledge, and sensitivity to navigate effectively the ever increasing governance challenges facing today's college and university decision makers.

Leading in a Bifurcated Organization

Leadership in an academic organization requires the ability to work in a highly professional environment. Central to the concept of professionalism are individual autonomy and creativity to exercise one's unique professional knowledge. The question for any administrator is how to maintain organizational control and direction without imposing undue influence on these embedded professional values. As Etzioni (1964) explained,

> Only if immune from ordinary social pressures and free to innovate, to experiment, to take risks without the usual social repercussions of failure, can a professional carry out his work effectively. It is this highly individualized principle which is diametrically opposed to the very essence of the organizational principle of control and coordination by superiors—i.e., the principle of administrative authority. (pp. 76–77)

Noted sociologist Blau (1974) focused on the inherent conflict between bureaucracy and professionalism when addressing the issue of authority in organizations:

> The various components of professionalism must be distinguished in analyzing its implications for hierarchical authority in organizations. Full-fledged professionalization entails not only expert skills but also a body of abstract knowledge underlying them, a self-governing association of professional peers, professional standards of workmanship and ethical conduct, and an orientation toward service. Some of these factors may easily come into conflict with the discipline required by bureaucratic authority. (p. 247)

In his research specific to academic organizations, Blau (1973) described colleges and universities as organizations bifurcated into two spheres, the bureaucratic and the academic, and outlined the organizational tension that arises between these centers of authority. Noting that academics claim exclusive authority over their own work, insist on professional independence, and set their own standards for competence in their disciplines, Blau stated,

> These claims to professional autonomy and self-regulation create potential conflicts with the bureaucratic authority of administrators, since administrative and professional considerations are often at variance, for example, when budgetary requirements conflict with optimum professional service to clients, or when administrative demands infringe upon the specialized responsibilities of experts. (p. 159)

This bifurcated system, which aptly describes the higher education organization as substantially different from other organizational types, provides a useful way to categorize the decision structures of colleges and universities.

The simplicity of Blau's (1973) bifurcated system does not fully account, however, for the differences in organizational structure and process that exist among different types of institutions. McKelvey (1982) noted that certain types of academic organizations respond differently to environmental change according to their specific structure and process, suggesting another possible method to understand colleges and universities. Using the term *organizational systematics* to describe this phenomenon, McKelvey recognized that understanding academic organizations could be facilitated by placing them in homogeneous groups based upon decision structures, a vastly different approach from the more traditional Carnegie Classification scheme.

Using this concept, Hendrickson and Bartkovich (1986) created a new taxonomy that built on the Blau (1973, 1974) and McKelvey (1982) constructs. They proposed that academic organizations could be arrayed on a continuum ranging from highly bureaucratic to highly academic (using Blau's bifurcated system), with assigned factors such as decision-making authority, functional differentiation, administrative configuration, and participation in operational procedures to determine where a particular type of institution would reside on this continuum.

Since bureaucratic organizations tend to be vertical in structure with decision making centralized at the top, whereas academic organizations are flatter with decision centers at lower levels, the locus of power provides a useful understanding of how a specific college or university reacts to change. So many permutations of structures and process exist among academic organizations that this approach to understanding academic organizations emphasizes again how vastly different they are from other organizational types, a key point highlighted in the work of Hendrickson and Bartkovich (1986).

Decision Making in Academic Organizations

So messy is decision making in academic organizations that it has been described as similar to a garbage can (Cohen et al., 1972). In their study of universities as organized anarchies, Cohen et al. suggested that academic organizations are collections of solutions looking for problems, issues and feelings looking for decision opportunities to be vented, and decision makers looking for something to do. Thus, decision making in academic organizations can be construed as a set of problems, solutions, and participants who move from one decision-making opportunity to another. The outcome of a decision is influenced by the availability of solutions, the people involved in the process, and the nature of the process. Cohen et al. argued that in such organizations, solutions are often uncoupled from decisions. While decision making is believed to be a process to find a solution for a given problem, it is actually a complicated dance to align problems, solutions, and decision makers to allow action to occur.

Clearly, leadership and decision making in a college or university is a highly fluid and dynamic process that assumes different characteristics depending on the particular role one holds in the organization. For example, decision making for department chairpeople is significantly different from that of a dean or provost, whose decision circumstances in turn are quite unlike the decision-making conditions faced by an institution's president. Though all operate within a shared governance environment in which spheres of influence and responsibility are allocated according to one's function, acceptance of a decision is determined by the legitimacy and authority ascribed to the decision maker by others inside and outside the organization. For example, among the most challenging of administrative positions on today's campuses is that of provost. Having most often risen to that position from within the professoriate a provost must precariously straddle serving as an advocate for the faculty and its interests and serving at the pleasure of the president in an executive administrative capacity. Provosts must deftly support faculty autonomy through shared governance while firmly asserting administrative accountability:

> As trust is the cornerstone of academic leadership, the Chief Academic Officer (CAO) must be vigilant about not letting faculty go around their department chairs or deans, must avoid sharing information with just one dean or having a backdoor for negotiations, and must be consistently even-handed in all matters. The CAO cannot undercut the authority of deans and department chairs by publicly second-guessing them or getting

involved in matters for which the deans and chairs are responsible. At times, this means supporting those to whom one delegates daily responsibility for academic affairs even if the CAO disagrees with their actions. (Ferren & Stanton, 2004, pp. 13–14)

Because the notion exists of shared governance in academic organizations where authority is divided or bifurcated among bureaucratic and academic spheres of responsibility, potential differences in the perception of roles within each sphere or at various levels within a sphere also exist. Effective leadership and decision making in academic organizations therefore requires congruence among and between members of these different spheres on how different organizational roles are perceived and exercised. Role theory explores the consistency between one's assigned organizational role and the perception of that role by others. Especially in academic organizations in which authority and decision making is widely distributed throughout the institution, successful leadership requires an appreciation and understanding of role differences between and across the multiple spheres of authority that exist and is a prerequisite to effective administration and management.

Effective administrators of academic organizations benefit when they possess high degrees of emotional intelligence (see chapter 10 for additional information). Golman (1995) argues that possession of certain social skills is a greater predictor of leadership and managerial success than IQ alone. He cites a portfolio of behavioral and emotional skills that have been shown to yield high emotional literacy and managerial success. These skills include emotional self-awareness, the ability to manage one's emotions, empathy and the ability to read others' emotions, deftness at handling relationships, and an ability to harness emotions productively. In organizational settings such as colleges and universities in which the definition of *smart* is most often attributed to a person's IQ, the qualities of emotional intelligence may be undervalued. Yet it is precisely because effective academic administrators must be sensitive to the conflicts inherent between the professional and administrative spheres of their organization and the differences in role expectations for administrators according to their position and function that those with higher levels of emotional intelligence will, in fact, achieve greater leadership success than those who are deficient in such skills, regardless of IQ level.

Learning to Frame Situations

Given the highly dynamic and complex nature of academic organizations, are there particular leadership styles that work best in these organizations?

Earlier in this chapter we briefly examined three models of academic governance: bureaucratic, collegial, and political. One could argue that certain leadership and managerial styles have historically been associated with each. For example, leaders of organizations resembling the bureaucratic model often assume the role of hero—visionary and highly goal-oriented individuals who by virtue of their vision, drive, and position at the top of the organization provide the guiding impetus behind the organization's growth. Figures such as former General Electric President Jack Welch or Microsoft's Bill Gates are examples. An entirely different leadership style is required for organizations mirroring the collegial model of governance in which academic professionalism dominates. Here the leader serves as colleague in that his or her authority is derived from the expertise attributed to that individual by professional peers. When the federal government organized the Manhattan Project in Los Alamos, New Mexico, during World War II to develop an atomic weapon, it recognized the importance of placing an individual in supervision over the scientists working on the project whom they would defer to professionally. Physicist Robert Oppenheimer served as the ideal choice in that instance given his high stature within the scientific community. Finally, in the political model, the leader acts as facilitator, which requires strong negotiating and social skills to manage and influence competing interest groups in support of a common objective. As chronicled by historian Doris Kearns Goodwin (2005), Abraham Lincoln effectively managed a "team of rivals" in his cabinet during the Civil War. Prior to his administration, some of these individuals had been bitter political enemies but emerged from the experience of serving on Lincoln's cabinet with the deepest admiration and respect for the president.

Just as one single governance model cannot effectively describe academic organizations (which actually contain elements of all three), no single style of leadership can be applied to the task of managing and administering colleges and universities. An excellent and useful guide for decision making and leadership was proposed by Bolman and Deal (2008), who argued that leadership style is situation specific according to the circumstances at hand. The authors suggested four frameworks to view leadership. The leader who employs each of these frames as it is needed will be a more effective leader.

- *Structural.* Decisions and solutions are achieved through the realignment of structures, tasks, roles, and operations. This framework is useful in organizations with high degrees of formalization and rationality with clearly defined goals and little organizational conflict. A structural leadership style is analytical and highly strategic.

- *Human resource.* A focus on empowering and assisting the organization's people is the dominant theme of this frame. Organizational process and movement are consequences of motivations stimulated by management toward the workers and are especially beneficial when morale is either high or very low. Ample resources to provide that motivation are important to this framework. The human resource leadership style is one of servant leadership and advocate of the individual employee.
- *Political.* Effective management under this framework requires the identification and understanding of the organization's various constituencies and their leaders with a focus on negotiating desired organizational outcomes through influence and compromise. Scarce or declining organizational resources often stimulate use of the political framework. The leadership style of this framework involves strength in coalition building and use of persuasion.
- *Symbolic.* Traditions and values of the organization predominate in this framework, and organizational loyalty is prized. Workers look to a visionary leader and motivator for support and guidance. The importance of the organization's culture is central. Leadership in the symbolic framework requires high energy, foresight, and a charismatic personality to motivate employee productivity.

The utility of Bolman and Deal's (2008) four frameworks for leadership in academic organizations is that leaders must consider employee motivational factors during decision-making processes. Given the myriad constituencies confronting academic leaders on a host of organizational issues, the model correctly suggests that leaders adjust their style according to the issue to be addressed and the decision to be made. In addition, the ability to consider complex issues through multiple frames can help leaders avoid (or at least prepare for) potential hazards and negative reactions to decisions. Indeed, research suggests that many university presidents use at least two frames when making decisions (Bensimon, 1989). Any holistic approach to the study of leadership, especially as it relates to academic organizations that are becoming increasingly consumed by external variables, must account for these emerging influences.

Conclusion

In chapter 1 we outlined several principles that serve as a foundation to our study of U.S. higher education: the understanding of the role of mission, the need for institutional adaptation to changing environmental and societal circumstances, and the value of democratic partnerships in the formation and operation of colleges and universities. Those entrusted with governance responsibilities as either fiduciaries or administrators in U.S. higher education institutions cannot effectively lead without embracing these principles and appreciating how each affects management decisions on an ongoing basis. This chapter suggests how issues of institutional mission and democratic partnerships have evolved over the centuries into a dynamic and complex array of thousands of separate and unique organizations, each requiring of its leadership a separate set of understandings and strategies equally unique to the organization. It is not nearly enough to understand how colleges and universities differ markedly from other organizational types. More important, informed administrators will be well served to understand how their institution distinguishes itself from any other, and what they must understand about themselves and those they serve to effectively manage it with success.

Notes

1. More information about open systems can be found in Scott and Davis (2007).

2. More comprehensive information about these and other organizational theories pertaining to academic organizations can be found in Bastedo (2012) and Bess and Dee (2007).

References

Almanac of Higher Education. (2011). *The Chronicle of Higher Education, 58*(1).

Austin, A. E. (1994). Understanding and assessing faculty cultures and climates. *New Directions for Institutional Research, 84*, 47–63.

Baldridge, J. V. (1971). *Power and conflict in the university*. New York, NY: Wiley.

Baldridge, J. V., Curtis, D. V., Ecker, G., & Riley, G. L. (1978). *Policy making and effective leadership*. San Francisco, CA: Jossey-Bass.

Barnard, C. I. (1938). *The functions of the executive*. Cambridge, MA: Harvard University Press.

Bastedo, M. N. (2012). *The organization of higher education: Managing colleges for a new era*. Baltimore, MD: Johns Hopkins University Press.

Bensimon, E. M. (1989). The meaning of "good presidential leadership": A frame analysis. *The Review of Higher Education, 12*(2), 107–123.

Bess, J. L., & Dee, J. R. (2007). *Understanding college and university organization: Theories for effective policy and practice*. Sterling, VA: Stylus.

Blau, P. M. (1973). *The organization of academic work*. New York, NY: Wiley.

Blau, P. M. (1974). *On the nature of organizations.* New York, NY: Wiley.

Bolman, L. G., & Deal, T. E. (2008). *Reframing organizations: Artistry, choice and leadership* (4th ed.). San Francisco, CA: Jossey-Bass.

Buckley, W. (1967). *Sociology and modern systems theory.* Upper Saddle River, NJ: Prentice Hall.

Carnegie Foundation for the Advancement of Teaching. (2012). *The Carnegie classification of institutions of higher education.* Retrieved from http://classifications.carnegiefoundation.org

Clark, B. R. (1972). The organizational saga in higher education. *Administrative Science Quarterly, 17*, 178–184.

Cohen, M., March, J., & Olsen, J. (1972). A garbage can model of organizational choice. *Administrative Science Quarterly, 17*(1), 1–25.

Etzioni, A. (1964). *Modern organizations.* Englewood Cliffs, NJ: Prentice Hall.

Ferren, A. S., & Stanton, W. W. (2004). Academic leadership: Collaborating for institutional effectiveness. In A. S. Ferren & W. W. Stanton (Eds.), *Leadership through collaboration: The role of the chief academic officer* (pp. 1–21). Westport, CT: Praeger.

Geiger, R. L. (2005). The ten generations of American higher education. In P. G. Altbach, R. O. Berdahl, & P. J. Gumport (Eds.), *American higher education in the twenty-first century: Social, political, and economic challenges* (pp. 38–69). Baltimore, MD: Johns Hopkins University Press.

Glassman, R. B. (1973). Persistence and loose coupling in living systems. *Behavioral Science, 18*, 83–98.

Golman, D. (1995). *Emotional intelligence.* New York, NY: Bantam.

Goodwin, D. K. (2005). *Team of rivals.* New York, NY: Simon & Schuster.

Gregorian, V. (2008, October). *How foundations and colleges can advance each other's agendas: Two perspectives on leadership—the campus and the foundation.* Keynote presentation and discussion at the meeting of the Council of Independent Colleges, New York. Retrieved from http://www.cic.edu/meetings-and-events/Annual-Conferences/Foundation-Conversation/PastPrograms/2008_agenda.pdf

Gumport, P. J. (2000). *Academic governance: New light on old issues* (Occasional Paper No. 42). Washington, DC: Association of Governing Boards of Universities and Colleges.

Hall, R. H. (1977). *Organizations: Structure and process.* Englewood Cliffs, NJ: Prentice Hall.

Hendrickson, R. M., & Bartkovich, J. P. (1986). Organizational systematics: Toward a classification scheme for postsecondary institutions. *The Review of Higher Education, 9*(3), 303–324.

Julius, D. J., Baldridge, J. V., & Pfeffer, J. (1999). A memo from Machiavelli. *The Journal of Higher Education, 70*(2), 113–133.

Kast, F. E., & Rosenzweig, J. E. (1970). *Organization and management: A systems approach.* Hightstown, NJ: McGraw-Hill Education.

Kerr, C. (1963). *The uses of the university.* Cambridge, MA: Harvard University Press.

Kezar, A., & Eckel, P. D. (2004). Meeting today's governance challenges. *The Journal of Higher Education, 75*(4), 371–399.

Lane, J. E., Kinser, K., & Knox, D. (in press). Regulating cross-border higher education: A case study of the United States. *Higher Education Policy.*

Lucas, C. J. (2006). *American higher education: A history* (2nd ed.). New York, NY: Palgrave Macmillan.

McKelvey, B. (1982). *Organizational systematics.* Berkeley, CA: University of California Press.

Millett, J. D. (1962). *The academic community: An essay on organization.* New York, NY: McGraw-Hill.

Mintzberg, H. (1979). *The structure of organizations.* Upper Saddle River, NJ: Prentice Hall.

Mortimer, K. P., & McConnell, T. R. (1978). *Sharing authority effectively.* San Francisco, CA: Jossey-Bass.

Newman, J. H. (1990). *The idea of the university.* South Bend, IN: University of Notre Dame Press. (Original work published 1852).

Perrow, C. (1970). *Organizational analysis: A sociological view.* Belmont, CA: Wadsworth.

Peterson, M. W. (1974). Organization and administration in higher education: Sociological and social-psychological perspectives. *Review of Research in Education, 2,* 296–347. Washington, DC: American Educational Research Association.

Pfeffer, J., & Salancik, G. R. (1978). *The external control of organizations: A resource dependence perspective.* New York, NY: Harper & Row.

Pondy, L. R., & Mitroff, I. I. (1979). Beyond open systems models of organization. In B. M. Staw (Ed.), *Research in organizational behaviors* (Vol. 1, pp. 3–29). Greenwich, CT: JAI Press.

Riley, G. L., & Baldridge, V. J. (1977). *Governing academic organizations: New problems, new perspectives.* Berkeley, CA: McCutchan.

Scott, W. R., & Davis, G. F. (2007). *Organizations and organizing: Rational, natural, and open system perspectives.* Upper Saddle River, NJ: Pearson Prentice Hall.

Simon, H. A. (1997). *Administrative behavior.* New York, NY: Macmillan. (Original work published 1947).

Smith, A. (1991). *The wealth of nations.* New York, NY: Prometheus Books. (Original work published 1776).

Stroup, H. (1966). *Bureaucracy in higher education.* New York, NY: Free Press.

Thelin, J. R. (2004). *A history of American higher education.* Baltimore, MD: Johns Hopkins University Press.

Veblen, T. (1918). *The higher learning in America: A memorandum on the conduct of universities by business men.* New York, NY: B. W. Huebsch.

Weber, M. (1947). *The theory of social and economic organizations.* New York, NY: Free Press.

Weick, K. E. (1976). Educational organizations as loosely coupled systems. *Administrative Science Quarterly, 21*(1), 1–19.

Wiener, N. (1954). *The human use of human beings: Cybernetics and society.* Garden City, NY: Doubleday Anchor.

3

GLOBAL ENGAGEMENT OF COLLEGES AND UNIVERSITIES

The internationalization of higher education institutions has been an issue of increasing debate and interest among colleges and universities over the past decade. Enhanced global interconnectivity has made it easier for students, faculty, knowledge, and academic institutions to move around the world. Indeed, this interconnectivity means that colleges and universities need to evaluate their mission and activities in light of the changing international environment. Similarly, institutions need to ensure that their internationalization efforts align with their institutional mission. The global marketplace in which graduates now pursue employment requires institutions to expose students to international perspectives and experiences. Indeed, nations' long-term growth and success will be based on their economic, political, and social leaders' ability to operate within diverse international organizations and environments. Many of the research problems now being addressed by scientists no longer are bounded by national borders. Issues such as climate change, energy production, and water scarcity are globally relevant, and higher education institutions should facilitate and lead collaborations of scientists around the globe to work on such challenges.

Beyond issues of mission, for better or for worse, globalization is transforming the economic and organizational models of many higher education institutions. International students have become important for many institutions in reaching enrollment targets, particularly in science and engineering graduate programs. Furthermore, colleges and universities are beginning to expand their physical presence beyond their own national borders, operating research sites, academic programs, and campuses in other countries. Despite the intensifying global environment, discussions persist in state governments and in the governing bodies of higher education institutions about the appropriateness of such engagements and the resources that should be allocated to support such endeavors.

While a renewed interest was evident in the past decade among U.S. colleges and universities to engage with the world beyond their nation's borders, few higher education institutions have ever operated in complete isolation from the broader world. Scholars and students have long crossed international borders in the pursuit of new experiences, new people, new jobs, and new knowledge. Even before the Internet, knowledge could hardly be limited to national borders. Books, academic journals, and scholars moved between nations, bringing new knowledge from one country to another. The past several decades, however, have witnessed an explosion in the number of individuals, programs, and institutions crossing borders. The increasing interconnectedness of economies, governments, and cultures has made it even more important for students to acquire the skills and knowledge necessary to be internationally engaged. Moreover, higher education institutions are now viewed broadly as economic drivers critical for nations to maintain or expand their economic competitiveness (Lane, 2012).

For the past two decades, internationalization of higher education in the United States has focused on attracting students from other countries, transforming curricula, providing opportunities for domestic students to study abroad, and hiring faculty members with degrees from institutions outside the United States. More recently, though, many educational institutions in the United States have been aggressively expanding their global footprint through engagements in joint partnerships with institutions in other nations, building research capacity abroad, and running offices and campuses in multiple countries. For some colleges and universities, the movement of students, faculty, and institutions across international borders is transforming the ways higher education institutions operate.

Such global engagements raise questions about the purpose and priorities of international education. For some advocates, such efforts have been about building collaborative environments, fostering intercultural development among students and scholars, and enhancing international relations between nations. Indeed, in the days following World War II, when calling for the creation of a new program to support the international exchange of scholars, U.S. Senator J. William Fulbright proposed the creation of a student exchange program in the fields of education, culture, and science for the purpose of promoting international goodwill (Dudden & Dynes, 1987).[1] However, in the nearly 70 years since the establishment of the Fulbright Program, a marked transition has occurred in the ways many governments are engaging with international higher education. While Fulbright (and similar types of governmental initiatives in other countries) supported international exchanges to foster great international harmony among nations, today international higher education remains no longer the exclusive domain of such entities. In many nations, higher education policy is being increasingly tied to economic development and competitiveness plans and policies. Even in the United States, the U.S. Department of Commerce plays a role parallel to that of the Department of State in promoting postsecondary educational opportunities in the United States for foreign students. This changing dynamic has led to tension between advocates of international education as a means to foster international diplomacy and advocates of the growing economic importance of the sector. Our purpose here is not to explore these tensions but rather make readers aware that such tensions exist. This chapter provides a broad overview of significant developments in the global higher education marketplace. It does not provide a framework for internationalizing a college curriculum or designing a study abroad experience. Instead, it introduces many of the current trends in internationalization, including policy developments in other regions that may affect the work of U.S. institutions. It also provides practical administrative advice to maximize the benefits and minimize the negative effects of such trends. This chapter is organized around the following themes:

1. Global growth and importance of higher education
2. Defining terminology
3. Organizing internationalization
4. Types of mobility: students, faculty, programs, and institutions
5. Accreditation and federal regulation

By necessity, this chapter is limited in breadth and depth. The growing global engagement of higher education institutions is vast, and no one book chapter can provide a comprehensive review of all relevant literature, trends, and issues. The noninclusion of certain institutions, individuals, and issues should not be perceived as an indication of importance or a lack thereof.

Moreover, this chapter is part of the introductory section of the book, as internationalization and globalization are not separate from other aspects of college and university administration; rather, they very much influence those aspects. As such, this chapter provides a context for the other chapters in this book.

Global Growth and Importance of Higher Education

The United States and its institutions of higher education are being buffeted by a number of international influences working to remake the global higher education landscape, and the increasing interconnectedness fostered by globalization ties the activities of U.S. colleges and universities to changes occurring outside the country. Many leaders of these American institutions have not, however, realized the full extent to which these phenomena may affect the operation of their institutions. In part, consideration of foreign perspectives could be lacking because of the same factors that created a similar situation for U.S. business. As Doug Ready (Dumaine & Ready, 1995), chief executive officer of the International Consortium for Executive Development Research, stated:

> Two generations of economic dominance, combined with a strong domestic market, have contributed to creating a colonial mentality in the U.S. companies. Why learn a second language or waste energy learning about other cultural preferences when people have to come to you? (para. 6)

There is a high degree of congruence between U.S. business and U.S. higher education in this aspect. American higher education has enjoyed decades of global dominance, significant government support, and a strong and growing student market. By some measures, U.S. research universities are considered the best institutions in the world, and most observers would agree that the American higher education system remains the strongest in the world.[2] Moreover, the United States has long been a favorite destination of students from other countries wanting to study abroad, and it has been considered by foreign institutions and governments as a model for creating a higher education system.

The global higher education market is changing rapidly, however. In 2009 almost 3.7 million students were studying outside their home country (Organisation for Economic and Cooperative Development [OECD], 2011). Böhm, Davis, Meares, and Pearce (2002) forecasted that given current trends, that number may rise to 7.2 million by 2025. Indeed, in 2009 international students accounted for 10% or more of higher education enrollments in Australia, Austria, New Zealand, Switzerland, and the United Kingdom (OECD). While the overall number of foreign students studying abroad is projected to increase, and the number of foreign students in the United States has continued to increase, the United States' global share of students studying abroad decreased from 26% in 2000 to 18% in 2009 (OECD). The declining proportion of those coming to the United States for their studies signals a strengthening of other higher education systems as well as increasing competition among nations and education providers. Indeed, a number of countries are strengthening their higher education systems to reduce the number of students leaving to study abroad and stem the brain drain of their best and brightest students (McBurnie & Ziguras, 2007; Wildavsky, 2010). Furthermore, many higher education sectors in Asia are beginning to reorient to India and China, away from the United States and western Europe. However, the dominance and worldwide prestige of the U.S. system have led many American higher education leaders and scholars to overlook the changing conditions outside their country.

The emergence of the knowledge-based society has anointed higher education as a critical component in cultural, political, and economic development. Indeed, the title of Wildavsky's (2010) book proclaimed his belief about the important role of higher education: *The Great Brain Race: How Global Universities Are Reshaping the World.* Wildavsky explained how nations such as China and India are increasingly investing in higher education to prevent brain drain and to attract the best and brightest students from other nations. In another study, Lane (2011) found that the governments of Malaysia and Dubai are importing higher education institutions from other nations with the hope, in part, of bolstering the international reputations of their higher education sector and position themselves as education hubs to attract more international students. Indeed, more than a decade ago, an article in the *Economist* noted the changing role of higher education institutions, describing the modern university as "not just a creator of knowledge, a trainer of young minds and transmitter of culture, but also a major agent of economic growth: the knowledge factory, as it were, at the center of the knowledge economy" ("The Knowledge Factory," 1997, p. 4).

Globalization has created an environment in which higher education is viewed as a tradable service, and some educational institutions have transformed into multinational enterprises (Lane & Kinser, 2011b).[3] While there has been worldwide acknowledgment of the importance of higher education, data about the global size or growth of higher education remains limited. From an economic perspective, the global education market was estimated by the Ministry of Trade and Industry of Singapore (2003) to be $2.2 trillion in 2002, a significant increase from an estimated $27 billion in 1995 (Patrinos, 2002). In 1999 education was included in one of the United States' top five service exports, producing about $10.7 billion in revenue (Moll,

Gates, & Quigley, 2001), and by 2009 the value of U.S. education exports had risen to $20 billion.[4] In 2009 education became Australia's leading service export, grossing about AUS$18.6 billion. However, demonstrating the fragility of the international market, international education trade in Australia shrunk 12%, about AUS$2.2 billion, in the following year (Australian Education International, 2011).

The growth in the international education sector's economic impact has been partially spurred by a growing demand for tertiary education, particularly in developing nations where access to and the need for higher education has been limited (Levy, 2006). This need is being driven by increasing numbers of secondary school graduates, heightened demand for educational opportunity among females, and changing workforce demands fostered by the movement toward a knowledge-based economy.

The importance of global engagement becomes even more significant when considered from a national perspective. Colleges and universities provide students with formative experiences that can affect their perspectives of other countries, their willingness to engage with them, and the ways in which they engage (James, 2005). International experiences are important for increasing appreciation of other cultures, learning languages, and instilling a long-term willingness to travel abroad. A U.S. report about the national importance of study abroad experiences began with this passage:

> On the international stage, what nations don't know can hurt them. In recent generations, evidence of that reality has been readily available. What we did not know about Vietnam hurt the United States. What we did not understand about the history and culture of the former Ottoman Empire has complicated our efforts in the Middle East for decades. Mistakes involving the Third World and its debt have cost American financiers billions of dollars. And our lack of knowledge about economic, commercial, and industrial developments in Japan, China, and India, successively, has undermined American competitiveness. Global competence costs, but ignorance costs far more. (Commission on the Abraham Lincoln Study Abroad Program, 2005, p. 3)

The argument of the Lincoln commission is that study abroad is much more than an institutional imperative. It is of national importance. The argument is that all American undergraduate students should have the opportunity to study abroad, and that such experiences should be the norm on college campuses and not an exception limited to the rich or privileged.

Defining Terminology

The term *internationalization* has been used since the 1980s to indicate a "process of integrating an international, intercultural, and global dimension into the purpose, functions (teaching, research, services) and the delivery of post-secondary education" (Knight, 2003, p. 2). Academic administrators should take note of two important components of this definition. First, being a process suggests that efforts in this arena should be ongoing and evolving, not static. The international environment continues to change, and institution officials who desire to be involved in such a dynamic environment should be prepared to respond to those changes. Second, the process involves international, intercultural, and global dimensions. *International* places great weight on the concept of nations being distinct entities that can be learned from and understood in a comparative fashion. *Intercultural* decouples the concept from being solely about nations by emphasizing the role of peoples and their cultural traditions. *Cultural* is not necessarily restricted by geopolitical boundaries. Rather, groups of people and their cultures can transcend such boundaries. *International* and *intercultural* highlight the comparative aspect of internationalization. This comparative perspective helps those involved to understand those different from them as well as their own nation and culture.

Globalization, on the other hand, is more focused on worldwide or global developments. In fact, *globalization* is a term that is now often used in higher education literature, although there is yet to be full agreement on its exact meaning in the higher education context (Guruz, 2008; McBurnie & Ziguras, 2007). Essentially, it is a process through which the world is becoming more interconnected and interdependent because of increasing flows of knowledge, people, culture, ideas, and trade. Most often thought of in terms of economic impact, globalization affects myriad areas, including education, environment, politics, and health.

The more specific terms *transnational, cross border*, and *offshore* are often used interchangeably to describe the movement of academic programs, projects, research initiatives, services, consulting assistance, and other activities across geopolitical borders (Davis, Olsen, & Böhm, 2000; Knight, 2004; Lane & Kinser, 2011b; McBurnie & Ziguras, 2007). Transnational education has been defined as education "in which the learners are located in a country different from the one where the awarding institution is based" (Council of Europe, 2001, p. 1). As noted by McBurnie and Ziguras, terms such as *transnational* (and, to a lesser extent, *cross border*) continue to recognize the involvement of the nation-state but also acknowledge the transcendence of educational institutions beyond national borders.

The increased mobility of students, programs, and institutions has necessitated new labels to denote the role or position of actors in cross-border education. *Education provider* is an inclusive term referring to all types of institutions offering an educational experience, usually with the opportunity for the student to earn a degree or comparable credential. The *home* or *exporting nation* refers to the country where the education provider is based and where the educational service is being exported from. The *host* or *importing nation* is where the education provider is offering the services to students.

In the area of study mobility, *international* or *foreign student* describes a student who is studying in another country. From the perspective of the academic administrator, an international student is usually a matriculated student whose permanent address is in a country other than where the campus is located. International students can be in attendance for only a few weeks, a semester, or the duration of an entire degree. While students may come from other countries to pursue some or all of their educational program at a college or university in the United States, they may also choose to pursue a portion of their academic program in another country. Such experiences, generally referred to as *study abroad*, include a range of activities such as classroom instruction, internships, research experiences (e.g., working on an archeology professor's dig in Egypt or helping to conduct interviews for a sociologist's study of the Roma in central Europe), or service-learning.

While administrators of some institutions are still deciding how international initiatives relate to their institutional missions, other institutions have developed into multinational colleges and universities. New York University has established a campus in Abu Dhabi, and Missouri University of Science and Technology has established a number of joint degree programs in countries throughout Asia. Despite these headline-grabbing endeavors, Patti McGill Peterson (2010), former executive director of the Council for International Exchange of Scholars and vice president of the Institute for International Education, argues that the faculty remains the central component of a globally oriented campus, yet the role of the faculty in the internationalization process is largely misunderstood. Professors in the United States have, however, long been one of the least internationally oriented faculties in the world.

In reviewing the findings of a 1992 international study of faculty by the Carnegie Foundation for the Advancement of Teaching and Learning, Finkelstein, Walker, and Chen (2009) concluded:

> Whatever their scientific and scholarly accomplishments, as reflected in a disproportionate share of international prizes such as the Nobel, American professors tended to be relatively insular and provincial in their orientation, turning inward in a kind of self-reflexive, if not narcissistic, gaze rather than outward to the larger world. (p. 113)

Moreover, Altbach and Lewis (1996) reported that a 14-nation study by the Carnegie Foundation found that U.S.-based academics were the least interested in reading scholarship by authors in other countries, engaging with international scholars, and internationalizing their curricula. In the 2007 follow-up survey, including 17 nations, U.S.-based faculty remained among the least likely to collaborate on or coauthor a publication with international researchers in other countries (Finkelstein et al., 2009). However, in that same survey, U.S. faculty reported above-average integration of international perspectives in teaching and research activities.

Understanding their faculties' orientation toward internationalization is important for institutional leaders, particularly as they seek to create undergraduate programs that require or strongly encourage students to gain international experience. While the scholarship about faculty motivations for participating in international work is limited, Klyberg (2012) found that professors at two comprehensive higher education institutions became interested in internationalization primarily because of experiences that happened outside of or before their institution adopted an internationalization initiative—not because of the introduction of a policy or incentives. That is, participants were more intrinsically than extrinsically motivated to engage in internationalization. While these faculty members expressed a desire for a formal acknowledgment or reward for their efforts to internationalize the curriculum, lead study abroad, and other such activities, their motivation to participate in this work, in essence, came from a belief in an academic and professional obligation to perform their teaching, research, and service responsibilities in an internationalized fashion. Klyberg's findings suggest that administrators of colleges and universities interested in internationalization need to identify creative ways to recognize participating faculty members and motivate uninvolved professors in their initiatives.

Organizing the Internationalization of Colleges and Universities

The concept of *internationalization* is difficult to define. It includes a range of initiatives from incorporating global perspectives into the academic curriculum to hosting international scholars to supporting the travel of students and faculty to other countries. There is no one right way to internationalize a campus or an institution, and internationalization efforts are not limited to a few elite institutions. Internationalization has been pursued by a range of institutions: two- and four-year, public and private, for-profit and nonprofit. What is important is that institution administrators remain focused on their mission when deciding how and when to internationalize.

For example, Houston Community College (HCC) is globally engaged with joint academic ventures and degree-granting operations in several countries, including Vietnam and Qatar. Historically, HCC was a domestically focused institution serving the students and communities in and around Houston. In the early 2000s, however, the institution's leadership decided it would be of benefit to its domestic students and the local communities for the institution to expand internationally (Spangler & Tyler, 2011). Rather than pursue every opportunity to expand, the institution's leaders examined each possibility in light of the college's mission and how the activity fit with the environmental context of HCC. Houston has one of the largest populations of Vietnamese immigrants in the United States, and its petroleum and health industries are linked to those in Qatar. Thus, the expansion of HCC into these countries was seen as an expansion of its mission in Houston.

Another example comes from a four-year public institution in the Northeast. Located in Boston, Northeastern University was once a local institution that primarily enrolled students from the surrounding region and whose alumni mostly settled in New England. During the first decade of 2000, Northeastern transformed itself into a globally engaged institution whose campus is covered with banners reminding faculty, staff, and students to pursue Engagement With the World. What is remarkable about this makeover is that it ensured that Northeastern's internationalization efforts helped to reinforce the institution's strengths. For more than 100 years, Northeastern has provided its students with opportunities to gain months of professionally related experience through its award-winning cooperative education program. When considering how to internationalize their campus, institutional leaders focused on the co-op program, deciding to offer students domestic and foreign experiences. In the 2009–2010 academic year the school reported it had provided 300 co-ops in 49 countries. According to *The Chronicle of Higher Education*, "Students have worked for a soft-drink maker in Lagos, Nigeria; with an electronics manufacturer in Shenzen, one of China's booming special-economic zones; and even at an Antarctic research station" (Fischer, 2011). Most importantly, internationalization has proven to be a success with students. Within a four-year period (2005–2009), Northeastern doubled the percentage of international students in its student body (to 10%) and increased the number of domestic students studying abroad by threefold. The success of the transformation has been credited to Northeastern's intent to remain mission driven as it engaged in internationalization.

In a more instruction-based approach, the State University of New York (SUNY) created the Center for Collaborative Online and International Learning (COIL) to provide its faculty (and faculty from non-SUNY campuses within and beyond New York's borders) with the opportunity to coteach a course with a colleague in another country. One of SUNY's new strategic initiatives, SUNY and the World, focuses on internationalizing SUNY campuses and providing new means for students to be exposed to meaningful international experiences. The purpose of COIL is

> to develop and implement online collaborative international courses at SUNY as a format for experiential cross-cultural learning, thereby sensitizing participating students to the larger world by deepening their understanding of themselves, their culture, how they are perceived and how they perceive others. ("About COIL," n.d.)

The program is meant to bridge study abroad and curriculum internationalization by allowing instructors in two countries to coteach a course. This innovative format allows students to collaborate with international colleagues in class discussions and group projects without having to leave their campus. By sponsoring COIL, SUNY hopes to expand the intercultural learning of students and faculty, many of whom may not otherwise have the opportunity to interact with people in other countries.

How institutions organize their international efforts also varies markedly. Many institutions now have offices or divisions that are responsible for various aspects of their international or global initiatives. Offices often hold responsibility for coordinating study abroad experiences, recruiting and retaining international students, facilitating research and academic partnerships with other countries, helping faculty with international travel, and so forth. Historically, these responsibilities were frequently dispersed throughout the administrative structure. For example, the admissions office would be responsible for recruitment, student affairs would work with international students on campus, and study abroad would operate as a stand-alone operation. Moreover, internationalization of curriculum or faculty research agendas was often left to the direction and desire of individual faculty members. Often, the decentralized nature of international programs would result in their being ghettoized rather than embraced throughout the institution's administrative and academic structures.

Many colleges and universities have begun to create structures that bring together various international programs in an attempt to infuse international efforts throughout their teaching, research, and service missions. One of the first institutions to create an integrated international programs division, Michigan State University (MSU) founded its International Studies and Programs (ISP) in 1956. ISP, which is led by a dean, is responsible for international students and visitors as well as area study centers and international offices such as MSU Dubai. ISP's mission has been to foster international understanding and activity throughout the university.

Internationalization has become more widely embraced in higher education institutions around the world, and its importance can be seen by its increased presence in institutional mission statements. Not all institutions (nor the stakeholders they serve) have embraced the concept, however. Indeed, fewer than 15 years ago, Mestenhauser (1998) decried, "Much of what I see in international education in the United States is minimalist, instrumental, introductory, conceptually simple, disciplinary reductionist, and static" (p. 7). Not all colleges and universities have the interest, resources, or faculty engagement apparent at HCC, Northeastern, the SUNY system, or MSU. Unfortunately, many administrators view international programs as something separate from their institution's core mission, and the people in local communities do not always understand why officials of a college or university may desire their institution to become more international in nature. Internationalization efforts should not be seen as something separate from the other roles of academic institutions. As Richard Levin (2008), president of Yale University, observed:

> In every nation, universities play a critical role in providing the human capital for business, government, and civil society, and the research generated by universities helps to drive the economy. . . . By adapting our curriculum and encouraging the flow of students across borders, we can better

prepare the next generation for leadership and citizenship in an independent world, developing in them the capacity for cross-cultural understanding that will be so important for the future peace and prosperity of the planet. By encouraging international collaboration in research, we can accelerate the advance of science and technology that will improve our health and material well-being. And, by utilizing modern communications technologies, we can provide the benefits of education to a far larger fraction of humanity. Such is the future of the global university.

Types of Mobility: Students, Faculty, Programs, and Institutions

International academic mobility is not a new concept. In fact, historically speaking, academics have been internationally engaged for decades. The international mobility of scholars can be traced to the fifth century BC, when wandering academics made a living by sharing their knowledge with others. Examples of such scholars include the Sophists of Greece (Welch, 1997) and the shih in China (Nakayama, 1984). Centuries later in western Europe when universities began to emerge, students and scholars often crossed borders to study at these educational institutions (Rait, 1931; Rashdall, 1895), and foreign enrollments at some institutions are estimated to have been as high as 10% of the student body (Neave, 2002). By the end of the 18th century, Britain, France, and Germany had become the knowledge centers of the world, and many educational institutions built elsewhere at that time were modeled after one or more of the universities in those countries. Consequently, scholars from the hubs were recruited to teach in other countries, and the students of other countries were sent to study in Britain, France, and Germany with the hope that they would return home as faculty members (Altbach & Teichler, 2001).

This brief history of the movement of international scholars and students demonstrates that internationalization of colleges and universities is not a new concept, although in the United States in the 19th and 20th centuries interest in higher education being internationally connected or engaged declined. While there are examples of U.S. institutions that maintain long-standing commitments to international perspectives and engagements, many have focused on educating students and producing research that would be relevant to local communities. The following provides an overview of the increasing mobility of individual members of colleges and universities and their institutions in their entirety.

Students

Universities in Asia, Australia, Europe, and the Americas are increasingly recruiting students from around the world to foster multicultural engagement while sending their own students abroad to prepare them to be successful in the global workforce. The number of students studying outside their own country has increased from 800,000 in 1975 to more than 3.7 million in 2009 (OECD, 2011). Most students travel from one developed country to another, although there has been an increasing flow of students from developing to developed countries, as well as the opposite, with students traveling from developed to developing countries. However, nearly 80% of those students studying abroad did so in OECD countries (OECD). Asian students account for more than 50% of all students who study abroad. The United States remains the most popular destination for study abroad students (OECD), with foreign students earning nearly 30% of the doctoral degrees awarded in the United States and with most students coming from China, India, and South Korea (National Science Board, 2010). The United States remains the leading destination for students to study abroad, although the nation has seen its share of the study abroad market shrink over the last several years. U.S. student participation in study abroad increased markedly over the past decade, and a growing number of academic programs are encouraging (some requiring) their students to study in another country prior to graduation. About 95% of all student experiences last one semester or less. The two most popular fields for study abroad are social sciences and business.

The first formal study abroad program in the United States likely began in the 1920s with a group of undergraduates from the University of Delaware sailing from New York to Paris (Munroe, 1986). That group of eight students was led by Raymond Kirkbride, a professor of modern languages, who believed that exposure to other cultures was important for increasing intercultural appreciation. More than 100 years later, the same university created the Institute for Global Studies, which oversees more than 80 study abroad programs in 45 countries.

While the University of Delaware may have been the first to offer a study abroad experience, it is clearly no longer the only one to do so. In the academic year 2009–2010, more than 270,000 American students pursued their academic studies in a foreign country (Institute of International Education, 2011)—a 3.9% increase over the previous year. This growth was part of a significant expansion in the number of students studying abroad in the first decade of the 21st century; during this decade, the number of American students studying overseas increased by more than 100,000 students (Institute of International Education, 2011). The decline reported in the most recent numbers will likely reverse itself, and many groups believe that interest in study abroad programs will continue to increase. Such declines, however, do illustrate how the unpredictability of international travel and instability in the domestic economy can affect such programs.[5]

There are three general types of study abroad programs. In faculty-led endeavors, students accompany a professor to another country usually to study a particular issue. The faculty member works with local businesses and organizations to provide students with opportunities to talk with local leaders, visit specific places, engage in a service project, and participate in other activities. These activities extend the theoretical aspects of the course and allow students the opportunity to experience more fully the challenges confronted by people of other nations. Another type of study abroad is institutional exchange. In these situations, historically, an institution develops an agreement with an institution in another country to allow its students to enroll in the partner institution for a period of time, often a semester. As of late, such arrangements have become part of multi-institutional agreements or are run by larger organizations that broker the relationships. These exchanges allow students to experience the academic structure of another nation as well as obtain a more in-depth cultural experience by living and learning among the students in another country.

A third set of study abroad experiences—internships, research, and service programs—has emerged more recently. These types of study abroad allow students to engage in some type of work or internship experience while overseas. According to the Institute of International Education (2010), 18,715 students had received credit for an internship experience in another country. A number of institutions are now tapping their alumni to help place students in international internships. Levin (2008), for example, noted that Yale University now has an alumni infrastructure to support summer internships in 17 cities: Shanghai, Hong Kong, Singapore, Delhi, Accra, Cape Town, Kampala, Montreal, Monterrey, Buenos Aires, João Pessoa, Brussels, Budapest, Istanbul, London, Madrid, and Athens.

Faculty

The faculty is the core of the academic enterprise and has always been an international profession. Intellectual curiosity and scientific inquiry rarely end at national borders. An increasing number of faculty members appear to be pursuing international careers, taking positions in countries other than where they obtained their graduate degrees, and where they obtained their degree may have been different from the country in which they grew up. Moreover, research has become an increasingly internationalized pursuit, with scholarly societies, academic journals, and research programs becoming internationally oriented. Indeed, many of today's most pressing research problems transcend nations and require cross-country collaboration of scholars and higher education institutions.

Unlike students, however, information about the international mobility of faculty is very limited. No international organization collects this data in any systematic way. However, the National Science Foundation does track a variety of statistics related to faculty in the fields of science, technology, engineering, and mathematics. It reported that in 2006 nearly 20% of all full-time faculty employed by U.S. colleges and universities were foreign born (National Science Board, 2010). However, the numbers varied significantly based on disciplines. In computer science, more than half of all full-time faculty and academic researchers were foreign born; that number drops to nearly 20% or less for full-time faculty and academic researchers in the life sciences, physical sciences, psychology, and social sciences.

Programs

While some students cross borders to pursue an education, a number of institutions are now moving their programs across borders to increase their availability to students in other countries. Knight (2005) defines *cross-border program mobility* as

> the movement of individual education/training courses and programs across national borders through face-to-face, distance, or a combination of these modes. Credits toward a qualification can be awarded by the sending foreign country provider or by an affiliated domestic partner or jointly. (p. 10)

According to Knight, such endeavors can take a variety of forms, although the prevalence of such forms is not known. It is likely that through such engagements people with different cultural, religious, and political beliefs will need to work together. Hereto, we believe that pursuing such collaboration through a democratic perspective is important. We emphasize, however, that this practice means allowing all parties to be freely and fairly engaged in the process and does not reflect a particular political philosophy.

In franchise arrangements, an institution in Country A allows an institution in Country B to offer its curriculum in Country B, and a credential is usually awarded by the institution in Country A. In contrast, twinning arrangements involve an articulation agreement between institutions in two different countries, whereby students can begin their study in one country and end it in another. In such arrangements, participating students receive their degrees from the institution providing the final year or years of study. Institutions in the United States rarely engage in franchising or twinning, preferring double/joint degree programs.

In double/joint degree programs, institutions in different countries form partnerships in providing a degree program, and students receive their degrees from both institutions or joint degrees from the collaborating institutions. With double degrees, students engage in course work that leads to degrees from two different institutions. Joint degree programs usually require students to take courses at two different institutions, but they receive one degree, usually with the imprimatur of both institutions. A study of 285 institutions in 28 countries revealed that almost all respondents (95%) saw such programs as part of their internationalization strategy, although only 55% had a clear policy related to joint/double degree program development (Obst, Kuder, & Banks, 2011). The United States offered the most double degree programs, preferring them over joint degree programs, and France was the top provider of joint degree programs. While the majority of double degree programs globally are at the master's level, most of these programs in the United States are at the undergraduate level. Moreover, U.S. institutions (along with those in China, France, India, and Germany) are among the most desired collaborators.

Institutions

Over the past 15 years the number of higher education institutions with campuses in more than one country has rapidly increased. An international branch campus (IBC) is an "entity that is owned, at least in part, by a foreign education provider; operated in the name of the foreign education provider; engages in at least some face-to-face teaching; and provides access to an entire academic program that leads to a credential awarded by the foreign education" (Lane, 2011, p. 5). These entities may be wholly owned by the home campus, operated in partnership with a foreign investor, or subsidized by the host government (Lane, 2010; Lane & Kinser, 2011c).

The earliest known IBC was built in Italy by Johns Hopkins University in the 1950s. Today nearly 200 IBCs are disbursed around the globe.[6]

According to a survey of IBCs, most U.S. institutions that are opening campuses abroad are private, although globally most non-U.S. schools opening IBCs tend to be public (Lane & Kinser, 2011a). IBCs mostly offer professional programs; the master's of business administration is the most common degree offered. Nearly half of all IBCs are operated by U.S. colleges and universities, while Australia and the United Kingdom are the other largest exporters of such entities. The largest importers (i.e., hosts) of IBCs are nations in the Middle East and Asia.

Accreditation and Federal Regulations

In addition to the organization of internationalization, higher education institutions must address or at least be aware of a number of operating issues. Here we address issues of accreditation, particularly when an institution undergoes a substantive change. In addition, myriad policies and regulations deal either directly or indirectly with internationalization efforts. We also address distinct areas of regulation: study abroad liability, federal financial aid, the Student and Exchange Visitor (SEVIS) Program, and export control laws.[7]

Accreditation

In the United States the institutional accreditation bodies do not pay much attention to issues of institutional internationalization, per se. However, if institutions choose to make internationalization a priority or an institutional goal, reviewers may assess the extent to which that goal is being implemented—but that goal is based on institutional decision making. Institutional accreditors have not reached the point of requiring institutions to internationalize. However, anytime a regionally accredited institution engages in a substantive change, such as offering an academic program in a foreign location, the institution is required to report the change to its accreditation body. An institution's regional accreditation body must provide approval for any substantive change, and for IBCs, an accreditor is now required to perform an on-site visit to ensure that the IBC meets its requirements. The substantive change should be approved prior to the change's actual occurrence, or the institution risks losing its accreditation. Operating in a foreign environment can bring many unanticipated challenges that could threaten institutional quality (e.g., lack of a qualified student market to draw enrollments from, inability to attract high-quality faculty, financial pressures, and disagreements with local partners or governments). Failing to meet the minimum requirements of the accreditation agency could lead to a choice between closing the campus or losing accreditation for the entire institution.

Study Abroad Liability

While we have argued the importance of study abroad programs, they do not come without risk to student, faculty, or institution.[8] Travel always presents safety concerns, but providing study abroad opportunities for students presents a host of additional issues ranging from unprepared or immature students; different laws and customs; different cultural expectations; varying levels of security; and in some cases the constant threat of harm from gangs, terrorists, and war. Institutions that prepare for the unforeseeable will best be able to serve and protect their students and staff.

According to Hoye and Rhodes (2000), the level of risk to the institution depends on its relationship with the program. "As the degree of ownership and control exercised over a particular program by the home campus increases, the potential liability exposure of the home campus also increases (in the absence of a contractual provision to the contrary)" (p. 155). Safety concerns can range from hitchhiking to terrorist bombings, but the U.S. courts have handled only limited legal questions relating to study abroad programs.

The courts are very clear that, to the extent possible, institutions and their on-site representatives have a duty to protect students and ensure their continued safety while participating in activities sponsored by the institution. In *Fay v. Thiel College* (2001), an undergraduate student participating in a school-sponsored trip to Peru in May 1996 was left to fend for herself after becoming ill during the trip. The student was taken to a clinic and left to the care of a missionary not connected with the college. At the clinic the student's requests to be transferred to better facilities and to call her parents were refused, and she was sexually assaulted by two members of the medical staff. While the suit was eventually settled confidentially out of court, the court did rule that the waiver signed by the student did not absolve the institution from its obligation of responsibility for the student's safety.

Similarly, a U.S. District Court in Michigan determined that institutions are obligated under Title IX of the Education Amendments of 1972 to reasonably protect students from environments that are sexually harassing or hostile (see *King et al. v. Eastern Michigan University*, 2002). This decision is not to suggest that institutions are responsible for changing entire cultures, particularly those that do not share beliefs about gender similar to those in the United States. However, colleges and universities do have a responsibility to provide students with a safe environment in situations when the institution or its representatives do have some control.[9]

Even though the law may not be entirely clear on the extent to which institutions may be legally responsible for student safety and access, institutional administrators should be diligent in creating and updating crises management and emergency preparedness plans. However, international education professionals need to be careful in how they present study abroad leaders and participants with information about liability issues. Too much of a focus on legal issues rather than on the educational experiences may scare away potential participants. Regardless of the legal liability or limits to responsibility, the ultimate task of institution officials should be to consider the educational experience being gained while ensuring the health and safety of their students, faculty, and staff who are traveling abroad.[10]

Federal Financial Aid

From the perspective of U.S. colleges and universities, there are two aspects to consider regarding financial aid and internationalization. First, how does financial aid work for international students? Second, how does it work for American students studying abroad? The answer to the first question is quite simple: International students are not eligible for federal financial aid. Indeed, for most international students, the federal government requires that they demonstrate they can afford the cost of their study in the United States before a visa is issued.[11] Some programs such as the Fulbright Program provide funding for foreign students, but the availability of government and private money in the United States for such students is limited.

For U.S. students who want to study abroad, they can apply their financial aid, such as Pell grants and federal Stafford loans, to cover educational-related costs associated with their overseas experience. In most cases, to be eligible for financial aid the student must be pursuing a degree and must earn credits from his or her home institution or earn credits from another institution that can then be transferred to the home institution. If no college-level credits are being earned, the student is not likely to be eligible for financial aid. There are also two federal scholarships designed to support study abroad. The David L. Boren Undergraduate Scholarships for Study Abroad support students interested in studying languages or cultures deemed important to U.S. national security. The Benjamin A. Gilman International Scholarship is available to students who receive a federal Pell grant. In addition, each institution may implement rules regarding student eligibility for financial aid, and specific questions should be addressed to the campus financial aid office.

SEVIS Program

Student and Exchange Visitor (SEVIS) is a web-based program to track foreign students and scholars who are in the United States on temporary, nonimmigrant visas to participate in the U.S. education system. SEVIS is used by the U.S. Department of State and the U.S. Department of Homeland Security, including the U.S. Customs and Border Protection, U.S. Citizenship and Immigration Services, and U.S. Immigration and Customs Enforcement, to collect information regarding a visitor's name, U.S. address, U.S. higher education institution, program of study, degree level being pursued, funding level (and any change in funding), and authorization for on-campus employment. All postsecondary educational institutions in the United States are required to comply with SEVIS reporting requirements.

After a foreign student has been admitted to an institution approved by the Student and Exchange Visitor Program, which administers the student portion of SEVIS, he or she should receive Form I-20 from the institution.[12] That form will be used by the student to apply for a visa to study in the United States. Students are required to pay a SEVIS processing fee, which varies according to the type of visa they are applying for. Once the fee is paid, the student can apply for a visa at a U.S. embassy or consulate. Upon beginning the student's study in the United States, the college or university becomes responsible for tracking and reporting any changes in the course of study or funding situation.

Export Control Laws

One area of federal involvement in cross-border education that is not often discussed, but may become of increasing importance for administrators to be aware of, is the nation's export control laws. Export control laws regulate the disbursement of information, products, and services deemed protected because of foreign trade policy and national security concerns to foreign nationals and nation-states. An export is any item that leaves the United

States, and imparting knowledge to foreign students, whether in the United States or abroad, is classified as exporting.[13]

For U.S. colleges and universities, most teaching and research activities are exempted from export control laws. However, a U.S. campus located in another country does not fall under the same exemptions as its home campus. It does not matter if an item is leaving permanently or temporarily, nor does it matter if it is being transferred to an organization wholly owned by a U.S. entity (such as an IBC) located outside the United States.

There are three primary aspects of export regulations campus administrators should be aware of. The International Traffic in Arms Regulations (1976) controls military or defense-related articles, technologies, and services. Except under special exemption or with authorization from the State Department, information about items listed on the U.S. Munitions List may be shared only with U.S. people. The Bureau of Industry and Security in the U.S. Department of Commerce enforces the export administration regulations, which regulate commercial and dual-use products and technologies (Commerce and Foreign Trade, 1982). Some items require a license before they can be exported, and export administration regulations restrictions on items may vary among destinations, based on the nature of the relationship between the United States and the importing nation. In addition, the Office of Foreign Assets Control in the Department of the Treasury prohibits transactions with countries subject to boycotts, trade sanctions, and embargoes.[14]

Conclusion

The international environment is changing quickly, and administrators of colleges and universities need to be aware of these changes and consider how they affect their institutional mission. Some institutions, such as Northeastern, may find ways to extend traditional services and activities into the international domain. Others may seek out new frontiers, as New York University did in its decision to build campuses in Abu Dhabi and Shanghai. In addition, intensifying international pressures may force some institutions to reinvest in their traditional mission, embracing it as a means for confronting the growing interconnectedness discussed in this chapter. Regardless of the direction an institution takes, its leaders need to be aware of the changing international dynamics and make purposeful decisions in partnership with the faculty and other stakeholders on the appropriate response.

Notes

1. More about the William J. Fulbright Program can be found in chapter 4.

2. According to the 2011 Academic Ranking of World Universities by Shanghai Ranking Consultancy, 17 of the top 20 universities in the world are American (see www.shanghairanking.com/ARWU2011.html).

3. Higher education institutions with presences in multiple countries confront a range of challenges and opportunities that are not dealt with by institutions with a presence in only one country. While providing an overview of the types of international engagements an institution may participate in, this book does not examine in depth the management of multinational colleges and universities. Those interested in this topic are directed to Lane and Kinser (2011b).

4. This number does not include branch campuses or other ventures established overseas by U.S. education providers. The calculation is mostly based on international students studying in the United States.

5. For example, in 2009 and 2010 several universities suspended their study abroad programs in certain parts of Mexico citing concerns about swine flu (Fischer, 2009). In addition, the U.S. Department of State issued a travel warning based on increasing drug-related violence in Mexico (Miller, 2010). Boston University cancelled a 20-year-old study abroad program in Niger in 2011 after two French citizens were abducted and killed in an area near where the university's students tended to live (Rocheleau, 2011).

6. See www.globalhighered.org/branchcampuses.php for an updated account of IBCs and other research on such institutions.

7. Those interested in regulatory and policy issues can find additional information at the website of NAFSA: Association of International Educators (www.nafsa .org).

8. Parts of this section are adapted from Lane (2007).

9. In the situation presented to the court, six African American women who participated in a study trip sponsored by Eastern Michigan University in South Africa complained to the supervising faculty member that several male students were making harassing remarks and at one point offered to sell one of the women to the bus driver. The faculty member declined to intervene. The court determined that to allow such conduct to occur could close such trips to female involvement because it would be "requiring them to submit to sexual harassment in order to participate" (221 F. Supp. 2d at 790).

10. Country-specific information and updates about travel advisories for U.S. citizens can be found at the U.S. Department of State website at http://travel.state .gov/travel/travel_1744.html.

11. More information about visas for foreign students studying in the United States can be found at http://travel.state.gov/visa/temp/types/types_1268.html.

12. The U.S. Department of State administers the exchange visitor (J Visa) portion of SEVIS.

13. According to the Department of Commerce, "'Items' include commodities, software or technology, such as clothing, building materials, circuit boards, automotive parts, blue prints, design plans, retail software packages and technical information." See www.bis.doc.gov/licensing/exportingbasics.htm for updated guidelines.

14. At the time of this writing, fully sanctioned nations include Belarus, Burma, Cuba, Iran, North Korea, Sudan, Syria, and Zimbabwe. See www.treas.gov/offices/ enforcement/ofac/programs for an updated list.

References

About COIL. (n.d.). Retrieved from http://coilcenter.purchase.edu/page/about-coil

Altbach, P. G., & Lewis, L. (1996). The academic profession in international perspective. In P. G. Altbach (Ed.), *The international academic profession: Portraits of fourteen countries* (pp. 3–48). Princeton, NJ: Carnegie Foundation for the Advancement of Teaching.

Altbach, P. G., & Teichler, U. (2001). Internationalization and exchanges in a globalized university. *Journal of Studies of International Education, 5*(1), 5–25. doi:10.1177/102831530151002

Australian Education International. (2011). *Export income to Australia from education services in 2010–2011: Research snapshot.* Retrieved from http://www.aei.gov.au/ research/Research-Snapshots/Documents/Export%20Income%202010–11.pdf

Böhm, A., Davis, D., Meares, D., & Pearce, D. (2002). *Global student mobility 2023: Forecasts of the global demand for international higher education.* Sydney, Australia: IDP Australia.

Commerce and Foreign Trade. (1982). (15 CFR 300 et seq; 700 et seq).

Commission on the Abraham Lincoln Study Abroad Program. (2005). *Global competence and national needs: One million Americans studying abroad.* Retrieved from http://www.nafsa.org/uploadedFiles/NAFSA_Home/Resource_Library_Assets/ CCB/lincoln_commission_report%281%29.pdf?n=6097

Council of Europe. (2001). *Code of good practice in the provision of transnational education.* Retrieved from http://www.coe.int/t/dg4/highereducation/recognition/ code%20of%20good%20practice_EN.asp

Davis, D., Olsen, A., & Böhm, A. (2000). *Transnational education providers, partners and policy: Challenges for Australian institutions offshore.* Canberra, Australia: IDP Education Australia.

Dudden, A. P., and Dynes, R. R. (Eds.). (1987). *The Fulbright experience, 1846–1986: Encounters and transformations.* New Brunswick, NJ: Transaction.

Dumaine, B., & Ready, D. (1995, October 16). Interview with Doug Ready: Don't be an ugly-American manager. *Fortune.* Retrieved from http://money.cnn.com/ magazines/fortune/fortune_archive/1995/10/16/206833/index.htm

Fay v. Thiel College. 55 Pa. D & C 4th 353 (2001).

Finkelstein, M. J., Walker, E., & Chen, R. (2009). *The internationalization of the American faculty: Where are we, what drives or deters us?* RIHE International Seminar Reports, Vol. 13 (pp. 113–142). Higashi-Hiroshima, Japan: Research Institute for Higher Education, Hiroshima University.

Fischer, K. (2009, April 28). Swine flu prompts more colleges to cancel study-abroad programs in Mexico. *The Chronicle of Higher Education.* Retrieved from http://chronicle.com/article/Swine-Flu-Prompts-More/42816/

Fischer, K. (2011, January 16). Northeastern, once local, goes global: University expands signature co-op program and foreign enrollment. *The Chronicle of Higher Education.* Retrieved from http://chronicle.com/article/A-Once-Local-University/125959/

Fulbright Program History. (n.d.). Retrieved from http://fulbright.state.gov/history.html

Guruz, K. (2008). *Higher education and international student mobility in the global knowledge economy.* Albany, NY: SUNY Press.

Hoye, W. P., & Rhodes, G. M. (2000). An ounce of prevention is worth . . . the life of a student: Reducing risk in international programs. *Journal of College and University Law, 27*(1), 151–167.

Institute of International Education. (2010). *Open Doors.* Washington, DC: Author.

Institute of International Education. (2011). *Open Doors.* Washington, DC: Author.

International Traffic in Arms Regulations. (1976). (22 CFR § 121.1 et seq.)

James, K. (2005). International education: The concept and its relationship to intercultural education. *Journal of Research in International Education, 4*(3), 313–332. doi:10.1177/1475240905057812

King et al. v. Eastern Michigan University, 221 F. Supp. 2d 783 (E.D. Mich., 2002).

Klyberg, S. G. F. (2012). *The faculty experience of internationalization: Motivations for, practices of, and means for engagement* (Doctoral dissertation). Center for the Study of Higher Education, Department of Education Policy Studies, Pennsylvania State University, University Park, PA.

Knight, J. (2003). Updated internationalization definition. *International Higher Education, 33,* 2–3.

Knight, J. (2004). Internationalization remodeled: Definition, approaches, and rationales. *Journal of Studies in International Education, 8*(1), 5–31. doi:10.1177/1028315303260832

Knight, J. (2005). *Cross-border education: Programs and providers on the move* (Millennium Research Monograph No. 10). Ottawa, Canada: Canadian Bureau for International Education.

The knowledge factory: Inside the knowledge factory. (1997, October 4). *The Economist,* p. 4. Retrieved from http://www.economist.com/node/600142

Lane, J. E. (2007). Student safety and institutional liability in study abroad programs. *ACPA Developments, 5*(2). Retrieved from http://www.myacpa.org/pub/developments/archives/2007/Summer/article.php?content=legal

Lane, J. E. (2010). Joint ventures in cross-border higher education: International branch campuses in Malaysia. In R. Sakamoto & D. W. Chapman (Eds.), *Cross border collaborations in higher education: Partnerships beyond the classroom* (pp. 67–90). New York, NY: Routledge.

Lane, J. E. (2011). Importing private higher education: International branch campuses. *Journal of Comparative Policy Analysis, 13*(4), 367–381. doi:10.1080/13876988.2011.583106

Lane, J. E. (2012). Higher education and economic competitiveness. In J. E. Lane & D. B. Johnstone (Eds.), *Colleges and universities as economic drivers: Measuring higher education's role in economic development* (pp. 221–252). Albany, NY: SUNY Press.

Lane, J. E., & Kinser, K. (2011a, November). *Findings from a global survey of international branch campuses.* Paper presented at the annual meeting of the Association for the Study of Higher Education, Charlotte, NC.

Lane, J. E., & Kinser, K. (Eds.). (2011b). Multinational colleges and universities: Leadership, administration, and governance of international branch campuses. *New Directions for Higher Education, 155.* doi:10.1002/he.440

Lane, J. E., & Kinser, K. (2011c). Reconsidering privatization in cross-border engagements: The sometimes public nature of private activity. *Higher Education Policy, 24,* 255–273. doi:10.1057/hep.2011.2

Levin, R. C. (2008, May 6). *The internationalization of the university.* Retrieved from http://communications.yale.edu/president/speeches/2008/05/05/internationalization-university

Levy, D. (2006). The unanticipated explosion: Private higher education's global surge. *Comparative Education Review, 50*(2), 217–240. doi:10.1086/500694

McBurnie, G., & Ziguras, C. (2007). *Transnational education: Issues and trends in offshore higher education.* London, UK: Routledge.

Mestenhauser, J. A. (1998). Portraits of an international curriculum: An uncommon multidimensional perspective. In J. A. Mestenhauser & B. J. Ellingboe (Eds.), *Reforming the higher education curriculum: Internationalizing the campus* (pp. 3–39). Phoenix, AZ: Oryx Press.

Miller, M. H. (2010, March 23). Universities suspend study-abroad programs in areas of Mexico hit by drug violence. *The Chronicle of Higher Education.* Retrieved from http://chronicle.com/article/Universities-Suspend/64809/

Ministry of Trade and Industry of Singapore. (2003). *Panel recommends global schoolhouse concept for Singapore to capture bigger slice of US$2.2 trillion world education market.* Retrieved from http://app.mti.gov.sg/data/pages/507/doc/DSE_recommend.pdf

Moll, J. R., Gates, S., & Quigley, L. (2001, May). International education and training services: A global market of opportunity for U.S. providers. *Export America,* 19–21.

Munroe, J. A. (1986). *The University of Delaware: A history.* Newark, NJ: University of Delaware Press.

Nakayama, S. (1984). *Academic and scientific traditions in China, Japan, and the West.* Tokyo, Japan: Tokyo University Press.

National Science Board. (2010). *Science and engineering indicators 2010.* Washington, DC: National Science Foundation.

Neave, G. (2002). The stakeholder perspective historically explored. In J. Enders & O. Fulton (Eds.), *Higher education in a globalising world: International trends and mutual observations* (pp. 17–37). London, UK: Springer.

Obst, D., Kuder, M., & Banks, C. (2011). *Joint and double degree programs in the global context: Report on an international survey.* Retrieved from the Institute for International Education website: http://www.iie.org/Research-and-Publications/ Publications-and-Reports/IIE-Bookstore/~/media/Files/Corporate/Publications/ Joint-Double-Degree-Survey-Report-2011.ashx

Organisation for Economic and Cooperative Development. (2011). *Education at a glance 2011: OECD indicators.* Retrieved from http://www.oecd.org/dataoecd/61/ 2/48631582.pdf

Patrinos, A. H. (2002, March). *The role of the private sector in the global market for education.* Paper presented at the meeting of Shifting Roles, Changing Rules: The Global Higher Education Market, The Hague, Netherlands.

Peterson, P. M. (2010). The centrality of faculty to a more globally oriented campus. In D. B. Johnstone, M. B. d'Ambrosio, & P. J. Yakoboski (Eds.), *Higher education in a global society* (pp. 134–148). New York, NY: TIAA-CREF Institute.

Rait, R. S. (1931). *Life in the medieval university.* Cambridge, UK: Cambridge University Press.

Rashdall, H. (1895). *The universities of Europe in the Middle Ages.* London, UK: Henry Frowde.

Rocheleau, M. (2011, January 17). BU cancels semester in Niger. *Boston Globe.* Retrieved from http://www.boston.com/news/local/massachusetts/articles/2011/ 01/17/bu_cancels_semester_in_niger/

Spangler, M. S., & Tyler, A. (2011). Identifying fit of mission and environment: Applying the American community college model internationally. *New Directions for Higher Education, 155,* 41–52. doi:10.1002/he.443

Welch, A. R. (1997). The peripatetic professor: The internationalization of the academic profession. *Higher Education, 34*(6), 323–345. doi:10.1023/A:1003071806217

Wildavsky, B. (2010). *The great brain race: How global universities are reshaping the world.* Princeton, NJ: Princeton University Press.

PART TWO

EXTERNAL CONSTITUENCIES

Organizations are inextricably connected to their environments and, as we have argued previously, colleges and universities need to adapt to changes in their external environment and collaborate with external constituencies through democratic principles to foster institutional growth and address societal needs. Part Two provides readers with an overview of key external constituencies and how they affect the work of academic organizations.

Chapter 4 discusses the constitutional role of the federal government in education, the historical evolution of federal involvement in higher education, and current federal policy. While the amendments to the U.S. Constitution reserve certain powers for the states, including the education of state citizens, the federal government was never completely removed from oversight of education from early childhood through postsecondary. The primary oversight mechanism used by the federal government is federal funding and the regulations that accompany those funds and regulations to protect constitutional rights. Through the allocation of billions of dollars annually for student aid and institutional improvement, and the federal support offered through the American Recovery and Reinvestment Act of 2009, the federal government has clearly entangled itself with higher education. Moreover, this involvement does not count the billions of dollars allocated to higher education through other departments and agencies such as the National Science Foundation, National Institutes of Health, Department of Defense, Department of Agriculture, and Department of Energy. This chapter provides readers with an overview of the relationship between higher education and the federal government and how that relationship affects academic leaders at all levels of the academic enterprise, and it offers insights to aid academic leaders to navigate the federal government's engagement with higher education.

In chapter 5 we discuss state governments' dominant authority when it comes to education in the United States. The Tenth Amendment to the U.S. Constitution confirms that education is a power reserved for the states. As a result, we now have 50 public higher education sectors regulated and partially funded by state governments. Further, many states have funded direct grants for student financial aid programs for private higher education institutions within their boundaries. State legislatures' influence on the operation of higher education organizations has been significant and varied over the years. Moreover, the states' role in supporting higher education has not been limited to the public domain but has also affected the private sector. Typically, community colleges are part of a state system of higher education, but in some cases states maintain community college districts with a governing board and local financing. Consequently, significant and subtle differences exist among and between all 50 states in terms of how they approach their role in higher education. This fact further contributes to the broad differentiation among public institutions on a state-by-state basis. In an era of financial strain upon state coffers, it is unclear how states will ultimately resolve their commitment to the principles of providing public access to higher education when the ability to afford it decreases. This chapter examines the nature of state involvement in higher education and local governance of community colleges, including historical antecedents, current issues, and future trends based on the contemporary operational and economic challenges confronting states today.

Chapter 6 analyzes the influence of the courts on higher education. Through the last half of the 20th century and into the 21st century, the courts have played a significant role in shaping higher education policy and practice. Some experts maintain that *Dixon v. Alabama* (1961) was the watershed decision that resulted in the judicial branch's entrance through the college gates and established significant constitutional, regulatory, and contractual challenges to policy and practice. As higher education adapts to present economic, social, and demographic changes, new threats to existing norms in the academic enterprise may give rise to new legal issues or challenges to existing ones. This chapter, while not being a comprehensive review, focuses on a number of legal issues that have a significant impact on academic leadership and management.

Chapter 7 explores town-gown relations, or the dynamics between an institution and its surrounding community. Town-gown relations are often very complicated because of years of strained interactions between postsecondary institutions and elected officials, many of whom may have competing goals and interests. Higher education has often been viewed as an ivory tower in which faculty members explore research topics of little relevance to society as a whole, and students pursue degrees apart from society and with little interaction with or connection to the local community. Many institutions are combating these stereotypes through involvement with their surrounding communities, especially in economically distressed areas where colleges and universities play significant roles in everything from promoting economic and community development to improving public K–12 education. We discuss the nature of an engaged campus that works democratically with its local community to address some of society's greatest challenges while strengthening its core academic commitments and mission.

In addition to interacting with federal, state, and local governments and their surrounding communities, colleges and universities collaborate with private voluntary associations and compacts such as foundations, accreditation associations, consortia, and national associations that influence policy and institutional practice. The diversity of U.S. higher education is mirrored in the diversity of external organizations and agencies that exist to assist them in meeting their mission, which we discuss in chapter 8. Collectively, these organizations and agencies represent an industry unto themselves, all sharing the common purpose of elevating higher learning and maintaining U.S. higher education's preeminent status in the world. They reflect the diverse interests, populations, and agendas that have made U.S. higher education a beacon among truly democratic institutions. Understanding these ancillary organizations and their distinct roles, along with the benefits and challenges they bring to higher education, is the subject of this chapter.

4

FEDERAL ENGAGEMENT IN HIGHER EDUCATION

T he federal government casts a long shadow over higher education. While the states retain primary authority over most of the nation's colleges and universities, the federal government has used its legislative power and purse strings to influence their development. As discussed throughout this chapter, federal involvement in higher education is complex and varied, although the extent to which an individual institution is involved with the federal government depends largely upon the institution's mission. Certain laws and requirements affect almost all colleges and universities. For example, higher education institutions are subject to laws and regulations pertaining to worker safety, employment discrimination, constitutionally protected freedoms, human and animal research protections, among other policies. Moreover, the federal government has used its investments in federal financial aid as a tool to leverage institutional compliance in a range of other activities. Now, all institutions that accept federal financial aid funds must comply with requirements pertaining to accreditation and data reporting. However, the federal government has also provided funding and support for basic and applied research, international engagements, and increased access to specialized programs of national need such as health, sciences, and languages.

The sprawling character of the federal government's involvement in higher education can make it difficult to understand the nature of such involvement. Generally, though, federal interaction with higher education can be grouped into five primary areas:

1. Access: programs and initiatives focused on increasing enrollments in specific programs as well as across all institutions;

2. Accountability and oversight: initiatives meant to ensure compliance with constitutional and other federal protections, requirements, and expectations;
3. Research and innovation: programs pertaining to building the nation's research capacity and fostering innovation;
4. Institutional development: initiatives designed to develop specific types of institutions such as land-grant institutions, historically Black colleges and universities (HBCUs), and tribal colleges; and
5. International engagements: programs that focus on the movement of individuals, programs, and institutions across international borders.

While most of the federal government's initiatives can be classified under one or more of these areas, the exact nature of federal involvement in higher education can vary significantly based on the interests and initiatives of elected officials and other environmental factors. For example, national service initiatives supported by Presidents George H. W. Bush and William J. Clinton encouraged the widespread engagement of colleges and their students in community service. President George W. Bush's interest in accountability brought about the No Child Left Behind Act and a subsequent national discussion about accountability in higher education. During President Barack Obama's administration, health-care reform has changed how institutions deal with student health insurance, a focus on urban renewal has involved institutions in the redevelopment of major metropolitan areas, and the Great Recession has raised questions about the sustainability of the federal government's support of higher education.

This chapter is designed to provide readers with a working knowledge of how the federal government is involved with higher education. It starts with a brief history of such interaction, chronicling the evolution of the relationship between the two entities. The chapter then goes into more depth on the five primary areas of federal involvement with higher education, describing the major types of involvements and discussing relevant federal agencies and legislation. In relating to the themes of this book, the mission of an institution should drive the types of involvement it has with the federal government, and yet the institution must also be able to adapt to changes in the environment—changes caused by the federal government and changes that cause the federal government to change its types of involvement. Ideally, the federal government and higher education should be viewed as partners in advancing national interests, but all too often the reality is far different. This chapter is not meant to be a road map to foster more democratic partnerships between the federal government and higher education but rather to provide readers with an introduction to how the federal government involves itself with higher education so that institutions are better able to manage this often complex relationship.

The Evolution of Federal Engagement in Higher Education

For many academic administrators, the federal government is viewed as a source of research funding, student aid, and protection for civil rights and other freedoms. Few may actually realize that the federal government plays a secondary, or supportive, role to state governments, which bear primary responsibility for education at all levels. The country's founders, such as George Washington, James Madison, and Alexander Hamilton, favored the creation of a federal university, but the vote to give Congress the power to create such an institution was narrowly lost in 1898 (Rainsford, 1972). While this early attempt to grant the federal government some participation in the nation's postsecondary education sector failed, the federal government's involvement would not be forestalled for long.

Only a few short years after the failed vote to create a national university, the federal government took a new interest in the postsecondary sector. The first major federal foray into higher education occurred with the creation of the U.S. Military Academy at West Point in 1802, and although the institution was not allowed to offer collegiate-level degrees until 1933, Francis Wayland, president of Brown University, noted its importance in 1850 when he suggested that every engineered bridge and highway in the United States to that point had been designed by West Point graduates (Babbidge & Rosenzweig, 1962). While a truly national university was never created, the federal government continues to sponsor several military academies that provide undergraduate education and leadership development for commissioned officers in the U.S. military.[1]

The first recorded significant congressional committee debate regarding higher education occurred on December 7, 1818, when Congressman John Floyd of Virginia suggested that the Public Lands Committee of the House of Representatives investigate the appropriation of federal lands to each state to endow a university (U.S. House Journal, 1818). While the committee did not immediately adopt the suggestion, Floyd started a several-decades committee debate about the role of the federal government in higher education that culminated in 1862 with the passage of the Morrill Act, also called the Land-Grant College Act, named after Representative Justin Morrill of

Vermont (a second Land-Grant College Act was passed in 1890 and is discussed later in the chapter). Indeed, the act spurred the creation of some of the nation's most productive research universities and thrust the federal government into becoming the most significant sponsor of agricultural research in the world.[2]

With the passage of the land-grant acts, Congress also established a precedent of involving itself in higher education when it needed the nation's colleges and universities to help with specific social or economic problems. The land-grant acts helped revolutionize agricultural production, manufacturing, and infrastructure development at a time when the industrial revolution was transforming many developed economies. The federal government's higher education engagement was mostly limited to land-grant institutions until World War I, when institutions became militarized to help support the war effort. Indeed, during times of war, the United States' colleges and universities have often played a significant role in the nation's story, serving as incubators for critics and protestors, trainers of military professionals, and providers of new research in national defense (Rudy, 1996). The years surrounding World War I were among the most active in the development of the relationship between higher education and the federal government.

In 1915 Congress authorized the creation of the Coast Guard Academy (following the creation of West Point and the Naval Academy). A year later in 1916, the National Research Council was created to coordinate the federal government's support of research and development. The following year, the Smith-Hughes Act of 1917 provided money for vocational training below the college level. Other federal policies affecting colleges and universities during the time included rehabilitation policies for disabled veterans, military training through the Student Army Training Corps and the Reserve Officer Training Corps (permanently established in 1920), and disposal of surplus military items (much of which was given to educational institutions).

At the start of World War I, the academic enterprise was largely insular, focused inward, and inadequate to support the needs of the modern military (Kolbe, 1919). In 1918, however, when the United States entered the war effort, the American Council on Education (ACE) was created by a group of college presidents to "coordinate the services which educational institutions and organizations could contribute to the Government in the national crisis brought on by World War I" (Quattlebaum, 1960, p. 41). Ultimately, the nation's colleges and universities mobilized to support national defense efforts.

In fact, the doctrine of "preparedness" had become a watchword in educational circles as the danger of war loomed nearer. With the actual outbreak the universities saw the horizon of their pre-war opportunities for useful cooperation infinitely widened, and their whole activity suddenly elevated from the plane of every-day education to that of national defense. (Kolbe, 1919, p. 21)

During World War I, U.S. colleges and universities forged a new union with society through their demonstrated usefulness in research, the training of military personnel, and the education of young men. These same institutions, however, confronted a number of challenges during the nation's war effort, including declining enrollments, shrinking budgets, and an increasingly militaristic social and academic culture (Levine, 1986). Despite the changes that occurred in higher education,

the subsequent proliferation of "reserve-officer training" and service academies themselves was but an extension of the principle established early in the Union, namely, that the expenditures of Federal funds for educational purposes and the use of educational institutions were justified in the effort to produce highly or uniquely trained personnel to meet identifiable needs of the National Government. Much of the subsequent history of Federal involvement in American higher education constitutes nothing more than a broadening of the definition embodied in this concept. (Babbidge & Rosenzweig, 1962, p. 7)

Indeed, for several more decades, the federal government continued to engage in using higher education to achieve other national goals (Morse, 1966; Russell, 1951). During the 1930s, President Franklin Delano Roosevelt turned to higher education as one of the mechanisms to implement his New Deal programs intended to lift the nation out of the Great Depression. In 1935 the Emergency Relief Appropriation Act funded many education-related programs, including the National Youth Administration, which provided funding to more than 620,000 students between the ages of 16 and 25 to continue their education. This program marked the first time the federal government supported private higher education institutions during peacetime.

While the First World War transformed the relationship between the federal government and higher education, the Second World War transformed higher education. First, the federal government took a leadership role in funding scientific inquiry, relying heavily on the nation's research institutions to support a number of research and development programs, such as the Manhattan Project, which created the first atomic bomb. Second, passage of the Servicemen's Readjustment Act of 1944 (commonly known as the GI Bill) greatly expanded higher education access, and institutions soon burgeoned with new enrollments as veterans returned to civilian life and could not find employment in the postwar economy. While veterans could use these benefits at private or public institutions, the result was a massive expansion of public sector enrollments.

The 1950s witnessed continued expansion of federal engagement in higher education, primarily because of the growing power of the Soviet Union. The Cold War fostered a national interest in the advancement of science and engineering, and the federal government wanted to build on the positive working relationship it had established with institutions of higher education during World War II. Indeed, in 1950 the National Science Foundation (NSF) was created, and an excerpt from its first annual report (1950–1951) indicates the importance of the nation's higher education institutions in helping to win the war:

> Penicillin, the proximity fuse, the atom bomb, among a host of other scientific contributions to American victory in the Second World War, brought home to many citizens the value of scientific research. In the continuing crisis after the war, there were few who opposed the proposition that sustained Federal support of science and research was essential to the defense and welfare of the United States. (NSF, 2009a)

The report goes on to state that Congress approved the creation of the NSF for such purposes as promoting science; advancing the nation's health, prosperity, and welfare; and securing the national defense.

The launch of Sputnik in 1957 intensified fears that U.S. scientists were falling behind their Soviet counterparts, and Congress passed the National Defense Education Act in 1958. The act provided general funding through the National Defense Student Loan program to increase the number of students enrolled in higher education. In addition, the act provided targeted funding to support foreign language studies, engineering students, and area study centers.

Not all federal involvement in higher education has stemmed from the legislative and executive branches. One significant action by the federal judiciary in the 1950s had long-reaching effects. In 1954 the U.S. Supreme Court ruled in *Brown v. Board of Education* that separate educational facilities for members of different races could not be considered equal. This ruling (discussed in more depth in chapter 6) caused dramatic changes in many public institutions, particularly in those states that had established separate land-grant institutions for Black and White students. Seemingly overnight, the federal judiciary set aside decades of institutionalized practice and case law supporting segregation and declared such practices illegal.

In the 1960s the federal government began to move away from interventions exclusively motivated by a desire to meet national needs. *Brown v. Board of Education* (1954) served as the foundation for the Civil Rights Act of 1964, which banned discrimination against minorities, such as Blacks and women. The act applied not just to higher education, but it specifically encouraged desegregation of public colleges and universities and authorized the federal attorney general to file lawsuits to enforce those provisions of the law.

Separately, Congress passed the Higher Education Act (HEA) of 1965, which created the Federal Student Aid Program, which has provided millions of students with grants or low-interest loans to help offset the cost of their education. These funds eventually supported the educational pursuits of hundreds of thousands of students each year. The HEA included a sunset clause, which meant that it needed to be reauthorized by Congress periodically. Thus, there have been nine reauthorizations, with another due in 2013. Under the 1968 and 1972 reauthorizations, Congress worked to consolidate many of the federal government's higher education engagements under one act. However, only about 25% of all federal engagements now fall under the HEA. While the HEA may not have consolidated all the federal government's higher education initiatives, it has served as a focal point for congressional interest in the topic. Indeed, in the past four decades, Congress's engagement with higher education issues occurred most frequently around the time of the reauthorization of the HEA (Lane & LeFor, 2007).

The HEA started a new era in the federal government's relationship with higher education. Higher education emerged as an important social institution in its own right, not merely a mechanism to help the federal government achieve other policy goals. For example, over the next several decades, the federal government became the most significant provider of financial aid to assist students with the cost of pursuing a college degree. It also continued to fund research, expanding existing sources and creating new ones. By the beginning of the 21st century, however, several members of Congress had begun to question (and challenge) the extensive support the federal government was giving to higher education. The Great Recession of

2008 (much like the passage of the HEA in 1965) may emerge as another pivotal moment in transforming this relationship. At the time of this writing, there are ongoing calls to defund several federally sponsored research programs, and the Department of Education announced the end of several support grants, particularly those focused on developing international education partnerships. Moreover, the American Recovery and Reinvestment Act of 2009 provided states (the primary funders of public higher education) with additional monies to offset declines in state support of higher education. Once that funding ran out, however, state support for higher education continued to decrease as well.

The remainder of this chapter provides readers with an overview of important federal policies and current engagements with higher education. These activities are so vast and diffuse that any treatment is certain to fail to provide a complete picture. As Knight (1960) noted in the introduction of a book in which he undertook a similar task:

> The temerity of writing a brief book on this subject is exceeded only by the necessity of it. None of us would pretend for a moment that we could do justice to that common ground of [federal] government and higher education, which is so confused and yet so critical a part of our national life. . . . Too many plans are in part the result of political expediency and compromise to allow us the comfort of knowing where the relationships of federal government and higher education are headed. We realize that a large amount of federal income is being invested in higher education of one kind or another; but we know surprisingly little beyond this fact. (p. 1)

Fifty years later, this passage remains remarkably relevant. While there is now greater understanding of the various involvements of the federal government with higher education, it remains practically impossible to inventory their full depth and breadth because of their scope across multiple departments and agencies.

Primary Areas of Federal Engagement

While the states retain primary financial and regulatory responsibilities for higher education, the importance of the nation's colleges and universities continues to attract the attention of the federal legislative, executive, and judicial branches. Moreover, one of the main means of support for U.S. higher education comes from federal financial aid programs, which provide students and families with loans and grants to offset the cost of attending a college or university. Various U.S. presidents have initiated their own institutional development programs and executive orders related to higher education, such as the White House Initiatives on Tribal Colleges and Universities (Executive Order No. 13,511, 2010); Educational Excellence for Hispanic Americans (Executive Order No. 12,900, 1994); and Promoting Excellence, Innovation, and Sustainability at Historically Black Colleges and Universities (Executive Order No. 13,532, 2010). Federal agencies support a range of programs that focus on research, international exchanges, and graduate-level training, among others. Congress, in addition to fulfilling its responsibility for creating and passing laws, engages in a range of monitoring activities that may not directly force change but can bring new attention to issues of concern. Finally, the federal courts have been involved in a range of cases covering issues such as discrimination, student privacy, academic freedom, and state sovereignty (most of these issues are discussed in chapter 6).

Since primary responsibility for education falls to state governments, no central federal authority ever emerged. Consequently, the federal government's involvement with higher education is diffused across several federal departments and agencies. The decentralized nature of federal involvement makes the task of describing it particularly difficult. In many nations, one national agency would have primary responsibility over the affairs of higher education—not so in the United States. While there is a federal Department of Education, the federal government engages in the funding and oversight of higher education through a cadre of departments and agencies such as the Departments of Agriculture, Energy, and State, among others. These engagements usually involve either oversight of federal mandates and laws or funding provided to institutions or individuals. For example, the Department of Education oversees a more than $100 billion grant and loan program designed to aid students pursue their postsecondary studies; the Department of State supports the international exchange of students and faculty; and the NSF, National Institutes of Health (NIH), Department of Defense, and others provide funding for research and development. In addition, millions of federal dollars have been earmarked for institutions for a range of programmatic and capital projects.

As previously mentioned, federal involvement with higher education can be grouped into five primary areas: (a) access, (b) accountability and oversight, (c) research and innovation, (d) institutional development, and (e) international engagements. The following provides an overview of each of the areas and describes relevant legislation, regulations, and federal agencies.

Access

One of the primary goals of the federal government regarding higher education is to increase access. The federal government is the primary provider of
financial aid meant to help students pay for their education. While some aid
programs target specific groups of individuals based on their background
(e.g., military service) or academic interest, most aid is allocated to students
based on need, regardless of their academic program or other characteristics.
The HEA (1965) was originally passed "to strengthen the educational
resources of our colleges and universities and to provide financial assistance
for students in postsecondary and higher education" and was designed to
expand access to higher education through the provision of various grant
and loan programs for students from lower- and middle-income families. It
also created programs (now known as the TRIO programs) to help at-risk
students pursue undergraduate degrees. The HEA was reauthorized in 1968,
1971, 1972, 1976, 1980, 1986, 1992, 1998, and 2008. The next reauthorization
is scheduled for 2013.

According to the latest *Digest of Education Statistics* (National Center for
Education Statistics [NCES], 2010) and the *2007–08 National Postsecondary
Student Aid Study* (NCES, 2009), about 66% of all undergraduate students
(80% of all full-time undergraduate students) received some type of financial aid in the 2007–2008 academic year. About 63% of all full-time undergraduates received aid from the federal government, and 63% of full-time
undergraduates also received aid from nonfederal sources such as state aid,
institutional scholarships, and private loans. At the federal level, students
may be eligible for three general types of aid: grants, loans, or work-study.

The general federal student aid programs are administered by the
Department of Education. To qualify for federal student aid, students must
complete the Free Application for Federal Student Aid.[3] When the HEA was
originally passed in 1965, most of the aid was allocated through grants as a
means to increase access to low-income students. For example, Pell Grants
support students with financial need by helping to defray the cost of college
and do not need to be repaid. Over the past several decades, however, loans
have emerged as the largest source of federal aid for students. The Stafford
Loan Program makes low-interest loans to students to assist them with covering college costs. Students are required to repay these loans after they
graduate or stop attending college. The work-study programs are by far the
smallest of all the general aid programs. They provide funding to higher
education institutions to subsidize the cost of employing student workers
from disadvantaged backgrounds.

Support for the nation's veterans to attend college comes through the Department of Veteran Affairs.[4] The 1944 GI Bill provided education and other benefits to veterans of World War II. While the law eventually transformed higher education by significantly expanding access, it almost did not survive congressional debates. One of the primary concerns was whether it was appropriate to send hardened veterans to college, a place historically reserved for societal elites. While the GI Bill bolstered college enrollments, it also helped forestall a potential economic recession similar to the one that followed World War I. The GI Bill provided veterans with numerous benefits, including unemployment payments, inexpensive housing loans, and grants to cover tuition and other education-related expenses. The law had an immediate impact, with veterans accounting for almost half of all college enrollments in 1947. When the original GI Bill ended in 1956, nearly half (7.8 million) of the 16 million veterans of World War II had pursued education or training programs through the bill. Updated versions of the GI Bill were subsequently authorized for veterans of the Korean and Vietnam Wars.[5]

The GI Bill was reauthorized in 1984 under the leadership of Representative Gillespie V. Montgomery of Mississippi, and it became known as the Montgomery GI Bill. The expanded law provides the opportunity for educational benefits to all who enlist in the U.S. armed forces as well to some members of the Selected Reserve. The amount of benefits is determined by the length of service, type of services, and other requirements. Generally, veterans have up to 10 years after the completion of their service to take advantage of the benefits.

A new benefit program for veterans was instituted in 2008. The Post-9/11 Veterans Educational Assistance Act of 2008 (often referred to as the Post-9/11 GI Bill), did not replace the Montgomery GI Bill. Veterans who completed service prior to September 11, 2001, may receive benefits in accord with the 1984 law; however, veterans and service members who meet the criteria for the 2008 bill may choose which program they want to participate in. The number of veterans who are taking advantage of these higher education benefits grows, and the complexity of facilitating the distribution of benefits has required many higher education institutions to create offices dedicated to handling their veteran students' affairs.

Accountability and Oversight

The members of the U.S. Congress, which comprises the Senate and House of Representatives, serve an important role in defining and developing the relationship between the federal government and higher education. While federal agencies and departments are often the primary intermediary between the government and institutions, Congress establishes the parameters of the interactions through the federal budget, legislation for programs, and definition of responsibilities of entities that receive federal aid. Beyond these basic legislative functions, Congress has also assumed a responsibility for oversight of federal actors and others engaged in activities of national interest. This section provides an overview of Congress's role in oversight of higher education and describes four key federal laws related to higher education.

Higher education serves a central function in the development of the nation's culture and economy, and the federal government directly contributes billions of dollars each year for research, student access, and a variety of other projects. Consequently, higher education now captures significant interest from many members of Congress. This interest, while sometimes resulting in legislation affecting higher education, often manifests itself solely through congressional hearings (Cook, 1998; Hannah, 1996; Parsons, 1997).

Congressional oversight hearings, while not always resulting in legislation, have led to altered institutional behavior. In one example of a congressional committee's oversight activities, the Senate Finance Committee's chairman, Charles E. Grassley of Iowa, "announced an investigation of American University and called the [governing] board a 'poster child for why review and reform are necessary' for governing boards of nonprofit organizations" (Fain, 2006, p. A25). The committee's investigation was a response to a financial scandal at American University in 2005 in which the institution's president was alleged to have misspent hundreds of thousands of dollars, and the institution's trustees were accused of not providing adequate oversight of the president's activities (Fain & Williams, 2005; Kinzie & Strauss, 2006). The scandal resulted in the firing of the president and resignation of four trustees. While Congress did not pursue any governance reforms for colleges or universities in response to this scandal, many observers feared that such an action could have been the next step for Congress had American University's leaders not responded in the way they did.

Occasionally, legislative committees investigate alleged federal abuses, such as the Veterans Administration overpaying institutions during the 1950s, and institutions' purposeful defrauding of the government through federal financial aid programs during the 1980s and 1990s. More recently, beyond the American University example, a *New York Times* article about possible academic integrity concerns at Auburn University resulted in a congressional investigation of that institution's athletic program (Wolverton, 2006). In line with an investigation of the tax-exempt status of several nonprofit organizations, the House's Ways and Means Committee also explored the commercialization of college athletics (Wolverton). Other hearings during the 108th Congress (2003–2005) focused on the regulation of foreign scholars visiting the United States, the role of Hispanic-serving institutions in Texas, consideration of a full-year academic calendar for higher education, and oversight of state-sponsored college tuition saving plans.[6] In many cases, these hearings are designed to give attention to an issue of national importance or of importance to the constituents of a particular member of Congress, not to influence new legislation.

Beyond congressional oversight and funding for higher education, the federal government assumes an active role in the protection of human and animal subjects used in research. Most colleges and universities now have an office of regulatory research compliance, which includes an Institutional Review Board (IRB) of academics and is intended to regulate research projects to ensure the safety and privacy of human and animal subjects. The genesis of most of these offices comes from federal initiatives in the 1970s to provide additional protections for subjects of research projects. The protections arose from concerns about reports of unethical research practices, including the Tuskegee Syphilis Study, a 40-year experiment conducted by the U.S. Public Health Service. The participants in the study, poor African American men, thought they were receiving free health services, but they were actually the subjects of a study tracking the untreated development of syphilis (Jones, 1981).

In response to the concerns raised by such projects, the National Research Act, passed in 1974, created the National Commission for the Protection of Human Subjects of Biomedical and Behavioral Research. In 1979 the commission released *Belmont Report: Ethical Principles and Guidelines for the Protection of Human Subjects of Research*. The report set forth the foundation of research protections in the United States, describing three fundamental ethical principles:

1. Respect for people: Researchers should protect the autonomy and self-direction of all individuals, giving particular consideration to participants with diminished capacities. Participants should have to give informed consent, and researchers should be truthful in all matters.

2. Beneficence: Research should be guided by the principle of "do no harm" and seek to maximize the benefits of the project while minimizing potential harm to participants.
3. Justice: Distribution of benefits and costs should be fair so that those who participate in the research are not denied the benefit of such research.

The commission was part of the U.S. Department of Health, Education, and Welfare (later renamed Health and Human Services [HHS]), which adopted a series of research regulations in the 1970s and 1980s that pertained to research funded by the Department of Health, Education, and Welfare. Most federal agencies have since adopted HHS's regulations, placing the burden of proof on higher education institutions to ensure that research conducted by their faculty members and students conforms to these guidelines. Indeed, most institutions now require all research projects, not just those funded by the federal government, to conform to these rules, and the *Belmont Report* remains an important reference item for many IRBs.

Research and Innovation

A major support function of the federal government is to provide colleges and universities with funding for research. The history of research funding is discussed earlier in the chapter, but in fiscal year 2009, the NSF found that 12 federal departments and eight agencies provided nearly $30 billion in research and development funding to the nation's colleges and universities. Most of this money came in the form of direct grants to institutions, although about 12% was allocated to federally funded research and development centers (FFRDCs) located in universities. For example, the Massachusetts Institute of Technology runs the air force's Lincoln Laboratory, the University of California oversees the Department of Energy's Lawrence Livermore National Laboratory, and the California Institute of Technology is responsible for NASA's Jet Propulsion Laboratory. Table 4.1 provides an overview of the federal research and development spending allocated to higher education from each agency in fiscal year 2009.

The federal government is one of the primary funders of academic research, and much of the federal funding is allocated through a competitive process in which individuals or institutions apply for support. Those requesting funds are usually required to submit an application to a relevant program area or in response to a call for proposals. While some program officers retain discretion over small pools of funding, most proposals are reviewed and rated

TABLE 4.1
Federal Obligations for Research and Development, by Agency and Performer: Fiscal Year 2009 (in Millions of Dollars)

Agency	Obligations to Universities and Colleges	Obligations to University FFRDCs
All agencies	25,723.8	3,502.8
Individual departments		
Department of Agriculture	538.8	0.0
Department of Commerce	146.1	15.3
Department of Defense	2,103.5	404.2
Department of Education	206.8	0.0
Department of Energy	943.9	1,632.6
Department of Health and Human Services	17,065.1	71.7
Department of Homeland Security	51.8	36.2
Department of Housing and Urban Development	0.4	0.0
Department of the Interior	38.1	0.0
Department of Justice	26.0	0.0
Department of Labor	11.6	0.0
Department of Transportation	58.8	12.0
U.S. Agency for International Development	16.2	0.0
Appalachian Regional Commission	0.3	0.0
Environmental Protection Agency	64.7	0.0
National Aeronautics and Space Administration	540.0	1,088.3
National Archives and Records Administration	2.9	0.0
National Science Foundation	3,900.6	235.0
Nuclear Regulatory Commission	0.6	7.5
Social Security Administration	7.5	0.0

Note. From *Survey of Federal Funds for Research and Development,* by the National Science Foundation, 2009. Retrieved from www.nsf.gov/statistics/seind12/append /c4/at04-31.xls/.

by a panel of experts. Those evaluations are then used to determine who receives the funding. Grant proposals usually include direct and indirect costs. The direct costs go to support the researcher and the project.

Indirect costs are those expenses that cannot be directly associated with a project but that an institution provides to support the work of that project. Such costs can include utilities, janitorial support, and building depreciation.

(In general, direct costs are those that can be clearly associated with the research or sponsored project.) An institution recovers indirect costs through a general surcharge on externally sponsored projects. The indirect cost rate is negotiated by each institution with the Department of Health and Human Services or the Office of Naval Research. The exact classification of costs is determined by the Office of Management and Budget's (2004) Circular A-21.

Though the rate is set by the institution with the federal government, most institutions establish a policy that all sponsored projects include indirect costs as part of their projects' budgets. These costs now often exceed 50% of the project's direct costs. However, some private foundations will not pay indirect costs or place a smaller cap on such costs than federally negotiated rates. Also, some federal programs pay lower indirect rates than those otherwise negotiated with the federal government. For example, many training grants will only pay an indirect rate of 8%. Most institutions will allow researchers to pursue grants with lower indirect cost rates, but they first need to obtain institutional permission to do so.

Institutional Development

As discussed previously, one of the federal government's earliest engagements with higher education was in institutional development through the Morrill Acts of 1862 and 1890, which transformed the nation's higher education landscape. In addition to creating some of the nation's greatest research universities, the 1890 act was instrumental in developing several HBCUs. Moreover, under the Elementary and Secondary Education Reauthorization Act of 1994, 32 of the nation's tribal colleges were granted land-grant status, making them eligible for funding designated for land-grant colleges and universities.[7]

In the middle of the 19th century, several members of Congress believed that the nation's economy was in the process of changing and that higher education could play an important role in creating that new economy. The Morrill Act of 1862 was an attempt to foster innovation in the agricultural and mechanical sciences as well as facilitate the private development of federal lands. Land-grant institutions,

> without excluding other scientific and classical studies and including military tactic . . . [were to] teach such branches of learning as are related to agriculture and the mechanic arts, in such manner as the legislatures of the

States may respectively prescribe, in order to promote the liberal and practical education of the industrial classes in the several pursuits and professions in life. (§ 304)

Each state was allocated a certain number of acres of federal land in the
western territories.[8] The states could then use the revenues produced by that
land (usually through its sale) to support the development of a higher education institution dedicated to the advancement of the agricultural and
mechanical arts as well as the liberal arts. Most states used the money to
support the development of new or existing public institutions, such as
Pennsylvania State University, Michigan State University, and North Carolina State University. Two notable exceptions were New York and Massachusetts, which designated Cornell University and Massachusetts Institute of
Technology (as well as the University of Massachusetts) as their land-grant
institutions. Today, four of Cornell's colleges are public and a part of the
State University of New York system.

A subsequent act expanded the number of institutions designated as
land-grant colleges or universities. The second Morrill Act was passed in
1890 with the intention of providing additional support for land-grant institutions. This act required that if race was considered as part of the admission criteria for a land-grant institution, a second land-grant institution had
to be created to serve those excluded by those admission policies. The act
created many of today's public HBCUs, such as Lincoln University (Missouri), South Carolina State University, and Prairie View A&M University
(Texas).

In addition to the Morrill Acts, the federal government has undertaken
a number of other initiatives designed to help build the nation's institutions
of higher education. For example, in the 1950s, during a time of severe short-
age of health care professionals, Congress allocated funds to build the capacity of medical and nursing schools. The National Defense Education Act of
1958 provided federal support for institutions to build foreign language and
international studies programs.

Many current institutional development initiatives fall under the
Department of Education. The undersecretary oversees the President's Advisory Board on Tribal Colleges and Universities and the President's Advisory
Board on Historically Black Colleges and Universities, which extend the
institutional development work started under the land-grant acts. The
department is also responsible for most of the development programs
authorized under the HEA, including the Fund for the Improvement of

Postsecondary Education; institutional development programs aimed at the nation's HBCUs and Alaska Native and Native Hawaiian institutions; programs designed to support Hispanic and other minority-serving institutions; and TRIO programs, which support students from disadvantaged backgrounds.

The Department of Education also serves an important role in institutional development through the collection of data. The NCES collects data about the nation's education system and provides research and analysis for public use. All institutions that accept federal financial aid are required to submit information to the NCES's Integrated Postsecondary Education Data System (http://nces.ed.gov/ipeds), which provides basic data about student enrollments, staff demographics, and institutional characteristics. These data, along with the others collected by the NCES, are important for understanding the development of the nation's higher education system and are often used by institutions for benchmarking and other purposes.

International Engagements

Another area in which the federal government can take clear leadership is international engagements, although like many other initiatives at this level, relevant policy and practices are spread across several agencies, and no coherent set of national policies and expectations related to internationalization has emerged. Historically, the U.S. Department of State has served as the primary federal intermediary between U.S. higher education institutions and individuals and institutions in other countries. This role began in 1946 after Congress created the Fulbright Program, which used the sale of surplus war property to support the international exchange of students to promote goodwill among nations. Through its Bureau of Educational and Cultural Affairs, the State Department now oversees numerous exchange programs for students and scholars, including the Fulbright Program, and through its EducationUSA centers abroad (http://educationusa.state.gov), it has become involved in promoting U.S. higher education overseas as well as in encouraging domestic students to study abroad. Primary financial support for the Fulbright Program comes from an annual appropriation to the Bureau of Educational and Cultural Affairs. In fiscal year 2010, Congress allocated $253.8 million to support Fulbright. The program also receives support from private foundations and foreign governments that help fund the binational commissions that support the program in other countries. In the United States, colleges and universities that host Fulbright participants will often provide some cost sharing as well. The Fulbright Program is administered by two nonprofit organizations, the Institute of International Education and the American-Mideast Educational and Training Services.

While the international engagements of the nation's colleges and universities have primarily focused on international exchanges of students and scholars, a growing number of institutions are participating in the export of educational services through the development of international branch campuses, joint degree programs, and foreign research sites. These increasing international engagements, along with the growing importance of higher education in domestic economic development, have begun to capture the interest of the Department of Commerce, which is increasingly including the sector in its trade development initiatives.

Finally, the U.S. Agency for International Development (USAID) is an independent agency designed to provide developing nations with support in the areas of health, economic growth, agriculture, and conflict prevention. It is intended to support capacity development in foreign nations and advance the foreign policy agenda of the United States. Many of the capacity-building projects supported by the agency involve the nations' higher education institutions and their staffs.

Primary Departments and Agencies for Federal Engagement

As previously discussed, the federal government began to invest significant amounts of money in research following World War II. During much of this time there was no unified policy regarding patents on new products that resulted from this federal support, although most patents ended up under the control of federal departments and agencies, which accumulated as many as 30,000 patents prior to 1980. However, only about 5% of these patents were commercially licensed, suggesting that much of the research output funded by the government was not being developed in ways that could broadly benefit the nation.

In 1980 Congress passed the Bayh-Dole Act, which allowed many recipients of federal research funding, including higher education institutions, to retain the patents on their research discoveries. It is widely believed that the passage of the Bayh-Dole Act sparked the creation of institutions' current emphasis on the development and marketing of inventions by their faculty members (Lane & Johnstone, 2012). Many institutions not only support the research of their faculty but have also created innovation centers, research parks, and incubation sites designed to help faculty and students commercialize and market the results of their research. Of course, institutions often retain control of the intellectual property and share in the profits of any successful products. The following is a description of some of the agencies that provide significant research support to higher education institutions that result in many innovations.

Department of Agriculture

Upon passage of the Morrill Acts (1862, 1890), many U.S. colleges and universities contributed to the transformation of the agricultural industry and made the United States the leading food producer in the world. The agricultural research and service work of these institutions continues to be supported primarily through funding from the U.S. Department of Agriculture, which was created in 1862, the same year as the first land-grant act. Through an array of grants and programs, the Department of Agriculture works to bring together farmers, ranchers, higher education institutions, and other public and private partners to advance agricultural production in the United States and abroad. Much funding comes through the Hatch Act (1887) and the Smith-Lever Act (1914), which provided financial support for the development and operation of agricultural experimentation stations and cooperative extension services in each state. The funding provided through these two acts is allocated to land-grant universities by the Department of Agriculture, and states are expected to provide matching funding for much of the federal funds.

Department of Energy

During World War II, the federal government created the Manhattan Project, which employed numerous university faculty members and graduate students to develop the atomic bomb. At the end of World War II, Congress created the Atomic Energy Commission to oversee research into atomic energy. The commission eventually evolved into the Department of Energy, which was created in 1977 to oversee energy-related programs, production, and regulation, including supervision of the nation's nuclear energy research facilities and power plants. Throughout the 1940s and 1950s, the commission created a network of laboratories, many of which were located in the nation's top universities.

Today, the research and development efforts of the Department of Energy are overseen by its Office of Science, which is the largest federal sponsor of physical science research, supporting about 27,000 investigators at nearly 300 academic institutions and department research laboratories. In addition, the Office of Science provides funding to academic programs that educate undergraduate and graduate students in the physical sciences. In fiscal year 2009, the Department of Energy allocated more than $2.5 billion to research and development at the nation's colleges and universities.

Department of Defense

Compared to many other federal agencies, the Department of Defense provides only a fraction of the federal dollars that support scientific research, but it has been one of the primary sources of funds for research in areas such as computer science and electrical engineering. Moreover, although the department's financial contribution to research at universities is not as high as that provided by the NIH and NSF, it does signal a rather rare partnership between the nation's military establishment and its colleges and universities. Indeed, the U.S. military has long relied on the nation's higher education institutions for research and planning support. Price (1954) noted:

> The United States is the only nation that has ever been willing to support and create private institutions to make studies on problems combining scientific and military considerations—problems of a sort that would elsewhere be considered the very heart of general staff planning. The private institutions . . . [receiving] military funds are the most important sources of independent, skeptical, and uninhibited criticism of military thinking today. (pp. 143–144)

The Department of Defense's support for higher education initiatives ranges from developing new research related to national defense to fostering advanced foreign language skills and knowledge about critical regions. For example, the National Security Education Program provides support for undergraduate and graduate students wanting to study languages and regions critical to national security. It also grants funding for institutional development of language and area study programs. In addition, the Multidisciplinary University Research Initiative funds basic interdisciplinary research projects and in 2010 allocated more than $200 million to academic institutions.

National Institutes of Health

The National Institutes of Health (NIH), part of the Department of Health and Human Services, is the federal agency primarily responsible for biomedical and health-related research. It invests more than $30 billion in medical research annually. The NIH campus is located outside Washington, DC, in Bethesda, Maryland. The agency comprises 27 separate institutes. The NIH provides extramural funding for research, mostly performed by researchers at the nation's colleges and universities. In addition, parts of the NIH, such as the National Institute of Aging, the National Institute on Drug Abuse, the National Institute of Environmental Sciences, and the National Institute of Allergy and Infectious Diseases, engage in their own research projects.

National Science Foundation

The National Science Founcation (NSF) provides support for research and education in a broad range of scientific and engineering fields (except for medical-related research, which is funded through the NIH). In 2010 the NSF had an operating budget of nearly $7 billion, which accounted for about 20% of all federally supported research conducted by U.S. colleges and universities. The leadership of the NSF (i.e., its director, deputy director, and the National Science Board) is appointed by the president and confirmed by the Senate. About 10% of the NSF's staff members tend to be academics who take leaves of absence from their faculty positions to work in its various program areas.

The Future of Federal Involvement

The Great Recession of 2008 created significant financial challenges for governments, businesses, and social organizations. Many of the United States' colleges and universities were affected by declining state appropriations, decreases in state aid programs, and significant losses in institutional endowments. In an attempt to stave off more drastic economic repercussions, the federal government passed a series of laws that would help sustain the nation's higher education system.

For example, the American Recovery and Reinvestment Act of 2009 was intended to invest public monies in the U.S. economy to spur economic recovery. The law included about $787 billion in federal tax incentives; expansion of social welfare benefits, including unemployment support; increased spending on infrastructure and energy projects; and investment in social organizations such as education and health care. Education funding included more than $30 billion to address college affordability and improve access to higher education. The law also included billions to fund scientific research via the NIH, the NSF, the Department of Energy, NASA, and other research-oriented agencies.

About a year later, Congress approved the Health Care and Education Reconciliation Act of 2010. This law also included the Student Aid and Fiscal Responsibility Act, which was added as a rider during the reconciliation process. The law increases the amount of support available to students who receive federal Pell Grants, provides $2 billion over four years to community colleges to expand educational access and enhance workforce training programs, and allocates $2.55 billion to support capacity-building efforts among the nation's minority-serving institutions.

It is uncertain, however, how the federal government's relationship with higher education will evolve in the future. At the time of this writing, the U.S. public is increasingly interested in a federal solution to the rising cost of higher education, and the government is looking for ways to reduce the federal deficit. Meanwhile, higher education's importance for the United States' global competitiveness continues to grow (Lane, 2012). How the nation's leaders meet these competing demands will likely have an important effect on higher education's development and competitive edge.

Notes

1. In addition, because Washington, DC, is controlled by the U.S. Congress, institutions within that territory have an unusually direct connection with the federal government.

2. The Morrill Act of 1890, also called the Agricultural College Act, was the second land-grant act and was intended to extend the provisions of the 1862 act to the Confederate states as long as they could prove that race was not a factor in admissions. Providing separate institutions for Blacks and Whites was permissible in meeting this requirement.

3. See www.fafsa.ed.gov for application information.

4. This discussion is intended to provide readers with a basic understanding of the requirements and benefits of the GI Bill. Readers are encouraged to contact the U.S. Department of Veterans Affairs for more detailed information regarding these matters, including additional programs, exemptions, and requirements.

5. These were the Veterans Readjustment Assistance Act of 1952, the Veterans' Readjustment Benefits Act of 1966, and the Post–Vietnam Era Veterans' Educational Assistance Act of 1977.

6. These are drawn directly from a review of congressional committee activity as recorded in the Congressional Information Service Abstracts passim.

7. The Elementary and Secondary Education Reauthorization Act of 1994 was not the federal government's first involvement in the affairs of tribal colleges. The passage of the Tribally Controlled Community College Assistance Act of 1978 marked the first time the federal government provided funding assistance for these institutions.

8. A state received 30,000 acres for each of its members of Congress. Thus, if a state had two representatives and two senators, it received 120,000 acres. More information about the Morrill Act of 1862 can be found in Williams (1991).

References

American Recovery and Reinvestment Act of 2009 (P.L. 111-5).

Babbidge, H. D., Jr., & Rosenzweig, R. M. (1962). *The federal interest in higher education.* New York, NY: McGraw-Hill.

Bayh-Dole Act (1980, 37 C.F.R. 401).

Brown v. Board of Educ., 347 U.S. 483 (1954).

Civil Rights Act of 1964 (P.L. 88-352, 78 Stat. 241).

Cook, C. E. (1998). *Lobbying for higher education: How colleges and universities influence federal policy.* Nashville, TN: Vanderbilt University Press.

Elementary and Secondary Education Reauthorization Act of 1994 (P.L. 103-382, 108 Stat. 3518).

Emergency Relief Appropriation Act of 1935 (Pub. Res. 11, 74th Cong.).

Exec. Order No. 12,900, 59 Fed. Reg. 9061 (1994).

Exec. Order No. 13,511, 3 C.F.R. (2010 comp.), 244–245.

Exec. Order No. 13,532, 75 Fed. Reg. 2053 (2010).

Fain, P. (2006, June 2). American University's chastened trustees approve wide-ranging reforms. *Chronicle of Higher Education,* p. A25.

Fain, P., & Williams, G. (2005, November 11). U.S. Senate probe begun at American U. *The Chronicle of Higher Education,* p. A30.

Hannah, S. B. (1996). The Higher Education Act of 1992: Skills, constraints, and the politics of higher education. *Journal of Higher Education, 67*(5), 498–527. doi:10.2307/2943866

Hatch Act of 1887 (7 U.S.C. § 361a et seq.).

Health Care and Education Reconciliation Act of 2010, Pub. L. No. 111–152.

Higher Education Act of 1965, Pub. L. No. 89-329 (1965).

Jones, J. (1981). *Bad blood: The Tuskegee syphilis experiment.* New York, NY: Free Press.

Kinzie, S., & Strauss, V. (2006, May 18). Senator questions school's governance. *Washington Post,* p. B2.

Knight, D. M. (Ed.). (1960). *The federal government and higher education.* Englewood Cliffs, NJ: Prentice Hall.

Kolbe, P. R. (1919). *The colleges in war time and after.* New York, NY: D. Appleton.

Lane, J. E. (2012). Global competitiveness, higher education, and the triple helix. In J. E. Lane & D. B. Johnstone (Eds.), *Colleges and universities as economic drivers* (pp. 1–30). Albany, NY: SUNY Press.

Lane, J. E., & Johnstone, D. B. (Eds.). (2012). *Colleges and universities as economic drivers.* Albany, NY: SUNY Press.

Lane, J. E., & LeFor, D. (2007, November). *Federal oversight of higher education: An analysis of Congressional committees, 1944–2004.* Paper presented at the annual meeting of the Association for the Study of Higher Education, Louisville, KY.

Levine, D. O. (1986). *The American college and the culture of aspiration, 1915–1940.* Ithaca, NY: Cornell University Press.

Montgomery GI Bill of 1984 (P.L. 78-346, 58 Stat. 284m).

Morrill Act of 1862 (7 U.S.C. § 301 et seq.).

Morrill Act of 1890 (26 Stat. 417, 7 U.S.C. § 321 et seq.).

Morse, J. F. (1966). The federal government and higher education: Old answers breed new questions. In W. J. Minter (Ed.), *Campus and capitol: Higher education and the state* (pp. 49–62). Boulder, CO: Western Interstate Commission for Higher Education.

National Center for Education Statistics. (2009). *2007–08 National postsecondary student aid study (NPSAS:08): Student financial aid estimates for 2007–08.* Retrieved from http://nces.ed.gov/pubs2009/2009166.pdf

National Center for Education Statistics. (2010). *Digest of education statistics, 2010.* Retrieved from http://nces.ed.gov/pubs2011/2011015.pdf

National Commission for the Protection of Human Subjects of Biomedical and Behavioral Research. (1979). *The Belmont report: Ethical principles and guidelines for the protection of human subjects of research.* Retrieved from the U.S. Department of Health and Human Services website: http://www.hhs.gov/ohrp/human subjects/guidance/belmont.html

National Defense Education Act of 1958 (P.L. 85-864, 72 Stat. 1580).

National Research Act (1974, Pub. L. No. 93-348).

National Science Foundation. (2009a). *NSF history–50th anniversary.* Retrieved from http://www.nsf.gov/about/history/50thanni.jsp

National Science Foundation. (2009b). *Survey of federal funds for research and development.* Retrieved from http://www.nsf.gov/statistics/srvyfedfunds/

Office of Management and Budget. (2004). *Circular A-21: Revised 05/10/04.* Retrieved from http://www.whitehouse.gov/omb/circulars_a021_2004

Parsons, M. D. (1997). *Power and politics: Federal higher education policy making in the 1990s.* Albany, NY: SUNY Press.

Post-9/11 Veterans Educational Assistance Act of 2008 (Pub. L. No. 110-252, Title V).

Post–Vietnam Era Veterans' Educational Assistance Act of 1977 (38 U.S.C. 1642).

Price, D. K. (1954). *Government and science.* New York, NY: New York University Press.

Quattlebaum, C. A. (1960). Federal policies and practices in higher education. In D. M. Knight (Ed.), *The federal government and higher education* (pp. 35–52). Englewood Cliffs, NJ: Prentice Hall.

Rainsford, G. N. (1972). *Congress and higher education in the nineteenth century.* Knoxville, TN: University of Tennessee Press.

Rudy, W. (1996). *The campus and a nation in crisis: From the American Revolution to Vietnam.* Cranbury, NJ: Associate University Presses.

Russell, J. E. (1951). *Federal activities in higher education after the Second World War: An analysis of the nature, scope, and impact of federal activities in higher education in the fiscal year 1947.* New York, NY: King's Crown Press.

Servicemen's Readjustment Act of 1944 (P.L. 78-346, 58 Stat. 284m).

Smith-Hughes Act of 1917 (P.L. 64-347, 39 Stat. 929).

Smith-Lever Act of 1914 (7 U.S.C. § 343).

Tribally Controlled Community College Assistance Act of 1978 (P.L. 95-471).

U.S. House Journal. (1818). 15th Cong., 2nd sess., 7 December.

Veterans Readjustment Assistance Act of 1952 (38 U.S.C. 997).

Veterans Readjustment Benefits Act of 1966 (P.L. 89-358).

Williams, R. L. (1991). *The origins of federal support for higher education: George W. Atherton and the land-grant college movement.* University Park, PA: Pennsylvania State University Press.

Wolverton, B. (2006, September 22). Congress broadens an investigation of college sports. *The Chronicle of Higher Education,* p. A36.

5

STATE AND LOCAL GOVERNMENTS' RELATIONSHIP WITH HIGHER EDUCATION

S tate governments play a critical role in how colleges and universities deal with the three themes of this book, as they are charged with primary oversight and regulation of education.[1] Moreover, states invest in higher education institutions, public and private, under the premise that such institutions will support the public policy goals of the state. In regard to public higher education, some state governments play an active role in determining the mission of institutions and approving the types of academic programs offered. Finally, as states are key players in changing economic environments, institutions have to respond to the ways their state governments fund and regulate the higher education sector.

In an era of growing financial strain on state coffers, it is unclear how states will ultimately resolve their commitment to the principle of providing public access to higher education when their ability to afford it decreases. Taking into consideration the contemporary operational and economic challenges confronting states, this chapter examines the nature of state involvement in higher education and the local governance of community colleges, including its historical antecedents, current issues, and future trends. Chapter 9 examines in more depth the operations, organization, and role of governing boards at public and private institutions. This chapter focuses on governing boards of public institutions, specifically in terms of their relationship with state and local governments.

State Actors and Institutions

Those working in higher education know that multiple actors, many not directly involved with the academy, influence policy and administrative decisions. Even those associated with these decisions, however, are not often aware of the full breadth of actors engaged or how they are engaged in higher education. Thus, before exploring the relationship between higher education and state governments, it is important to identify state and local actors commonly involved with a state's higher education sector. This section introduces readers to the relevant actors. Their activities are reviewed briefly, and readers are encouraged to seek out additional information about the role of these actors in their particular state. The section draws on and adapts the typology developed by Fowler (2000).

Government Actors

This chapter is largely focused on expanding readers' knowledge of a state government's role in higher education. In this section, we provide an overview of the actors directly aligned with the legislative and executive branches of government. These entities, while often without a specific focus on higher education, influence higher education policy and governance.

Legislative branch. State legislatures are similar across the nation. Each state has a bicameral legislative system (with the exception of Nebraska, which has a unicameral system) largely based on the model established by the U.S. Congress. The primary responsibilities of a legislature include developing state statutes; passing resolutions; allocating state resources; and overseeing the actions of state entities, including public colleges and universities. Committees perform much of the work of a legislature.

A legislature's involvement with higher education comes in multiple ways. Occasionally, a legislature will involve itself in discussions on appropriate educational governance structures and regulations regarding quality assurance, faculty workload, and student conduct. However, the primary entanglement usually occurs over state funding of higher education. In some states each public institution proposes its budget to the legislature, and the institution's leader is required to attend a budget review hearing with a legislative committee. In other states, a coordinated budget is proposed by the head of a system or an agency, and that person is responsible for handling the hearings, though often with support provided by individual institutions. Beyond budgeting, legislatures, or more often a legislator or group of legislators, may engage in inquiries of specific institutional activities, such as student-sponsored events, salaries of executives or coaches, tuition increases, and the like. Such oversight is often triggered by media reports or constituent correspondence, and an institution is forced to defend itself before legislative committees or through written responses to legislative inquiries (Lane, 2007).

While state legislatures are often quite influential on higher education policy, individual legislators can be even more influential (Marshall, Mitchell, & Wirt, 1989). The most influential tend to be members of budget and higher education committees (sometimes higher education is subsumed under other committees dealing with broader mandates such as education from early childhood through graduate degrees or workforce development). These committees hold hearings and draft legislation related to higher education policy or budgeting. Thus, the committee members, particularly the chairs, can exert a great deal of influence on the higher education sector.

Many state legislators now have professional support staff who play an important role in the development of policy and directing the focus of the legislators they work for. Historically, state legislators were part-time and had limited access to staff. However, as expectations of state legislatures increased, efforts were taken to professionalize the role of legislators by increasing their salaries, providing office space, and funding staff for legislative offices (Bowman & Kearney, 1988). Thus, in many states, legislators are now full-time public servants with their own staffs who help support the work of the legislative office. It is important to note, though, that in some states, mostly in the western United States, legislatures remain nonprofessional, with the legislative role being part-time (a small number of state legislatures meet only for one session every two years) and without dedicated staff, instead sharing centralized staffing pools (Patterson, 1996).

Fowler (2000) notes three types of legislative staff. Clerical staff handle scheduling and correspondence and can be important for gaining access to a legislator or professional staff. Professional staff members tend to possess professional expertise and provide substantive research and counsel on legislative issues, in addition to handling case work such as responding to major requests from constituents. Finally, many states provide centralized staff services to support the entire legislature. These offices provide assistance in drafting bills, providing legal advice, and tracking legislative histories. All staff members play important roles in the policy-making and budgeting processes because of their positions as gatekeepers as well as their responsibility for processing information and providing advice to the legislator (Patterson, 1996).

Executive branch. The governor heads the executive branch of government in each state. Depending on their institutional power and interest in education, governors can play an influential role in their states' higher education sector. Many governors have the authority to appoint members of institutional governing boards and statewide coordinating boards. In some states, the state higher education executive officer is also appointed by the governor, and that position is occasionally considered part of the governor's cabinet. In addition, some states grant the governor power to propose the initial state budget to the legislature, giving that office substantial influence over higher education appropriations. If higher education is a significant policy interest of the governor, he or she may champion legislation or governance reform, in addition to using the bully pulpit to influence institutional behavior such as keeping tuition as low as possible or focusing institutional efforts on economic development.

The power of the governor depends on a variety of factors. Those governors who win by a wide margin over their opponents tend to be more powerful than those who win by smaller margins. Beyond elections, state constitutions can either constrain or empower those who hold the position. "The strongest governors are elected to serve a four-year term and can be reelected at least once, have the power to appoint numerous state officials, have considerable control over the state budget, and can veto legislation" (Fowler, 2000, p. 147). Not all governors have such expansive powers, however. For example, Texas has been frequently regarded as having a constitutionally weak governor. While the Texas governor has the power to make numerous appointments, he or she has limited influence over the budget and policy processes. In that state, the lieutenant governor is viewed as the most powerful statewide elected leader, particularly in influencing higher education, as that person is the head of the state senate and has the power to appoint committees and their chairs (Bracco, 1997).

The executive branch also comprises numerous state agencies with influence over higher education. Many of these agencies have limited direct oversight of higher education, but their collective engagement creates a web of oversight that can be quite burdensome and constraining to institutions (Lane, 2007). Most of this direct oversight comes from statewide boards or higher education commissions that are charged with the coordinating, regulating, and licensing of higher education institutions (these functions are discussed in more depth later). Some states also have state education departments, which are bureaucracies charged with regulating multiple aspects of the educational sector but with no direct governing authority.

Nongovernmental Actors

In addition to the governmental actors, a number of state-level nongovernmental actors also influence higher education. The media tend to hold a great deal of sway over setting agendas, as well as the perceptions of local and state civic leaders (McCombs & Shaw, 1972). In a review of state oversight of higher education, Lane (2007) found that state policy makers' perceptions of higher education were heavily influenced by the media. The attention of the media can be a double-edged sword. It may serve as a means for highlighting successful endeavors, outstanding students and faculty, and exciting new programs. Such coverage, casting the institution in a positive light, can influence legislators, prospective students, and alumni. Media attention can quickly turn critical, however, particularly when an incident is likely to cause controversy with the local population. Such coverage can result in increased scrutiny from external stakeholders. While the media seem to hold great influence over policy makers and others, institutional leaders need to be aware of the drawbacks of such coverage. McLendon and Peterson (1999) expressed concerns about the legitimacy of the media in informing higher education policy making because of the press's reliance on partisan sources and tendencies to create "realities that appear singular, objective, and certain, although they are, in fact, multiple, subjective, and permeable" (p. 242). Such concerns have become even more prevalent with the rise of the Internet. Now there are news websites and quasi-news sites that report on campus events, particularly potentially negative ones, sometimes with very little fact checking. Blogs and social networking sites allow nearly anyone to provide commentary about campus activities or policy decisions. The advent of such "news" outlets has made it more difficult for institutions to influence media messages and have fed into the enhanced accountability expected by external stakeholders.

Beyond the media and the Internet, education and noneducation interest groups influence a state's relationship with higher education. Those groups directly interested in higher education tend to focus on labor issues, often in the form of unions. (See the discussion in chapter 6 that differentiates between federal regulation of labor relations of private corporations and state labor relations laws that govern public employees in the state.) For example, national groups such as AFT Higher Education, the American Association of University Professors, and the National Education Association have chapters in many states and represent higher education faculty and staff. In many institutions, there are separate unions for faculty, staff, and graduate assistants. In addition to bargaining for a legally binding labor agreement, these groups sometimes engage in lobbying over other education-related policy issues such as state funding and state regulation of higher education institutions. In addition to unions, some states have other higher education interest groups, many of which are designed to support the causes of specific institution types such as private institutions, for-profit or proprietary schools, and religiously affiliated institutions.

While some interest groups specifically focus on higher education, others may have indirect interests in the sector. National groups such as the National Governors Association and the National Conference of State Legislators have been increasingly engaged in policy work related to higher education, even producing reports on a range of issues from increasing degree production to enhancing higher education contributions to economic development (e.g., Bautsch, 2011; Sparks & Waits, 2011). In some states, agricultural groups such as the farm bureau can be quite active in lobbying on behalf of agricultural education efforts, which are usually undertaken by the state's land-grant universities. In light of the growing recognition of higher education's contributions to economic development, there has been a surge in businesses' and service groups' efforts to optimize accountability mechanisms, provide adequate funding to support colleges and universities, and encourage workforce-oriented training certificate and degree programs (Lane & Johnstone, 2012).

State Governance of Higher Education

Public higher education is generally overseen by two types of boards: governing and coordinating. Governing boards assume operational authority for an institution or a group of institutions. These boards, commonly referred to as a board of regents or a board of trustees, assume authority for hiring (and, if needed, firing) the chief executive officer (e.g., president or chancellor), ensuring the financial integrity of the institution, and establishing policies. (See chapter 10 for an extended discussion of the role of governing boards.) Depending on the state, these boards may also handle personnel issues, such as promotion and tenure, and other management functions.

Coordinating boards, on the other hand, are designed to perform functions such as limiting the duplication of degree programs, facilitating budget requests to the state government, licensing educational institutions, overseeing quality assurance mechanisms, and approving institutional missions. The role of these entities is not to handle the operational aspects of educational institutions, which is the role of governing boards. Rather, they are meant to ensure collaboration among a state's educational institutions and ensure that those institutions operate in a way that is aligned with state priorities and is in the best interest of the public.

States vary markedly in how they design their governing and coordinating structures. In some states, governing boards operate separately from coordinating boards. In others, a combined board serves both functions, having operational authority for several institutions and responsibility for coordinating operations among them. The following sections provide an overview of the basic types of governing boards and coordinating boards used by states.

Governing Boards

U.S. higher education has evolved in such a way that authority for institutions commonly rests in a corporate board. Essentially, a multitude of lay individuals assume responsibility for a college or university (Duryea, 2000). Particularly in the public sector, however, not all institutions have their own boards. Indeed, while most governing boards in the United States oversee one institution, most students in the United States actually attend a college or university that shares its governing board with other institutions (MacTaggart, 1998).

In *The Guardians: Boards of Trustees of American Colleges and Universities,* Kerr and Gade (1989) categorize modern public governing boards in three general types. Public institutions may have a campus-level board with full authority over a single institution. Some states use consolidated governance systems, where one board governs multiple institutions. Such a board may have responsibility for all public institutions in a state (e.g., New York and North Dakota), or it may only oversee a subset of institutions in the state. For example, in Missouri the Board of Curators of the University of Missouri governs four distinct campuses that operate fairly separately from each other, but each of the state's other public four-year institutions has its own board (e.g., Southeast Missouri State University and Truman State University). In the third category, institutions may be governed within segmented systems that have different governing boards for different types of institutions. In California, each of the three systems—the University of California system, the California State University system, and the California Community Colleges system—has its own governing board.

In terms of membership, the composition of public boards has remained fairly homogeneous. According to a 2010 survey by the Association of Governing Boards of Universities and Colleges (2010), public board membership remained mostly male (71.6%), White (76.9%), and over the age of 50 (69%). Nearly half the members (49.4%) had a background in business. In some states efforts have been made to increase the diversity of membership of these boards, but the composition is often dependent on how membership is determined. The survey also reported that the average number of voting board members is about 11, and the average length of a term is six years.

Whereas private institutions generally have boards that are self-sustaining (i.e., they select their own members), the leaders and board members of public institutions usually have limited direct involvement in the selection of new board members. Depending on the selection mechanisms, however, these individuals may be able to exert some influence in the process.

While structures differ across the states, the members of public institutions' governing boards are generally either appointed or elected, although some serve ex officio. Members come from the state, and it is likely many are "beholden to external political interests" (Kerr & Gade, 1989, p. 40). Increasingly, membership also includes individuals who represent internal stakeholders, such as students and faculty. Those who study governing boards suggest, however, that all members should view themselves as guardians of the institution rather than champions of particular groups or interests (Chait, Holland, & Taylor, 1996).

Beyond who constitutes the membership of a governing board, how a board is structured can influence its operations. Toma (1990) found,

> The structure of the boards is important because it helps to define the constraints on the board members and on the internal agents of the universities. . . . Public universities can be made to function more like private ones by placing them under separate governing boards. (p. 7)

Moreover, a board's scope of responsibility can affect how it relates to the institution or institutions under its control. For example, while a board of a single institution can focus all its efforts on advancing that institution, multicampus boards must make decisions about how to balance institutional needs and distribute resources. In the latter case, a board's attention is divided among multiple institutions, and institutional leaders may have to compete for consideration.

How members are selected can also influence board operations. Elected and appointed members often see their roles differently. Most appointments are made by the governor, though some come directly from the legislature. Appointments are generally favored over elections, as the vetting process tends to be more advanced, to ensure that dedicated and knowledgeable individuals are appointed, although there are numerous examples of political appointments being based on cronyism rather than relevant characteristics or skills (Kerr & Gade, 1989). Elected board members, on the other hand, may wield more political influence and have a greater opportunity to challenge unfriendly politicians, but they may also take a similar approach toward institutional leaders (Kerr & Gade). The selection process may not only affect how members interact with others, but also influence their priorities. Empirical studies in this area are quite limited, but Lowry (2001), for example, found that elected rather than appointed boards generally result in lower tuition rates at public institutions. The reason may be that elected boards are more attuned to the demands of the public, which often are focused on keeping tuition low.

Coordinating Boards

The entities charged with coordinating a state's higher education institutions can be separate from institutional governing boards or subsumed into them. While sometimes operational overlap occurs, governance and coordination are generally viewed as separate responsibilities. In *Statewide Coordination of Higher Education*, Berdahl (1971) argued that states have an appropriate role to play in the oversight and coordination of public higher education systems. As the source of significant funding and the representative of the people, a state government is obligated to ensure that public institutions operate in a manner consistent with the priorities and policies of their state. Berdahl cautioned, however, that while states have an obligation to deal with some administrative and procedural issues, it is important that institutions retain academic autonomy to handle matters related to the curriculum and other academic issues.

The idea of statewide coordination attracted great interest during the 1960s and 1970s and was widely adopted during the 1980s and 1990s. When Berdahl (1971) did his study, he found that some states had almost no coordination, or the coordination occurred voluntarily. The formal coordinating bodies that did exist focused on master planning and budgeting for their state's institutions, often with a particular focus on facilities planning. Moving into the 1980s and 1990s, the focus of coordinating boards began to evolve into more "market-driven 'strategic investment' approaches" designed to influence institutional behavior (MacTaggart, 1998, p. 12).

Today, almost all states have an entity designated to oversee statewide coordination.[2] Most states operate with a statewide coordinating board (e.g., Colorado, Illinois, Tennessee, and Texas) or a consolidated governing/coordinating board (e.g., Arizona, Georgia, South Dakota, and New Hampshire). Statewide coordinating boards are separate from institutional governing boards and focus on a system as a whole as opposed to the separate interests of institutions. Some coordinating boards have more power to engage in the coordination process than others. For example, regulatory boards may have the authority to approve academic programs and institutional missions as well as coordinate institutional budget requests to the state government. Advisory boards may have only the authority to "review and make recommendations" to institutional boards in regard to academic programs, while others may have powers limited to institutional licensure or administration of student aid funds (MacTaggart, 1998, p. 20). Some boards also prioritize institutional requests for capital improvements or new construction.

With consolidated governing/coordinating boards, one or more entities are charged with governing and coordinating a system of institutions. In some states with segmented systems (e.g., community colleges vs. four-year institutions), multiple boards may be charged with governing and coordinating. In this structure, the board fulfills coordination and planning functions and is also charged with helping to build and manage the institution, as previously discussed.

Community College Governance

Most community colleges developed along a separate path than four-year institutions, resulting in different governance arrangements. Some institutions were created as two-year branch campuses affiliated with four-year institutions, so they are generally governed by the same board as the four-year institutions. These institutions were initially meant to serve as feeder schools so that the students would take some of their early course work at the branch before coming to the larger institution. Alternatively, many two-year institutions were founded by school districts or local communities as a means to provide technical and vocational training beyond high school. Today, regardless of their origins, most two-year institutions have evolved into comprehensive community colleges that provide an array of vocational programs, transfer programs, continuing education courses, and other services (Cohen & Brawer, 2009).

While in some states two-year colleges are included in a comprehensive public system, in others community colleges are governed separately. For example, the Illinois Community College Board serves as the coordinating entity for 48 community colleges. Each community college has its own board of trustees, whose members are elected from the local community college district. Less frequently, the governance remains entirely local with a school board or local tax district retaining control over an institution, as is the case in South Dakota, which is the only state without statewide community college coordination (Tollefson, Garrett, Ingram, & Associates, 1999).

Tollefson et al. (1999) identified five models of state-level coordination of community colleges. These models are a combination of separate and combined governing and coordinating boards. In the first model, a state board of education provides some limited coordination but has little direct control over the colleges, which have their own boards (e.g., Alabama, Kansas, and Pennsylvania). In the second model, state higher education commissions have degree/program approval authority, but local boards govern the institutions (e.g., Arkansas, Missouri, and New Jersey). The third model is a statewide community college board that typically has budgetary and programmatic control (e.g., California, New Hampshire, and Wyoming). With the fourth model, state community college governing boards retain coordinating and governing responsibilities only for community colleges (e.g., Delaware, Kentucky, and Maine). Finally, in some states community colleges are overseen by a consolidated governing/coordinating board that supervises all higher education institutions in the state (e.g., Alaska, North Dakota, and Vermont).

Institutional Licensure

A primary characteristic of higher education institutions that distinguishes them from other organizations is their ability to confer an academic degree. A degree is widely recognized but sometimes difficult to define, particularly in terms of what it confers upon its recipient. The Supreme Court of Vermont stated:

> In practical affairs, [a degree] introduces its possessor to the confidence and patronage of the general public. Its legal character gives it moral and material credit in the estimation of the world, and makes it thereby a valuable property right of great pecuniary value. (*Townshend v. Gray*, 1890, p. 636)

In many ways, the value of the degree is tied to the legitimacy of the institution granting it.

While the primacy of state governments in regulating educational institutions is widely acknowledged, their legal authority to license educational institutions has been little explored. Contreras (2009) wrote an overview of this issue in which he argued there are three legitimate sources of degree-granting authority in the United States: tribal, state, and federal governments. Because of their semisovereign status in the United States, tribal governments have licensed several tribal colleges, mostly providing educational offerings to Native Americans.[3] At the federal level, a handful of institutions, such as the nation's military academies, received their degree-granting authority from the U.S. Congress.

Nearly all postsecondary educational institutions in the United States receive their degree-granting authority from their state government.[4] Contreras (2009) stated there are three types of state-conferred authorizations: (a) public institutions owned or operated by the state government or a subunit of the government (such as a community college taxing district), (b) institutions exempted from state regulation on religious grounds, and (c) nonpublic (nonprofit and for-profit) institutions with a formal authorization to operate in the state.

The authority for public institutions to grant degrees comes directly from a state government when it creates the institution. In many ways, establishment of public colleges and universities is the epitome of democratic partnerships. There is a fundamental belief, particularly in states with limited private higher education sectors, that the state has an obligation to make higher education opportunities available to its citizens. Public institutions are generally created (or recognized) through either statutory or constitutional provision.[5] In some states, public institutions were actually created prior to statehood, so their mention in their state's constitution or statutes reflects recognition of their special relationship with the state rather than an actual chartering of the institution. Many others were created after statehood was granted, and their existence was authorized through some form of state approval. Institutions that are enshrined in a state constitution tend to have more freedoms from state government than peers mentioned in state statutes (Blackwell, 1961). Legislators and governors have power over statutes, but it takes broad approval by a state's citizens to amend the constitution.

Regardless of affiliation or orientation, the courts have largely held that states have the right to regulate all degree-granting institutions within their borders (*New Jersey State Board of Higher Education v. Board of Directors of Shelton College*, 1982; *State ex rel. McLemore v. Clarksville School of Theology*, 1982). However, in some states—fewer than half—religiously based educational institutions are largely exempt from requirements regarding licensure as well as other regulations (Contreras, 2009).[6] The reason originates with the free exercise clause of the First Amendment of the U.S. Constitution. This clause can prohibit the judiciary and legislature from entertaining lawsuits or laws pertaining to religiously based educational organizations. While the clause is meant to ensure neutrality, the courts have long held that noninvolvement is one of the surest ways to maintain nonentanglement between the government and religious organizations. While the protection of religious institutions is not absolute (see *Bob Jones University v. United States*, 1983), some state governments have adopted this premise when it comes to institutional licensure, essentially conceding their authority to accreditation agencies and relying on an institution's accreditation as a signal that the state should allow the institutions to operate within its borders. The exemption, however, is explicitly granted by the state and can be withdrawn by the state. These laws in some states have led to concern about the proliferation of diploma mills under the guise of religious freedom, and many states are now reviewing how they handle such institutions.

Most colleges and universities in the United States are nonpublic entities with some form of state authorization.[7] This authorization comes in three forms. First, many institutions, particularly the oldest in the United States, were authorized through some form of state-issued charter or "some other kind of *sui generis* state action that approves specific schools by name" (Contreras, 2009, p. 6). Many of the colonial colleges, for example, were authorized by royal degree. These charters define the relationship between the institution and the state, and in some cases grant special rights to the institution, such as freedom from paying property taxes. Furthermore, some states have delegated license authority to a religious body that has to approve affiliated institutions. In most states, authorization is regulated by a set of policies enforced by a state agency (although not always an education-related agency). If an institution meets the necessary requirements, then a license to operate is issued. Many agencies make a distinction between nonprofit and for-profit higher education, administering a more active licensing review in the case of for-profit institutions.

As Contreras (2009) explained, "To be valid, a degree must be issued by an entity that has the legal authority to do so" (p. 20). In the United States, state governments retain primary authority in this area. They may choose to abdicate this authority by shifting responsibility to a religious organization or an external accrediting body, such as California has attempted to do by empowering the Western Association of Schools and Colleges as its licensor.

However, it ultimately remains the responsibility of a state to approve and regulate the educational institutions within its borders, and it is this responsibility that sets the foundation for all of its other engagements with its colleges and universities.

Quality Assurance and Accountability

In addition to licensure, states have assumed an increasing role in holding colleges and universities accountable for their performance, particularly in the area of teaching and learning. In the United States, quality assurance has historically been left to nongovernmental accreditation agencies (see chapter 8). These agencies, which have no direct oversight from either federal or state governments, have assumed quasi-regulatory status, particularly in states that largely abdicate their licensure authority to them. This arrangement has caused some confusion for students, particularly those from outside the United States who do not understand the multifaceted regulatory environment for education-related quality assurance.

The advent of more centralized coordinating boards since the 1970s has led some state governments to assume a more active role in the quality assurance process. At the state level, such engagements are commonly referred to as accountability measures (Burke, 2005). The accountability efforts of many states have moved beyond academic efforts to include financial and regulatory issues. Many institutions, particularly those in the public realm, are now required to submit a host of reports to their state government as well as comply with an array of regulations and oversight meant to hold the institution accountable to the state government (Lane, 2007).

The term *accountability* has become so common that it means everything and nothing. Public officials use the term to describe vaguely defined notions such as trustworthiness, fidelity, and justice (Bovens, 2006). Neither scholars nor policy makers have been able to develop a common definition (Dubnick, 2005), and attempts to do so have only resulted in a proliferation of models, typologies, analogies, and the like. For example, in his review of the higher education literature, Burke (2005) identified multiple models of accountability: bureaucratic, professional, political, managerial, market, and managed market. Higher education accountability has been represented as a triangle (Clark, 1983), a sphere (Behn, 2001), and a diamond (Middlehurst, 2011). It also has been noted to face upward, downward, inward, and outward (Vidovich & Slee, 2000). Lane (2007) referred to multiple types of state accountability mechanisms as a spider-web that comes to envelop an institution.

State-level accountability processes can take passive and active forms. Many states now have sunshine laws designed to allow the public broad access to higher education information and meetings (McLendon & Hearn, 2004). Consequently, most governing board meetings, except those that deal with personnel or other exempted matters, must be announced in advance and be held in a public forum. Moreover, salaries, reports, and other documents are usually covered by freedom of information laws, which require educational institutions and other public organizations to allow outsiders access to their work products and other data. The idea behind such laws is to increase transparency and therefore improve accountability. With these initiatives, institutions tend to be mostly passive participants, facilitating the public's access to their meetings and documents.

States have also instituted many more active accountability requirements. These programs require institutions to report their performance to their state governments, and at times to the general public. These initiatives have been called performance reporting, performance funding, and performance budgeting (Burke & Associates, 2002). Performance reporting requires institutions to report performance outcomes along a range of common measures. Increasingly, these measures are being made available to the public via the Internet. Performance funding and performance budgeting tie financial allocations to performance reporting. Performance funding is intended to reward institutions financially for their performance on predetermined measures, while performance budgeting allocates money to institutions as an enticement for them to engage in new initiatives aligned with their state's policy agenda. Currently, most states operate only performance reporting programs, although some states are looking to resurrect performance funding programs.

State Funding

States play a significant role in the funding of public (and some private) higher education institutions. While the federal government provides substantial loans to students and grants for research, the amount of federal funds directly allocated for institutional support is limited. States provide funds to higher education in three primary ways: operating funds, capital funds, and student aid. In fiscal year (FY) 2010 state and local governments allocated a total of $88.5 billion to support higher education, with about 78% directly supporting institutional operating budgets (State Higher Education Executive Officers, 2011). Twelve percent of the funds supported special projects such as research, agricultural extensions, and medical education. Student aid programs supporting attendance at public institutions accounted for another 7%, and the remaining 3% went to support private institutions and their students.

While public expenditures at the state level increased overall during the second half of the first decade of the 21st century, the years following the Great Recession have seen a retrenchment in state funding. Between FY 2006 (before the Great Recession of 2008 began) and FY 2010, overall state support for higher education across the nation increased by 12.5%. Following the recession, however, states began to pull back on their funding. Total state and local support of higher education, including monies from the federal American Recovery and Reinvestment Act of 2008, decreased by 1.9% between FY 2009 and FY 2011. However, the impact was disparate across the nation. Between FY 2009 and FY 2011, 32 states reported modest (0.3%) to significant (13.5%) declines in state funding, while 16 states reported modest (0.2%) to significant (24.7%) increases in state support (State Higher Education Executive Officers, 2011).

The financial picture becomes bleaker when one considers the amount of money allocated per full-time equivalent student. Because of the slow economy, enrollments increased by 6% between 2009 and 2010. Thus, institutions served more students without more state financial support. In FY 2010, state and local governments allocated an average of $6,451 per full-time equivalent student (not including appropriations for research, agricultural extension, and medical education), which was a $500 (or 7%) decrease from 2009, the lowest rate since 1985 (State Higher Education Executive Officers, 2011).

State Aid to Students

Historically, most states have not provided state aid directly to students. This trend has changed, though, in the last few decades. As the cost of public higher education increased, some states opted to provide aid directly to students in addition to appropriations to institutions. State aid programs provide only a small amount of the total aid given directly to students, however. The federal government provides 49% of all student aid; state governments provide only 9% (College Board Advocacy & Policy Center, 2010).[8] In the 2009–2010 academic year, states allocated $10.8 billion in state funding to student aid programs, which represented an increase from $10.4 billion the year before (National Association of State Student Grant & Aid Programs, 2010).

State student aid policies differ considerably across the nation. States use a variety of methods to distribute aid, such as grants, loans, scholarships, work-study, and tuition waivers, although the most common approach is grants (National Association of State Student Grant & Aid Programs, 2010). Aid policies differ in two primary ways. In the first, in terms of how much money is allocated to student aid programs, all states now appropriate at least a small amount of money to student aid programs, but the amounts vary significantly. New Hampshire, South Dakota, and Wyoming allocated less than $5 million to aid programs, whereas 21 states allocated more than $100 million—including California, which allocated in excess of $1 billion (National Association of State Student Grant & Aid Programs). A number of reasons explain these differences, including state fiscal culture, institutional tuition levels, and the number of students in each system.

The second difference concerns how eligibility for aid is determined. Eligibility is often defined in terms of merit or need, although states vary markedly in their aid policies, which directly affect who benefits. Merit-based aid is allocated to students according to their previous academic performance or other types of exceptional achievements. Need-based aid is intended for students with financial need. Eligibility for need-based aid, even at the state level, is usually determined by the federal Free Application for Federal Student Aid (www.fafsa.ed.gov). All 50 states provide undergraduate programs with a need-based component, and 30 states also have aid programs exclusively based on merit (National Association of State Student Grant & Aid Programs, 2010).

State Support of Private Institutions

While all states provide some funds to public postsecondary institutions, only a handful provide support to private institutions.[9] In FY 2010, 14 states provided more than $200 billion to their private colleges and universities. With the exception of Louisiana, all these states are east of the Mississippi River (see Figure 5.1), and state support of private higher education in these states is likely because of the strength of the private sectors there. Those states

FIGURE 5.1
States Providing Public Aid to Private Institutions (2010)

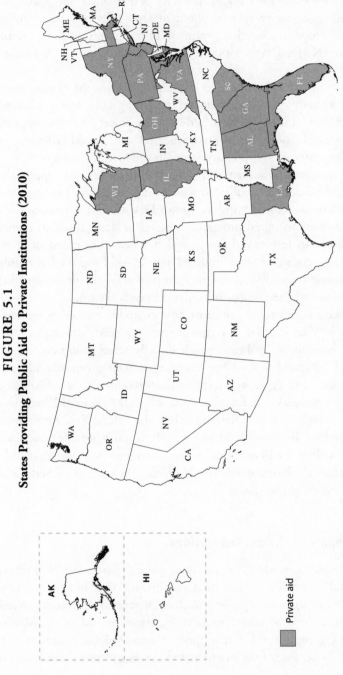

Private aid

Note. Data from *State higher education finance FY 2011*, by State Higher Education Executive Officers, 2011, www.sheeo.org/pubs/pubs_results.asp?issueID=20.

allocating institutional aid to private colleges and universities are Alabama, Florida, Georgia, Illinois, Louisiana, Maryland, Massachusetts, New Jersey, New York, Ohio, Pennsylvania, South Carolina, Virginia, and Wisconsin. The amount of private aid varies markedly across the nation, however. Half the states allocated less than $6 million, with several of those states providing closer to $1 million. In four states, however, aid to private institutions totaled more than $20 million. How this money is allocated varies from state to state.

As an example, New York, which hosts the second highest number of higher education institutions in the United States, provides the largest amount of aid to private institutions. The Bundy Aid program began in 1968 on the recommendation of a select committee chaired by McGeorge Bundy and charged with advising "how the State can help preserve the strength and vitality of our private and independent institutions of higher education and at the same time, keep them free" (Steck, 1994, p. 275). In FY 2010 New York allocated $42.7 million of Bundy Aid to its private institutions.[10] Bundy Aid comes from an annual appropriation from the state legislature and is intended to provide unrestricted financial support to a number of private institutions. Funding is allocated based on the number of degrees granted in the previous year. Not all private institutions in New York State are eligible for the aid; institutions must apply and meet a set of criteria. About 100 institutions now participate in the Bundy Aid program.

Future Issues

States are the primary organizing structure for the nation's higher education sector. State governments retain primary responsibility for licensing and regulating a state's colleges and universities. In addition, state governments have historically served as the primary funders of their public institutions. However, the Great Recession of 2008 solidified a new normal in many states' relationships with their higher education institutions. Reductions of state revenues resulted in many state leaders' cutting state appropriations to colleges and universities. Effectively navigating higher education's relationship with state governments requires knowledge of key actors as well as the state's governance structure and the functions of the state government.

Since 2008 many state governments have been significantly decreasing their support of public higher education to help abate their structural budget deficits (State Higher Education Executive Officers, 2011). It is not unusual for states to decrease their financial support for higher education during times of fiscal austerity, but the significant size of recent rounds of reductions resulted in some of the most substantive changes to the higher education sector in decades. Indeed, the multiyear cutting of state support has resulted in many institutions' raising tuition significantly, eliminating academic programs, and slashing administrative support. The dramatic nature of the most recent cuts is prompting much discussion about the future of the public higher education sector and its relationship to state government. What will happen when tax revenues begin to recover? Will states take a lead in revitalizing their public colleges and universities? Or will new revenues be directed to other state needs, further shifting the cost of education to students and their families?

States have been fortunate that traditional higher education institutions have been largely place bound. That is, no matter how much or how little a state supports its public higher education sector, the institutions remain in the state to educate students, provide cultural opportunities, attract new businesses, and so forth. As Shaffer and Wright (2010) found in their study of the role of higher education in economic development,

> From Springfield, Massachusetts, where a technical college has converted an abandoned factory into an urban tech park, to Raleigh-Durham, North Carolina, where research universities worked to turn a sleepy backwater into a global powerhouse of innovation and manufacturing, to Sidney, Nebraska, where a community college operates a training academy that has helped keep the headquarters of a growing national company in its rural hometown, communities today recognize that their hopes for the future are tied to higher education. (p. 1)

As states have decreased their funding of higher education, however, their public institutions have begun to look for new revenue streams outside state borders. A common strategy has been to attract out-of-state students, who usually pay higher tuition rates than in-state students. More recently, states have been crossing borders in more significant ways. In fact, dozens of public colleges and universities have engaged in joint partnerships with foreign institutions as well as opened campuses in other states and countries (Lane, Kinser, & Knox, in press). The emergence of multistate and multinational educational institutions is but one example of how some institutions may be decoupling themselves from their state governments.

James Duderstadt (2011), former president of the University of Michigan, framed the issue this way: "Overburdened with legacy economic and political burdens, state governments are less and less influential in determining prosperity in the new economy. . . . Today's economic activities are no longer constrained by traditional geopolitical boundaries, such as states and nations" (p. 13). This quote comes from a report intended to be a new strategic plan for higher education in the Midwest. In it Duderstadt argued that because of the waning dominance of the states in economic planning and in higher education, public institutions need to find ways to advance their own efforts to bolster local economies through regional collaborations and compacts that allow for sharing resources and expertise across state borders (see chapter 8).

However, a report from the National Governors Association, issued about the same time as Duderstadt's (2011) master plan, continues to operate on the assumption of the primacy of the state in the organization of the economy and higher education. The report suggested that the two policy priorities for higher education should be increasing the number of college graduates and aligning degree production with areas with demand for jobs (Sparks & Waits, 2011). The emphasis here is that state leaders need to do a better job of aligning higher education outputs with state economic priorities. Surprisingly, there is no mention of the need for states to reinvest in higher education to support these policy priorities.

Notes

1. As discussed in this chapter, the amendments to the U.S. Constitution give control of education to state governments. The federal government, however, has always maintained some interest in these affairs.

2. In most states, such coordination applies only to public institutions, although a few states such as New York permit their coordinating body to exert some authority over private institutions. In addition, Pennsylvania has only a state agency with very little authority, and Michigan has no such statewide entity.

3. According to the American Indian Higher Education Consortium, there are 36 tribal colleges. The federal government has been involved with tribal colleges. For example, the Tribally Controlled Community College Assistance Act of 1978 provides federal funding to Tribal Colleges, and the Equity in Educational Land-Grant Status Act of 1994 designated them as federal land-grant institutions, making them eligible for additional funding. More information about tribal colleges can be found in chapter 4 and at www.aihec.org.

4. The Education Commission of the States maintains a list of state licensure agencies on its website, www.ecs.org.

5. A handful of institutions also attained public status after first operating as private entities. For example, Temple University and the University of Pittsburgh

were created as private institutions, but when they became financially troubled, the Commonwealth of Pennsylvania began to provide them with annual appropriations because of the important roles they played in Pittsburgh and Philadelphia. Though these institutions fought to maintain their private status, the state supreme court ruled that "a symbiotic relationship between the institution and the Commonwealth exists," so "action taken by those institutions are, therefore, actions taken under color of state law" (*Krynicky v. University of Pittsburgh*, 1984).

6. In most cases these institutions exclusively offer religious degrees. Institutions such as the University of Notre Dame (Roman Catholic) and Valparaiso University (Lutheran), which offer nonreligious degrees, are usually regulated in the same fashion as other private nonprofit institutions.

7. According to the *Digest of Education Statistics*, as of 2009–2010, there were 4,495 accredited institutions in the United States awarding associate's degrees or higher. Of this number, 1,672 were public, 1,624 were private nonprofit, and 1,199 were private for-profit institutions (Snyder & Dillow, 2011, p. 283).

8. Institutions provide 36% of aid, while employers and other private sources cover 11% (College Board Advocacy & Policy Center, 2010).

9. Unless otherwise cited, the information in this section was provided by the State Higher Education Executive Officers staff and is from the State Higher Education Finance Study (State Higher Education Executive Officers, 2011).

10. Like all higher education funding in New York State, Bundy Aid experienced a significant cut the following year.

References

Association of Governing Boards of Universities and Colleges. (2010). *Policies, practices, and composition of governing boards of public colleges, universities, and systems.* Washington, DC: AGB Press.

Bautsch, B. (2011). *Investing in higher education for Latinos: Payoffs for state economies.* Denver, CO: National Conference of State Legislators.

Behn, R. D. (2001). *Rethinking democratic accountability.* Washington, DC: Brookings Institution Press.

Berdahl, R. O. (1971). *Statewide coordination of higher education.* Washington, DC: American Council on Education.

Blackwell, T. E. (1961). *College law: A guide for administrators.* Washington, DC: American Council on Education.

Bob Jones University v. United States, 461 U.S. 574 (1983).

Bovens, M. (2006). *Analysing and assessing public accountability: A conceptual framework* (European Governance Papers No. C-06-01). Retrieved from http://www.connex-network.org/eurogov/pdf/egp-connex-C-06-01.pdf

Bowman, A. O., & Kearney, R. C. (1988). Dimensions of state government capability. *Western Political Quarterly, 41*(2), 341–362. doi:10.1177/106591298804100208

Bracco, K. R. (1997). *State structures for the governance of higher education: Texas case study summary*. Retrieved from the California Higher Education Policy Center website: http://www.capolicycenter.org/texas/texas.html

Burke, J. C. (2005). The many faces of accountability. In J. C. Burke (Ed.), *Achieving accountability in higher education* (pp. 1–24). San Francisco, CA: Jossey-Bass.

Burke, J. C., & Associates. (2002). *Funding public higher education for performance: Popularity, problems, and prospects*. Albany, NY: Rockefeller Institute Press.

Chait, R., Holland, T. P., & Taylor, B. E. (1996). *The effective board of trustees*. Washington, DC: Oryx Press.

Clark, B. R. (1983). *The higher education system: Academic organization in cross-national perspective*. Berkeley, CA: University of California Press.

Cohen, A., & Brawer, F. (2009). *The American community college* (5th ed.). San Francisco, CA: Wiley.

College Board Advocacy & Policy Center. (2010). *Trends in student aid*. Retrieved from http://trends.collegeboard.org/student_aid/

Contreras, A. L. (2009). *The legal basis for degree-granting authority in the United States*. Boulder, CO: State Higher Education Executive Officers.

Dubnick, M. J. (2005). Accountability and the promise of performance: In search of the mechanisms. *Public Performance & Management Review, 27*(3), 376–417.

Duderstadt, J. J. (2011). *A master plan for higher education in the Midwest: A roadmap to the future of the nation's heartland* (Heartland Papers Series No. 3). Retrieved from the Chicago Council on Global Affairs website: http://www.thechicagocouncil.org/files/Studies_Publications/HeartlandPapers/A_Master_Plan_for_Higher_Education_in_the_Midwest.aspx

Duryea, E. D. (2000). *The academic corporation: A history of college and university governing boards*. New York, NY: Falmer Press.

Equity in Educational Land-Grant Status Act of 1994, Pub. L. No.103-382, 108 Stat. 4048 (1994).

Fowler, F. C. (2000). *Policy studies for educational leaders: An introduction*. Upper Saddle River, NJ: Prentice Hall.

Kerr, D., & Gade, M. (1989). *The guardians: Boards of trustees of American colleges and universities*. Washington, DC: Association of Governing Boards.

Krynicky v. University of Pittsburgh, 742 F.2d 94 (3rd Cir. 1984).

Lane, J. E. (2007). Spider web of oversight: Latent and manifest regulatory controls in higher education. *The Journal of Higher Education, 78*(6), 1–30.

Lane, J. E., & Johnstone, D. B. (Eds.). (2012). *Colleges and universities as economic drivers*. Albany, NY: SUNY Press.

Lane, J. E., Kinser, K., & Knox, D. (in press). Regulating cross-border higher education: A case study of the United States. *Higher Education Policy*.

Lowry, R. C. (2001). Government structures, trustee selection, and public university process and spending: Multiple means to similar ends. *American Journal of Political Science, 45*(4), 845–861. doi:10.2307/2669328

MacTaggart, T. J. (1998). *Seeking excellence through independence: Liberating colleges and universities from excessive regulation.* San Francisco, CA: Jossey-Bass.

Marshall, C., Mitchell, D., & Wirt, F. (1989). *Culture and education policy in the American states.* Bristol, PA: Falmer Press.

McCombs, M. E., & Shaw, D. L. (1972). The agenda-setting function of the mass media. *Public Opinion Quarterly, 36*(2), 176–187. doi:10.1086/267990

McLendon, M. K., & Hearn, J. C. (2004). Why "sunshine" laws matter: Emerging issues for university governance, leadership, and policy. *Metropolitan Universities, 15*(1), 67–83.

McLendon, M. K., & Peterson, M. W. (1999). The press and state policy making for higher education. *The Review of Higher Education, 22*(3), 223–245.

Middlehurst, R. (2011). Accountability and cross-border higher education: Dynamics, trends and challenges. In B. Stensaker & L. Harvey (Eds.), *Accountability in higher education: Global perspectives on trust and power* (pp. 179–202). New York, NY: Routledge.

National Association of State Student Grant & Aid Programs. (2010). *2009–2010 41st annual survey report on state-sponsored student financial aid.* Retrieved from http://www.nassgap.org/viewrepository.aspx?categoryID=332#

New Jersey State Board of Higher Education v. Board of Directors of Shelton College, 90 N.J. 470, 448 A.2d 988 (1982).

Patterson, S. C. (1996). Legislative politics in the states. In V. Gray & H. Jacob (Eds.), *Politics in the American states* (6th ed., pp. 159–206). Washington, DC: Congressional Quarterly Press.

Shaffer, D. F., & Wright, D. J. (2010). A new paradigm for economic development: How higher education institutions are working to revitalize their regional and state economies. Retrieved from the Rockefeller Institute of Government website: http://www.rockinst.org/pdf/education/2010-03-18-A_New_Paradigm.pdf

Snyder, T. D., & Dillow, S. A. (2011). *Digest of education statistics 2010.* Washington, DC: U.S. Department of Education.

Sparks, E., & Waits, M. J. (2011). *Degrees for what jobs? Raising expectations for universities and colleges in a global economy.* Retrieved from the National Governors Association Center for Best Practices website: http://www.nga.org/files/live/sites/NGA/files/pdf/1103DEGREESJOBS.pdf

State ex rel. McLemore v. Clarksville School of Theology, 636 S.W.2d. 706, 5 Ed. Law Rep. 1294 (1982).

State Higher Education Executive Officers. (2011). *State higher education finance FY 2010.* Retrieved from http://www.sheeo.org/pubs/pubs_results.asp?issueID=20

Steck, H. J. (1994). How good and how large a state university? Dilemmas of higher education policy in New York state. In J. M. Stonecash, J. K. White, & P. W. Colby (Eds.), *Governing New York state* (pp. 289–332). Albany, NY: SUNY Press.

Tollefson, T. A., Garrett, R. L., Ingram, W. G., & Associates. (1999). *Fifty state systems of community colleges: Mission, governance, funding and accountability.* Johnson City, TN: Overmountain Press.

Toma, E. F. (1990). Boards of trustees, agency problems, and the university output. *Public Choice, 67,* 1-9.

Townshend v. Gray (1890) 62 Vermont 373. *Atlantic Reporter, 19,* 635–637.

Tribally Controlled Community College Assistance Act of 1978. 25 U.S.C. 1802 et seq. (1978).

Vidovich, L., & Slee, R. (2000). *The unsteady ascendancy of market accountability in Australian and English higher education.* Paper presented at the conference of the Australian Association for Research in Education, Sydney University, Sydney, Australia.

6

THE COURTS AND
HIGHER EDUCATION

T he judicial branch of government has overt and hidden effects on
higher education, and the courts' influence directly relates to the
three themes of this book.[1] By defining the legal relationship of
employees and students with their colleges and universities, the courts have
determined how an institution's core mission and values must be applied to
its relationship with its various constituencies. Legal interpretations have
affected how institutional mission and values are applied to policy and practice, our first theme, and have established the legal parameters that dictate
how an institution interacts with and adapts to its environment, our second
theme. Our third theme, creating and fostering democratic partnerships, is
directly affected by court oversight of the relationships between institutions
and their constituencies. While much of this oversight emanates from the
Constitution and laws passed by Congress, the courts' interpretation of these
laws has a direct impact on shared governance. As we discuss the courts'
influence on higher education, we will return to these three themes.

This chapter discusses the evolution of judicial involvement in U.S.
higher education. Following an overview of the constitutional and legal
authority of the federal and state governments, we discuss various issues in
the last several decades' worth of court decisions relevant to higher education.[2] We continue with student issues such as student-institution relationships and student rights. We then address employee concerns, including
faculty employment issues and the development of collective bargaining in
the private sector and at the state level with public employees. We conclude
with a discussion of the legal responsibilities of boards of trustees.

The Legal System in the United States

The system of courts in the United States functions on two levels: the federal court system and a state court system in each state. Federal courts adjudicate issues involving the U.S. Constitution; federal statutes, laws, and regulations; and treaties between the United States and sovereign entities. In the federal court system, the Supreme Court is the highest court that interprets the laws through the Constitution of the United States and is the final arbitrator of requests for redress (Alexander & Alexander, 2011, p. 14). The Supreme Court also can, through a writ of certiorari, agree to hear a case from any federal or state court that requires interpretation of constitutional and federal law. Once the interpretation of the law has been established by the Supreme Court, the court will remand the case to a lower court to address the issues raised by the aggrieved party.

The court of original jurisdiction (where suits originate) at the federal level is the federal district court. Federal district courts are located in each state, with the number of courts in a state depending on population. Cases appealed from the federal district court will be heard in the federal circuit court of appeals, which interprets the law but also may address the issues of the aggrieved party. There are 11 circuits in the United States, and when there is disagreement between two or more circuit courts of appeals on the interpretation of the law, the Supreme Court will often become involved in deciding the issue.

States have a structure similar to that of the federal court system, although the names of the different levels of the court may vary.[3] The highest state court is the interpreter of state law through the state constitution. States also have a court of original jurisdiction but also may have small claims courts or courts with special jurisdiction. States also have appellate courts. A state court's decision is the law in that state and may point to how another state might rule on a similar issue. For example, a ruling in the state of California may point to how another state might rule, but it would not be law in Florida, for example, unless the Florida court reached a similar conclusion.

The Courts' Historical Involvement With Higher Education

Dartmouth College v. Woodward (1819) recognized the existence of two sectors of higher education, a private sector and a public sector, and established the basic structure of corporate law. For a long time after the Dartmouth Case, however, the courts were reluctant to engage in legal disputes involving higher education. Colleges and universities were viewed as a realm in which the courts lacked expertise, and the judiciary often deferred to the judgment of academics and their administrators. Moreover, the relationship between institutions and their students was viewed similarly to that of parents and their children, legally referred to as in loco parentis, and the courts preferred to remain uninvolved in that relationship. In one notable case the court stated: "College authorities stand *in loco parentis* concerning the physical and moral welfare and mental training of pupils, and we are unable to see why, to that end, they may not make any rules or regulations for the government or betterment of their pupils than a parent could for the same purpose" (*Gott v. Berea College*, 1913, p. 204).

Beginning in the 1930s, however, the courts increasingly involved themselves in student-institution relationships in a number of cases concerning African Americans' access to historically White public institutions. When African Americans challenged the legitimacy of the doctrine of "separate but equal," which was established in *Plessy v. Ferguson* (1896) and allowed states to establish separate institutions for Black and White students, the courts began to peer through the college gates to consider those segregation policies. The legality of segregation in public institutions ended with *Brown v. Board of Education* (1954), when the Supreme Court ruled that separate educational institutions could not be considered equal. With this rebuff of *Plessy v. Ferguson*, the courts eventually moved through the college gates and began to oversee the student-institution relationship.

One of the last cases to take a hands-off position toward the student-institution relationship was *Steier v. New York State Education Commissioner* (1959), in which the court ruled that the dismissal of a student from a public institution was a state matter over which the federal courts lacked jurisdiction, although the student claimed that his speech rights protected by the First Amendment were being violated. Whether a public or private institution, the courts were reluctant to enter campus and regulate colleges' and universities' decisions.

The seminal case that began the courts' now long-standing scrutiny of higher education policies and practices was *Dixon v. Alabama State Board of Education* (1961). In *Dixon*, students at a public historically Black college, Alabama State University, were involved in a series of protests against segregated facilities and services inside the state capitol. George Wallace, the governor of Alabama, had insisted these students be dismissed and the protests cease. Students were expelled and claimed that their constitutional rights to due process and equal protection under the 14th Amendment were violated. This case established that the rights and protections of citizens in the U.S. Constitution, such as freedom of speech, due process, and protection against discrimination, applied to the relationship between public colleges and universities and their students. While this decision specifically applied to a public institution, it established a standard that private institutions also generally embraced in their own policies.

In the last half of the 20th century, the courts began to exert judicial oversight of postsecondary institutions not only because of the civil rights movement but also because of higher education's role in addressing societal problems. Colleges and universities met society's needs by providing a path for upward mobility, generating research and development, and competing in the Space Race and fighting the Cold War. As higher education's profile became increasingly linked to a middle-class lifestyle in the 1950s and 1960s (Carnevale & Rose, 2012), Americans' demand for access accelerated. College and university enrollments grew by around 200% during this time, and the state and federal policies and programs that followed this expansion increased expectations for accountability at the state and federal levels. For example, the federal government established programs for student financial aid, facilities grants and loans, and research funding (see chapter 4). To receive this support, public and private institutions had to submit to increased federal regulation and oversight.

Federalism and State Authority in Public Education

One of the underlying premises of law is that governments are sovereign entities; that is, they have supreme, independent power over a given geographic area. State and federal governments in the United States operate with dual sovereignty in that the federal government retains sovereignty over certain functions on behalf of the entire nation, and state governments retain sovereignty over other functions within their borders.

The U.S. Constitution delineates the powers of the three branches of the federal government: The congressional branch creates the law, the executive branch administers the law, and the judicial branch interprets the law. The Bill of Rights (the first 10 amendments to the Constitution) defines the rights of U.S. citizens in their relationship with the federal government. The 10th Amendment declares that those rights and powers not delegated to the federal government or its citizens fall under the sovereignty of the states. Because education is not addressed in the Constitution, it is one of the rights that states historically have retained sovereignty over. For example, the concept of sovereign immunity, or states' rights to fiscal integrity and to govern themselves, has been upheld since the inception of the United States (Hendrickson, 1999, p. 10). However, as discussed in chapter 4, the federal government has found ways through regulations and financial inducement to involve itself in higher education.

In addition to defining the relationship between the state and federal governments, the U.S. Constitution defines the fundamental relationship between the citizens of the United States and their government. Initially, the individual protections (e.g., freedom of speech, press, and religion) granted in the Constitution applied only to the relationship between the federal government and the individual. The passage of the 14th Amendment mandated that those protections govern the relationship between the individual and the state government as well:

> All persons born or naturalized in the United States, and subject to the jurisdiction thereof, are citizens of the United States and of the state wherein they reside. No state shall make or enforce any law which shall abridge the privileges or immunities of citizens of the United States; nor shall any state deprive any person of life, liberty, or property, without due process of law; nor deny to any person within its jurisdiction the equal protection of the laws. (U.S. Const. Amend. XIV, § 1)

The 14th Amendment has also become the vehicle to protect constitutional rights at public institutions of higher education, as they are deemed agents of the state government and subject to the same laws as states. However, the relationship between private institutions and their constituencies is governed by contract law.[4] Since constitutional rights have become a societal norm, however, most private institutions have incorporated these rights into their policies and practices. Thus, there is little practical difference today between the legal rights of students at most private and public higher education institutions in the United States. Additional federal laws have been passed to enhance and clarify the rights of higher education constituencies (including students), and other federal regulations and initiatives have been established to regulate state activities such as education, with federal funding based on institutional compliance. Therefore, beyond the enforcement of constitutional rights, the federal government can withhold funds as a means to compel states and public and private institutions to comply with federal regulations (see chapter 4, pp. 89–102, and chapter 5 for a discussion of federal and state authority over higher education institutions).

Student Issues

A mission-driven institution should focus on how it defines its duties and obligations to its students, who are the focus of most colleges' and universities' goals, values, and missions. Historically, the student-institution relationship has been interpreted in four different ways: contract, fiduciary, in loco parentis, and constitutional. First, when students enroll at a college or university and pay tuition and fees, they enter into a *contract* with the institution. In return for their payment of tuition and fees, the institution agrees to provide students with the opportunity to pursue an educational experience that most often results in an academic credential. The terms of the contract are defined by the institution's student handbook, course and degree catalog, schedule of courses for that academic year, and other policies. However, it is not a simple transactional contract, as students are not automatically awarded a degree in return for their payments. Rather, students must also abide by institutional policies and perform well enough in their academic work to earn academic credits and, eventually, a degree. Second, the *fiduciary* relationship places the institution in a position of trust to act in the best interest of its students, similar to the relationship between a doctor and patients. Students are the beneficiaries in the trust relationship, and a college or university must "exercise a high standard of care in managing another's [student's] money or property" (Garner, 2009, p. 1402). By accepting students, an institution is obligated to provide them with a quality educational experience. Much as with doctors or lawyers usually knowing more than their patients or clients about what is in their best interest, the faculty and administrators at an academic institution know better than their students about the nature of the educational experience and the course content to be delivered. In this case, students trust their institution to provide them with a high-quality academic experience, as they do not normally have the experience necessary to evaluate the academic decisions of their institution.

Third, the courts have historically viewed the relationship between an institution and its student as *in loco parentis*, meaning that the institution stands in place of the parent and may make any rules or policies a parent would make in the care of his or her children. As noted earlier, the courts were historically hesitant to insert themselves between the institution and the student, much like they are resistant to interfere between a parent and a child. However, the strength of that relationship has wavered over the past several decades, as Lake (1999) has argued:

> The story of the twentieth century higher education student safety law is the gradual application of typical rules of civil liability to institutions of higher education and the decline of insulating doctrines, such as *in loco parentis*, which traditionally protected institutions of higher learning from scrutiny in the legal system. (p. 1)

That being said, a recent barrage of liability lawsuits brought against colleges and universities has caused many scholars to reconsider whether the institution-student relationship is undergoing yet another change. These cases evidence a growing interest among parents that colleges and universities retain some responsibility for the safety and well-being of their students.

While a legal consensus has yet to emerge, Henning (2007) has argued that this era of increased liability does not represent a return to in loco parentis, per se. Rather, it is an acknowledgment that institutions and parents have a joint obligation to protect students. We should also note that this type of relationship typically deals with traditional age students, and the growing number of adult and other nontraditional learners also challenges many established conceptions of the student-institution relationship.

Fourth, in the 1960s a new student institutional relationship emerged. This *constitutional* relationship was established between students and their colleges and universities with the *Dixon* (1961) case. Subsequent legal decisions clarified that students had constitutional rights as enumerated in the amendments to the Constitution. Since the focus of this book is on academic administration, our focus here is on the due process and equal protection clauses of the 14th Amendment.

Student Due Process Rights

Due process is a right acquired through the constitutional relationship. The courts have determined that once students have matriculated at an institution, they possess what the courts commonly refer to as a *property right*. That is, the institution cannot deprive students of their right to pursue an education unless certain procedural requirements are met. In addition, challenges to one's good name and reputation represent a *liberty interest* and also require due process. For example, the courts require that student violations of behavioral standards or charges of cheating, lying, fraud, or criminal acts that may lead to institutional disciplinary action must be adjudicated using due process. In addition, charges of cheating and plagiarism require disciplinary due process even though they involve academic matters. In these situations, the charges affect the accused person's good name or character, which implicates a liberty interest and requires the same level of due process as a property right.[5]

Dixon (1961) stated that a student's due process rights required the rudiments of fair play but not "a full dressed judicial hearing" (p. 159). The following due process requirements are still considered the standard of procedural due process on campuses today:

1. The student should receive written notice containing a statement of specific charges and grounds as well as possible disciplinary action. If suspension or expulsion is an option, that must be indicated.
2. The student has a right to a formal hearing. The nature of the hearing may vary according to the circumstances of the case but should be more than an informal interview with an administrator. Some institutions convene boards of students or faculty and staff to adjudicate the hearing.
3. The rudiments of an adversarial proceeding should include the names of witnesses testifying against the student and an oral or written statement of the facts testified. Also, according to *Nash v. Auburn University* (1987), the student does not have a right to be present when the testimony is given nor to cross-exam witnesses. The accused should be given the opportunity to present a defense and witnesses on his or her behalf.
4. A written report of the decision should be made available to the student.[6]

Subsequent case law such as *Goss v. Lopez* (1975) refined the process and established that a student who is found to be a danger to others can be suspended from the institution pending a due process hearing. Students are allowed to bring legal counsel to hearings only under limited circumstances. *The University of Houston v. Sabeti* (1984) determined that a student could bring legal counsel into a hearing only if the institution's legal counsel was present. Finally, the decision of the disciplinary body must be consistent with the evidence, as demonstrated in *Jackson v. Hayakawa* (1985), where the evidence did not support the presumption of guilt and was viewed by the court as arbitrary and capricious. If an institution is found to violate a student's due process rights, the remedy is a new hearing and not reinstatement as a student.

Academic Dismissal

Courts are reluctant to evaluate the quality of students' academic performance. These evaluations are left to faculty members with expert knowledge in their fields. This practice of deferring to the expertise of academics has been called "academic deference" (Hendrickson, 1999, p. 202). The benchmark case in academic dismissal is *Board of Curators of the University of Missouri v. Horowitz* (1978), in which the Supreme Court stated:

> Academic evaluations of a student, in contrast to disciplinary determinations, bear little resemblance to the judicial and administrative fact-finding proceedings to which we traditionally attached full hearing requirements. . . . The decision to dismiss respondent, by comparison, rested on academic judgment of school officials that she did not have the necessary clinical ability to perform adequately as a medical doctor and was not making sufficient progress toward that goal. Such a judgment is by its nature more subjective and evaluative than the typical factual questions presented in the average disciplinary action. Like the decision of an individual professor as to the proper grade for a student in his course, the determination whether to dismiss a student for academic reasons requires an expert evaluation of cumulative information and is not readily adapted to the procedural tools of judicial or administrative decision making. (pp. 90–91)

In *Regents of the University of Michigan v. Ewing* (1985) the court strengthened the notion of academic deference: "This narrow avenue of judicial review precludes any conclusion that the decision to dismiss Ewing from the Interflex program was a substantial departure from accepted academic norms as to demonstrate that the faculty did not exercise professional judgment" (p. 514). While the majority of cases have upheld academic deference, faculty members who make arbitrary or capricious decisions regarding a student's performance cannot rely on a claim of deference. Most institutions have established processes for students to challenge academic decisions based on claims of discrimination or an arbitrary or capricious judgment.

Discrimination in Admissions

The courts have given great latitude to institutions in the formulation of admissions policies and the resulting selecting of students. According to

Kaplin and Lee (2006, p. 317), admissions policies are only constrained in three general ways. First, the process of selecting new students must not be arbitrary or capricious. Second, contract theory may bind institutions to adhere to published admission policies and honor admissions decisions. Third, admissions policies may not unjustifiably discriminate on the basis of race, sex, age, disability, or citizenship.

One of the most contested areas of law in this arena is the use of affirmative action.[7] Some of the courts' earliest engagements with academe focused on the issue of segregation, attempting to overturn a legacy of discrimination that had been taking place on many college campuses. The passage of Title VI, and Title VII of the Civil Rights Act of 1964 and Title IX of the Education Amendments of 1972 resulted in the development of affirmative action policies meant to aid those who had been the focus of historic discriminatory activities and that would significantly affect access to higher education. The creation of affirmative action also brought claims of reverse discrimination by those who believed they were negatively affected by such policies.

DeFunis v. Odegaard (1974) was the first case that addressed reverse discrimination in admissions. A White male claimed discrimination after being denied admission to the University of Washington Law School, which had a special admissions program for minority applicants. The Supreme Court ruled the case moot, but Justice William O. Douglas wrote a dissenting opinion that would provide a road map for a subsequent Supreme Court decision on this issue (Hendrickson, 1999, p. 167).

In *Regents of the University of California v. Bakke* (1978), a White male claimed race discrimination in the denial of his admission to the Medical School at the University of California, Davis (UC Davis). UC Davis had a dual admissions process—a special admissions process for minority applicants who did not meet admissions criteria, and a general admissions process for everyone else. Since race was a factor in this case, the Supreme Court applied the strict scrutiny test and found that the state of California could not show a compelling state interest in providing preferential treatment based on race.[8] If the state—through a legislative, administrative, or judicial proceeding—had found past evidence of discrimination, it could have implemented a narrowly tailored remedy, without harming others, to right the past wrong. In this case, there was neither a finding of past discrimination at UC Davis nor a narrowly tailored remedy. Thus, the dual admission process at UC Davis was found to be in violation of the Equal Protection Clause of the 14th Amendment. In a five-four split decision, the Supreme

Court found that race could be a factor—but not the *sole* factor—in admissions decisions. This decision would change the processes that institutions use in admissions, and a great deal has been written about equal access and Bakke (see, for example, Sindler, 1978). Controversy over affirmative action and admissions has continued, however.

After *Bakke* (1978), a number of lower court cases sought to overturn the decision, including an unprecedented decision by the Fifth Circuit Court of Appeals, which overturned Bakke, at least in the Fifth Circuit (*Hopwood v. Texas*, 1996). Subsequent Supreme Court decisions nullified Hopwood, however. The use of race as a criterion for admission was settled by a set of companion cases, *Gratz v. Bollinger* (2003) and *Grutter v. Bollinger* (2003), which involved the admissions processes of two colleges at the University of Michigan. *Gratz* concerned the undergraduate admissions process of the College of Literature, Science, and the Arts (LSA). Jennifer Gratz and Patrick Hamacker, White in-state students who were denied admission, claimed violation of their 14th Amendment equal protection rights under the Constitution and federal statutes. The Supreme Court ruled that the LSA admissions process, which assigned points for various applicant attributes, violated the Equal Protection Clause because using weighted points for race as the sole factor in admissions decisions guaranteed admission to minority applicants.

In *Grutter* (2003), however, the Supreme Court found that the admissions process did not violate applicants' equal protection rights. Barbara Grutter had been denied admission to Michigan's law school, whose admissions policy focused on academic ability coupled with a flexible assessment of applicants' talents, experiences, and potential to contribute to the learning of those around them. The policy required admissions officers to evaluate each applicant based on all application information, including a personal statement, letters of recommendation, and an essay describing the ways an applicant will contribute to the life and diversity of the law school. The policy was intended to achieve diversity in the student body, with the idea that such diversity would potentially enrich the experience of the entire law school class. The policy did not limit the types of diversity that would be rewarded, nor did it dictate the weight they would play in admissions decisions, although the law school was committed to enrolling a critical mass of students from diverse backgrounds, including minority students.[9]

In its opinion, the Supreme Court noted the educational advantages of a diversified student body citing Bowen and Bok (2000). The justices also found that the goal of achieving a critical mass of minority students was not a quota system. The admissions policy was narrowly tailored to use race as a factor, but not the sole factor, in decisions. In the *Grutter* (2003) decision, Justice Sandra Day O'Connor expected that admissions programs would be able to adopt racially neutral policies within 25 years (p. 311), and it remains to be seen whether her prediction will come true in the next two decades. In the meantime, to implement the admissions process endorsed by the Supreme Court in *Grutter,* institutions must expand their admissions staff to perform individual evaluations of each application to determine each applicant's potential contributions to institutional diversity.[10]

Gender Discrimination

Title IX of the Education Amendments (1972) prohibits discrimination based on gender in all programs or activities receiving federal financial assistance and applies to employees and students. Title IX's most controversial and well-known implementation occurred in college athletic programs. After 30 to 40 years of haggling over the regulations passed to implement the laws that apply to athletics, the National Collegiate Athletic Association and the federal government ruled that it was not the intent of the law to integrate teams in individual sports. While there is still much disagreement concerning the notion of equal treatment under this law (Suggs, 2005), institutions are now required to give men and women equal opportunities to participate in athletic activities. For example, women do not have to be given the opportunity to participate in football, but other women's sports must equal the opportunities provided to men (Brake, 2010).

A number of gender discrimination cases have addressed admissions issues. In *Cannon v. University of Chicago* (1979), the Supreme Court established a private right of action under Title IX to allow individuals to sue in federal court.[11] The most active gender discrimination litigation has concerned the admission of women to state military academies (*United States v. Commonwealth of Virginia*, 1996; *United States v. Massachusetts Maritime Academy*, 1985). In the Virginia case, the Supreme Court overturned a lower court decision, finding that a program at Mary Baldwin College did not provide an opportunity for women that would be comparable to the experience provided by the Virginia Military Institute.

Faculty Employment Issues

Understanding the employment relationships between staff and faculty members and their institution is key to defining the nature of democratic partnerships in higher education. We begin this section with a discussion of the concept of academic freedom and then move into a discussion of different types of faculty contracts and the legal rights and responsibilities associated with each employment relationship. While the job responsibilities of different types of faculty members are discussed in chapter 13, the legal relationship between an institution and its faculty is discussed in this section.

Academic Freedom and First Amendment Speech

While the American Association of University Professors (AAUP, n.d.) maintains that academic freedom is a constitutional right under the First Amendment, Hendrickson (1999) has asserted that academic freedom is a contractual right granted by an institution. Supreme Court opinions lend support to this notion of academic freedom as a contractual right such as *Minnesota State Board for Community Colleges v. Knight* (1984). In this section, we discuss the differences between academic freedom rights and First Amendment rights, as well as the contractual rights and responsibilities of a faculty member under academic freedom and the rights of a faculty member as an employee at a public institution guaranteed by the First Amendment.

Academic freedom. The concept of academic freedom was established around the turn of the 20th century by the AAUP, although it originated in the German university traditions of *Lehrfreiheit* (freedom to pursue truth) and *Lernfreiheit* (freedom to learn). The purpose of these freedoms was to protect faculty members from religious, political, and societal interference in the pursuit of truth, wherever that might lead (Toma, 2011, p. 95). Building on this practice, the AAUP (1940) policy on academic freedom defined the rights and responsibilities of faculty members in teaching and research in their area of expertise. These rights include freedom from interference by administrators and board members in what a faculty member teaches, researches, or writes within his or her area of expertise. However, the rights also come with certain restrictions. For example, when making public comments on issues outside their specific area of expertise, professors should be clear they are doing so as private citizens, not in their faculty roles. Hence, in such situations, they should not identify themselves by their professional titles. Academic freedom does not generally apply to such things as when or where a class is scheduled, the attire a faculty member wears in the classroom, the courses taught, or the number of students enrolled in a class. Academic freedom is a right generally given to all academic faculty members regardless of status. However, the vehicle to protect faculty academic freedom has been tenure, which is discussed in more depth in later sections. Readers should note, though, that as institutions have moved to employ more contract faculty members, colleges and universities have extended academic freedom guarantees to contract faculty members, who usually do not benefit from the employment protections granted by tenure. Thus, despite such guarantees, some observers have expressed concern that it is extremely difficult to ensure contract faculty members' academic freedom because of how easily they can be let go at the end of a contract period (Toma, p. 98).

First Amendment employee rights. Faculty members at public institutions have First Amendment speech protections.[12] Several court cases have addressed which First Amendment speech protections apply to faculty members at public institutions. In *Connick v. Myers* (1983), the Supreme Court differentiated between speech on matters of public concern, which is protected speech by the First Amendment, and speech on matters of employee concern, which is not protected. Speech on matters of public concern includes issues that address the academic quality of the institution or that might jeopardize health, safety, and the welfare of the public. In any dismissal case, the institution must show that protected speech was not the motivating factor for its decision. Rather, it must document that valid employment criteria were the motivating factor.

Speech on matters of employee concern is generally not protected under the First Amendment; this type of speech addresses issues solely of interest to the employee. For example, complaints about the lack of air-conditioning in a classroom or public criticism of the large number of students in a particular lecture section, course schedules, committee assignments, verbal interpersonal conflicts, or other matters of concern only to the employee are not considered protected speech. Some employment-related speech, however, could be protected by the concept of academic freedom, such as a debate on the content of a particular course.

Disruptive speech. In *Waters v. Churchill* (1994), the Supreme Court ruled that a public employee could be dismissed for disruptive speech or speech that inhibits the normal and effective operations of the organization where the employee works.

The key First Amendment analysis of government decisions, then, is this: The government's interest in achieving its goals as effectively and efficiently as possible is elevated from a relatively subordinate interest when it acts as sovereign to a significant one when it acts as employer. The government cannot restrict the speech of the public at large just in the name of efficiency. But where the government is employing someone for the very purpose of effectively achieving its goals, such restrictions may well be appropriate. (p. 1088)

In *Waters*, a nurse had made comments to fellow employees and was spreading rumors about her supervisor's skills and performance that created a negative work environment in the unit. This speech was found to be disruptive to the public organization that employed her and was determined to be legitimate reason for her dismissal. That is, public employees can be terminated for disruptive speech, but only after due process when the dismissal is taking place during the term of the contract.

Faculty Contracts

Faculty contracts typically range from one to five years. Most institutions clearly define in their contracts the expectations for contract renewal, including the date by which a contract faculty member will be notified whether his or her contract will be renewed. Contract faculty members on a tenure track are treated similarly to other contract faculty in that their institution is under no obligation to renew their contract—even though they received a probationary tenure-track contract. A faculty member has the right to due process if the institution seeks termination during the term of the contract, which is a form of property. Tenured faculty members have contracts without term, or continuous contracts, so ending that contract always requires a form of due process by the institution. A college's or university's due process requirements are outlined in its faculty handbook or policies for the discipline of the faculty.

The controlling Supreme Court case on this issue is *Board of Regents of State Colleges v. Roth* (1972). Roth, a probationary tenure-track faculty member, held a one-year contract with the understanding that if this contract was renewed five times, he would be reviewed for the award of tenure. He was notified during his second year, by the date specified in his contract, that his contract would not be renewed. No reasons were given for the decision. The court found that Roth had no property right in the renewal of his contract; therefore, no reasons needed to be provided for the nonrenewal decision. Nonrenewal without reasons would not implicate a liberty interest, while a publicly stated reason might stigmatize Roth's reputation. The court noted that institutions should have the right to decide not to renew an employee's contract as long as they follow their own policies governing notification of the employment decision.

In many cases, reasons for the nonrenewal of probationary tenure-track faculty are offered as part of these faculty members' evaluation process. Formal policies that define the requirements and steps to achieve tenure do not establish a property right for probationary faculty (see *Goodisman v. Lytle*, 1984). Similarly, the existence of performance evaluations of pretenure faculty members does not implicate a liberty interest (see *Wells v. Doland*, 1983). While no due process right exists that requires the opportunity to appeal a nonrenewal decision, some institutions have established an appeals process. Sometimes this appeals process is part of collective bargaining grievance procedures. Typically an appeals process will determine whether the decision not to renew was based on inappropriate reasons and followed institutional policies.

When an institution fails to evaluate a probationary faculty member at the time prescribed in the contract, the result is not de facto tenure (*Sabet v. Eastern Virginia Medical Authority*, 1985). Public and private institutions have developed policies and specific contract provisions that clearly state that faculty members can achieve tenure only through a formal review process (Hendrickson, 1999, p. 57).

Denial of Tenure

There are occasions when tenure-track faculty members are denied tenure and are usually required to end their employment with the institution. Courts are reluctant to become involved in actual decisions to award or deny tenure because of the tradition of academic deference, not wanting to substitute a court decision for one reached via the peer review process. Courts will hear cases, however, in which the question is whether the institution followed its policies and procedures in the tenure decision or whether the decision was based on valid job performance criteria. Academic deference comes into play even in these cases in that while courts will discern whether the relevant job criteria were used in the decision, they will not determine the quality of the job performance.[13] These academic decisions usually do not lend themselves to the administrative or judicial analysis available to the courts (Hendrickson, 1999, p. 61).

The courts have also considered breach of contract issues raised in denial of tenure cases. Courts have found that a breach of contract existed when the institution failed to review a faculty member's performance during his sixth probationary year as required by his contract (*Smith v. University of Arizona*, 1983) and when it attempted to force a probationary faculty member to resign before the end of the contract (*Lowe v. Beaty*, 1984). However, the courts have determined that no breach of contract existed when a faculty member was denied tenure for deficient interpersonal skills or because the department had reached its tenure quota as long as the school followed its tenure review policies (*Waring v. Fordham University*, 1986).[14] In another case (*Brumback v. Rensselaer Polytechnic Institute*, 1987), the vice president of academic affairs granted through a letter a one-year extension of the probationary period to allow a female faculty member to improve her research record. While she showed improvement, her research record was still insufficient, and tenure was denied. The court found that the letter was either a bad-faith contract or a breach of contract. Institution administrators need to make sure they clearly spell out terms of employment and expectations of performance, but they also need to be diligent in following those terms and performance requirements.

Many denial-of-tenure challenges involve claims of gender and race discrimination.[15] One of the most significant outcomes of the challenges is the rights that candidates for tenure have regarding access to their own performance reviews and the applications of other comparable candidates for tenure. In *University of Pennsylvania v. EEOC* (1990) the court granted a female faculty member access to her review materials and those of comparable males, including access to redacted peer review letters. Other cases gave faculty members access to the promotion and tenure committee's deliberations and votes (*EEOC v. Franklin and Marshall College*, 1985; In re *Dinnan*, 1981).

When evaluating claims of discrimination, the courts have primarily focused on how the treatment of the individual compares with that of others in a similar set of circumstances or how performance reviews align with the job description. For example, when four females were denied tenure, they sued the institution, claiming the promotion and tenure process had a disparate impact on women (*Maguire v. Marquette University*, 1987). The court acknowledged that measures of performance vary across disciplines and that tenure recommendations were decentralized across individual disciplinary departments in the institution. A broad sampling of faculty at the institution that showed only 42% of women received tenure as opposed to 65% of men did not yield a prima facie (superficial appearance) case of discrimination, and the case was dismissed.

An example of the three burden of proof strategies (see note 15) under Title VII of the Civil Rights Act (1964) is *LaFleur v. Wallace State Community College* (1996). However, when an African American female tenure-track faculty member was denied tenure at a predominantly White community college in Alabama, the courts found evidence of discrimination based on the institution's seemingly capricious decision. The college claimed the reason for the denial of tenure was based on the faculty member's doctorate being from a nonaccredited institution, nonconformity with the prescribed work schedule, and incompatibility with college administrators. However, the court found that the faculty position she held required only a master's degree, that her immediate supervisor had threatened her in a discriminatory and racially motivated manner, and that there was discriminatory intent in the employment decision.

What administrators need to remember is that all employees have the right to be treated fairly and respectfully, and that employment decisions and performance evaluations need to be based on valid job criteria and be free of discriminatory intent.

Tenure and Termination for Cause

After a faculty member is granted tenure, he or she receives a contract without term, meaning there is no predetermined end to the contract. While tenure grants an additional level of job security, faculty members must continue to meet job performance expectations. Tenured faculty members can be terminated for cause for reasons delineated in the institution's specific policies and guidelines. Due process to terminate a tenured faculty member usually begins with notification of the charges against the faculty member and a preliminary meeting with his or her unit head or academic vice president. Then there is a hearing before faculty peers, who make a recommendation to the president. In turn, the president makes a recommendation to the governing board. If the recommendation of the hearing panel is termination, there is usually an appeals process involving either or both the president and the board. Most termination for cause proceedings do not move past the institutional due process procedures. The court cases in this area represent a small number of termination proceedings at colleges and universities during the past few decades.

Termination of a tenured faculty member can occur for a number of reasons (Hendrickson, 1990, pp. 78–82). One of the causes for termination is *insubordination*, or failure to implement the directives of a superior (Garner, 2009, p. 870). Examples might be refusal to teach a course assigned by the department chair; failure to keep office hours as directed; or the use of abusive and threatening speech that results in uncooperative behavior in interactions with superiors, peers, or students (see *Gressley v. Deutsch*, 1994). *Breach of duty*, or failure to meet the responsibilities outlined in the employment contract, is another cause for termination (Garner, 2009, p. 214). Failure to submit grades or use the prescribed procedure to file grades or meet a scheduled class are examples of breach of duty.[16]

Incompetence, or lack of "fitness to discharge required duties" (Garner, 2009, p. 833), is another cause for termination. One form of incompetence is continuous poor student evaluations of teaching, but in such a context the faculty member should be notified of the deficiency and given the opportunity to improve. Failure to remedy the situation would make the faculty member eligible for a termination process (*Dhuria v. Trustees of the University of the District of Columbia*, 1993). *Moral turpitude*, or "conduct contrary to honesty, modesty or good morals" (Garner, 2009, p. 1101), provides another reason for termination of a tenured faculty member. Examples of moral turpitude would be fraud, theft, plagiarism, selling of illegal drugs, and solicitation of sexual activity in public areas (*West Valley-Mission Community College Dist. v. Concepcion*, 1993). Ethical and professional standards violations, which are defined by disciplinary areas, round out the list of causes that could lead to termination. One example would be the case in which a faculty member held full-time faculty appointments at two institutions and because of this arrangement was found to be in violation of professional and ethical standards (*Zahavy v. University of Minnesota*, 1996). This type of violation is a more recent addition to the list. It is important in all of these cases that the supervisor has thorough documentation of the problem and the action taken.

Collective Bargaining

The National Labor Relations Act (NLRA) (1935) applies to employees of business corporations, and since 1970 it has applied to faculty and staff employed by private higher education institutions (In re *Cornell University*, 1970).[17] The National Labor Relations Board (NLRB) is the administrative agency responsible for adjudicating labor disputes. After a decision has been reached by the NLRB, a party may sue in federal court to challenge the NLRB's decision. For employees at an institution to have a bargaining unit, they must first complete a petitioning process. Once a specified number of signatures are collected and verified, an election by the employees is certified and held. If a majority of the employees vote for unionization, a bargaining unit is certified to negotiate collectively. Managers and supervisors are typically not part of the bargaining unit.

Since the NLRA is based on a corporate business model, it does not always easily fit an academic setting where faculty members can be part of the decision-making processes often reserved for managers in the corporate setting. For example, faculty members sometimes will vote for collective bargaining if they feel their shared governance authority has been eroded in their institution. Faculty union bargaining processes may then result in the negotiation of decision-making prerogatives as well as salary and benefits. Over time, the result of these negotiations is that faculty members acquire many of the previously eroded shared governance decision-making prerogatives.

This ebb and flow of faculty decision making resulting from collective bargaining led to a Supreme Court decision, *NLRB v. Yeshiva University* (1980). After a number of years working under a collective bargaining agreement, the faculty at Yeshiva University had acquired most of the decision-making prerogatives of a shared governance structure. Since the faculty was involved in hiring, promotion and tenure, setting the calendar, determining the curriculum, and 10 other decision points, the court agreed with Yeshiva University that faculty members were managers. Since managers and supervisors are not normally part of a collective bargaining unit, the court decided that the faculty union at Yeshiva University should be terminated (decertified). After this decision, a number of other faculty unions at private institutions were decertified, a process not seen in the corporate setting.[18]

Employment Discrimination

In the 1960s and 1970s, federal legislation was passed to eliminate discrimination in employment and bring equity to the workplace. Title VII of the Civil Rights Act of 1964 prohibited discriminatory employment practices such as hiring, promotion, and termination based on race, color, religion, sex, or national origin. In 1963 Congress also passed the Equal Pay Act, which prohibited inequality based on sex in pay for equal work or for jobs requiring equal skills, effort, and responsibilities or performed under similar conditions. These regulations were followed by the Age Discrimination in Employment Act of 1967 (ADEA) (29 U.S.C. 641-34 et seq.) and the Rehabilitation Act of 1973, which prohibited discrimination based on a handicap. In addition, as discussed previously, Title IX of the Education Amendments of 1972 prohibited gender discrimination in educational programs or activities receiving federal financial assistance. Each of these regulations was heavily litigated, which has provided a clear understanding of the federal government's regulation of employment practices. Colleges and universities should designate an affirmative action officer to comply with federal law in all employment decisions.

Title VII of the Civil Rights Act of 1964

Title VII prohibits discrimination in employment based on race, gender, religion, and national origin and is designed to reinforce the Equal Protection Clause of the 14th Amendment. Employment practices at public, private, nonprofit, and business corporations are covered by Title VII. The law provides an administrative remedy for alleged violations and requires an employee with a claim to file a complaint with the Equal Employment Opportunity Commission (EEOC). The EEOC then investigates the claim to determine if there is potential for employment discrimination, in which case it issues a right to sue letter. The regulation requires that a claim be filed with EEOC within 300 days' tolling (the number of days of eligibility to file a complaint) from the date of the last act of discrimination that occurred. Failure to meet the tolling requirement bars a claim before the EEOC and litigation in the courts. There are two types of claims: a "disparate impact" suit in which the claim is that the "employment practice has negative impact or effect on minority opportunities" and a "disparate treatment" suit, which requires proof of intent to discriminate against an individual or a group of similar individuals (Hendrickson, 1999, p. 108).

Disparate impact or disparate treatment cases use a shifting burden of proof strategy (*McDonnell Douglas Corporation v. Green*, 1973). The plaintiff must first establish a prima facie claim of discrimination. The burden then shifts to the employer, who must show that valid job performance reasons resulted in the employment decision. The burden then returns to the plaintiff to prove that the employer's reasons for the decision were a pretext for discrimination. Given this proof strategy, it behooves employers to make sure employment decisions are driven by valid job performance criteria.

Disparate impact. Discrimination that has a disparate impact on a class of employee can best be explained by discussing specific cases. The use of a salary formula based on discipline or field was the issue in *Donnelly v. Rhode Island Board of Governors for Higher Education* (1997) in which female faculty members claimed that the three-tier salary formula used for humanities, natural sciences, and business had a disparate impact on female faculty members. The court found that the women failed to establish a prima facie case for discrimination when the salary plan was based on national market factors.

The preference of one race in hiring was the issue in *Craig v. Alabama State University* (1978). A White faculty member was passed over for a faculty position when an African American faculty member returned from a study leave having achieved a doctorate. Sending employees on study leave to improve the quality of the university's faculty did not overcome the institution's historic hiring practices that preferred Black applicants. The institution's hiring practices thus were found to have a disparate impact on White applicants. Since the institution failed to show valid reasons for the employment decision, there was no need for the plaintiff to show pretext for discrimination.

Performance criteria used in hiring were at issue in *Peters v. Lieuallen* (1984). The institution successfully maintained that the hiring criteria of good written and oral communication skills were valid job criteria without disparate impact on minority applicants. Similarly, *Hassan v. Auburn University* (1994) found that requiring faculty hires to have English fluency was not national origin discrimination. In addition, another case found that requiring that a faculty member at a Catholic college be Catholic to teach theology was not religious discrimination (*Pime v. Loyola University of Chicago*, 1986).

Each of these examples shows how institutions need to ensure that the criteria used in faculty hiring and rewards do not discriminate on the basis of race, gender, national origin, or religion and are free of disparate impact.

Disparate treatment. Discrimination against a specific employee is labeled disparate treatment under Title VII. The three-part burden of proof strategy uses slightly different criteria to establish a prima facie case for discrimination under disparate treatment. The plaintiff must show that he or she is a member of a protected class and qualified for the position he or she sought. The burden then shifts to the employer to provide reasons for the hiring decision and then back to the plaintiff to show that the reasons were a pretext for discrimination. For example, in *Fields v. Clark University* (1987), a female assistant professor was denied tenure and sued claiming disparate treatment under Title VII. She met her burden by showing that an all-male faculty committee made the tenure decision. The institution in turn met its burden by claiming that the reason for the negative decision was the poor quality of her teaching and scholarship. The female professor met her burden again, proving that the institution's reason was a pretext for discrimination by showing that a male faculty member from her academic unit who received tenure had a weaker teaching and scholarship record than hers.

An example in which pretext was not proven is *Namenwirth v. Board of Regents of the University of Wisconsin System* (1985). In this case, a female faculty member could not show that her promotion and tenure dossier was comparable to that of a male faculty member who received tenure. In addition, hiring the top-ranked male for an endowed chair instead of the third-ranked female was not a pretext for discrimination (*Lamphere v. Brown University*, 1986). When an institution can establish valid job criteria free of discriminatory impact in employment decisions, it will survive claims filed under Title VII.

Retaliation

It is a violation of Title VII for an institution to make an employment decision in response to a claim filed by an employee—that is, retaliate against the employee. An employee complaint should not, however, trump an institution's valid employment decision. For example, in *Smart v. Ball State University* (1996) a valid negative evaluation of job performance was not deemed to be retaliation for the faculty member's claim of discrimination under Title VII.

Title VII Summary

As demonstrated in the preceding discussion, Title VII regulations require careful consideration as college and university officials make employment decisions. Employment decisions should always be based on valid job requirements and applied in a fundamentally fair and just way, and to that end, institutions should employ an affirmative action officer to guide them through the requirements of Title VII. Despite an institution's best efforts to adhere to the law, it is impossible in our litigious society to keep individuals bent on suing from going to court. Making exceptions to institutional policy out of fear of a lawsuit should be avoided at all cost. These exceptions to policy would become precedent and prevent campus administrators from effectively addressing nagging personnel problems.

Equal Pay Act of 1963

The Equal Pay Act requires equal pay for equal work. While appearing to be a simple concept, it has resulted in some of the most complex litigation the courts have seen (Hendrickson & Lee, 1983). Similar to Title VII, the Equal Pay Act mandates the time to file a complaint (tolling) as no more than 300 days from the time an employee becomes aware that there may be inequity in pay. Courts have ruled there is no violation of the First Amendment Establishment and Free Exercise Clauses when the Equal Pay Act is enforced at private religiously affiliated educational institutions (*Russell v. Belmont College*, 1982).[19]

A challenge of the equal pay for equal work statute involves the definition of equal skills, equal effort, and equal responsibilities. To establish a prima facie case for pay discrimination, an employee must show that his or her job requires comparable skills, effort, and responsibilities to other employees' work. Courts have allowed pay differentials when positions require equal skills but differing levels of expertise and responsibility, such as between a nurse and a physician's assistant in a hospital (*Beall v. Curtis*, 1985).

Equal skills, effort, and responsibilities lead to the legal concept of comparable worth. Comparable worth is an attempt to show that two different jobs are comparable even if they involve different types of work. For example, using the argument of comparable worth, one could argue that the work of a garbage collector and the staff assistants is comparable, or that faculty work across different disciplines is comparable and faculty members should receive the same pay for comparable work. However, *Spaulding v. University of Washington* (1984) ended the viability of comparable worth. Female nursing faculty members argued that the pay differential between female-dominated disciplines and male-dominated disciplines constituted salary discrimination by gender. The court stated: "Every employer constrained by market forces must consider market value in setting labor costs. Naturally, market prices are inherently job-related, although the market may embody social judgment as to the worth of some jobs" (p. 708). When employers use market factors to arrive at salaries, they are free of culpability in salary discrimination. Based on this decision, comparable worth is no longer argued in Equal Pay Act litigation.

After a plaintiff establishes a prima facie case for salary discrimination, the burden shifts to the employer to provide valid reasons for the salary differential. Such reasons could include the quality of a faculty member's scholarship, teaching, level of productivity, level of training or experience, and market value. In *Covington v. Southern Illinois University* (1987), for example, the court found for the employer, which had paid a higher salary to the plaintiff's predecessor, who had five more years of experience than the new hire. In another example, the court found that a salary differential based on market value was not salary discrimination, since the salary increase being questioned was offered in response to a female faculty member's new job offer and the institution's desire to discourage her from leaving (*Winkes v. Brown University*, 1984). These decisions indicate that salary determinations based on valid market value factors, qualifications, and job performance will be upheld.

Attempts to prove that differential pay was a pretext for discrimination have been unsuccessful. These failed claims have included challenges to higher education institutions' decisions and processes on recruitment, hiring, credentials, productivity, and promotion. Other unsuccessful challenges have involved claims that faculty criteria to measure productivity—such as journal publications, market value of disciplines, and doctoral programs in some disciplines—are gender biased and, therefore, a pretext for discrimination. Just as with Title VII, pretext for discrimination is almost an insurmountable argument in equal pay litigation.

Equal Pay Class Action Suits

The Equal Pay Act allows a class of employees to sue for discrimination in pay. Examples of a class of employees would be all the male or all the female faculty members at a higher education institution. Typically, multiple regression analysis is used to determine whether a salary disparity is because of gender or other job performance criteria. In one of the early equal pay class action cases (*Mecklenburg v. Montana State Board of Regents*, 1976), the institution failed to counter the multiple regression analysis brought by the female plaintiffs by conducting an analysis using a broader number of valid measures of faculty performance. Subsequent cases, however, saw the institutions conducting regression analyses using additional variables such as rank, publications, and grants (*Chang v. University of Rhode Island*, 1985; *Ottaviani v. State University of New York at New Paltz*, 1988; *Sobel v. Yeshiva University*, 1983). The regression analysis either eliminated or reduced the variance (relative strength) of gender as the determinant of salary. The technical and complicated discussion surrounding multiple regression analysis resulted in courts' throwing out regression evidence and relying instead on anecdotal information.

Many institutions now use regression analysis to address gender salary disparities. The key to using regression analysis to achieve salary equity is the extent and quality of the variables included in the analysis. Use of an insufficient set of performance criteria variables has resulted in litigation by male faculty members claiming reverse discrimination, such as in *Smith v. Virginia Commonwealth University* (1995). Virginia Commonwealth University had traditionally awarded merit increases based on teaching load, teaching quality, and quantity and quality of publications. However, a salary committee chose not to use those criteria in the regression analysis and found that female faculty members experienced salary discrimination. After male faculty members sued, the court found that the regression analysis was flawed because it falsely assumed that male and female productivity was equal and should have included the productivity measures. It is good practice for institutions to conduct regression analysis to determine salary equity, but they should make sure that all factors used to measure performance and determine salaries are included in the analysis.

Age Discrimination

The ADEA prohibits institutions from refusing to hire an individual, firing an individual, and discriminating on salary and benefits based on age. When the ADEA was enacted, mandatory retirement ages for tenured faculty members were allowed to continue to be enforced for 20 years, but on December 31, 1993, mandatory retirement at age 65 or 70 of tenured faculty members was eliminated. These cases use the same shifting burden of proof strategies of Title VII cases. If the employment decision is based on valid job criteria and not age, plaintiffs will not meet their burden to prove that the reasons are a pretext for discrimination.

Claims of retaliation are also litigated under ADEA.[20] If an institution makes an employment decision after an employee files an ADEA claim, it can be considered retaliation if it is not based on valid job criteria. Retaliation has been found to exist when an employer fires, reassigns, or changes the job responsibilities of an employee who has filed an ADEA complaint without evidence that such decisions are warranted based on job performance. In many cases, it is best for the employer to postpone a decision until a decision is reached on the ADEA complaint. The courts have also determined that certain human resources policies can also constitute retaliation. For example, in one case, *EEOC v. Board of Governors of State Colleges and Universities* (1992), the faculty's collective bargaining agreement mandated that faculty members must file complaints through the union contract grievance process. If professors used the grievance process but also filed a claim with another agency (federal or state agency), they could be dismissed. The court found retaliation when a faculty member who was denied tenure filed a grievance through the union process, then filed an ADEA claim, and subsequently was dismissed by the institution's board of trustees. In this case, the threat of losing one's employment if he or she files a claim with the ADEA while going through or after the union grievance process was preemptive retaliation as it could be used to prevent an employee from filing such a claim out of fear of penalty from the employer. Employers cannot have a policy prohibiting filing such claims with the appropriate government agency.

Discrimination Based on a Disability

The Rehabilitation Act of 1973 states: "No otherwise qualified handicapped individual shall, solely by reason of his handicap, be excluded from participation in, be denied the benefits of, or be subject to discrimination under programs or activities receiving federal financial assistance" (29 U.S.C. 701). The definition of programs and activities was expanded by the Civil Rights Restoration Act (1987) to include the entirety of any organization in which a unit receives federal financial assistance.[21] The law was also reinforced by the Americans with Disabilities Act of 1990, which states:

> No individual shall be discriminated against on the basis of disability in full or equal enjoyment of goods, services, facilities, privileges, advantages, or accommodations of any place of public accommodation by any person who owns, leases (or leases to), or operates a public accommodation. (42 U.S.C.A. 12182[1])

Barriers to access that do not directly interfere with an employee's job performance or a student's ability to engage in a future profession must be accommodated for disabled individuals. Accommodations could include ramps between sidewalks and the street, ramp entrances to buildings, and elevators. Other accommodations include providing wheelchair access to laboratory tables; changing patient bed height and access to hospital equipment for physically handicapped doctors and nurses; and modifying the settings for academic examinations for students who are blind, deaf, or have learning disabilities. Employees with disabilities may be provided with special software programs and keyboards to facilitate their use of computers or technologies. Moreover, institutions must make appropriate accommodations for service animals that aid individuals in performing professional duties or personal tasks; however, institutions do have certain rights to limit the presence of therapy animals that may help an individual deal with certain mental ailments but have limited recognition under the law.

Most colleges and universities now have an office that provides assistance to students with physical and mental impairments to ensure that faculty and staff are providing appropriate accommodations and students are provided with appropriate support. As teaching and learning strategies change, these offices become increasingly important for ensuring that students have appropriate opportunities to pursue their education. This is particularly relevant with the increasing adoption of online learning methods, which can create additional barriers for those with various impairments. For example, web pages need to be designed to be accessible by those with visual impairments, and students with malformed fingers may have a difficult time typing on a keyboard; However, regardless of the academic setting, instructors are not required to provide alternate accommodations unless they receive official notification from the institution; and it is the responsibility of the student to ensure that the institution knows of his or her impairment and that the instructor is appropriately notified.

There are limits to institutions' accommodating a student's impairment. The seminal case that addressed disability issues in higher education was *Southeastern Community College v. Davis* (1979). An applicant who was deaf applied for admission to a nursing program, and the school asked its state board of nursing to determine whether she could perform the duties of the job in spite of her handicap. The board determined she could not, and the school denied her admission. The Supreme Court supported this decision, ruling that the law required that an individual with a handicap must meet all admissions requirements in spite of his or her disability. Candidates who can meet all performance criteria would be termed "an otherwise qualified handicapped individual" (p. 406). Davis was not an otherwise qualified handicapped applicant because her hearing loss prevented her from meeting the job performance requirements of a nurse.

Sexual Harassment

Under Title VII of the Civil Rights Act of 1964, sexual harassment is "unwelcome sexual advances, requests for sexual favors or other verbal or physical conduct of a sexual nature" (§ 1604.11[a]) that is aimed at only one gender. Sexual harassment developed as a legal concept under Title VII, and the U.S. Supreme Court confirmed the legitimacy of gender-based sexual harassment claims. The two bases for sexual harassment are a hostile work environment, or behavior in the workplace that is of a sexual nature and is unwelcome and offensive; and quid pro quo sexual harassment, or a demand for the performance of uninvited sexual acts in exchange for positive employee advantages.

Initially it was thought that only females could be harassed sexually, but the courts have expanded the notion of who can be sexually harassed. Now sexual harassment claims may involve harassment of males or females (*Chiapuzio v. BLT Operating Corp.*, 1993). Moreover, harassment may include interactions between different or same sexes. Same-sex sexual harassment was found to be covered by Title VII (*Oncale v. Sundowner Offshore Services, Inc.*, 1998).

Hostile Work Environment

The standards for a hostile work environment have four parts: The employee (plaintiff) must prove that the defendant's overtures were unwelcome, and that the harassing speech or conduct was gender based. In addition, the harassment should be *sufficiently severe and pervasive* to create a hostile workplace, and the employer must have had knowledge of the harassment and either condoned it or failed to initiate a remedy. In Title VII of the Civil Rights Act, sexual harassment that involves contested speech at public institutions is not speech protected by the First Amendment, as it is private speech and not speech on matters of public concern. Further, even though the harassing speech at a private institution is controlled by federal law (Title VII), it is also not protected speech under the First Amendment.

The question of what constitutes a severe and pervasive hostile environment can best be understood through the case law. An extreme example is *Harris v. Forklift Systems, Inc.* (1993), in which the Supreme Court described the hostile environment in this way:

> Throughout Harris' time at Forklift, Hardy (the president of the company) often insulted her because of her gender and often made her the target of unwanted sexual innuendos. Hardy told Harris on several occasions, in the presence of other employees, "You're a woman, what do you know" and "we need a man as the rental manager"; at least once, he told her she was "a dumb ass woman." Again in front of others, he suggested that the two of them "go to the Holiday Inn to negotiate a raise." Hardy occasionally asked Harris and other female employees to get a coin out of his pants pocket. He threw objects on the ground in front of Harris and other women and asked them to pick the objects up. He made sexual innuendos about Harris' and other women's clothing. [Hardy told Harris he would stop when she complained but the harassment continued.] While Hardy was arranging a deal with one of Forklift's customers, he asked her, again in front of other employees, "What did you do, promise the guy . . . some [sex] Saturday night?" (p. 19)

The court found that the four-part test for a hostile work environment had been met: This situation was a severe and pervasive hostile environment.

Claims of a hostile environment in the classroom involve issues of academic freedom. In *Silva v. University of New Hampshire* (1994), a technical writing instructor used sexual analogies to describe the process of topic selection and development of a thesis statement, and described Jell-O on a vibrator as an example of a good metaphor for belly dancing. In another example, *Cohen v. San Bernardino Valley College* (1996), the court found that an instructor's statements were based in pedagogy and did not create a hostile environment in a college-level writing class. This case concerned a remedial English class in which the instructor required students to write on controversial topics such as consensual sex with children, pornography, obscenities, and cannibalism. He also tried to be provocative by using profanity for its shock effect. The court found that a vague sexual harassment policy used to discipline the professor violated his academic freedom and First Amendment rights. His controversial teaching methods, which the institution had considered sound in the past, did not create a severe and pervasive hostile environment.

Quid Pro Quo Sexual Harassment

Quid pro quo sexual harassment involves the offer of benefits in exchange for sexual favors and usually involves a power gradient in which the harasser has some control over the award of benefits that the harassed needs or wants. In one case (*Simon v. Morehouse School of Medicine*, 1995), an individual entered into a relationship with an immediate supervisor because of coercion, which eventually included rape. Since superiors were knowledgeable about the situation but did not intervene, the institution was found to be liable. In another case (*Karibian v. Columbia University*, 1994), a staff member, out of romantic interest, entered into a consensual relationship with a supervisor, but the relationship went sour. The supervisor wanted to continue the relationship, and the staff member refused, after which the supervisor used benefits or threats to coerce the staff member into continuing the sexual activity.

When administrators of an institution fail to investigate a claim of sexual harassment that they have knowledge of, the institution will be subject to liability. If there is no knowledge of the claim, or if the harassed individual tells someone at the institution about the relationship but asks for confidentiality, there is no institutional liability (*Slater v. Marshall*, 1995).

Institutions have established sexual harassment training programs and policies to educate employees on what constitutes sexual harassment. Supervisors who are aware of incidents of sexual harassment and fail to take action to stop it will put their institution in jeopardy of liability claims. The removal of individuals who harass other employees should follow the same procedures and processes established for the termination of employees; there should not be a separate procedure for sexual harassment. Student-to-student sexual harassment is also covered under the law, and the disciplinary procedures used for student behavioral issues should be followed in student-to-student sexual harassment cases.

Title IX of the Education Amendments of 1972

Title IX prohibits discrimination based on gender. When the law was originally passed, it was not thought that Title IX covered employment, but several U.S. Supreme Court decisions confirmed that Title IX did cover employment at educational institutions. *North Haven Board of Education v. Bell* (1982) narrowed the coverage to employees working in programs or activities receiving federal financial assistance. *Grove City College v. Bell* (1984) narrowed the coverage to a specific program receiving federal funds, although as mentioned previously, the Civil Rights Restoration Act (1987) expanded the meaning of programs and activities to include the entirety of an organization containing a unit that receives federal financial assistance. Gender discrimination claims involving employment decisions have been litigated under Title IX, and the courts have required a burden of proof similar to that used for Title VII of the Civil Rights Act (1964) cases. Other cases have combined Title IX claims with Title VII or Equal Pay Act (1963) claims.

Legal Issues and Board Governance

While the roles, selection, duties, and responsibilities of boards of trustees are covered in chapter 9, this section focuses on legal issues involving membership selection and the authority of boards of trustees. Before addressing these matters, though, it is important to note that public and private institutions' boards of trustees differ in terms of the source of their authority and their role. Boards of trustees of public colleges and universities obtain their authority through their state's constitution or statutes. Typically, a state legislature and governor have oversight power over these institutions. In some states each public institution has its own board of trustees with legal authority over that institution, while other states have developed a coordinating board to coordinate these institutions (see chapter 5, pp. 118–122). Private colleges or universities are normally granted a charter by the state where the main campus is located. They usually have a board of trustees whose legal responsibility is to protect the original goals and purposes of their institution's charter.

Board Member Selection

The questions of selection processes and terms of service of board members have been before the courts. In the context of public higher education, legislatures must conform to legally defined selection processes and cannot remove an elected board member, as that action would be a violation of citizens' voting rights (*Tully v. Edgar*, 1996). In contrast, a state legislature may prevent a governor's board appointees from taking positions on a board. In Alabama, the governor's nominees were rejected by the state senate as authorized under the law and thus could not be appointed to a state institution's board (*Dunn v. Alabama State University Board of Trustees*, 1993). These cases illustrate that the appointment of members to state boards can be contested, especially if prescribed procedures under state law have not been followed.

Boards of trustees have the legal authority to own property, enter into contracts, hire personnel, and approve programs and degrees. The authority of the board to make funding and academic program decisions has been challenged. In *Espinosa v. Board of Trustees of Community College District No. 508* (1994), for example, a taxpayer was not allowed to challenge an Illinois community college board that eliminated 500 courses for financial reasons. In another case that concerned finances (In re *Polishook v. City University of New York*, 1996), the court found that the board of trustees' decision to reduce degree credit requirements to reduce costs to students was an arbitrary and capricious decision but upheld its other retrenchment decisions that were intended to reduce operating costs. These examples illustrate a board of trustees' authority over the fiscal integrity of its institution, including the elimination of degree programs with low enrollments or because of a financial exigency.

The board has the authority to establish new degree programs in consultation with the institution's governing body. A school district challenged the decision of the local community college and the California Community Colleges Board of Governors to develop an adult education program at the college. In *Orange Unified School District v. Rancho Santiago Community College District* (1997), the court found that agreement from the school district was not required to implement the new program. In matters surrounding the integrity of degree programs and course and degree requirements, however, boards must share decisions with the faculty as *Polishook* (1996) indicates. A board has the authority to protect the academic integrity of its institution, enter into contracts, and hire and terminate employees as long as it follows established policies and precedent practices, and consults with administrators and faculty in the spirit of shared governance (as discussed in chapter 12, pp. 270–274). In all other employment decisions—such as rank, tenure, salaries, and benefits—a board has the ultimate authority to make these decisions as long as it does so by following institutional policies and past practice or precedent.

Fiduciary Duty

Members of boards of trustees have a fiduciary duty to their institution and must not gain personally from institutional decisions. For example, if a board member is the head of a contracting company that might bid on a construction project or is a service provider for the institution, he or she should have no involvement in the development of the bidding process and should recuse himself or herself from any decisions about the contract. It is important that board members avoid any appearance of impropriety and clearly avoid conflicts of interest.

Fiduciary duty also means that board members will take due diligence to protect the integrity of their institution. There is no excuse for any board member to abdicate his or her fiduciary duty; it is always a board member's role to protect the mission, health, well-being, and founding goals and principles of the institution. Trusting another board member to take care of a certain aspect of the institution's health and well-being will not satisfy a trustee's fiduciary duty and could yield a finding of negligence and a breach of fiduciary duty.

Open Meeting and Sunshine Laws

Boards of trustees of public institutions are often subject to sunshine laws. These laws require that with the exception of personnel matters such as employee misconduct, salary disputes, and grievances, institutions must operate under the eye of public scrutiny. That is, boards of trustees' decisions, including hiring decisions, must be made in public view. An example of a violation of a sunshine law occurred at the University of Michigan, when the chair of the Board of Regents, after consulting other board members by phone, narrowed the presidential search to one finalist, and members of the board visited the finalist at his current place of employment. *Booth Newspapers, Inc. v. University of Michigan Board of Regents* (1993) successfully challenged the regents' actions as a violation of the state's freedom of information and open meeting laws. This consultation with board members by phone was actually a vote, so it was violation of the open meeting law. Moreover, failing to reveal the travel records for the visit to the candidate's home community, which were public information, was a violation of the freedom of information laws.

In another example of a sunshine law case related to an employee search, *Federated Publications, Inc. v. Board of Trustees of Michigan State University* (1997), the court found that the Presidential Selection Committee of the board of trustees had violated the state's open meeting act. The committee members had narrowed their list of presidential candidates, and the court agreed that a newspaper should have access to this information. Searches at public institutions for key leadership positions such as the presidency must be conducted in the sunshine, particularly when the search is winnowed to a small list of finalists.

Other board decisions must also be made in public, particularly when a vote is taken. While in many states deliberations surrounding personnel matters can be conducted behind closed doors, the ultimate decision—the vote (although not the rationale for the decision)—must be made in public view. For example, the board of trustees for a New Jersey public college voted in a closed session to provide a housing allowance to two vice presidents (*Council of New Jersey State College Locals v. Trenton State College Board of Trustees*, 1995). The court agreed with the union that the vote in private violated the state's open meeting law. However, the violation was corrected when in a subsequent open meeting the board ratified the vote.

Conclusion

Through their interpretation of federal and state law as it applies to colleges and universities, and by clarifying the legal relationships between institutions and their constituencies, the courts have had a direct impact on higher education. Specifically, the courts have affected how institutions address the three themes of this book—being mission driven, adapting to changes in the environment, and practicing democratic partnerships. The following are some key points and issues discussed in this chapter.

Under the U.S. Constitution, individual states are responsible for public education. Violations of 14th Amendment protections by the state or its institutions allow citizens to sue states in federal court for violations of constitutional rights. Federal laws and regulations that expand and clarify 14th

Amendment protections have resulted in suits in federal courts against states and public institutions. The result is that the constituencies of a public college or university have constitutional rights in their relationship with their institution. Private institutions do not come under these constitutional requirements, but because these rights have become societal norms and expectations, they have been incorporated into private institutions' contracts, policies, and practices.

Student, faculty, and employee rights have been expanded and clarified by federal laws and legal decisions. When dealing with students, institutions need to be cognizant of the due process procedure they have agreed to or are required to follow. Faculty and employee policies should be free of discrimination and designed to achieve fairness and equity. Employment decisions should be based on valid job performance criteria and follow the policies, procedures, and practices as defined in contracts and past precedent.

There is no way for an institution to eliminate risk and avoid litigation. In our litigious society, people are going to sue. If administrators make decisions that are fundamentally fair and just, informed by all available facts, and consistent with institutional policy and practice, however, they will find themselves on the right side of an issue should the courts become involved. Making a fair and just decision may not be the easiest decision, but in the long run it will be in the best interest of all the parties involved. Ignoring personnel issues will have negative consequences and create flawed exceptions to sound institution policy. It is better to address personnel issues directly as they occur.

Notes

1. It is not possible in a chapter such as this to provide a thorough review of all aspects of the legal issues associated with higher education. For readers with an interest in topics not included here or who desire more expansive coverage of the included topics, associations such as the Education Law Association and the Council on Law in Higher Education and gatherings such as the National Conference on Law and Higher Education can serve as additional resources. Moreover, laws can change quickly. In this chapter we have sought to provide readers with an understanding of the legal issues and requirements in place at the time of our writing that are the most relevant to academic administrators.

2. References to all court cases cited in this chapter can be found in the section titled "Cases and Statutes" beginning on p. 174.

3. For example, in New York, the Supreme Court is the lowest court in the system.

4. Contract law incorporates policies and practices that define legal obligations between parties.

5. See *Crook v. Baker* (1987) and *University of Texas Medical School v. Than* (1995).

6. These requirements are derived from *Dixon* (1961) and reaffirmed in *Henson v. Honor Committee of the University of Virginia* (1983). Additional discussion of these requirements can be found in Hendrickson (1999, p. 198).

7. In the 1960s and early 1970s, U.S. presidents issued executive orders to enforce the practice of affirmative action among government contractors. John F. Kennedy first used the phrase *affirmative action* in Executive Order No. 10,925 (1961) to ensure that federal contractors would not discriminate on the basis of race, creed, color, or national origin. Lyndon B. Johnson subsequently issued Executive Orders No. 11,246 (1965) and No. 11,375 (1967), which required companies with 50 or more employees and holding federal contracts of $50,000 to practice affirmative action. Richard M. Nixon expanded Executive Order No. 11,246 in Executive Order No. 11,478 (1969) to apply affirmative action to all companies holding federal contracts and to labor unions whose workers were engaged in those projects. Nixon also issued Executive Order No. 11,625 (1971), which, in the spirit of affirmative action, encouraged awarding federal contracts to minority businesses.

8. A strict scrutiny test is required when a public entity, such as a state, is either providing services or withholding services based on a suspect classification (race, creed, national origin, or gender). The state has the high burden to show a compelling state interest through a legislative, judicial, or administrative finding of past discrimination in order to use the suspect category. The state must also show that the remedy is the least intrusive means to right the wrong and is narrowly tailored to eliminate wrong without harm to others (*American Jurisprudence*, 2012).

9. Critical mass is defined as enough to ensure that students have the ability to make contributions to the law school in *meaningful* numbers or representation.

10. At the time of this writing, the Supreme Court had agreed to hear *Fisher v. University of Texas at Austin* (2012), which focuses on the use of race-based admissions policies by the University of Texas. The outcome from this case may again alter the legal use of affirmative action by colleges and universities.

11. That is, an individual can sue in federal court.

12. As mentioned previously, the 14th Amendment is the vehicle for applying constitutional rights to citizens of a state. First Amendment protections apply only to faculty members at public institutions, while the speech of faculty members at private institutions is governed primarily by contractual agreements, which at most institutions include AAUP academic freedom principles. Since many of these constitutional rights have become societal norms, private institutions have embraced some of these rights and protections through their student and employee contracts.

13. See, for example, *Ganguli v. University of Minnesota* (1994) and *Spiegel v. Trustees of Tufts College* (1988).

14. A tenure quota is a prescribed percentage of tenured faculty members in a department. The AAUP opposes tenure quotas; see www.cabrini.edu/facultysenate/Pages/Docs/AY0607/AAUP_Statement_On_the_Imposition_of_Tenure_Quotas.html).

15. These claims usually fall under Title VII, which is explained starting on p. 158.

16. However, it is not a breach of duty to refuse to teach a course in which a student has repeatedly disrupted the class, and the institution has failed to discipline the student adequately (*McConnell v. Howard University*, 1987).

17. The NLRA does not cover state public employees; each state has established laws to govern labor relations of public employees.

18. For more information, see the National Center for the Study of Collective Bargaining in Higher Education and the Professions at www.hunter.cuny.edu/ncscb hep.

19. Government can neither establish religion nor inhibit the free exercise of religion (U.S. Const., amend. Establishment and Free Exercises Clauses).

20. Retaliation is a negative employment action on the part of an employer because an employee filed, in this case, an ADEA claim.

21. The Restoration Act amended the following existing federal statutes: Title IX of the Education Amendment of 1972, Title VI of the Civil Rights Act of 1964, Age Discrimination in Employment Act of 1967 and 1975, Section 504 of the Rehabilitation Act of 1973, and the Americans with Disabilities Act of 1990, all of which contained the provisions of "programs or activities receiving federal financial assistance."

Cases and Statutes

Age Discrimination in Employment Act, 29 U.S.C. § 621 et seq. (1967).

Americans with Disabilities Act, 42 U.S.C. § 12101 et seq. (1990).

Bd. of Curators of Univ. of Mo. v. Horowitz, 435 U.S. 78 (1978).

Bd. of Regents of State Colls. v. Roth, 408 U.S. 564 (1972).

Beall v. Curtis, 603 F. Supp. 1563 (M.D. Ga. 1985).

Booth Newspapers, Inc. v. Univ. of Mich. Bd. of Regents, 507 N.W. 2d 422 (Mich. 1993).

Brown v. Board of Educ., 347 U.S. 483 (1954).

Brumback v. Rensselaer Polytechnic Inst., 510 N.Y.S. 2d 762 (N.Y. App. Div. 1987).

Cannon v. Univ. of Chicago, 441 U.S. 677 (1979).

Chang v. Univ. of Rhode Island, 606 F. Supp. 1161 (D. R.I. 1985).

Chiapuzio v. BLT Operating Corp., 826 F. Supp. 1334 (D. Wyo. 1993).

Civil Rights Act, Pub. L. No. 88-352, 78 Stat. 241 (1964).

Civil Rights Restoration Act, U.S. P.L. 100-259 (1987).

Cohen v. San Bernardino Valley Coll., 92 F. 3d 968 (9th Cir. 1996).

Connick v. Myers, 461 U.S. 138 (1983).

Council of N.J. State Coll. Locals v. Trenton State Coll. Bd. of Trustees, 663 A.2d 664 (N.J. Super. Ct. Law Div. 1995).

Covington v. Southern Ill. Univ., 816 F. 2d 317 (7th Cir. 1987).

Craig v. Ala. State Univ., 451 F. Supp. 1207 (11th Cir. 1978).

Crook v. Baker, 813 F. 2d 88 (6th Cir. 1987).

Dartmouth College v. Woodward, 17 U.S. 518 (1819).

DeFunis v. Odegaard, 416 U.S. 312 (1974).

Dhuria v. Trustees of the Univ. of the Dist. of Columbia, 827 F. Supp. 818 (D.D.C. 1993).

Dixon v. Alabama State Bd. of Educ., 294 F. 2d 150 (5th Cir. 1961).

Donnelly v. Rhode Island Bd. of Governors, 110 F. 3d 2 (1st Cir. 1997).

Dunn v. Ala. State Univ. Bd. of Trustees, 628 So. 2d 519 (Ala. 1993).

EEOC v. Bd. of Governors of State Colls. and Univs., 957 F. 2d 424 (7th Cir. 1992).

EEOC v. Franklin & Marshall Coll., 775 F. 2d 110 (3d Cir. 1985).

Equal Pay Act, 29 U.S.C. 206(d) et seq. (1963).

Espinosa v. Bd. of Trustees of Cty. Coll. Dist. No. 508, 632 N.E. 2d 279 (Ill. App. Ct. 1994).

Exec. Order No. 10,925, 26 Fed. Reg. 1977 (1961).

Exec. Order No. 11,246, 30 Fed. Reg. 12319 (1965).

Exec. Order No. 11,375, 32 Fed. Reg. 14303 (1967).

Exec. Order No. 11,478, 34 Fed. Reg. 12985 (1969)

Exec. Order No. 11,625, 36 Fed. Reg. 19967 (1971).

Federated Publ'ns., Inc. v. Bd. of Trustees of Mich. State Univ., 561 N.W. 2d 433 (Mich. Ct. App. 1997).

Fields v. Clark Univ., 817 F. 2d 931 (1st Cir. 1987).

Fisher v. Univ. of Texas at Austin, 2012 WL 538328 (U.S. 2012).

Ganguli v. Univ. of Minn., 512 N.W. 2d 918 (Minn. Ct. App. 1994).

Goodisman v. Lytle, 724 F. 2d 818 (9th Cir. 1984).

Goss v. Lopez, 419 U.S. 565 (1975).

Gott v. Berea Coll., 161 S.W. 204 (Ky. Ct. App. 1913).

Gratz v. Bollinger, 539 U.S. 244 (2003).

Gressley v. Deutsch, 890 F. Supp. 1474 (D. Wyo. 1994).

Grove City Coll. v. Bell, 465 U.S. 555 (1984).

Grutter v. Bollinger, 539 U.S. 306 (2003).

Harris v. Forklift Sys., Inc. 510 U.S. 17 (1993).

Hassan v. Auburn Univ., 15 F. Supp. 1097 (11th Cir. 1994).

Henson v. Honor Comm. of Univ. of Va. 719 F. 2d 69 (4th Cir. 1983).

Honore v. Douglas, 833 F. 2d 565 (5th Cir. 1987).

Hopwood v. Texas, 78 F. 2d 932 (5th Cir. 1996), *cert. denied,* 518 U.S. 1033 (1996).

In re Cornell University, 183 N.L.R.B. 329 (1970).

In re Dinnan, 661 F. 2d 426 (5th Cir. 1981).

In re Polishook v. City Univ. of N.Y., 651 N.Y.S. 2d 459 (N.Y. App. Div. 1996).

Jackson v. Hayakawa, 761 F. 2d 525 (9th Cir. 1985).

Karibian v. Columbia Univ., 14 F. 3d 773 (2d Cir. 1994).

LaFleur v. Wallace State Cmty. Coll., 955 F. Supp. 1406 (M.D. Ala. 1996).

Lamphere v. Brown Univ., 798 F. 2d 532 (1st Cir. 1986).

Lowe v. Beaty, 485 A. 2d 1255 (Vt. 1984).

Maguire v. Marquette Univ., 841 F. 2d 1213 (7th Cir. 1987).

McConnell v. Howard Univ., 818 F. 2d 58 (D.C. Cir. 1987).

McDonnell Douglas Corp. v. Green, 411 U.S. 792 (1973).

Mecklenburg v. Mont. State Bd. of Regents, 13 F.E.P. 462 (D. Mont. 1976).

Minn. State Bd. for Cmty. Colls. v. Knight, 465 U.S. 271 (1984).

Namenwirth v. Bd. of Regents of U. of Wis. Sys., 769 F. 2d 1235 (7th Cir. 1985).

Nash v. Auburn Univ., 812 F. 2d 655 (11th Cir. 1987).

National Labor Relations Act, 29 U.S.C. §§ 151-169 (1935).

NLRB v. Yeshiva Univ. 444 U.S. 672 (1980).

North Haven Bd. of Educ. v. Bell, 456 U.S. 512 (1982).

Oncale v. Sundowner Offshore Servs., Inc., 523 U.S. 75 (1998).

Orange Unified School Dist. v. Rancho Santiago Cmty. Coll. Dist., 62 Cal. Rptr. 2d 778 (Ca. Ct. App. 1997).

Ottaviani v. State Univ. of N.Y. at New Paltz, 679 F. Supp. 288 (S.D.N.Y. 1988).

Peters v. Lieuallen, 746 F. 2d 1390 (9th Cir. 1984).

Pime v. Loyola Univ. of Chicago, 803 F. 2d 351 (7th Cir 1986).

Plessy v. Ferguson, 163 U.S. 537 (1896).

Regents of Univ. of Cal. v. Bakke, 438 U.S. 265 (1978).

Regents of Univ. of Mich. v. Ewing, 474 U.S. 214 (1985).

Rehabilitation Act, 29 U.S.C. 701 et seq. (1973).

Russell v. Belmont Coll., 554 F. Supp. 667 (M.D. Tenn. 1982).

Sabet v. Eastern Va. Med. Auth., 775 F. 2d 1266 (4th Cir. 1985).

Silva v. Univ. of N. H., 888 F. Supp. 293 (D. N.H. 1994).

Simon v. Morehouse School of Med., 908 F. Supp. 959 (N.D. Ga. 1995).

Slater v. Marshall, 906 F. Supp 256 (E.D. Pa. 1995).

Smart v. Ball State Univ., 89 F. 3d 437 (7th Cir. 1996).

Smith v. Univ. of Ariz. *ex rel.* Bd. of Regents, 672 P. 2d 187 (Ariz. Ct. App. 1983).

Smith v. Va. Commonwealth Univ., 62 F. 3d 659 (4th Cir. 1995).

Sobel v. Yeshiva Univ., 566 F. Supp. 1166 (S.D.N.Y. 1983).

Southeastern Cmty. Coll. v. Davis, 442 U.S. 397 (1979).

Spaulding v. Univ. of Wash., 740 F. 2d 686 (9th Cir. 1984).

Spiegel v. Trustees of Tufts Coll., 843 F. 2d 38 (1st Cir. 1988).

Steier v. N.Y. State Educ. Comm'r., 161 F. Supp. 549 (E.D.N.Y. 1959).

Title VI of the Civil Rights Act, 42 U.S.C. 2000d to 2000d-7 (1964).

Title VII of the Civil Rights Act, 42 U.S.C. 2000I et seq. (1964).

Title IX of the Education Amendments, 20 U.S.C. 1681(a) (1972).

Tully v. Edgar, 664 N.E. 2d 43 (Ill. 1996).

United States v. Commonwealth of Va., 518 U.S. 515 (1996).

United States v. Mass. Maritime Academy, 762 F. 2d 142 (1st Cir. 1985).

Univ. of Houston v. Sabeti, 676 S.W. 2d 685 (Tex. Ct. App. 1984).

Univ. of Pa v. EEOC, 493 U.S. 182 (1990).

Univ. of Tex. Med. School v. Than, 901 S.W. 2d 926 (Tex. 1995).

Waring v. Fordham Univ., 640 F. Supp. 42 (S.D.N.Y. 1986).

Waters v. Churchill, 511 U.S. 661 (1994).

Wells v. Doland, 711 F. 2d 670 (5th Cir. 1983).

West Valley-Mission Cmty. Coll. Dist. v. Concepcion, 21 Cal. Rptr. 2d 5 (Cal. Ct. App. 1993).

Winkes v. Brown Univ., 747 F. 2d 792 (1st Cir. 1984).

Zahavy v. Univ. of Minn., 544 N.W. 2d 32 (Minn. Ct. App. 1996).

References

Alexander, K. W., & Alexander, K. (2011). *Higher education law: Policy and perspectives.* New York, NY: Routledge.

American Association of University Professors. (n.d.). *1940 statement on academic freedom and tenure.* Retrieved from http://www.aaup.org/AAUP/pubsres/policy docs/contents/1940statement.htm

American Jurisprudence (2nd ed.). (2012). 328 Am. Jur. 2d Constitutional Law § 403. Eagan, MN: West Publishing.

Black's Law Dictionary. (2009). St. Paul, MN: West Publishing.

Bowen, W. G., & Bok, D. (2000). *The shape of the river: Long-term consequences of considering race in college and university admissions.* Princeton, NJ: Princeton University Press.

Brake, D. (2010). *Getting in the game: Title IX and the women's sport revolution.* New York, NY: New York University Press.

Carnevale, A. P., & Rose, S. J. (2012). The convergence of postsecondary education and the labor market. In J. E. Lane & D. B. Johnstone (Eds.), *Colleges and universities as economic drivers: Measuring and building success* (pp. 163–190). Albany, NY: SUNY Press.

Garner, B. A. (Ed.). (2009). *Black's Law Dictionary.* St. Paul, MN: West Publishing.

Hendrickson, R. M. (1999). *The colleges, their constituencies and the courts* (2nd ed.). Dayton, OH: Education Law Association.

Hendrickson, R. M., & Lee, B. A. (1983). *Academic employment and retrenchment: Judicial review and administrative action.* Washington, DC: Association for the Study of Higher Education.

Henning, G. (2007). Is "In consortio cum parentibus" the new in loco parentis? *NASPA Journal, 44*(3), 538–560.

Kaplin, W. A., & Lee, B. A. (2006). *The law of higher education* (4th ed.). San Francisco, CA: Jossey-Bass.

Lake, P. (1999). The rise of duty and the fall of in loco parentis and other protective tort doctrines in higher education law. *Missouri Law Review, 64*(1), 1–28.

Sindler, A. P. (1978). *Bakke, DeFunis, and minority admissions: The quest for equal opportunity.* New York, NY: Longman.

Suggs, W. (2005). *A place on the team: Triumph and tragedy of Title IX.* Princeton, NJ: Princeton University Press.

Toma, J. D. (2011). *Managing the entrepreneurial university: Legal issues and commercial realities.* New York, NY: Routledge.

7

THE ENGAGED COLLEGE OR UNIVERSITY

The idea that institutions of higher learning should exist for the betterment of society and the promotion of democratic ideals is as old as the founding of this nation. It can be argued that the oldest college in the United States, Harvard, was founded to promote the advancement of societal goals. Evidence of this purpose is found in the earliest account of its creation, an article written in the 1643 publication *New England's First Fruits*, where it was stated, "After erecting shelter, a house of worship, and the framework of government, one of the next things we longed for, and looked after, was to advance Learning and perpetuate it to Prosperity" (as cited in Rudolph, 1962, p. 4).

Rudolph (1962) noted that the establishment of Harvard, and indeed all the colonial colleges, was born both out of necessity and a sense of community responsibility for future generations. If the colonists' communities, governments, and churches were to continue to flourish, they would need to train individuals to lead these critical institutions. The colleges' creation was not simply based on a need for vocations or a sense of order, however. As Rudolph pointed out, with the establishment of William and Mary, its founders specifically identified the need to ensure "that the youth were piously educated in good letters and manners from which the colony would draw its public servants" (p. 7). In other words, to our nation's founders, higher education was necessary to produce the next generation of citizens who would lead and be engaged in society.

The vision of a college and its graduates engaged in society was manifest in myriad ways during the colonial period and the creation of the United States. In fact, many believe that promotion of the democratic ideals that led to the American Revolution was partly fueled by the number of men of learned professions who were educated either in Europe or at one of the colonial colleges. Berkin (2002) described those leaders who directly participated in the creation of the U.S. Constitution as "men with a near monopoly on formal education and professional training in a predominantly agrarian society" (p. 49), and Ellis (2007) believed the American people were the beneficiaries of an "accumulated wisdom" (p. 4) to which the founders had been exposed through their formal education and training. A case can be made that without this extraordinary collection of college-educated people, the founding of this country may have taken a different course. Based on the democratic foundation that was laid by these learned men, it is easy to understand how an education—and especially a college education—came to be viewed as part of the American ethos. By the middle of the 19th century, there was a strong belief that colleges were essential to the promotion of American democracy, and a commitment to fostering these ideals became a part of the mission of most U.S. colleges (Rudolph, 1962, p. 61).

By the end of the 19th century, with the egalitarian nature of the land-grant movement and the advancement of the German research university model in the United States, the promotion of democratic ideals became intertwined with discussions on the true aims of education. Should the focus be on liberal education, research, the advancement of industry and agriculture, the promotion of democracy, or could it be all of the above? John Dewey (1916), the influential educational philosopher of the late 19th and early 20th centuries, emphasized a pragmatic approach to education and described the connection between education and democracy. Dewey believed that all education that "develops power to share effectively in social life is moral" (p. 360), making him one of the first commentators to identify the importance of democratic partnerships in advancing educational aims.

Dewey (1916) promoted the idea that theory and practice are not merely compatible but highly interconnected. Moreover, he argued that the greater aims of society could be accomplished only through participatory democracy. He emphasized that major advancements in knowledge occurred most often when the focus was on solving significant societal issues. These advancements most often occurred, according to Dewey, when learning in the classroom was contiguous with learning outside the school in the real world.

Unfortunately, as was the case in Dewey's time, the real world outside the classroom today is complicated, unpredictable, and difficult to control. It is filled with politics, shifting economic realities, and changing societal mores, all of which influence how education institutions interact with or relate to the world outside the ivory tower. Developing mutually beneficial democratic partnerships with constituents outside the academy (whether local or global) to advance knowledge and enhance student learning is certainly challenging, but developing these partnerships is paramount if a college or university is to thrive in the 21st century.

Three Educational Movements

In this chapter we discuss the intersection of three important educational movements of the 21st century. We believe the confluence of these movements presents a unique opportunity for higher education to reassert its value to society by engaging more deeply in societal issues, particularly at the local level. First, we describe what led colleges and universities to take more seriously their role in educating responsible citizens and reaffirm that educating students for citizenship is one of the primary aims of higher education. Second, we address how service-learning pedagogy has grown and transformed higher education. Third, we consider the rising expectation for colleges and universities to be more democratically engaged in their local communities while focusing on global issues. Throughout this chapter we have incorporated information on organizations and national engagement initiatives involved in this work.

Educating Responsible Citizens

Evidence that U.S. citizens' participation in their democracy has been in decline since the middle of the 20th century is abundant. In numerous studies conducted in recent years (Putnam, 2000; Sax, 2004; Zukin, Keeter, Andolina, Jenkins, & Delli Carpini, 2006), the declining participation rate of Americans in civic acts such as voting or involvement in a local community organization is alarming.

As stated earlier, from its inception American higher education has been viewed as a key instrument for promoting democratic values that are essential to the health and well-being of the republic. By the end of the 20th century, however, there was broad concern that higher education had lost its focus on the greater good and its commitment to civic virtues. Specifically, a widespread debate began to emerge by the middle of the 1980s over what the priorities of U.S. higher education ideally should be in an ever changing and pluralistic society. Some felt that higher education's primary aim was economic development. For example, in 1983 the National Commission on Excellence in Education, appointed by President Ronald Reagan, produced a report, *A Nation at Risk,* that attempted to identify the knowledge, abilities, and skills high school and college graduates should possess to promote economic prosperity but it said little about the promotion of democratic ideals as being key to prosperity. Others, however, felt colleges and universities needed to do more than fuel America's economic engine; higher education needed to support and sustain our democracy.

In response to these conversations, the Carnegie Foundation for the Advancement of Teaching sponsored a report (Newman, 1985) that called for the nation's schools to take more responsibility for educating students for citizenship. This report prompted the presidents of several leading U.S. universities to form an association called Campus Compact, aimed at encouraging institutions to instill a greater sense of social and civic responsibility in their students. The response to this initiative was tremendous. Within five years, the membership of Campus Compact exceeded 500 institutions, and today over 1,100 colleges and universities serving over six million students are part of this dynamic organization.

The Carnegie Foundation for the Advancement of Teaching continued to explore the priorities of U.S. higher education with the publication of a special report on the state of the professoriate (Boyer, 1990). Written by Carnegie Foundation president Ernest Boyer, the report suggested a new way of thinking about higher education. Rather than perpetuate the traditional debate about whether research or teaching should be valued more in faculty work, Boyer focused on the larger idea of scholarship, identifying four broad categories: the scholarship of discovery, integration, application, and teaching (p. 25).

This new way of thinking about academic work changed the nature of the debate over priorities and how faculty work should be categorized and rewarded, but it was Boyer's (1990) definition of the aim of education that ignited a broader discussion on higher education's civic role:

> The aim of education is not only to prepare students for productive careers but also to enable them to live lives of dignity and purpose; not to generate new knowledge but to channel it to humane ends; not merely to study government, but to help shape a citizenry that can promote the public good. (pp. 77–78)

Several years later, Boyer (1996) added a fifth element of scholarship, which he described as the scholarship of engagement. He added this category to emphasize the critical need for U.S. higher education to commit to public service anew.

In 1993 a group of U.S. higher education leaders known as the Wingspread Group on Higher Education proposed that administrators of institutions of higher education needed to take a closer look at their purpose and ask how their entering freshman classes in the next year would become "more sensitive to the needs of community, more competent in their ability to contribute to society, and more civil in their habits of thought, speech and action" (p. 9). In an open letter, the group called on institutions of higher education to raise their sights and take difficult steps to promote national health.

Other observers also expressed concern about the United States' national health. Putnam (1995), for example, described what he perceived to be a disturbing downward trend in civic, social, and political engagement among American citizens from the 1960s through the 1990s. Putnam had previously studied regional governments in Italy and discovered that local governments worked better—and communities were more likely to prosper—where there was "organized reciprocity and civic solidarity" (p. 2). Putnam argued that the health of a democracy depended on active participation of its citizens in everything from voting to membership in choral societies to bowling. In the United States he discovered a large percentage of Americans were disconnected from their neighbors and their local communities. To counter this trend, he argued that development of strategies to improve social capital and reverse political apathy among citizens should be high on the American agenda.

Although Putnam (1995) never suggested that higher education was the only solution, his findings and recommendations resonated in academic circles and were part of the impetus for some national organizations and higher education associations to call for greater involvement by colleges and universities in their local communities. By the beginning of the 21st century, these discussions led to the establishment of working groups and national programs such as the Association of American Colleges and Universities' (AAC&U's) Greater Expectations initiative, which articulated the aims and purposes of a liberal education and emphasized the importance of civic engagement in a diverse democracy. In spite of the widespread conversation about social and civic responsibility, however, the term *civic engagement* was not clearly understood. Since civic engagement was not clearly defined, it often was used as a catchphrase for a plethora of initiatives.

The difficulty with terminology stems from different interpretations of the word *civic*. A traditional understanding of the term is that it refers to the duties of a municipal or government worker rather than the responsibilities of all citizens. To others, it may have a political meaning and is often confused with student or political activism. Gradually, though, the term began to incorporate a more inclusive meaning. In 2003, for example, Colby, Ehrlich, Beaumont, and Stephens spelled out what they believed constituted a morally and civically responsible individual—one who sees himself or herself as

> a member of a larger social fabric and therefore considers social problems
> to be at least partly his or her own; such an individual is willing to see the
> moral and civic dimensions of issues, to make and justify informed moral
> and civic judgments, and to take action when appropriate. (p. 17)

In 2009 Jacoby and associates offered a simpler definition of *civic engagement*: "acting upon a heightened sense of responsibility to one's communities" (p. 9). For this book, we define it as the preparation of students to be informed, active, and responsible citizens in a democratic society who are committed to work for positive social change locally, nationally, and globally.

Some of the work for positive social change may take place in a traditional educational setting under the leadership of a faculty member, or it may occur when students engage in a community learning experience such as conducting research on an environmental issue tied to their course work. Other civic engagement activities, including voluntary service at a food bank or active participation in a political campaign, may have a positive impact on society and students but sometimes the lack of structure prevents students from having an experience that has a lasting impact on their development. The key to meaningful engagement is that those experiences are structured in ways that help students reflect on their experiences and make it more likely they will continue to participate in a significant way in the future. The more support mechanisms an institution has in place for such activities, the more likely the institution and its students will be civically engaged.

To recognize exemplars in the field of civic engagement, in 2006 the Carnegie Foundation for the Advancement of Teaching created an elective classification system for higher education institutions concerned with community engagement, or "the collaboration between institutions of higher education and their larger communities (local, regional, state, national, global) for the mutually beneficial exchange of knowledge and resources in a context of partnership and reciprocity" (Carnegie Foundation for the

Advancement of Teaching, n.d.). Colleges and universities can earn this recognition based on their work in three categories: curricular engagement, outreach and partnerships, or a combination of the two. By 2010 over 100 colleges and universities—public and private, large and small—were included on the list.

Several other associations and organizations have emerged to assist colleges and universities with civic engagement. For example, Project Pericles was founded by philanthropist Eugene Lang in 2001 to promote social responsibility and participatory citizenship as essential elements of the educational programs at its 30 member institutions, all of which are independent colleges and universities. Two elements of Project Pericles worth noting are the high level of institutional cooperation and academic partnerships that exists among member institutions and the commitment and involvement of member presidents in the organization.

While Project Pericles is limited to private schools, the American Democracy Project, created in 2003, is a multicampus initiative sponsored by the AAC&U to prepare the next generation of engaged citizens. Over 200 public institutions are part of this program, which has emphasized the importance of students becoming citizens who are deeply engaged in local community issues that have global impact. Furthermore, the AAC&U, which includes public and private institutions in its membership, sponsors several initiatives involving hundreds of institutions focused on personal and social responsibility as well as civic and democratic learning.

Strong evidence exists that the civic engagement movement in higher education has affected college students' participation in our democracy over the past two decades. For example, a 2006 report noted that current students, as well as those who recently attended college, are among the most engaged of all young people (Carnegie Foundation for the Advancement of Teaching and CIRCLE, 2006). For example, 28% of college graduates under the age of 25 reported being active in their communities, as compared to 13% of young people who did not attend college (Carnegie Foundation for the Advancement of Teaching and CIRCLE).

Voter participation of college graduates in the past two national elections has been almost double that of young people who did not attend college. According to a 2007 CIRCLE report, college students were far more active in their communities than their counterparts from the 1990s, although the later generation found the political system less accessible and felt traditional politics was not the best mechanism for change (Kiesa et al., 2007). Nevertheless, since the 1990s there has been a noticeable increase in voting participation and community involvement among young people aged 18–25 who are attending or have attended college as compared to those who do not attend college. We next explore the community-based learning and service-learning initiatives believed to have helped achieve these results.

Service-Learning and Community-Based Learning

Service-learning's roots can be traced to Dewey and his emphasis on the importance of school and community cooperation to address society's most pressing issues. Benson, Harkavy, and Puckett (2007) argued that Dewey's commitment to community was influenced by his work at the University of Chicago and by its first president, William Rainey Harper. Harper suggested that universities must guide American democracy, and that urban universities had a unique opportunity to collaborate with their cities to bring about remarkable societal transformations (Benson et al.).

Dewey, however, expanded on this idea to create a new educational paradigm that emphasized a union between the traditional contemplative approach to learning and a more vocational or applied method of learning. The experiential learning movement grew out of his philosophy and in turn led to the development of cooperative education, practicum experiences, and internships across myriad academic disciplines—especially in the professional schools that emerged in the middle of the 20th century.

Service-learning also emerged from the experiential learning movement in the late 1960s. According to Giles and Eyler (1994), the term *service-learning* was first coined by Sigmon and Ramsey in 1967. The early service-learning movement gained rapid popularity in U.S. institutions of higher education, but by the end of the 1970s it had largely disappeared because most programs were not tied to their academic institutions' missions, and the relationships between colleges and universities and their community partners were uneven or unequal (Jacoby & Associates, 1996; Kendall & Associates, 1990). Furthermore, little evidence was collected to demonstrate that this pedagogical approach truly had an impact on student learning.

By the early 1990s, service-learning reemerged at colleges and universities across the country, but this time its goals were more clearly developed. Institutions could not expect learning to occur simply by arranging for students to engage in service activities. Instead, programs had to emphasize service and learning. Moreover, leaders had to assess initiatives' impact on student learning outcomes. The new generation of service-learning advocates also recognized that to promote the practice of democratic principles among students, their institutions had to be more democratic in their approaches to education and relationships with community partners. Service-learning initiatives were further buttressed by the growing realization that students would need to be able to work collaboratively across cultures in a global society—a skill that service-learning programs were ready to develop (Spiezio, Baker, & Boland, 2006).

As is the case with civic engagement, service-learning suffers from the lack of a simple definition. Questions abound such as, How is service-learning different from community service? and Does a service experience have to be directly tied to a formal curriculum to count as service-learning? One of the pioneers of modern service-learning, Sigmon (1994), developed a typology to answer these and other questions. In his typology, Sigmon identified four distinct forms of the service-learning experience.

Sigmon's (1994) first type of service-learning is service-*Learning*, where the emphasis is on traditional classroom learning outcomes. For example, a student may be enrolled in a course on urban education, and as part of the course the student may serve as an assistant to an urban school teacher. In this role, however, the student functions only as an observer and does not actively engage with the teacher's students.

In contrast, Sigmon's (1994) second type is *Service*-learning, where the emphasis is on service. In this context, a student may learn about a particular community issue in a class, such as the rise of teenage pregnancy in rural communities, and be encouraged to do volunteer work on the issue outside the classroom. In the class, however, there is limited organized reflection on that experience, and the quality of the student's service activity is not evaluated as part of the course.

Traditional community service or volunteerism would be considered service-learning in Sigmon's (1994) typology (the third type) because the activity is not tied directly to any learning outcomes or classroom experience. This categorization can be confusing to people unfamiliar with Sigmon's typology because this type of service-learning experience is not always associated with the educational mission of the institution.

The fourth and most desirable form of service-learning in Sigmon's (1994) typology is *Service-Learning*, with equal emphasis on service and learning as they relate to academic course work. In this scenario, a marketing student might study the challenges associated with promoting a nonprofit organization's services to indigent populations in a depressed urban environment and then volunteer at the agency to develop a marketing plan. The plan would be devised under the supervision of the agency as well as the classroom professor, and the student would be evaluated on the quality of the plan and its perceived value to the nonprofit.

For this book, an ideal service-learning experience refers to the fourth type identified by Sigmon (1994). Beyond *Service-Learning*'s equal emphasis on service and learning and its explicit understanding that course work and engagement are integrated, it also assumes a mutually beneficial partnership exists between the institution of higher learning and the community organization, and both have agreed to measurable outcomes prior to the beginning of the service-learning experience.

Research on the impact of service-learning on students' learning and civic involvement has grown exponentially in recent years. In *Executive Summary: How Service-Learning Affects Students,* Astin, Sax, Ikeda, and Yee (2000) discovered after studying a number of service-learning programs that this pedagogical method did have a profound impact on several dimensions of student learning. They found that service-learning had a positive impact on grade point averages, writing skills, self-efficacy, critical thinking, and a future commitment to community service.

Eyler and Giles (1999) have been leaders in the assessment of service-learning and have advanced the field in significant ways. In a research study including over 1,500 college students, they discovered significant evidence of the effects of participating in service-learning on achieving a variety of learning outcomes across disciplines. With regard to civic engagement, or the development of citizenship in students, Eyler and Giles's findings demonstrated that students who participated in service-learning had an increased willingness to participate in service in the future, a stronger sense of community connectedness, an increased desire for social justice, and an interest in political change.

The research of Daynes and Wygant (2003) has also indicated a connection between service-learning and civic engagement. In a study of 2,200 students enrolled in an American Heritage course at Brigham Young University, they discovered that although service-learning was not necessarily a better predictor of civic engagement than voluntary membership in an association or following politics in the media, it was influential in helping students shape their opinions on how citizens should act in a democracy.

Simons and colleagues (2010) at Widener University discovered that participation in two different service-learning courses influenced student development in areas such as communications, problem solving, and attitudes regarding social justice issues. This study was one of the largest of its kind, involving 600 students over six years, and reinforced the importance of the relevance of service performed to the content of the associated course as well as the significance of the cooperating community organization in helping design the service activities.

A Campus Compact report (Cress, Burack, Giles, Elkins, & Stevens, 2010) also documented a clear connection between civic engagement and student academic success, particularly increased student access to college. For example, the report cited a study by Gallini and Moely (2003) that demonstrated that college students engaged in intensive service-learning experiences scored higher on five key learning outcomes than peers who did not enroll in a service-learning course. Several other studies included in the report found links between participation in a service-learning course and an increased likelihood of persistence and graduation by students from traditionally underserved populations. Moreover, the report presented evidence that college-level civic engagement activities targeting at-risk high school students through mentoring and tutoring programs improved the likelihood that those students would pursue postsecondary education (Cress et al., 2010).

The evidence is clear that service-learning has a positive influence on a wide range of student learning outcomes. Although a single definition of the practice does not seem to exist, three key elements appear to be involved in all meaningful service-learning experiences: research, relevance, and reflection. The first element, research, is a thoughtful preparation for learning prior to the service experience. In other words, the professor must prepare students for what they will encounter in the community, and students need to understand what the underlying societal issues are that contribute to the problems they will be addressing. This preparation requires advance research on the part of everyone involved, including research on the community partner, the university's history of community engagement, and the political realities associated with the issues to be addressed.

The second element, relevance, is a clear understanding of the relationship between the work students will be doing in the community and the academic subject they are studying. It is not enough to encourage students to commit to community service as part of a course. Rather, the faculty member must ensure that students understand the connection between the objectives of the service activity and the course. Students need to appreciate how their work in the community will advance their knowledge of the subject under study and help them develop skills to be active citizens.

The third element, reflection, may be the most critical for student learning. Eyler and Giles (1999) make the case that effective reflection on service-learning must include the five *C*s: connection, continuity, context, challenge, and coaching (p. 183). In Eyler and Giles's model, the faculty member plays a critical role in helping his or her students through their service-learning experience. They also note that the faculty member will not be able to fulfill this role without broader institutional support.

Several national organizations have been developed to support service-learning efforts across the country. In addition to Campus Compact, the Corella and Bertram Bonner Foundation supports 75 colleges and universities in a service-learning network. Starting in 1990 with the Bonner Scholars Program at Berea College in Kentucky, the Bonner Foundation has led several national conversations and administered federally funded programs aimed at increasing opportunities for students at its member institutions to engage in high-quality community service initiatives and service-learning endeavors.

The federal government has also increased its involvement in service-learning. The Clinton administration established the Corporation for National and Community Service, through which the Learn and Serve America program was specifically created to foster and encourage service-learning in K–12 educational institutions across the country. The program continues to emphasize the importance of reciprocal relationships between educational institutions and community partners as well as research and the collection of data on the impact of service-learning. Under President George W. Bush, the corporation created the President's Higher Education Community Service Honor Roll to recognize colleges and universities for their promotion of community service opportunities for their students.

A number of other organizations, including the National Center for Learning and Citizenship, the National Service-Learning Clearinghouse, and the International Association for Research on Service-Learning and Community Engagement, have also been established to promote service-learning. In addition, several academic journals have emerged to promote scholarship on service-learning, including *Journal of Higher Education Outreach and Engagement* and *Michigan Journal of Community Service Learning*. The work of such organizations, agencies, and publications provides evidence that service-learning positively affects student learning and longer-term civic involvement. It also suggests that service-learning as a pedagogical tool as well as an educational movement will remain an important part of the higher education agenda for decades to come.

Engaging the Community Through Democratic Partnerships

A traditional way to view a college's or university's engagement with society has been through the lens of town-gown relations. Despite the myriad benefits associated with the presence of a college or university in a community, colleges (gown) and their communities (town) continually have to work to resolve the conflicts that arise when a college and its community have differing goals and interests.

Conflicts between colleges and local municipalities have existed in the United States since the establishment of the colonial colleges. Whether it is concern over the behavior of students and whose responsibility it is to monitor them, or the physical growth of institutions to meet surging student demand, or intercollegiate athletic events and the thousands of spectators that flow into a community to watch their favorite college team, town-gown relations are complicated and require considerable time and effort on the part of every stakeholder to resolve difficult issues.

The literature on higher education is replete with examples of colleges and universities and their relationships with the communities where they reside (Gallo & Davis, 2008; Harris, 2011; Hartley, Harkavy, & Benson, 2006; Maurrasse, 2001). These relationships, positive and negative, have been categorized under a broad range of headings, such as community partnerships, town-gown relationships, and neighborhood collaborations. The nature of the relationship—and, therefore, the type of engagement—vary according to the history, current circumstances, and economic conditions of the institution and its community.

Many institutions across the country became increasingly involved in local community issues that can broadly be placed in three categories: economic development, community development, and public education initiatives. Economic development refers to universities' efforts to form partnerships with local municipalities, businesses, financial institutions, and federal and state agencies to encourage and promote the economic well-being of a region or city. These initiatives can take the form of workforce development, targeted purchasing, capital investments, neighborhood revitalization projects, corporate research, and the development or even creation of business incubators to encourage and support entrepreneurial ventures.

Community development typically refers to the efforts of the administrators of an institution to work with government officials and agencies as well as community-based organizations to address problems that affect the living conditions (e.g., housing, violence, homelessness) of the community where the university is located. Likewise, public education initiatives focus on how an institution can become a partner with the local public school district and other organizations to improve the quality of K–12 education. The ultimate aim of this work is to improve student learning outcomes and prepare a greater percentage of students from underrepresented groups for college-level study.

To articulate their commitment to advancing these three broad issues, leaders of colleges and universities, particularly urban and metropolitan institutions, are increasingly describing their institutions as being place bound or anchored to a particular location. According to a report on university engagement published by the Democracy Collaborative (Axelroth & Dubb, 2010), officials of anchor institutions who wish to enhance the long-term viability of their communities can play many roles but typically their institution follows one of three patterns: facilitator, leader, or convener.

When a college or university acts as a facilitator, the institution works to connect faculty members and students with local community organizations through academic service-learning opportunities. In addition, it arranges conversations between various organizations to build capacity to address societal issues (Axelroth & Dubb, 2010). Usually these institutions have supportive administrative and academic leadership but limited resources to contribute as a major investor in significant community development projects.

A college or university is considered a leader when it attempts to address a specific societal concern, such as crime or failing schools, by taking a leadership role in discussions about the issue and making a significant financial commitment to efforts to resolve it (Axelroth & Dubb, 2010). In this context, the institution's administration may take a very active and visible role in addressing a particular topic and use its influence to attract additional partners and resources.

An institution functions as a convener when it builds alliances with local organizations, government agencies, and other partners to set an agenda focused on long-term strategies for improvement of living conditions in particular neighborhoods, establishment of community health goals, or encouragement of economic development (Axelroth & Dubb, 2010). In this situation, administrators view the college or university itself as part of its mission as a partner and may invest its own resources to advance the initiative, but usually only if others are willing to work with the institution on the particular issue.

At any time a college or university may be playing one or all three roles through engagement in any number of activities. Syracuse University is an example of an institution that has served as a facilitator, leader, and convener in community and economic development. Syracuse has exhibited its commitment to being an anchor institution in several ways. Under the leadership of Chancellor Nancy Cantor, Syracuse's anchor mission is articulated through its vision, "Scholarship in Action" (Axelroth & Dubb, 2010, p. 141). Syracuse's vision includes "forging bold, imaginative, reciprocal and sustained engagements" locally and globally (p. 141). To date, members of the university community have engaged in a diverse range of activities including participating in neighborhood revitalization projects, implementing economic inclusion principles by hiring local contractors, and changing tenure and promotion guidelines to support engaged scholarship by the faculty (p. 98).

Hostos Community College, a two-year institution created specifically to serve the poor, mostly Latino South Bronx community in New York City, has focused its involvement in the neighborhoods that provide the vast majority of its students. For example, in response to an identified need in the community to address issues of domestic violence and the spread of HIV and AIDS among immigrant populations, the college created a women's center to coordinate outreach by the faculty and students to the community and to serve as a portal for local residents to connect to the college (Maurrasse, 2001, p. 159). Years later, because of funding cuts, the college worked with local nonprofits to ensure that these efforts continued to be supported. In these ways the college served as an anchor to the community.

After years of frustration in dealing with the bureaucracy and changing leadership (four different superintendents in six years) of the lowest performing school district in Pennsylvania, Chester-Upland, officials at Widener University made the bold decision to open their own charter school. The Widener Partnership Charter School was the first of its kind in Pennsylvania and was the outgrowth of years of discussions and failed negotiations between Chester-Upland and the university to address educational reform issues throughout the district. When the university turned to the community for input and feedback, it found strong support of and strong resistance to the idea of a charter school. Once the school opened and produced the best statewide testing results in the district, the school gained broader support, but it took strong and sustained commitment as well as political resolve from the university's administration and faculty to make it work (Ledoux, Wilhite, & Silver, 2011).

California State University, Fresno, has engaged with its community through a series of university-led initiatives and partnerships with key regional and state stakeholders. One of its largest projects was the creation of the Regional Jobs Initiative, a public-private partnership aimed at improving the local economy of the surrounding eight-county region, known as the San Joaquin Valley, by connecting the university with community and business leaders to create sustainable economic growth through broad-based job creation (Welty & Lukens, 2009, p. 59). The university became a leader and a convener by bringing together business, community, and government leaders to set a course of action.

One example of the results of this university collaboration is the identification of 10 industry clusters that had strong potential for growth in the region. As of 2008 over 600 business leaders had been involved in the clusters and provided direction for the development of training to meet workforce needs (Welty & Lukens, 2009, p. 65). It is important to note that Fresno's president, John Welty, was a driving force in this initiative, using his considerable political connections and influence to help this project succeed.

A number of national movements have emerged over the years to help colleges and universities make sense of these relationships in view of their particular mission or location. Most of these movements coalesce around specific institution types or within particular Carnegie Classifications. As noted previously, some of the best examples of this work have revolved around urban universities and their efforts to deal with the changing economic, social, and political landscape of urban America. For example, the Coalition of Urban and Metropolitan Universities was established in 1990 to use the power of its campuses in education, research, and service to enhance the communities where they are located. Originally made up exclusively of public universities, today the coalition includes public and private institutions whose administrators are focused on fully understanding the distinctiveness of their institution's mission through conferences, a journal, research projects, creation of a policy agenda, and regular networking opportunities.

Throughout this book, we have made the argument that to prosper in the 21st century, institutions of higher learning need to be mission driven, adaptable, and predisposed to form democratic partnerships inside and outside the academy. However, is it reasonable to expect that a college or university be held to the higher standard of democratic engagement and the challenges associated with coming to consensus over difficult issues in all that it does internally and externally? Given the difficulty associated with community engagement because of the conflicting goals and interests of a university and myriad participating community stakeholders, it could be argued that no one should expect these institutions to act democratically in everything they do.

The idea of a truly democratic partnership between a higher education institution and community partners is desirable, but many institutions fear committing to a democratic approach to engagement because they know that sustainable university community partnerships take time to evolve. Over the years, leaders move on, priorities are modified, and funding opportunities fluctuate. Within this ever changing environment, is it realistic to expect democratic engagement with stakeholders whose priorities and visions for the future may not be consistent with those of the university?

More authors have increasingly called for a rethinking of the approach colleges and universities take in engagement in their communities (see, for example, Colby et al., 2003; Hartley et al., 2006; Maurrasse, 2001). Their reasoning is that it is not enough for leaders of institutions of higher learning to express their support for reciprocal, democratic alliances and then do what is in their best interest in the end, saying that they had no choice but to act unilaterally. Rather, colleges and universities need to make a commitment to do the heavy lifting necessary to build trust and true democratic partnerships because it is better for the institution and the community in the long run. Furthermore, if college and university officials wish to encourage their students to develop into responsible citizens equipped to work collaboratively in a global society, it is paramount that institutions of higher learning model the same behavior.

Hartley, Saltmarsh, and Clayton (2010) called for a deeper examination of the implications of democratic civic engagement and what it will require of colleges and universities in the future. First, they proposed that administrators of institutions of higher learning must accept that these institutions do have "a responsibility to our democracy" (p. 292). Second, they suggested that true democratic engagement will require a change in how students are taught, so that greater emphasis is placed on demonstrating how democracy works by creating more reciprocal relationships between students and faculty (p. 294). Furthermore, they argued that a new type of collaboration between an institution and the communities it serves needs to be developed, whether locally or globally. This collaboration should be one in which the future is cocreated, and all partners are viewed as bringing valuable expertise and resources to the table. This approach contrasts with the traditional view in which academic knowledge is valued over community-based knowledge (Hartley et al., 2010).

Fostering democratic partnerships to address the most pressing issues facing society has local and global implications. With less than 1% of U.S. college students studying abroad at any time, the most likely place where they will have the opportunity to address societal issues and practice the skills necessary to function in a democratic society is in the community surrounding their campus. Therefore, it is the responsibility of a college or university to model democratic practices and provide students with opportunities to prepare for their role as citizens by engaging them on and off campus in structured, meaningful, and truly democratic learning opportunities.

References

Astin, A. W., Sax, L. J., Ikeda, E. K., & Yee, J. A. (2000). *Executive summary: How service learning affects students.* Retrieved from University of California, Los Angeles, Graduate School of Education and Information Studies, Higher Education Research Institute website: http://heri.ucla.edu/PDFs/rhowas.pdf

Axelroth, R., & Dubb, S. (2010). *The road half traveled: University engagement at a crossroads.* Retrieved from the Democracy Collaborative at the University of Maryland website: http://www.community-wealth.org/_pdfs/news/recent-articles/10-10/report-axelroth-dubb.pdf

Benson, L., Harkavy, I., & Puckett, J. (2007). *Dewey's dream: Universities and democracies in an age of education reform.* Philadelphia, PA: Temple University Press.

Berkin, C. (2002). *A brilliant solution: Inventing the American constitution.* New York, NY: Houghton Mifflin Harcourt.

Boyer, E. (1990). *Scholarship reconsidered: Priorities of the professoriate.* Princeton, NJ: Carnegie Foundation for the Advancement of Teaching.

Boyer, E. (1996). The scholarship of engagement. *Journal of Public Outreach, 1*(1), 11–20. doi:10.2307/3824459

Carnegie Foundation for the Advancement of Teaching. (n.d.). Community engagement. Retrieved from http://classifications.carnegiefoundation.org/descriptions/community_engagement.php?key=1213

Carnegie Foundation for the Advancement of Teaching and CIRCLE. (2006). *Higher education: Civic mission and civic effects.* Retrieved from Center for Information & Research on Civic Learning & Engagement website: http://www.civicyouth.org/PopUps/higher_ed_civic_mission_and_civic_effects.pdf

Colby, A., Ehrlich, T., Beaumont, E., & Stephens, J. (2003). *Educating citizens: Preparing America's undergraduates for lives of moral and civic responsibility.* San Francisco, CA: Jossey-Bass.

Cress, C. M., Burack, C., Giles, D. E., Jr., Elkins, J., & Stevens, M. C. (2010). *A promising connection: Increasing college access and success through civic engagement.*

Retrieved from Campus Compact website: http://www.compact.org/wp-con tent/uploads/2009/01/A-Promising-Connection-corrected.pdf

Daynes, G., & Wygant, S. (2003). Service-learning as a pathway to civic engage- ment: A comparative study. *Metropolitan Universities, 14*(3), 84–96.

Dewey, J. (1916). *Democracy and education: An introduction to the philosophy of educa- tion.* New York, NY: Free Press.

Ellis, J. J. (2007). *American creation: Triumphs and tragedies at the founding of the republic.* New York, NY: Knopf.

Eyler, J., & Giles, D. E., Jr. (1999). *Where's the learning in service-learning?* San Francisco, CA: Jossey-Bass.

Gallini, S., & Moely, B. (2003). Service-learning and engagement, academic chal- lenge, and retention. *Michigan Journal of Community Service Learning, 10*(1), 5–14.

Gallo, R., & Davis, R. (2008). Research on the impact of HBCUs on African Ameri- can communities. *Metropolitan Universities, 19*(2), 102–120.

Giles, D. E., Jr., & Eyler, J. (1994). The theoretical roots of service-learning in John Dewey: Towards a theory of service-learning. *Michigan Journal of Community Service Learning, 1*(1), 77–85.

Harris, J. T. (2011). How Widener developed a culture of civic engagement and fulfilled its promise as a leading metropolitan university. In M. W. Ledoux, S. C. Wilhite, & P. Silver (Eds.), *Civic engagement and service learning in a metropolitan university: Multiple approaches and perspectives* (pp. 1–12). New York, NY: Nova Science.

Hartley, M., Harkavy, I., & Benson, L. (2006). Building Franklin's truly demo- cratic, engaged university: Twenty years of practice at the University of Pennsyl- vania. *Metropolitan Universities, 17*(3), 22–37.

Hartley, M., Saltmarsh, J., & Clayton, P. (2010). Is the civic engagement movement changing higher education? *British Journal of Educational Studies, 58*(4), 391–406. doi:10.1080/00071005.2010.527660

Harvard University Institute of Politics. (2008). *Executive summary: The 14th biannual youth survey on politics and public service by Harvard's Institute of Politics.* Retrieved from Harvard University Institute of Politics website: http://www.iop.harvard.edu/ Research-Publications/Survey/Spring-2008-Survey/Executive-Summary

Jacoby, B., & Associates. (1996). *Service-learning in higher education: Concepts and practices.* San Francisco, CA: Jossey-Bass.

Jacoby, B., & Associates. (2009). *Civic engagement in higher education: Concepts and practices.* San Francisco, CA: Jossey-Bass.

Kendall, J. C., & Associates. (Eds.). (1990). *Combining service and learning: A resource book for community and public service* (Vol. 1). Raleigh, NC: National Society for Internships and Experiential Education.

Kiesa, A., Orlowski, A. P., Levine, P. L., Both, D., Kirby, E. H., Lopez, M. H., & Marcelo, K. B. (2007). *Millennials talk politics: A study of college student political engagement.* Retrieved from Center for Information & Research on Civic Learn- ing & Engagement website: http://www.civicyouth.org/PopUps/CSTP.pdf

Ledoux, M. W., Wilhite, S. C., & Silver, P. (Eds.). (2011). *Civic engagement and service learning in a metropolitan university: Multiple approaches and perspectives.* New York, NY: Nova Science.

Lopez, M. H., & Brown, B. (2006). *Civic engagement among 2-year and 4-year college students.* Retrieved from Center for Information & Research on Civic Learning & Engagement website: http://www.civicyouth.org/PopUps/FactSheets/FS06_comm_coll.pdf

Maurrasse, D. J. (2001). *Beyond the campus: How colleges and universities form partnerships with their communities.* New York, NY: Routledge.

National Commission on Excellence in Education. (1983). *A nation at risk: The imperative for educational reform.* Retrieved from http://www2.ed.gov/pubs/NatAtRisk/index.html

Newman, F. (1985). *Higher education and the American resurgence: A Carnegie Foundation special report.* Lawrenceville, NJ: Princeton University Press.

Putnam, R. D. (1995). Bowling alone: America's declining social capital. *Journal of Democracy, 6*(1), 65–78. doi:10.1353/jod.1995.0002

Putnam, R. D. (2000). *Bowling alone: The collapse and revival of American community.* New York, NY: Simon & Schuster.

Rudolph, F. (1962). *The American college and university: A history.* New York, NY: Random House.

Saltmarsh, J., & Hartley, M. (Eds.). (2011). *"To serve a larger purpose": Engagement for democracy and the transformation of higher education.* Philadelphia, PA: Temple University Press.

Sax, L. J. (2004, Summer). Citizenship development and the American college student. *New Directions for Institutional Research, 122,* 65–80. doi:10.1002/ir.110

Sigmon, R. (1994). *Linking service with learning.* Washington, DC: Council of Independent Colleges.

Simons, L., Fehr, L., Blank, N., Connell, H., DeSimone, R., Georganas, G. M., & Thomas, D. (2010). A comparative analysis of academic service-learning programs: Students' and recipients' teachers' perspectives. *Metropolitan Universities, 20*(3), 77–92.

Spiezio, K. E., Baker, K. Q., & Boland, K. (2006). General education and civic engagement: An empirical analysis of pedagogical possibilities. *Journal of General Education, 54*(4), 273–292. doi:10.1353/jge.2006.0012

Welty, J. D., & Lukens, M. (2009). Partnering with state government to transform a region. *Metropolitan Universities, 20*(1), 59–74.

Wingspread Group on Higher Education. (1993). *An American imperative: Higher expectations for higher education.* Racine, WI: Johnson Foundation.

Zukin, C., Keeter, S., Andolina, M., Jenkins, K., & Delli Carpini, M. X. (2006). *A new engagement? Political participation, civic life, and the changing American citizen.* Oxford, UK: Oxford University Press.

8

EXTERNAL INFLUENCES AND THE ROLE OF SUPPORTING ORGANIZATIONS

The vast number of colleges and universities in the United States pales in comparison to the number of organizations that exist to support, represent, and evaluate them. Today's colleges and universities are associated with a host of ancillary organizations that reflect the myriad interests, missions, and aspirations they represent. Some serve the academic disciplines as represented by the faculty. Others provide grants in support of institutional priorities or directions. Still others perform quasi-governmental functions by coordinating educational services of multiple institutions to meet specific regional educational needs. Many play policy and programmatic support roles to administrators or aid in governmental relations, and others perform the important function of evaluating the quality of education and its effectiveness in meeting an academic organization's stated educational purposes. Regardless of their purpose, these external organizations significantly influence institutional direction and outcomes and serve as a fluid and dynamic web linking the United States' diverse universe of colleges and universities.

Three primary reasons account for the existence of these external organizations. The first and most important reason is that the U.S. Constitution is silent on the matter of education, which by default refers the issue to the states. In the absence of centralized governmental control and authority, more decentralized mechanisms of supervision and influence emerge and proliferate. This diffused system permits multiple external groups to assume roles of varying importance in the life of an academic institution. A second reason rests in the nature of professionalism and the autonomy it demands. (See chapter 2 for a full discussion of this topic.) Given the multiple goals and various constituencies served by higher education, those individuals possessing personal expertise for meeting specific goals will demand primacy in how those goals are fulfilled, and they will collectively affiliate with peers with similar expertise and interests to provide support and leverage to realize their collective interests. The third reason relates to resources. Numerous funding entities, be they private or public, have a vested interest in ensuring that their agendas are realized. As important organizations of societal and individual change, colleges and universities benefit significantly from funding entities whose administrators recognize how valuable their resources are to the financial well-being and programmatic growth of institutions of higher education—while simultaneously fulfilling their own organizational missions.

External organizations that hold influence over colleges and universities can be understood in different ways. Harcleroad and Eaton (2005) broadly classified them into three sectors, providing an excellent overview on the role of influential external organizations. First, they identified the voluntary enterprise sector, which comprises thousands of independent nonprofit organizations serving higher education and its multiple constituencies in varied and important ways. Second is the public enterprise group, which consists of all local, state, and federal government agencies. Third, the private enterprise group includes all for-profit entities, such as corporations, that exercise influence through donations and sponsored research to meet specific goals of mutual benefit to themselves and the colleges and universities to which they provide funding. Together these entities wield an enormous, yet often unseen, influence over academia, which led Harcleroad and Eaton (2005) to refer to them as "the hidden hand" (p. 253).

Another way of categorizing these external groups is by function, and this chapter will examine external influential organizations accordingly. First, some organizations serve an evaluative role, meaning that their responsibility is to ensure colleges' and universities' compliance with standards of educational quality. Accrediting bodies constitute the largest group in this sector. Second, some associations serve an affiliate role that allows the collective professional interests and values of the membership to be expressed and acted upon. These are the many hundreds of professional membership organizations, consortia, and compacts that exist to serve colleges and universities; the various constituencies within them; or governments seeking regional solutions to educational needs. Third, some external entities serve a funding role, allocating resources to meet programmatic or societal outcomes. Because they are discussed in chapters 4 and 5, government agencies and the role they assume in funding higher education are not discussed here. Rather, in this chapter we primarily focus on private organizations that provide funding to colleges and universities. Together, these three roles provide a framework for understanding the vast network of organizations that influence, support, and sustain U.S. higher education.

The diversity of functions that these influential external organizations represent mirrors the three principles of this book. Each is reflective in some way of the diverse missions of today's higher education institutions. Each is tailored in purpose to conform to the special needs and issues of the institutions or constituencies they are designed to serve, and they promote the democratic values that are the hallmark of U.S. higher education. These external organizations also assist colleges and universities in adapting to their changing environments by analyzing, interpreting, and addressing the issues and challenges before them, as well as by facilitating organizational change through the allocation of targeted resources. All these efforts are pursued to maintain currency, accountability, and institutional quality. Ensuring accountability and quality is a task assigned to those organizations empowered to perform an evaluative role—the subject we now turn to.

Evaluation and the Role of Accrediting Bodies

In the absence of any single centralized governmental authority overseeing the affairs of U.S. higher education, who or what body is responsible for ensuring that the education being provided meets certain minimum standards? Likewise, who defines those standards and is granted the legitimacy to establish quality benchmarks and then evaluate and enforce their attainment across the wide array of institutional types?

As we will see in chapter 14 in our discussion of the student experience and the role of college, divergent views exist in our society on the purpose of college, what should be taught, and how student outcomes should be measured. Such disagreement does little to guide us in terms of who should make important determinations on matters of educational content and quality. Clearly, the United States' founding fathers felt it prudent to leave such matters to others apart from federal control. Rather, the notion of self-regulation by those professionals who are expert in and responsible for education was viewed as the most appropriate means of setting and enforcing standards. How this conclusion was reached is an interesting study in the formative forces that shaped American higher education and the political struggles that accompanied it.

The term *accreditation* has a variety of meanings and resonates differently with various constituencies depending on how the term is applied. According to Harcleroad (1980), accreditation is a concept, a process, and a status, and he uses the definition first employed by the former Council on Postsecondary Accreditation (COPA):

> First, it is a concept unique to the United States by which institutions of postsecondary education or professional associations form voluntary, nongovernmental organizations to encourage and assist institutions in the evaluation and improvement of their educational quality and to publicly acknowledge those institutions, or units within institutions, that meet or exceed commonly agreed to minimum expectations or educational quality.
>
> Second, it is a process by which an institution of postsecondary education formally evaluates its educational activities, in whole or in part, and seeks an independent judgment that it substantially achieves its own objectives and is generally equal in quality to comparable institutions or specialized units. Essential elements of the process are: (1) a clear statement of educational objectives, (2) a directed self-study focused on these objectives, (3) an on-site evaluation by a selected group of peers, and (4) a decision by an independent commission that the institution or specialized unit is worthy of accreditation.
>
> Third, it is a status of affiliation given an institution or specialized unit within an institution which has gone through the accreditation process and has been judged to meet or exceed general expectations of educational quality. (p. 12)

Harcleroad noted that numerous terms have been used to describe the process of evaluating and recognizing academic organizations and makes a distinction between the terms *approve* and *accredit*. The term *approve* connotes a qualitative judgment and may suggest that an institution is being granted an endorsement, whereas *accredit* carries a more neutral tone and has been adopted by educators as the term most frequently used to describe the concept, process, and status used in recognizing that an institution has met a certain predefined minimum standard.

The self-monitoring of educational standards is a relatively recent phenomenon given the long history of higher education in the United States. The need to introduce a structure and process to determine standards and quality emerged in the late 1800s during a profound era of change in higher education. As the United States made the transition from the age of the college to the age of the university, many new forms of institutions emerged to meet the needs of an increasingly pluralistic society and to respond to the scientific and technological developments of the day. This period in history also witnessed the decline of the classical curriculum in favor of the elective system and greater student choice in course selection. New academic disciplines and majors arose, and with them came a need to coordinate content and consistency in preparing students for the new professions required for an ascendant nation.

Minimum educational criteria for college admission also emerged as an issue during this time, as a lack of consistency in the quality of preparation for college resulted in wide disparities among students seeking higher education. Also, the distinction between institutional types and their educational rigor raised new questions on what actually constituted college-level work. Amid this period of enormous transition and growth, educators rapidly identified the need for a mechanism to address these vast changes and the competing standards they revealed.

The challenges educators faced transcended state boundaries and institutional types. On a voluntary basis, educators in specific geographic regions came together to advocate collectively for shared goals, a process that launched the current regional accreditation structure. First came the New England Association of Schools and Colleges and the North Central Association of Colleges and Schools, both founded in 1885, followed soon thereafter by the Middle States Association of Colleges and Schools in 1887. Though different in small ways, these early accrediting bodies shared the goals of influencing legislation favorable to their institutions, promoting common educational interests, and especially evaluating educational effectiveness and academic preparedness at the high school level. Similar motivations led to the subsequent founding of the Southern Association of Colleges and Schools in 1895, the Northwest Association of Schools and Colleges in 1917, and the Western Association of Schools and Colleges in 1924. These six organizations today serve as the major regional accrediting bodies responsible for ensuring the standards followed by our colleges and universities.

These organizations operated in coordinative and support roles early in their histories, and their scope and importance expanded considerably after World War II, when higher education experienced profound growth because of burgeoning veteran enrollments and the U.S. response to the threats posed by the Cold War. The need for more and better instructors, coupled with the creation of many new graduate programs in a host of new disciplines and fields, prompted calls for greater professional oversight to ensure consistency in academic quality. Parallel to these developments affecting the regional accrediting bodies was the creation of scores of specialized national accrediting associations in a variety of disciplines.

Each of these developments was of strong interest to the federal government, which invested heavily in veteran education with the passage of the Servicemen's Readjustment Act of 1944 (the GI Bill). By virtue of the federal government's heavy investment in higher education through that initiative, as well as through subsequent legislation that primarily concerned financial aid issues, the government's interest in educational outcomes began to increase. In a defensive move to keep the government from encroaching too deeply into higher education affairs, educators sought to strengthen the volunteer accreditation process, but the government opted to use accreditation structures to assist in determining institutional eligibility for receipt of federal funds. This governmental policy led the six regional accrediting organizations and over 70 specialized associations to increase coordination in 1975 under the auspices of the already existing COPA, which had been established earlier to develop continuity of accreditation practices and policies nationally. An excellent history of the development of accreditation can be found in Harcleroad (1980), which also provides an illuminating overview of the issues and problems associated with it.

Accreditation is essentially a partnership between three vested interests: institutions of higher education, represented by college and university presidents and their membership associations; accrediting bodies, which represent the professional expertise to render judgment on standards of performance; and state and federal governmental entities, which allow states to charter institutions, license programs, and provide state aid, and allow the federal government to provide resources in support of legislated programs.

Given the inherent conflict between bureaucratic principles and professionalism, this triumvirate is bound to have conflicts, and so it did with COPA. According to Bloland (1999), in the early 1990s,

> accreditation was confronting a series of conflicts and pressures: a rancorous debate on multicultural guidelines, increasing pressure by the federal government to use accreditation as a regulating device to reduce high default rates on federally guaranteed student loans, and progressive transfer of federal responsibilities to the states, which encouraged states and state governors to become more activist in all things educational, including accreditation. (p. 363)

Exacerbating these problems were dysfunctions within COPA itself, whose regional accrediting commissions, specialized accrediting associations, and presidential associations representing the interests of the colleges and universities were at odds on a variety of issues:

> The national associations, led by ACE (American Council on Education), sought to curb excessive visits and demands and unwarranted proliferation of specialized accreditors. The regional accrediting commissions complained of paying too large a proportion of the COPA dues without a commensurate voice in COPA decision making. The regionals thought the specialized and professional agencies had too much power. (Bloland, 1999, p. 364)

In short, the conflict in COPA demonstrated the challenges of balancing multiple interest groups in a highly pluralistic and democratic organization that was attempting to define and execute the difficult process of setting uniform academic standards on a national level.

What arose from the termination of COPA in 1993 was a new and restructured organization that sought to address the concerns of all parties and involve all major constituencies. More important, however, was what emerged—an organization that would be viewed as a legitimate voice on matters pertaining to higher education standards. Called the Council for Higher Education Accreditation (CHEA), its mission is to "serve students and their families, colleges and universities, sponsoring bodies, governments, and employers by promoting academic quality through formal recognition of higher education accrediting bodies and will coordinate and work to advance self-regulation through accreditation" (Eaton, 2011, p. i).

CHEA (2011) "is an association of 3,000 degree-granting colleges and universities and recognizes 60 institutional and programmatic accrediting organizations." The jurisdiction of CHEA extends beyond the United States to institutions and programs in 113 other countries that have chosen to be governed by CHEA's accreditation standards and processes. The organization oversees four types of accrediting organizations, including the six regional accreditors described earlier; national faith-related accreditors that focus on religiously affiliated institutions such as seminaries; national career-related accreditors that review degree-granting and nondegree, career-based, often for-profit institutions; and the many programmatic accreditors that evaluate professional schools and special programs such as those focused on business, music, medicine, law, engineering, and health professions, among others.

In 2009 there were 19 recognized institutional accrediting organizations and 61 programmatic accrediting organizations in the United States (Eaton,

2011, p. 6). Each accrediting body has a decision-making council known as a commission composed of faculty members, administrators, and some members of the public who review and affirm recommendations for accreditation or reaccreditation. The legitimacy of the accreditation process is granted by the participating colleges, universities, and academic programs that collectively support this peer evaluation process.

According to Eaton (2011), there are four roles of accreditation. Accreditation is intended to ensure quality in the academic offerings of an institution and the fiscal stability to sustain them; provide access to federal funding, since the government will provide student financial aid or other programmatic resources only to recognized accredited institutions; engender private sector confidence by ensuring to prospective employers a proper level of credentialing; and ensure quality to facilitate the transfer of credits between institutions. It is important to note that the government also performs an important function through the process of recognition, in that CHEA and the U.S. Department of Education collaborate to develop evaluation standards of the various accrediting organizations. This "evaluation of the evaluators" ensures a level of internal validity that helps to maintain the integrity of the entire accreditation process.

In the four-step process to accreditation, first administrators of an institution prepare a written evaluation of the institution called a self-study, based on specific standards established by the accrediting organization. Second, an evaluation team of faculty members and administrators from other institutions trained in a review protocol conducts a peer review. Third, the evaluation team conducts a multiday site visit to the institution. The team examines the level of consistency between the self-study and actual practice as determined through personal observation and document review. Fourth, the evaluation team issues a report to the accrediting organization commission in which it cites the strengths and weaknesses of the institution under review, as well as any relevant recommendations. Periodic reviews and updates may be required of the institution prior to the next regularly scheduled review. Most evaluations occur every 10 years, often with two interim reports required (Eaton, 2011).

As with any process that involves control and influence or yields such important consequences as the continuation or noncontinuation of an institution or a program, accreditation can be misused. Specifically, particular social or educational agendas can be advanced through the inappropriate application of accreditation. Young, Chambers, Kells, and Associates (1983) cited several instances when such abuse could occur:

The groups that have most particularly attempted to use accreditation in ways that depart from generally accepted principles are (1) government bodies, both federal and state, that have seen accreditation as a potentially useful regulatory adjunct, (2) professional organizations that have viewed accreditation as a tool for association advancement, and (3) institutions of postsecondary education, or units within them, that have recognized that accreditation can be used as a lever for accomplishing certain institutional purposes. (p. 75)

Governmental entities can misuse accreditation processes to gain compliance with certain federal or state agendas or social policies. As providers of funds, usually in the form of student financial aid, governments place accrediting bodies in the position of serving a quasi-public function. Accreditors are tasked with ensuring that institutions are meeting certain legislative or administrative goals, or in the case of states that institutions are meeting some minimum standard of institutional or programmatic quality to meet state funding or licensing requirements.

Professional organizations can advance their individual agendas through accreditation at the programmatic or disciplinary level. Faculty members and administrators can use the accreditation process to influence evaluators on certain institutional deficiencies and the need for resources to correct them, even if they are not central to the overall quality of the institution. Despite these potential areas of mistreatment, Mayhew, Ford, and Hubbard (1990) exhaustively examined accreditation and concluded that "voluntary accreditation is still the best mechanism for certifying undergraduate quality" (p. 231), despite flaws in the system and the process.

Any discussion of accreditation must mention the role of assessment, as the two concepts are interrelated. Both accreditation and assessment refer to quality assurance and speak to the requirement that each institution and program be accountable for the education it delivers. Assessment, or the measurement of success in achieving desired educational outcomes, emerged as a prominent issue in the late 1980s when former U.S. Secretary of Education William Bennett supported the creation of criteria for student outcomes in the accreditation process. Since then, the practice of assessment has gained momentum and now represents an important component of the overall accreditation process (Ratcliff, Lubinescu, & Gaffney, 2001). Building on others' research, Ratcliff et al. identified four reasons for the focus on assessment: political, economic, educational, as well as societal.

Political reasons include the need of government officials to ascertain that funds allocated to higher education are being used effectively for programs and services. Assessment is seen as a tool to ensure that colleges and universities produce graduates who constitute a well-trained, competent, and competitive workforce—the economic reason. Educational reasons for assessment often come from within higher education and are reflected in the various national reports. In these reports, quality is most often the primary educational reason for implementing assessment. The societal reason refers to the broader public aspect of higher education. Society needs to understand what higher education is offering and how it meets the needs of the public. (p. 14)

The assessment process is intensive and involves professional judgments on a variety of factors. Since assessment processes are intended to collect and interpret information on how effective an institution is in realizing the stated educational outcomes desired of its students, disagreements will occur over why assessment needs to occur, what is to be assessed, how it will be done, how results will be interpreted, and what shall be done with the findings (see Rowntree, 1987). Given today's challenges to improve student outcomes, increase college graduation rates, and respond to society's demands for more accountability in a competitive world, assessment is becoming an important component of the overall accreditation process.

Membership Organizations

We have noted that democratic partnerships within and among colleges and universities are a defining feature of higher education in the United States. Few entities demonstrate the breadth of those partnerships better than the thousands of representative organizations that have been created over the years to support the professional interests of the many and varied constituencies within academe and the shared educational interests of the institutions they serve. In addition to accrediting organizations, three other types of membership organizations exercise important influence over the direction of higher education: regional compacts, consortia, and voluntary institutional membership organizations. Each plays a unique but important role in providing educational services, guidance, and professional development to sustain and propel the higher education enterprise.

Regional Compacts

These organizations were created out of a shared need by multiple states in a geographic region to provide and coordinate certain types of educational services within and across state boundaries. Compacts are legislatively created and are contracted by the states within a region to provide specific educational programs usually not available at traditional colleges or universities. These services can include, but are not limited to, research and policy studies to understand regional educational needs, seminars and workshops on topics of regional interest, and coordination and administration of interstate arrangements to meet specific programmatic goals. Each compact is supported financially by its member states along with private foundations and federal agencies. Membership is derived through acts of individual states' legislatures that are signed by their governors. Each agency maintains a small staff and is governed by a board or commission appointed by the governors of the member states. Today four such regional compacts exist. Listed in order of the dates of their creation, they are the Southern Regional Education Board, 1949; the Western Interstate Commission for Higher Education, 1953; the New England Board of Higher Education, 1955; and the Midwestern Higher Education Commission, 1991. Only New York, New Jersey, and Pennsylvania are not affiliated with one of the four compact organizations.

States' cooperation in these compacts extends to collaboration and cost-cutting measures in a variety of areas, including research and policy studies, international education and student exchanges, graduate and professional education, cooperative purchasing programs, and many others. Harcleroad and Eaton (2005) provide excellent examples of some of the more successful collaborative programs and note the flexibility these compacts provide to their regions as they continually adapt their educational offerings to the changes occurring in our society.

Consortia

Individual colleges and universities can benefit from aligning in consortia as well. Advantages may include building successful legislative lobbying efforts, entering into purchasing collaboratives for utilities or campus services to reduce expenditures, linking computer services in wide-area networks, generating data for institutional decision making, sharing academic programs or faculty expertise, promoting a certain educational goal (such as service-learning), enhancing faculty and administrative development, and a host of other purposes that depend upon mutual support to achieve articulated shared goals.

Consortia, therefore, may assume many forms for many purposes. What they all share is that they are voluntary, derive most of their income from dues or fees paid by member institutions, and generally maintain a small staff headed by a director. Member colleges and universities may be of the same institutional type or may align because of a shared interest in some particular purpose. The value of participation in a consortium rests in the influence the group lends to achieving collective institutional goals, be they political, economic, or programmatic.

The nature of consortia can be tenuous or concrete, depending on the goals to be achieved and the relative usefulness these institutional collectives bring to their member institutions. For example, the former East Central College Consortium in Ohio existed for several decades to promote best practices and collaborative opportunities for the faculty and administrators at about 10 similar private colleges in Ohio and Pennsylvania. In 2009, at a time of tight budget constraints, the consortium was disbanded as its functions were no longer viewed by many of the member institutions' presidents as having the value they did in earlier days.

Conversely, the Association of Independent Colleges and Universities of Pennsylvania continued to enjoy strong member support during a similar time of budget constraints because of its mission as primarily a lobbying organization directed at members of the Pennsylvania state legislature whose votes were essential to continued state support for student financial aid through the Pennsylvania Higher Education Assistance Agency, a program that significantly benefited enrollment figures for the association's member institutions. Though the association serves numerous other important functions for its members, its influence on state government is crucial for its member institutions. These two examples demonstrate how the success of consortia depends on the value ascribed to them by member organizations and how environmental factors can alter that value at any time.

Consortia are not new. The first consortium in higher education was the Ohio College Association, founded in 1867. Other consortia appeared throughout the early 20th century as the need for collaboration became apparent for programmatic and economic purposes. Only in the latter half of the 20th century was there significant growth in these groups, coinciding with the rapid expansion of higher education in the 1960s and 1970s and the emergence of new opportunities for institutions to align on a variety of programmatic and political issues. This increase in the number of consortia prompted the creation in 1965 of an umbrella membership organization called the Council of Interinstitutional Leadership, now known as the Association for Consortium Leadership, which provides a venue for consortia leaders to share ideas, services, and projects and stimulate information sharing between consortia.

The 2011 edition of the *Higher Education Directory* lists 89 major consortia-serving organizations throughout the United States. These groups range in scope from serving institutions of the same type (e.g., independent colleges and universities, community colleges, elite private institutions, state-owned universities) in the same state to providing specific services to meet different individual and organizational needs. For example, in 1982 the state of Connecticut, in conjunction with Connecticut colleges and universities, established the Connecticut Higher Education Supplemental Loan Authority to provide supplemental student loans separate from student financial aid packages. The program enhances opportunities for students to complete their degrees when faced with financial challenges. The Consortium of College and University Media Centers, based at Indiana University, serves as a forum for the improvement of instructional media delivery and academic technology. In addition, the Midwest Universities Consortium for International Activities represents a consortium of three land-grant research universities: Ohio State University, Michigan State University, and University of Minnesota. Founded in 1964 with a grant from the Ford Foundation, its purpose is to provide a variety of educational and technical services to international students and foreign governments and universities. These are but three examples of the varied nature of consortia and the important purposes that are fulfilled through joint cooperation made possible by formalized relationships.

Institutional Membership Organizations

Voluntary membership organizations exist to support the mission and interests of all types of colleges and universities and their disciplines and academic programs. While compacts represent the collective interests of certain states within a region as they relate to the provision of shared educational services, and consortia tend to be alliances of a limited number of institutions benefiting from a collaborative relationship, institutional membership organizations tend to be more national in scope with a broader base of participation and a more focused agenda conforming to the specific needs and issues confronting like institutions. Consequently, these collectives mostly reflect specific institution types as well as the various constituencies that serve them. As they most often represent institutions and constituencies on a national and even an international level, their influence is significant and their impact on the improvement and growth of higher education is considerable. Many of the largest and most powerful of these organizations are based in Washington, DC.

The impact that these organizations have on the direction of higher education in general and their member institutions in particular is significant. Organizations that serve an umbrella function to represent the collective interests of all of higher education are especially powerful. For example, the American Council on Education (ACE) serves as the singular voice of over 1,800 accredited colleges and universities and provides a host of programs and services to improve U.S. higher education. Founded in 1918, ACE has sponsored numerous commissions and committees to address such issues as educational quality and access, gender equity, and institutional leadership. It plays an important role in influencing legislation on higher education and helped to pass the Post-9/11 GI Bill, otherwise known as the Yellow Ribbon Program, to provide financial aid for veterans of the Iraq and Afghanistan conflicts. ACE also developed and administers the General Education Development high school educational equivalency testing program, and in conjunction with the Carnegie Foundation and the College Board, it founded the Educational Testing Service. In addition to its role as a membership organization for so many colleges and universities nationwide, ACE performs the role of consortium, serving as coordinator for about 50 national higher education membership organizations that collectively meet monthly to discuss issues and policies affecting higher education nationally. Called the Washington Higher Education Secretariat, the group produces work that holds significant importance as Congress continues to examine the federal government's role in such matters as student financial aid, support for research, institutional accountability, and student outcomes, and higher education's collective response to the policies that it may propose.

Numerous other major membership associations represent the interests of subsets of institutions. These organizations include the Association of Public and Land-Grant Universities (formerly the National Association of State Universities and Land-Grant Colleges), the National Association of Independent Colleges and Universities, the Council of Independent Colleges, and the American Association of Community Colleges, to name a few. Occasionally referred to as *sector associations*, they exist to promote the mission and interests of the institutional types they represent, including representing their sectors to legislators and policy makers, sponsoring national forums for members to exchange ideas and best practices, and representing their sectors to the public at large.

Promoting institutional mission can also be an important function of associations such as the Association of American Colleges and Universities, which has responded to the growing national focus on vocationalism by taking an active role in highlighting the value and importance of liberal learning and the unique place liberal arts colleges have in building an educated citizenry. Most associations provide ongoing communication and updates for their membership on a host of issues and developments, and those associations, whose primary purpose is influencing national higher education policy, involve their members in lobbying messages to members of Congress. These associations derive their funding predominantly through membership dues, grant support, and sponsorships by vendors whose products and services may benefit the operations of member institutions.

Professional Membership Organizations

Still other associations focus on constituencies in higher education and support their professional interests. The Association of Governing Boards of Universities and Colleges, for example, serves as a national resource for institutional governance issues and trusteeship, with special focus on the relationship between trustees and presidents. In addition to producing the monthly magazine *Trusteeship*, the association sponsors conferences and forums on effective institutional governance and provides professional experts for consulting services. The National Association of College and University Business Officers (NACUBO) is the representative voice of chief financial officers and controllers. In addition to its regular meetings at which members can share best practices, NACUBO provides research and data on a host of topics to support institutional financial decision making. This is especially useful to campus leaders who must make a variety of financial decisions but lack comparative data with other institutions that can lend a point of reference. The work of NACUBO is essential in providing these data. Moreover, admissions professionals have the National Association for College Admission Counseling; development officers, communications professionals, and alumni directors can tap the services of the Council for the Advancement and Support of Education; and registrars often belong to the American Association of Collegiate Registrars and Admissions Officers. Beyond this sample of the hundreds of professional membership associations that support higher education and its administrative functions, scores of membership associations exist for faculty members and the many academic disciplines they represent. Such associations often possess strict criteria for individual membership and lend considerable influence in maintaining the currency and quality of academic content taught in the classroom.

Together, these associations represent a significant influential force on the future direction of higher education, which could not be realized without them. They provide a venue for the professional exchange of ideas, issues, and best practices among their members; they influence how governmental policy is developed; and they offer their members a variety of services and resources to support the missions and functions they represent.

Foundations

Foundations are playing an increasingly important role in furthering individual, organizational, and national goals for postsecondary education that are consistent with their philanthropic purposes. Colleges and universities serve as engines of social change and therefore are a significant beneficiary of the resources foundations provide. According to the Giving USA Foundation (2011), foundations provided all grantees about $41 billion in 2010 or 14% of the total dollars donated. Of that, $8.4 billion was donated to colleges and universities, which represented 30% of all gifts to higher education in 2010 (Council for Aid to Education, 2011). This impressive level of support was made possible by a variety of foundations, including independent, corporate, community, and operational foundations established to support special purposes. The funds provided to U.S. colleges and universities from these sources help institutions shape their programs and educational outcomes in meaningful ways.

Foundations in some form have existed in the United States since colonial days, but they rose in prominence and impact following the Civil War, when wealthy industrialists employed vast discretionary personal assets to meet a variety of philanthropic interests. According to Kiger (2000), Benjamin Franklin is credited with creating the earliest form of a foundation when he established two trusts, one in Boston and the other in Philadelphia, the earnings from which were to provide loans to young inventors of "good character" (p. 40). Around 40 years later in 1829, Englishman James Smithson left a large bequest to the United States to promote the creation and dissemination of knowledge; an act of Congress established a museum and research programs with his gift. Because of Smithson's philanthropy, U.S. citizens enjoy free exhibits and services at the Smithsonian Institution in Washington, DC.

At the end of the 19th and beginning of the 20th centuries, wealthy industrialists such as George Peabody, Andrew Carnegie, and John D. Rockefeller provided sizable sums of their vast fortunes to create foundations expressly intended to meet a variety of social needs, most prominent among them education and research. Carnegie is most often viewed as the father of the philanthropic foundation, having established a prototype with the Carnegie Institution of Washington in 1902 with an initial corpus of $10 million, soon followed by the Carnegie Corporation of New York in 1911–1912. Over the next 40 years, many of today's most prominent national foundations—many of which provide significant support to higher education—were established, including the Russell Sage Foundation, created in 1907; Rockefeller, in 1913; Kellogg, in 1930; and Ford, in 1936. Together, these earliest major foundations significantly contributed to the improvement of society in general, and colleges and universities have been among their many beneficiaries.

There are four types of foundations, each of which is distinguished by its purpose and source of funds. Independent foundations represent the largest group, and most of the wealthiest and well-known national foundations are of this type, such as the Kresge Foundation, the Kellogg Foundation, and the Bill and Melinda Gates Foundation. These independent foundations possess significant assets and provide grants to a wide range of programs and purposes and are reflective of the philanthropic interests of the benefactors who created them. Smaller family foundations that dispense less substantial grants for charitable purposes can also be classified under the heading of independent foundations.

Community foundations serve an urban or regional area and derive their assets from multiple sources, most often residents and businesses in their vicinity. These foundations are repositories for philanthropic dollars intended to meet local needs in either a restricted (earmarked) or unrestricted fashion and play an important role in furthering the philanthropic climate of many communities. Corporate foundations are formed to meet corporate philanthropic interests, and often do so on a quid pro quo basis, meaning that the recipient of corporate foundation funds is engaging in an activity that also benefits the company itself, either directly or indirectly. Operating or special purpose foundations are established to provide a funding stream to a single organization and occasionally may make grants to outside interests. Over the years colleges and universities have derived grant funding from all four types of foundations, often with the most influential grants being made by the large national independent foundations that share specific programmatic interests and goals.

According to McIlnay (1998), foundations are among the least understood of organizations: "Inaccessibility, secrecy, and uncooperativeness have long characterized the behaviors of foundations" (p. 6). In part, this lack of understanding stems from the personal nature of foundations, since they represent the application of private funds to meet the specific interests of their benefactors. One could argue that the need for discretion and privacy by foundations results from the significant influence they exert in society and the favored tax status they enjoy, even when the government may not share the specific goals some foundations promote. This lack of transparency had been particularly challenging for nonprofit organizations applying for foundation funding in earlier decades. However, the emergence of a grant-seeking profession in which specialists identify and seek funding for the nonprofit sector, together with more centralized information sources about grantors and their giving priorities, has aided in fostering greater understanding and transparency of foundations. "In the 1970's the lack of information on foundations became so pronounced that a whole grantsmanship industry sprang up to provide information to grantseekers that foundations could not or would not furnish" (McIlnay, 1998, p. 7).

McIlnay (1998) identified six roles or faces foundations assume as they carry out their philanthropic missions: judges, editors, citizens, activists, entrepreneurs, and partners. They are active participants in the process of social change and through their philanthropy can direct policy, shape outcomes, and improve society in important ways on global and local levels. For example, the Bill and Melinda Gates Foundation (2012) held over $33 billion in assets in 2009 and is focusing much of its significant wealth on issues of global health and economic development worldwide. The foundation's U.S. programs center on enhancing social mobility and opportunity with special emphasis on projects to improve public education.

But local and regional foundations are making enormous impacts as well. With over $20 million in assets, the much smaller Marion G. Resch Foundation of economically depressed Youngstown, Ohio, is making enormous strides in helping underserved inner-city children prepare for and access higher education. The Resch Foundation is a partner with several area colleges that work with elementary and high school students to provide a variety of early intervention programs designed to enhance future college matriculation. Scholarship support from the foundation is also provided for those students who successfully advance to college. As the focus on educational outcomes grows, the role of foundations will become even more important to colleges and universities in the future as reduced government funding places greater demands on academic institutions to secure private funding to support their varied educational missions.

Conclusion

Colleges' and universities' diverse missions; the numerous higher education constituencies that must interact in a democratic and shared fashion; and the ever changing social, political, and economic environment in which academic institutions operate all serve as reasons for the emergence and growth of external organizations that orbit the higher education enterprise. Higher education institutions depend on these ancillary organizations for the direction, coordination, and resources to fulfill their educational purposes.

The very presence of these external organizations reinforces the three main principles that serve as the foundation for this book, and their influence is substantial. The many challenges confronting U.S. higher education today can be resolved not through the independent efforts of each college or university, but through collective efforts to identify those challenges, research responses, implement solutions, and assess outcomes. Ongoing concern for and commitment to ensuring access and affordability, enhancing educational quality, improving graduation rates, and producing an enlightened citizenry require ongoing attention by external organizations and stronger partnerships between them and the institutions they serve.

References

Bill and Melinda Gates Foundation. (2012). *2009 annual report.* Retrieved from http://www.gatesfoundation.org/annualreport/2009/Pages/consolidated-state ments-of-financial-position.aspx

Bloland, H. G. (1999). Creating CHEA: Building a new national organization on accrediting. *The Journal of Higher Education, 70*(4), 357–388.

Council for Aid to Education. (2011). *Voluntary support of education, 2010.* New York, NY: Author.

Council for Higher Education Accreditation. (2011). *The condition of accreditation: U.S. accreditation in 2009.* Retrieved from http://www.chea.org/pdf/Condi tion_US_Accreditation_in_2009.pdf

Eaton, J. S. (2011). *An overview of U.S. accreditation.* Retrieved from Council for Higher Education Accreditation website: http://www.chea.org/pdf/Overview% 20of%20US%20Accreditation%2003.2011.pdf

Giving USA Foundation. (2011). *Annual report on philanthropy for the year 2010.* Chicago, IL: Giving USA Foundation.

Harcleroad, F. F. (1980). *Accreditation: History, process, and problems* (AAHE-ERIC/ Higher Education Research Report No. 6). Washington, DC: American Association for Higher Education.

Harcleroad, F. F., & Eaton, J. S. (2005). The hidden hand: External constituencies and their impact. In P. G. Altbach, R. O. Berdahl, & P. J. Gumport (Eds.), *American higher education in the twenty-first century* (pp. 253–283). Baltimore, MD: Johns Hopkins University Press.

Higher Education Directory. (2011). Reston, VA: Higher Education Publications.

Kiger, J. C. (2000). *Philanthropic foundations in the twentieth century*. Westport, CT: Greenwood Press.

Mayhew, L. B., Ford, P. J., & Hubbard, D. L. (1990). *The quest for quality: The challenge for undergraduate education in the 1990s*. San Francisco, CA: Jossey-Bass.

McIlnay, D. P. (1998). *How foundations work*. San Francisco, CA: Jossey-Bass.

Post-9/11 Veterans Educational Assistance Act of 2008, Pub. L. No. 110-252, H.R. 2642.

Ratcliff, J. L., Lubinescu, E. S., & Gaffney, M. A. (2001). *How accreditation influences assessment*. San Francisco, CA: Jossey-Bass. doi:10.1002/he.1.abs

Rowntree, D. (1987). *Assessing students: How shall we know them?* New York, NY: Nichols.

Servicemen's Readjustment Act of 1944, Pub. L. No. 78-346, 58 Stat L.284.

Young, K. E., Chambers, C. M., Kells, H. R., & Associates. (1983). *Understanding accreditation*. San Francisco, CA: Jossey-Bass.

PART THREE

THE BOUNDARY SPANNERS

The important role colleges and universities are assigned in our society and the tradition of internal shared governance they operate under prompts a corollary that is particularly salient for leaders of higher education organizations. The corollary states that multiple interest groups, within and beyond the organization, will hold a vested interest in the decisions rendered in fulfillment of each institution's mission. The task of understanding and accommodating constituencies' interests in support of the institution will fall to the president and board of trustees, who must interpret the institution's goals, values, and direction even when they may not be in alignment with constituent preferences. Presidents and boards must effectively navigate the political waters of interorganizational and intraorganizational interest groups in fulfilling their operational and fiduciary responsibilities to achieve success. As each constituency in the higher education decisional framework operates in its own sphere of influence and self-interest, adept leaders must carefully span the boundaries that separate them and tactfully coordinate and fashion unity toward a common cause that takes into account not only the mission of the institution but the multiple agendas it serves.

Boundary-spanning activity requires sensitivity and fortitude. A thorough understanding of one's role as chief executive or trustee is a prerequisite to success in managing and overseeing the disparate groups that constitute today's colleges and universities. But effectiveness is also determined by an understanding and appreciation of the self-interests and constituent agendas that underlie the organization's total stakeholder universe. Guided by strong determination and conviction to support the mission of the institution, even in instances where doing so can result in significant conflict, boundary spanners must fundamentally be able to anticipate the consequences of any decision based upon their knowledge of the players and the motivations that guide their behaviors. Part Three of this book attempts to provide the reader with useful insights and tools to do so.

Chapter 9 addresses the roles and responsibilities of the men and women who serve on boards of trustees and in whose hands the life of an institution legally rests. Following a brief overview of the history of lay governance—a history unique among higher education organizations throughout the world—different types of boards are discussed. Recognizing the importance of understanding the role of boards in the governance structure, we give considerable attention to the responsibilities boards assume when responding to the call for service and the need to assess their effectiveness periodically in meeting those responsibilities. A central theme throughout is the importance that board members must lend to the relationship between them and their principal boundary-spanning partner, the president.

Chapter 10 accelerates the momentum of our discussion of boundary spanners to the point of central impact on any college campus, the academic presidency. Though some would argue that the power and influence of college presidents is limited within the framework of shared governance, few sitting presidents today would concur. The college or university president sits in a unique position to mold and guide his or her institution in important ways, while serving as the crucible for all whose parochial demands beg to be considered. As in chapter 9, attention is given to the concept of role, how the academic presidency has changed over the years, and what lies ahead for those aspiring to its rewards and challenges. Boundary-spanning behaviors will be addressed as part of our ongoing theme of creating democratic partnerships in fulfillment of institutional missions. Finally, the chapter speaks to the need for mentorship of future academic leaders given the rising challenges confronting U.S. higher education. The demands upon the presidency are increasing, and fewer people are aspiring to the position given the rising stress-benefits ratio. This trend is regrettable because the opportunity to make an important difference in the lives of many resides with those willing and able to serve in this exciting and dynamic role.

9

TRUSTEESHIP

The theme of this book is that the adoption of three essential principles contributes significantly to a college's or university's success: adherence to institutional mission, skill at adapting to environmental change, and encouragement of democratic partnerships with the constituencies being served. These themes collectively represent a fundamental pursuit of an alignment of organizational goals and values with educational purposes, and the consequential benefits to society for which the institution was originally created. Colleges and universities serve the public good as influential centers of intellectual, social, cultural, and economic development. The importance society ascribes to higher education and the benefits derived from it cannot be overstated, yet the ultimate responsibility for the operation, growth, and success of our nation's colleges and universities falls not to professionally trained administrators but to a special group of volunteers: the men and women who make up each institution's board of trustees.

Boards of trustees hold in trust the financial, physical, and intellectual assets of the institution, a responsibility that cannot be delegated to others. Boards must approve and execute the institution's mission, interpret the institution to its publics, and span boundaries between and among internal and external constituencies served by the organization. As Novak and Johnston (2005) explained,

> Trustees are guardians of the public trust in that boards of trustees, rather than government officials, govern our colleges and universities. They are responsible for ensuring that the institutions will serve the purpose for which they were designed, that they will fulfill their missions and serve the public good by creating an educated citizenry, contributing to the creation of knowledge, and preserving cultural heritages. [Trustees] serve as the bridge between higher education and society. (p. 89)

That we have entrusted the welfare of these complex and highly professional-ized organizations to a group of volunteers who quite often lack the academic credentials or educational administrative experiences to render informed judgment over the affairs of the academy strikes some as inappropriate. For example, Brown University President Francis Wayland asked in 1855, "How can colleges prosper, directed by men, very good men to be sure, but who know about every other thing except about education?" (as cited in Rudolph, 1962, p. 172). Despite such doubts, this model of governance is based in centuries-old tradition and utilitarian purpose that have actually reinforced and nurtured the unstated social contract that exists between colleges and universities and the society they serve.

A board must adhere to its institution's mission, interpret the environ-ment to the institution, and ensure strategic linkages to the many consti-tuencies it serves. It is unrealistic, however, to assume that volunteer board members—who often lack intimate knowledge of the nuances of shared gov-ernance, most often are not educators themselves, and convene in board meetings only infrequently—can fully understand and execute decisions in the best interests of the college or university they serve without some mecha-nism of expert support. That support is most often manifested through the institution's president.

The central relationship for effective lay governance and institutional operation, therefore, is found between the board and the institution's chief executive officer. This relationship represents the fulcrum institutional gov-ernance primarily hinges on, and the literature on boards of trustees is replete with references to the criticality of the symbiosis between the two. Any dis-cussions of lay governance and the service that volunteer boards render to higher education are essentially also discussions of presidential leadership and the interaction that exists, or in some cases may not exist, between a board and a president.

This chapter provides an overview of trusteeship and the unique and important role lay governance plays in U.S. higher education governance. This review deals primarily with the role of volunteer boards in independent and public nonprofit institutional settings rather than corporate board struc-tures and issues associated with proprietary and for-profit institutional mod-els. We begin with an overview of the historical foundations lay governance in U.S. higher education was built on, from the earliest colonial colleges through the emergence of public institutions. Key differences between pri-vate and public boards are addressed, along with the role of multicampus coordinating boards. Contemporary board models and characteristics are also explored briefly, as are typical roles and responsibilities of trustees. We then address the issue of board effectiveness, especially relationships that exist between a board and its institution's president. Finally, we review challenges facing governing boards today, as higher education adapts to changing economic and governmental conditions.

Historical Foundations of Lay Governance

The concept of lay governance is a societal and organizational manifestation of the value that people have placed on education over the ages. It answers this fundamental question: If education serves as the primary mechanism to advance humankind, then who should be responsible for ensuring the fulfillment of that purpose? The answer to this question has varied depending on the specific goals of education over the millennia, the types of organizations created to achieve those goals, and the historical contexts that have shaped human intellectual expression.

The importance of educational institutions to the advancement of society required a body charged with performing fiduciary oversight of them, entrusted with the responsibility of perpetuating human progress through these institutions. The presence of a fiduciary implies there is also a beneficiary. Throughout the history of higher education, that beneficiary has been society itself, while the role of the fiduciary has been ascribed to an institution's governing board. The terms *governing board, board of trustees, directors, regents,* and *overseers* are often used interchangeably to denote fiduciary groups responsible for lay governance. The term *lay* is derived from the Greek word *laos,* which means "people" and refers to individuals who are not clergy or professionally trained in a specific discipline. Lay governance, therefore, involves a group of nonprofessionals performing a public responsibility.

Lay governance originated in the early Middle Ages in Europe and was developed to provide a system of checks and balances to thwart the formation of an intellectual monopoly and to preserve the public's interest as a counterbalance to faculty self-interest. The period following the Protestant Reformation of the 16th century was most noteworthy in the development of educational governance structures that served as future models in the North American colonies of the 17th and 18th centuries. Prototypes of early American colonial boards emerged in Italy, the Netherlands, and Scotland following the Reformation, when lay leaders replaced clergy in the control and exercise of religious policy (Zwingle, 1980). Dutch Protestants in Leyden created governance mechanisms that were important precursors to modern lay boards. According to Duryea and Williams (2000),

> In effect, Leyden and three subsequent Dutch universities set a pattern of organization that anticipated much of the organization later employed in American higher education. The curators represented the government and, at the same time, conveyed to it the interests of the colleges. They were chosen from the higher official ranks, renowned lawyers and members of parliament, not unlike the American pattern. (p. 74)

The U.S. pattern of lay governance emerged with the founding of Harvard College in 1636 and served as a precedent for governance structures at subsequent colleges and universities. Hofstadter (1955) noted three factors that contributed to this development. First, strong Roman Catholic clerical influence over medieval society and its institutions was supplanted by greater lay control with the rise of the Protestant Reformation, a trend that carried over to the New World when settlers first came to our shores. Just as authority in the fledging churches of the colonies was shared between laypeople and clerics, the early Protestant-formed colleges also followed this model. Second, the very limited resources of that era required the colonial colleges to embrace the involvement of wealthy merchants and people of societal prominence to support their educational mission and growth. Third, unlike the established universities of Europe, which enjoyed an influential and highly learned faculty, early American colleges employed relatively young people as teachers who viewed teaching as a means of ascension to more lucrative and influential positions in society. Oversight of these young teachers was thereby relegated to laypeople of greater maturity and stature in cooperation with a college's president.

Central to any discussion of the history of lay governance is the nexus between public and private purposes and the exercise of authority in the oversight of an academic institution. It was emphasized earlier that societal benefits served as the impetus for the founding and growth of higher education institutions in the American colonial period, and the earliest trustees were empowered to ensure that colonial colleges fulfilled this role. These institutions operated within a broader societal context despite their decidedly sectarian affiliation.

> Neither the colonial governors nor the legislators looked upon the colleges as private associations removed from control by the state; rather, they considered them to be public agencies. Leaders of that time had no basis for

thinking otherwise; English law had yet to recognize a distinction between public and private corporations. (Duryea & Williams, 2000, p. 64)

That distinction effectively changed in 1819 when the U. S. Supreme Court handed down a landmark decision in *Dartmouth College v. Woodward* (1819), better known as the Dartmouth College Case (see chapter 6, pp. 139–140). The Supreme Court ruled in favor of Dartmouth, affirming the authority of its independent governing board in overseeing the institution. That seminal decision established a distinction between nonprofit private corporations (e.g., private colleges and universities) and public sector institutions, which had been created and funded by state governments (Hendrickson, 1999). The case also supported the legitimacy, and ultimately the permanent and subsequent practice, of lay governance in both private and public U.S. higher education.

Since the Dartmouth Case, the practice of lay governance has evolved substantially as higher education itself has changed over the years. This evolutionary process has been marked by periods of significant tension as boards and their members have adjusted to monumental changes to U.S. higher education, such as the rise of the public university, the maturation and changing role of faculty in institutional decision making and its subsequent challenges to lay authority, and the demise of the doctrine of in loco parentis as a more consumerist and pluralistic society supplanted older, more traditional norms of authority on campus. A major consequence of these changes has been a shift in the scope of interactional relationships required of boards of trustees. Early boards largely served in an authoritarian manner, unencumbered by challenges or demands from others within and beyond their institution. Today's boards of trustees must be adept boundary spanners in the context of shared governance, responding to constant internal and external challenges to an institution's mission, direction, and fiscal viability over which trustees hold final control. The consequent increasing difficulty of trusteeship has prompted greater attention and devotion to the understanding and improvement of trusteeship in recent decades. Whereas the earlier literature on lay governance appeared to center on a board's roles and responsibilities, later scholarship has demonstrated greater concern for issues of practice and effectiveness.

Public, Private, and Coordinating Boards

Three primary types of governing boards are predominant. They include single-campus boards that oversee an individual public or private institution.

Next, some boards govern multicampus systems in a state, often in conjunction with a single systemwide executive. Finally, most states now maintain coordinating boards or councils that serve a broader state policy function but operate independently of any individual college or university or state system. As their name implies, they play a coordinative rather than governing role and are linked to a state's legislative educational agenda. A relatively recent addition to higher education governance, coordinating boards differ significantly among the states in terms of their purpose, responsibility, structure, and authority, but most share in some budgeting and resource oversight, especially in matters of implementing budget policy to meet specific state purposes.

Community colleges often fall under the control of coordinating boards. Such control may exist separate from or in conjunction with local jurisdictional oversight, as some community colleges operate under local governance and fiscal control. Given the fiduciary rather than public policy role single- and multicampus boards perform, our focus here is on these types of boards rather than coordinating boards.

Some significant differences exist between boards of private, independent institutions and public institutions. Most notable is the selection method for board members:

> Self-perpetuating boards (those that select themselves) govern most independent, private institutions of higher education. Trustees determine the structure and stature of the board and select individuals to fit institutional or system-wide needs. Most public college or university boards, on the other hand, serve explicitly for and at the request of an external public constituent or set of constituents. (Longanecker, 2006, pp. 95–96)

The greatest challenge for public board members is the political environment they operate in, which often influences their selection to the board in the first place. Selection to public boards is most often performed through the state governor's office and may be based on the meritorious qualifications of an appointee or as a function of political patronage. "Publicly appointed governing boards serve multiple masters, but the expectations of those different masters are not always clear" (Longanecker, 2006, p. 106). For appointees, difficulties arise when

> boards are beholden to the governor as the appointing authority but legally and ethically beholden to their institution or system. This is a complex role, for two reasons. First, many governors are uncomfortable with their

relationship with their state's higher education system. . . . Second, higher education often is not a high priority for governors. (p. 105)

This discomfort was confirmed by Dorman (1990), who measured higher levels of role stress in trustees who were appointed to board service than in those serving on a self-perpetuating board.

Another difference between private and public boards rests with the institutional agenda. During times of fiscal stability, all types of boards have relative autonomy in serving the fiduciary function of the institution. As resources for higher education diminish and budgets tighten in the wake of the United States' growing national debt and recessionary times, public board decision making is becoming more constrained and susceptible to external constituent and legislative pressures. The environmental circumstances facing public boards today are increasingly calling their institutions' missions and identities into question: "One of the biggest challenges resulting from decreased state funding for public universities is to what extent they will remain public" (Novak & Johnston, 2005, p. 91).

Although independent boards are less susceptible to the state policy vagaries faced by public institutions, they also face challenges in governance in times of economic uncertainty. According to an Association of Governing Boards of Universities and Colleges survey (AGB, 2009a), private boards' operational effectiveness and ability to recruit new board members for service is increasingly compromised as resources become more constrained. Generally speaking, governance differences between public and private boards are based "on the size of their institutions' annual budgets. Often those with the smallest budgets reported fewer of the best practices the survey covered" (p. 2).

Roles and Responsibilities of Governing Boards

That a group of laypeople serving on a volunteer basis possesses ultimate control over an enterprise as vital to society as higher education introduces a set of organizational dynamics that has challenged college and university administration since the doors of Harvard College opened in the 17th century. These challenges have frequently originated from the ambiguity of board members' roles—to exercise legal responsibility over an organization that requires expertise they often do not hold, engage with campus power structures they often do not understand, and take actions on management decisions they often did not participate in. Board members rightly question the value and impact they as individuals bring to their board's operation, and how they conduct themselves separately or with their colleagues as a corporate body serves as the basis for the majority of scholarship about boards of trustees.

The notion of role is more than a set of job descriptors or responsibilities. Rather, Banton (1965) defined role as "a set of norms and expectations applied to the incumbent of a particular position" (p. 29). These norms and expectations can be assigned by the incumbent in the position, by others related to the position, or both. A lack of agreement between the incumbent and others related to a particular position can inhibit optimum board function, a subject explored by Dorman (1990) as it related to trusteeship at four major research universities. Though Dorman's study was represented as an initial examination of board perceptions of the trustee role as it related to role effectiveness, subsequent research suggests that enhanced efforts to articulate and orient trustees to their appropriate role significantly enhances board effectiveness (see, for example, AGB, 2009a; Dika & Janosik, 2003; Kezar & Tierney, 2006).

The issue of trustee role is best addressed at the outset of the selection process, with reinforcement through a comprehensive orientation prior to the start of board service. At Westminster College in Pennsylvania, a full-day board orientation program includes an extensive examination of the trustee role with particular attention to how trustees (most being business-people) must adapt to a shared governance environment and the significant differences between higher education organizations and other organizational types. Since understanding one's role requires an understanding of the context in which that role is exercised, trustee understanding of the nuances of the academic enterprise with all its constituencies and competing interest groups provides new trustees with a richer experience during their tenure on the board.

An individual's decision to volunteer for a college's or university's governing board carries with it the obligation that the person will suspend individual self-interest in favor of what is best for the institution as a whole. Colleges and universities are among the most enduring organizational creations, and an important role of the trustee is to perpetuate that endurance:

> Whether a board serves public or private higher education or governs a single or a multi-campus system, trustees often lack continuity of perspective—that is, the recognition that they are not simply individuals but part of an ongoing process of institution-building. (AGB, 2002, p. 379)

Too often, individual trustees bring to their board their personal predispositions on how an organization should be run; focus on only one or two issues that elicit personal passion; or, as is frequently the case with alumni serving on their alma mater's board, approach the oversight of the institution through the prism of their own collegiate experience from years past. These trustees perform a disservice to the institution because they neglect the fiduciary responsibility of trusteeship entrusted to them. "Many trustees understand neither the concept of service on a board as a public trust nor their responsibilities to the entire institution" (AGB, 2002, p. 376). It is imperative, therefore, for trustees to be sensitized to this possibility so they may better serve the entire institution and not undermine the work of its president.

A useful list of the main responsibilities of boards of trustees, in an order that approximates the priorities highlighted in subsequent literature on trusteeship (AGB, 2009a; Kezar, 2006), was offered by Nason (1980):

1. Appointing the president
2. Supporting the president
3. Monitoring the president's performance
4. Clarifying the institution's mission
5. Approving long-range plans
6. Overseeing the educational program
7. Ensuring financial solvency
8. Preserving institutional independence
9. Enhancing the public image
10. Interpreting the community to the campus
11. Serving as a court of appeal
12. Assessing board performance (pp. 27–46)

These responsibilities represent five broad governance domains: leadership, mission, finances, external relations, and self-assessment. Of these responsibilities, the selection, support, and evaluation of the president are the most critical.

Ensuring Outstanding Leadership

The articulation of an institution's mission is a fundamental role of its board, while the execution of policies and practices in fulfillment of that mission is the responsibility of its president. As noted earlier in this chapter, the board/president relationship is the fulcrum on which an institution's performance is ultimately hinged. Consequently, selection of the right individual for a college's or university's presidency cannot be overstated as the single most important role of a board. This process must be conducted with the greatest care and attention, beginning with board members' understanding and acceptance of their institution's unique qualities and personality as well as the challenges and aspirations that face the organization. It is not enough for a board to hire a strong leader with the diverse skills necessary to handle the complex challenges inherent in today's academic presidency; a board must also ensure that the presidential candidate's personality is a good fit with the institution's organizational and operational ethos. Members of the entire board, therefore, must be clear and unified in their thinking about the type of leader that will be able not only to advance the institution but reflect the values and norms that distinguish it from its academic peers.

Once a new president is hired, a board must integrate the new president into the life of the institution and monitor that progress to ensure a smooth transition and optimum cooperation between the board and the president. Rita Bornstein (Bornstein & AGB, 2006), retired president of Rollins College and consultant and writer on the president-board relationship, places strong emphasis on the processes that must occur for successful synergy between a president and his or her board. She said, "Strong relationships between presidents and boards are built on communication, education, transparency, and accountability" (p. 1). These relationships are crucial to the long-term success of college and university presidents. Bornstein warned there are

> reports of presidents who undermine their own leadership and sometimes lose their jobs because of errors of omission or commission they make with their boards. These presidents tend to treat their boards in one of two ways: They "protect" trustees and maximize their own authority by providing limited screened information about institutional problems or they overwhelm trustees with excessive, nonessential information and involve them in inappropriate decisions about operations. The first option leads to disengaged and inattentive boards, the second to boards that micromanage. (p. 1)

While the primary responsibility for maintaining a sound board-president relationship falls to the president as the compensated professional responsible for the overall health of the institution, the role of the board's leadership—and most specifically the board chair—in fostering and ensuring a constructive working relationship between the board and the president is also important. Developing and maintaining such a relationship is no easy task, especially for one who serves as a volunteer, with only a tangential comprehension of the key issues and challenges the president faces daily. Despite this tenuous understanding, a board chair serves multiple roles in relation to his or her institution's president. The chair is the primary spokesperson for and representative of the board and functions as the president's direct supervisor. At the same time, he or she must also serve as a colleague to the president in the mutual task of advancing the mission of the institution, and as friend and confidant when the president needs informed counsel, support, or just a sympathetic ear. In short, the board chair must work equally as hard on building his or her relationship with the president as the president does with the board chair.

Boards also hold an important responsibility for monitoring the president's annual performance, preferably against preestablished, mutually agreed-upon benchmarks or goals. Presidential performance is directly correlated to the health and improvement of the institution he or she is responsible for, and a board must monitor not only the professional behavior of the president but the organizational metrics that are a product of the president's leadership. Two glaring failures of proper board oversight of presidential actions in the past two decades are illustrative of the damage that can befall an institution when a board does not fulfill this responsibility. Eckerd College in Clearwater, Florida, experienced a two-thirds decline in its endowment—from $34 million to $13 million—in the 1990s, a time of substantial market gains, because of administrative mismanagement and a lack of proper board supervision. Trust and overconfidence in Eckerd's entrepreneurial president at the time resulted in a failure by the board to question the administration's actions and reports until the financial and reputational damage had become overwhelming (Pulley, 2000). In Washington, DC, actions by American University's board of trustees were the subject of a 2005 Senate investigation into abuse of the institution's nonprofit status when its president was found to have charged hundreds of thousands of dollars of personal expenses to the university and was subsequently granted millions in a severance package upon his termination (Williams, 2005). Although these are among the more newsworthy examples of board inattention to presidential performance, such instances are avoidable with proper board oversight mechanisms. A more complete discussion of presidential performance issues can be found in chapter 10.

Articulating the Institution's Mission

Regardless of institution type and public or private status, the definition and maintenance of institutional mission are the responsibility of the board of trustees, not the administration or the faculty. As the institution's fiduciaries, trustees must ensure that alignment exists among the historical purposes of the institution, the programs it offers, and its academic and other outcomes. The process of institutional accreditation focuses on this alignment to ensure that an institution's stated purposes, as found in its legal and public documents, are in fact being fulfilled. Careful attention is given by accrediting bodies to an institution's mission statement and the degree to which congruence exists between the written statement and the policies, procedures, and practices that support it.

Instances may occur when the trustees, administration, or faculty wish to pursue a new and different institutional direction to meet a programmatic desire or a financial imperative. Such changes should occur following a significant review by the board as part of the institution's overall planning process. Failure to accommodate change through deliberate planning can cause an institution to drift from its stated mission. When the mission statement of an institution requires updating or alteration out of institutional or external necessity, a board should appropriately direct its president to engage the entire campus community in that process to ensure general acceptance of any change. Although a board owns its institution's mission, the campus community must execute it. It is therefore prudent to enter such a process with full deliberation and care to guarantee that the practice of shared governance is respected.

Moreover, throughout any deliberations over institutional mission, a college's or university's board and broader community should remain mindful of the customary view that higher education exists to serve the public good and advance society. Novak and Johnston (2005) describe how trustees can maintain this traditional role in their institution's mission:

> It is appropriate for the board both to promote and to oversee the institution's commitment to public service through the mission. Conversations at the board level can make a significant difference in how institutions serve the public good by adhering to and fulfilling their missions or adapt their missions when appropriate. (p. 93)

Maintaining Financial Solvency

Trustees are responsible for the financial stability of their institution, which they execute in three ways: approving the budget, monitoring the investment performance of the endowment (at private institutions), and establishing a strong philanthropic program while personally contributing to the institution annually at levels commensurate with financial ability. Increased scrutiny of nonprofit organizations' finances by the federal government in recent decades has added an additional layer of responsibility for boards in the area of audits and compliance. Revised federal Form 990, which requires of all institutions a level of documentation of a college's or university's annual financial operations heretofore unseen, has vastly increased the reporting burdens of institutions and has yielded unprecedented transparency into the financial operations of academic institutions.[1] These new requirements were prompted, in part, by nonprofit organizations whose elaborate management and spending practices violated the normative behaviors generally associated with organizations serving the public good.

In addition to federal financial reporting, the annual completion of disclosure statements outlining any potential conflicts of interest by individuals serving on college and university boards has also become accepted practice. The impetus behind this and other efforts to provide greater transparency in college and university governance can largely be attributed to the enactment of the Sarbanes-Oxley Act of 2002, which placed new and more restrictive standards on for-profit corporate boards and accounting firms in the wake of a series of high-profile corporate management and governance malfeasance scandals. Although the law did not extend to nonprofit entities, certain practices and policies stemming from the legislation have been voluntarily adopted by a majority of nonprofit boards as a preventative measure to improve governance and avoid future controversies.

External Relations

A board of trustees has a special obligation to the various constituencies, internal and external, served by its institution. As fiduciaries, trustees must serve as the campus community's interpreters of the environmental context of the institution for consistency between the institutional mission and the educational outcomes required by the environment. Likewise, boards must serve as boundary spanners between the institution and the broader society by representing the institution to its various publics.

These interpretive roles require trustees to be accountable in their duties. According to the AGB (2007),

> boards are accountable to (1) the institution's mission and cultural heritage, (2) the transcendent values and principles that guide and shape higher

education, (3) the public interest and public trust, and (4) the legitimate and relevant interests of the institution's various constituencies. (pp. 2–3)

The scope of institutional accountability has grown in recent years as higher education has been scrutinized over issues of decreasing affordability, diminishing access, and increasing questions over the assessment of educational outcomes. Boards have been forced to assume greater prominence in understanding and confronting these issues as part of their routine governance responsibilities. These conditions have convinced some trustees to assume a more activist position in fulfillment of their board responsibilities.

The rise of trustee activism as a reaction to perceived ills in higher education was examined by Bastedo (2006), who argued that "activist trustees see themselves as protectors of a public trust, one that must be reconceptualized in light of what they see as declining academic standards and broad failures of shared governance" (p. 128). Often associated with a conservative political agenda or a desire to implement corporate governance models to counter liberal faculty self-interest, trustee activism is a recent phenomenon that has emerged to diminish the perceived excessive control of faculty members of their own conditions of employment and evaluation of performance (p. 133). At issue is the balance between institutional and public interests, a debate that requires trustees to assume an uncomfortable but necessary boundary-spanning role. This dialogue is important, and it must be conducted in a manner that acknowledges and respects the various spheres of authority that exist on campus. As Bastedo explained,

> If the concept of the public interest remains contested, the real issue of activist trusteeship is not academic standards or tenure or any other specific policy problem. The issue is how these preferences are expressed by activist trustees and what these preferences mean for the power dynamic among faculty, administrators, and trustees. (p. 137)

Self-Assessment

The ambiguities and tensions inherent in service on a board of trustees suggest that mechanisms need to be in place to promote ongoing introspection to ensure that the roles and responsibilities of the board in general, and its members in particular, are being fulfilled. Board self-assessment serves numerous functions, including building cooperation and coherence among and between board members who share in this unique and highly rewarding experience. In addition to examining the functional aspects of a board, self-assessment provides a board with the opportunity to reflect upon its corporate culture, which represents the sum of its many diverse personalities. Board self-assessment seeks to answer these open-ended questions:

1. In what ways are we performing our roles and responsibilities most effectively?
2. What functions of the institution require further understanding?
3. How well are we working collectively as a board?
4. In what ways can our meetings be more productive and substantive?
5. How can we improve our overall effectiveness as a board?
6. How can communication between and among board members improve?
7. How can communication between the president and the board improve?
8. What mechanisms exist to measure our progress as a board?
9. How effective are we in setting and meeting annual goals for the board?
10. In what ways can board leadership be enhanced?

Board self-assessment should occur on a periodic basis. The frequency of such assessments varies by board and can be conducted in association with a standing meeting or at a special board activity such as a retreat. The AGB maintains an extensive library of reference materials at its Washington, DC office and provides consulting services to assist boards in planning and conducting board assessment exercises. According to the AGB (2009a), two thirds of boards assess their overall performance, with public boards doing so more frequently than private boards.

Assessments are not limited to boards in their entirety. Boards are also encouraged to conduct periodic reviews of individual board members or invite members to participate in individual self-assessments of their service, often in conjunction with completion of a term of service and consideration of continuance on the board. Inherently more delicate and personal a process, individual assessments can take many forms and are highly useful and instructive in isolating issues and concerns so that board members may focus on improving their participation on the board. The combination of assessment activities for an entire board and its individual members serves an important purpose in enhancing the quality and effectiveness of trusteeship and is considered a best practice.

Board Effectiveness

The challenges facing U.S. higher education today are among the most acute in our nation's history and will require informed and inspired decision making in the days ahead. Arguably, at no time in the history of higher education has the need for effective board leadership been greater. The increasing price of a college education, decreasing availability of public resources, diminishing access to higher education among all groups, expanding regulatory requirements, burgeoning competition from the for-profit higher education sector, emerging technologies that affect communications and learning modalities, and growing public outcry over the overall worth and effectiveness of higher education are just some of the major issues confronting trustees today. Successful responses to these challenges depend on the effectiveness of governing boards to understand and address such issues in a societal context vastly altered from what it was just a decade ago.

A recurring theme on board effectiveness is collaboration between the president and the board and among the board members themselves (see Bowen, 2008; MacTaggart, 2011). Such collaboration must take into account an appreciation and understanding of the specific roles of the board and the president, and both parties must be adept at executing those roles consistently. With these fundamental relationships operating in harmony, board functionality and, ultimately, effectiveness, are enhanced. The responsibility for achieving this positive relational state among board members and between the board and the president rests with three governance entities: the president; the board chair; and the trustee committee responsible for board membership and orientation, often referred to as the committee on trustees, the membership committee, or the governance committee. It is axiomatic that the selection of the right president, board chair, and individual board members is the most crucial first step in creating an effective board.

Wilson (2005) affirmed the value of a collaborative environment by noting the importance of creating a culture of interconnectedness among board members and the president. Wilson offers 10 governance habits that distinguish a highly effective board from its more typical counterparts: select the right president, select the right board chair, empower the committee on trustees, insist on a strategic vision, set goals and assess performance, understand and monitor academic policy, develop future board leaders, structure the board strategically, embrace board education, and make trusteeship enjoyable. It is important to note Wilson's 10 habits emphasize the composition of a board and the roles of its members, not board processes. This distinction is important because insufficient care and attention to building a collaborative culture on a board can undermine the operational effectiveness of the board as a whole. The president and board chair must devote sufficient time to this task. A collaborative and positive working dynamic in a board can be seriously compromised by the presence of rogue board members or an autocratic chair.

Collaboration between the president and the board, and among the board members themselves, is achieved when it is accompanied by a collective sense of ownership in governance decisions, respecting the roles and responsibilities of both parties. "Trustees must make a conscious decision to create a governance partnership with the president. Moreover, the board's leadership must organize and motivate the trustees as strategic contributors by creating an environment in which the work of the board is integrated" (Wilson, 2007, p. 10). According to Wilson, it is important that this sense of partnership be embedded into the culture of the board:

> The partnership begins to take on character and strength when the president's strategic vision moves from an owned and approved plan to active implementation. The trustees owe the president four things:
>
> 1. A commitment to generate the strategic resources
> 2. Active, assertive and constructive oversight
> 3. Alignment of the work of the board with the president's goals and objectives
> 4. A fair and supportive process of presidential performance appraisal as part of an institutionalized culture of accountability. (p. 12)

The success of this partnership rests in board members' shared commitment to involve, inform, and commit one another to the operational success of their board's strategic vision. Some partnerships fail, Wilson notes, because insufficient effort is applied by either the president or the board to identify and reconcile differences or to adjust individual styles to accommodate the greater good of the partnership relationship.

Harvard's Richard Chait (2006), perhaps the United States' best known authority on lay governance, has observed that the greatest cause of poor board effectiveness centers on how board members interact with the president and with one another. He identified two "culprits" that most often account for substandard governance: boards that are "orchestras of soloists" and boards "which either lionize or trivialize the president" (pp. 10–11). Regarding board members operating in a noncollaborative fashion, Chait argued that "difficulties ensue not because trustees think independently, a hallmark of effective boards, but because trustees proceed independently, based on a self-declared role and a self-determined scope of authority" (p. 10). On how boards conceptualize the president, he noted,

> When a board perceives a president as an indispensable, heroic leader, then trustees disengage from governance or accord the chief executive undue deference—tendencies that some presidents are keen to reinforce. In short order, the trustee's overestimation of presidential importance leads to over-dependence on the chief executive and underperformance by the board. (p. 11)

Both these conditions reinforce the aforementioned need to exercise great care in the selection of a president and board members. These individuals' personal operating styles should value and support the collaborative behaviors that will encourage enhanced board effectiveness.

An example of a relationship between a board and a president in which the board relinquished some of its responsibility for oversight was the controversy that erupted at Pennsylvania State University in late 2011. At that time a retired assistant football coach was indicted on charges of child molestation, some of which allegedly took place on university grounds. The president of the university, Graham Spanier, had been a long-term successful leader of Penn State and had the complete support and trust of the board of trustees. However, when two senior university officials were indicted for perjury in the case, Spanier failed to keep the board fully apprised of the seriousness of the situation and publicly stated his unconditional support for the administrators in question. When the grand jury findings were made public, several questions arose regarding what people knew and when, including the revered head football coach, Joe Paterno. Under great pressure from the public and the media, the board called an emergency meeting and decided to fire Paterno and Spanier, leaving the university without a leader or recognized spokesperson. Based on reports at the time, our understanding is that the chaos that ensued may have been partly avoided if the board had had a better line of communication with the president and had made clear their expectations for full disclosure about pending legal issues. Likewise, if the board had had in place an emergency management plan for handling such a crisis, the university may have avoided the serious damage that was done to its reputation.

The necessity of having the right people in place was noted by Rogers (2005), who emphasized that creating exceptional boards requires exceptional people. It is essential for the president and the board to actively cultivate positive, supportive relationships and act as partners while being sensitive to each other's roles. The importance of institutional leadership as it relates to the special relationship that exists between a college's or university's president and its governing board was further highlighted by a report of the AGB (2006) Task Force on the State of the Presidency in American Higher Education titled *The Leadership Imperative*. The report acknowledged the increasingly challenging and complex environment facing U.S. higher education and asserted that a more symbiotic leadership partnership must characterize future relationships between presidents and their boards. A heightened level of "support, candor, and accountability" (pp. vi–vii) between both entities was viewed as essential in the years ahead if colleges and universities are to effectively address the challenges before them. Substandard or dysfunctional governance practices will interfere with the process of addressing educational and institutional shortcomings that face our nation's colleges and universities. *The Leadership Imperative* is a clarion call to strengthen the board/president relationship: "A president's ability to foster integral leadership . . . inescapably depends upon the board's support and effective oversight. The Task Force is concerned that too few presidents receive from their governing boards the degree of support necessary for courageous and visionary leadership" (pp. 9–10).

In light of the enormous challenges facing higher education today and the growing responsibility of fiduciaries to navigate these perilous waters, Chait, Ryan, and Taylor (2005) argued that institutional leadership should reframe how governance and lay leadership are viewed. Though the concepts of leadership and governance have different meanings, the authors linked the two to assert that lay leaders traditionally empowered with governance responsibilities can assume important roles as institutional leaders without undue encroachment on traditional executive authority. Whereas previous governance literature focused on best practices with an emphasis on process, Chait and his colleagues asserted that we should divide the role of governance into three domains: fiduciary, strategic, and generative. The first two are traditional roles of lay leaders, as described earlier. The third suggests lay leaders adopt practices that anticipate future issues and organizational directions in light of emerging challenges and environmental change. In the past, boards have used committee structures to address organizational operations that are largely managerial in nature, while chief executives have focused on more visionary and planning activities. The authors observed:

> While non-profit managers have gravitated toward the role of leadership, trustees have tilted more toward the role of management. The shift has occurred because trusteeship, as a concept, has stalled while leadership, as a concept, has accelerated. The net effect is that trustees function, more and more, like managers. (p. 4)

A more generative function for trustees refocuses their time and energy on issues relative to the broader context in which their college or university operates, thereby emphasizing their unique place as objective but informed fiduciaries whose primary interest is in the long-term viability of, and vision for, their institution.

Trustee effectiveness can best be achieved when a collaborative environment for governance exists and when trustees themselves are confident and secure in knowing and acting appropriately in their roles. Presidents and board leaders, therefore, must ensure that trustees understand the answer to one fundamental question: What is our purpose as a board? A shared understanding of that answer—along with a team identity resulting from carefully selecting board members and leaders who will operate in a collective, and not individual manner—will significantly contribute to stronger leadership and governance of the institution.

Future Challenges

Numerous conditions challenge U.S. higher education today. In the AGB's (2009b) periodic review of major higher education policy issues facing governing boards, it noted several conditions that will have a profound effect on the character and viability of higher education institutions going forward, such as the recession and weakened financial state of the nation; heightened scrutiny of nonprofit organizations by the federal government; accountability and assessment of student learning; the United States' global competitiveness, changing demographics, and workforce; diminishing federal research support; and more transparency and accountability in higher education governance. As fiduciaries responsible to the institution and the publics served by the institution, boards of trustees will assume heightened importance in the years ahead as they address these environmental challenges within the context of their institutions' missions. The three main principles woven throughout this book—adherence to institutional mission, skill at adapting to environmental change, and encouragement of linkages to the constituencies being served—depend upon good governance to be preserved, and effective governance rests within each trustee.

Note

1. The information provided on these forms can be accessed by the public at www.guidestar.com.

References

Association of Governing Boards of Universities and Colleges (2002). The role of governing boards: Issues, recommendations, and resources. In R. M. Diamond (Ed.), *Field guide to academic leadership* (pp. 375–387). San Francisco, CA: Jossey-Bass.

Association of Governing Boards of Universities and Colleges. (2006). *The leadership imperative: The report of the AGB Task Force on the State of the Presidency in American Higher Education.* Washington, DC: Author.

Association of Governing Boards of Universities and Colleges. (2007). *AGB statement on board accountability.* Retrieved from http://agb.org/sites/agb.org/files/u3/AccountabilityStatement2007.pdf

Association of Governing Boards of Universities and Colleges. (2009a). *The AGB survey of higher education governance.* Washington, DC: Author.

Association of Governing Boards of Universities and Colleges. (2009b). *AGB top public policy issues for higher education in 2009 and 2010.* Washington, DC: Author.

Banton, M. (1965). *Roles: An introduction to the study of social relations.* New York, NY: Basic Books.

Bastedo, M. N. (2006). Activist trustees in the university: Reconceptualizing the public interest. In P. D. Eckel (Ed.), *The shifting frontiers of academic decision making: Responding to new priorities, following new pathways* (pp. 127–141). Westport, CT: Praeger.

Bornstein, R., & Association of Governing Boards of Universities and Colleges. (2006). *The president's role in board development.* Washington, DC: Association of Governing Boards of Universities and Colleges.

Bowen, W. G. (2008). *The board book: An insider's guide for directors and trustees.* New York, NY: Norton.

Chait, R. P. (2006). Why boards go bad. *Trusteeship, 14*(3), 8–12.

Chait, R. P., Ryan, W. P., & Taylor, B. E. (2005). *Governance as leadership: Reframing the work of nonprofit boards.* Hoboken, NJ: Wiley.

Dartmouth College v. Woodward, 17 U.S. 518 (1819).

Dika, S. L., & Janosik, S. M. (2003). The role of selection, orientation and training in improving the quality of public college and university boards of trustees in the United States. *Quality in Higher Education, 9*(3), 273–285.

Dorman, R. (1990). Perceptions of role conflict and role ambiguity held by members of boards of trustees of four research I-type universities (Unpublished doctoral dissertation). Pennsylvania State University, University Park, PA.

Duryea, E. D., & Williams, D. (Eds.). (2000). *The academic corporation: A history of college and university governing boards.* New York, NY: Falmer Press.

Hendrickson, R. M. (1999). *The colleges, their constituencies and the courts.* Dayton, OH: Education Law Association.

Hofstadter, R. (1955). *Academic freedom in the age of the college.* New York, NY: Columbia University Press.

Kezar, A. J. (2006). Rethinking public higher education governing boards performance: Results of a national study of governing boards in the United States. *Journal of Higher Education, 77*(6), 968–1008. doi:10.1353/jhe.2006.0051

Kezar, A., & Tierney, W. G. (2006). 7 elements of effective public-sector boards. *Trusteeship, 14*(6), 29–32.

Longanecker, D. A. (2006). The "new" new challenge of governance by governing boards. In W. G. Tierney (Ed.), *Governance and the public good* (pp. 95–115). Albany, NY: SUNY Press.

MacTaggart, T. (2011). *Leading change: How boards and presidents build exceptional academic institutions.* Washington, DC: AGB Press.

Nason, J. W. (1980). Responsibilities of the governing board. In R. T. Ingram (Ed.), *Handbook of college and university trusteeship* (pp. 27–46). Hoboken, NJ: Jossey-Bass.

Novak, R., & Johnston, S. W. (2005). Trusteeship and the public good. In A. Kezar, T. C. Chambers, & J. C. Burkhardt (Eds.), *Higher education for the public good: Emerging voices from a national movement* (pp. 87–101). San Francisco, CA: Jossey-Bass.

Pulley, J. L. (2000, August 18). How Eckard's 52 trustees failed to see two-thirds of its endowment disappear. *The Chronicle of Higher Education,* pp. A31–A33.

Rogers, B. (2005). View from the board chair: Moving beyond oversight to active board engagement. *Trusteeship, 13*(5), 7.

Rudolph, F. (1962). *The American college and university.* New York, NY: Knopf.

Sarbanes-Oxley Act (2002). Pub. L. No. 107-204, 116 Stat. 745.

Williams, G. (2005, October 31). U.S. Senate to investigate board of American U. over Ladner's compensation. *The Chronicle of Higher Education.* Retrieved from http://chronicle.com/article/US-Senate-to-Investigate/121437

Wilson, E. B. (2005). It all boils down to this . . . *Trusteeship, 13*(5), 8–13.

Wilson, E. B. (2007). Row, row, row the same boat. *Trusteeship, 15*(3), 8–13.

Zwingle, J. L. (1980). Evolution of lay governing boards. In R. T. Ingram (Ed.), *Handbook of college and university trusteeship* (pp. 14–26). San Francisco, CA: Jossey-Bass.

THE ACADEMIC PRESIDENCY

I t can be argued that no single individual in a college or university is more important to the advancement of the institution's mission, adaptation to environmental changes, and development of democratic partnerships than its president. Given these and myriad other expectations of a college or university president, few people can fulfill the role successfully. Clark Kerr (1964), the 12th president of the University of California system and first chancellor of the University of California, Berkeley, had this to say about the academic presidency:

> The university president in the United States is expected to be a friend of the students, a colleague of the faculty, a good fellow with the alumni, a sound administrator with the trustees, a good speaker with the public, an astute bargainer with the foundations and the federal agencies, a politician with the state legislature, a friend of industry, labor, and agriculture, a persuasive diplomat with the donors, a champion of education generally, a supporter of the professions (particularly law and medicine), a spokesman to the press, a scholar in his own right, a public servant at the state and national levels, a devotee of opera and football equally, a decent human being, a good husband and father, an active member of a church. Above all he must enjoy traveling in airplanes, eating his meals in public, and attending public ceremonies. No one can be all of these things. Some succeed at being none. (pp. 29–30)

The role of the academic president has changed dramatically over the centuries. Indeed, it is doubtful that a president of a colonial college would even recognize the presidency today. Whereas in the early years presidents would have played a significant and direct role in the education and training of their institutions' students, guided the curriculum, and had great latitude in the selection of tutors and faculty, today's presidents may never teach a single class, engage in the development of academic curricula, or have a specific role in the recruitment of faculty members. A contemporary college or university president is expected to be first among equals with the faculty, an institutional ambassador to the world, an institution's principal fundraiser, and most of all chief executive officer of a complex enterprise.

Scholars have written widely about the changing role of the academic presidency over the years (Bensimon, 1989; Ikenberry, 2010). Based on the economic, political, and social environments that all colleges and universities are confronting in the 21st century, however, higher education faces a major dilemma. During a time when the need for strong leadership has never been greater, the ability to attract, support, and prepare the next generation of academic presidents has never been more difficult.

Increasing Demand and Diminishing Interest

According to a 2006 study of 2,148 college and university presidents conducted by the American Council on Education (ACE, 2007), the academic presidency will face a major crisis by the end of the second decade of the 21st century. Based on the data collected for this study, the average age of an academic president in the United States has increased from 52 years in 1986 to 60 years in 2006, and the percentage of presidents over the age of 61 grew from 14% to 49% over the same period. It is interesting to note that the study found that other senior leaders of academic institutions are of a similar age. This shift in the average age of college and university leaders suggests that from 2010 to 2020 there will be a large number of retirements and a great demand for professionals prepared to succeed them. While the ACE report noted that a higher percentage of presidents are women and minorities today than 20 years ago, the pipeline for the next generation of leaders is not growing at a pace to keep up with the expected demand.

The position most academic presidents hold prior to becoming the chief executive officer of an institution is provost or chief academic officer (ACE, 2007). Although a higher percentage of presidents, particularly at smaller independent colleges, are coming from nontraditional backgrounds than ever before, the most likely pathway to the academic presidency remains the role of provost (ACE). That being said, a study released by the Council of Independent Colleges reported that fewer provosts are interested in pursuing presidencies than in years past (Hartley & Godin, 2010). According to the study, less than 25% of current chief academic officers at smaller independent colleges and only 30% of provosts overall plan to seek an academic presidency in the future. Their lack of aspiration to the academic presidency seems to stem from the unappealing nature of the president's work, including fund-raising, board relations, and financial management (p. 2).

Even among individuals who have prepared for and successfully obtained an academic presidency, the demands of the job often overwhelm the ablest among them. McLaughlin (1996) found that new presidents are often shocked by the expectations of the position, the exhausting pace they are expected to keep, and the range of issues they are required to address. Because of their close proximity to their presidents, provosts and chief academic officers experience a taste of what it is like to be the chief executive officer of a college or university, and they increasingly say that the job is less appealing than ever before. What has changed over the years to bring about such a negative response from those individuals who historically were most likely to fill the role of president, and what are the implications of this change?

The Changing Nature of the Academic Presidency

Academic presidents have been described in myriad ways over the years. Kerr (1964) referred to them as giants and McLaughlin (1996) called them living logos. Others have gone so far as to suggest that the academic presidency is an illusion (Cohen & March, 1974), and that presidents are the most universal fakers (Sinclair, 1923) who at best might become good bureaucrats. Clearly there exists a panoply of views about the academic presidency, but most agree that the role of the president has changed over the years, and the pace of change has accelerated.

The evolution of the academic presidency parallels major shifts in the academy over the centuries. By the middle of the 19th century, the typical institution of higher education was religiously affiliated, and its leader could be best described as a learned clergyman. In contrast, by the turn of the 20th century, the rise of the secular research university required a new type of leadership—individuals who could deal with increasingly complex organizations with broader goals and enlarged responsibilities (Kerr, 1964; Rudolph, 1962). The transition from a religious focus to a secular orientation, coupled with the increasing desire for new sources of financial support, led to a demand for academic leaders who were financially astute and able to convince foundations and wealthy benefactors that their institution was worthy of investment.

These new responsibilities required an academic leader who could keep one foot on campus dealing with student and faculty concerns and the other foot in the world outside the academy, a world that demanded the university be more relevant to the times. As the university grew more complex, a greater need for organization, standardization, and centralized control emerged. These changes necessitated more administrative oversight and required a new, more sophisticated type of academic leader (Rudolph, 1962).

This reorientation came at a cost, however. Whereas earlier academic presidents could be expected to be deeply engaged in the daily life of the institution they served, this new administrative model gave way to the type of leader Rudolph (1962) described as someone "whose remoteness from the students would be paralleled by his remoteness from learning itself" (p. 418). The remoteness described by Rudolph became the sine qua non of the 20th-century academic president, a leader academically prepared but professionally detached from the daily work of the academy, instead addressing the pressing matters of enrollment, finances, and fund-raising.

By the end of the 1920s the academy had changed dramatically again. The growth of specialized academic departments and the increasing expectation for faculty research productivity were changing the relationship between institutions and their faculties, as well as between their faculties and their students. Universities were being asked to advance knowledge using more sophisticated research techniques and to address global events precipitated by the Great Depression and World War II, such as expanding international commerce and national aspirations.

The societal needs and economic prosperity of the second half of the 20th century in the United States created another set of expectations for higher education. After World War II, U.S. colleges and universities witnessed an unprecedented increase in enrollments as veterans returned from the conflict eager to earn a degree and pursue the American dream. This new national interest in pursuing a college degree, prompted by the GI Bill and perpetuated by changing workforce expectations, produced a growth in student demand that could not be accommodated by existing higher education institutions. This trend led to new models of state and federal funding for student aid and research and expansion of colleges and universities across the nation.

Kerr (1964) described what developed from this changing landscape as a new model of higher education, something he called the "multiversity." To Kerr, this new entity was governed in a fashion similar to "a system of government, like a city or a city-state: the city-state of the multiversity"

(p. 20). He went on to state that this organization may "be inconsistent but it must be governed—not as the guild it once was, but as a complex entity with greatly fractionalized power. There are several competitors for this power" (p. 20), including students, faculty, administrators, and public authority.

This competition for power led to the need for a new type of academic leader who was agile enough to deal with emerging changes in institutional structure and governance—a leader who had the skills and abilities to work with government officials, handle the changing nature of faculty relations, and respond to the increasing demands of students. At the same time, this new academic leader had to possess the financial and managerial skills necessary to deal with the greatest period of expansion and growth in the history of higher education.

The remarkable growth and expansion of higher education that marked the middle of the 20th century gave way to more austere times, during which increasing demands on state and federal funding caused a reduction in the resources available for higher education. This reduced support coincided with an increasing call for greater institutional transparency and accountability. In addition, during this period, colleges and universities experienced increased competition for faculty, funding, and students from sectors outside the academy, including corporations, foundations, and government agencies as well as a growing for-profit higher education sector. This new competition, coupled with an explosion in technological innovations and communication tools, created a new set of expectations for colleges and universities to remain current. When set against a backdrop of a progressively more complicated legal environment, a whole new era for higher education had emerged by the turn of the 21st century.

In light of these rapid changes, it is perhaps not surprising that by the end of the first decade of the 21st century the nature of the academic presidency had changed once again. Twenty-first-century presidents, as an extension of the institution they serve, face far more demands than their predecessors did, including greater competition, increased accountability, and an expectation to be visibly connected to their constituencies, all of which complicates the role. The president whose remoteness from his or her institution was described by Rudolph (1962) in the middle of the last century had been replaced with a new type of president whose connectivity to his or her institution had not yet been envisioned.

Stanley O. Ikenberry (2010) provided a great example of the new level of connectivity expected of a president. After a highly successful tenure as president of the University of Illinois from 1979 to 1995, and as president of ACE for six years, Ikenberry returned to the faculty in 2001. In 2010 after the unexpected departure of the new president of the University of Illinois, he was asked to serve as interim president for one year. At that time, Ikenberry (2010) described how the academic presidency had changed during his 15 years serving on the faculty. He said the greatest change he experienced upon his return to the presidency was the "unrelenting tsunami of electronic communication that now floods the president's office and personal life" (p. 26).

Unlike in previous generations, today's presidential communications are often unfiltered, and given public expectations for a response, the need to react is immediate (Ikenberry, 2010). Ikenberry also cited a more constrained environment in which presidents and governing boards face more ambiguous and daunting challenges than he experienced 20 years ago. Though the challenges are greater and the demands have grown, in Ikenberry's eyes, the most important role of the president has not changed, which is to "help the institution find itself, articulate and embrace its mission and mobilize others toward that vision" (p. 27).

The Role of the Academic President

If we are to understand the role of an academic president in advancing the mission of an institution, we need to understand the limits and uses of presidential power and influence. In the words of Ikenberry (2010), can an academic president really play a major part in helping a college or university find itself? Or is a president only one of many players in a complex web of institutional governance whose impact on the future success of the institution is predicated on how well he or she manages the interests of competing constituent groups?

Several authors have weighed in on this subject. For example, Robert Birnbaum (1988), who studied the academic presidency and then served as chancellor of the University of Wisconsin Oshkosh, has asserted that academic leaders, while important as a group, may have far less influence than most believe. Birnbaum suggested viewing the academic president's role in terms of James MacGregor Burns's theory on leadership that says leaders approach power in two ways, through transformational or transactional leadership. Burns (1978) viewed transformational leadership as when leaders and followers raise one another to higher levels of motivation and morality

(p. 20). Transactional leadership occurs when a leader makes contact with others for the purpose of an exchange of valued things (p. 19).

Birnbaum (1988) viewed transformational academic leaders, therefore, as being able to significantly change the institution they serve if the circumstances are right (p. 205). He believed that those circumstances were often when an institution is facing a crisis and is willing to allow the president to exert extraordinary influence over the decision-making process (p. 205). This type of leader is characterized by self-confidence and an ability to remain aloof from others in the institution to be able to make tough decisions when necessary. Furthermore, Birnbaum (1999) said that transactional academic leaders, on the other hand, emphasize the principle of approaching their work with others as a "fair social exchange" (p. 17) where there is mutual regard and influence. Leaders who use this approach also demonstrate respect for institutional culture and history and recognize that only after fostering a collegial approach to governance can their institution make significant progress (Birnbaum, 1999). While Birnbaum was open to the idea that an academic president can be a transformational leader, he believed that it is the exception, not the rule, and that true institutional transformation in academia usually occurs through good transactional leadership.

Kerr (1964) viewed the academic presidency in a similar fashion. He agreed that as the nature of universities changed over time, the presidency followed suit, with presidents needing to establish a balance of power between their institutions' constituencies, including the board, faculty, and students (p. 34). Unlike Birnbaum, however, Kerr believed that academic presidents could and do have great influence over the institutions they serve. He preferred to see the successful academic president as a highly functional "mediator-initiator," an individual who can "keep the peace and further progress" (p. 38). He promoted the ideas that an academic president should use his or her power delicately, and that the "opportunity to persuade" (p. 40) constituent groups should be commensurate with the responsibility each group possesses.

Kerr (1964) acknowledged that each institution has its own unique history and set of circumstances. Moreover, he recognized that various groups in and outside an institution wield power over it. In Kerr's eyes, successful presidents fostered an environment in which no single constituent group had too little or too much power, and none used that power unwisely. In the end, according to Kerr, effective presidents must encourage cooperation among constituent groups in the hope of moving the whole enterprise forward while reconciling themselves to the harsh realities of a job in which failures are highlighted more often than successes (pp. 40–41).

One of the best ways academic presidents can persuade others to follow the vision they have set for an institution is to surround themselves with a team of executives, often known as a cabinet, who agree on the institution's direction and work collaboratively to promote it. In a study of higher education senior management teams, Bensimon and Neumann (1993) discovered that effective teams viewed leadership as a collective and collaborative process. Too often in higher education most administrators join a group and subsequently assert "their independence from it" (p. 107). In highly functioning teams, the leader creates an environment where members open each other's eyes to new realities, make connections across administrative and academic functions, and forge new understandings about the organization (p. 102). In other words, members of effective collegiate cabinets or teams learn from each other and use that collective knowledge to advance their institution.

Beyond their function as a team leader, academic presidents play several roles, real and perceived. One of the most important roles a president can play is to become a personal symbol of his or her institution's mission, goals, and aspirations, or at least understand how to use appropriate symbols to advance the mission of the institution. Pfeffer (1977) believed all leaders are actors in part who need to learn how to manipulate symbols if they wish to have their roles legitimized by others in the organization. Dill (1982) also found symbolic leadership to be critically important in nourishing and maintaining the culture of an academic organization. The idea that leaders need to act symbolically is important for understanding the role of academic presidents in their institutions, where power and influence must often be shared to advance institutional goals (Dill, 1982; Pfeffer, 1977).

The actions of leaders in an academic environment are open to interpretation by others (Tierney, 1989). Successful leaders understand that everything they do (or do not do) may have meaning to some constituent group, intended or not (Tierney). In this environment, academic presidents can become the personification of institutional goals and objectives by using structural and personal symbols that demonstrate what they value (Tierney). The difficulty, however, is that leaders must interpret the institutional culture correctly, because if they fail to do so, the symbols they use may not make sense to organizational participants, which could send the wrong message and be detrimental to the leader's intended outcome (p. 387).

Demonstrating Respect for Mission and Culture

If the essential role of an academic president is to foster democratic partnerships with key constituents to achieve organizational goals that align with and ultimately support the core mission, then it makes sense that a leader in this context would need to possess certain skills to succeed. Chief among those skills are the ability to demonstrate respect for the university's mission and culture, using personal and structural symbols to advance and achieve the collective institutional vision, and sharing governance effectively and responsibly.

Whenever an academic president makes a decision, the mission and values of his or her institution should be reflected in that decision. This requirement can appear to complicate matters and even make decision making more difficult, but in reality, leaders who understand their institution's mission and can demonstrate that they are living it in their words and deeds are more likely to gain support for the choices they make.

When academic presidents align their actions with institutional values, it can have a powerful and lasting impact on those they serve. Deal and Kennedy (2000) found that corporate leaders who better understand an institution's "culture and core values" (p. 24) are able to create greater unity and a sense of purpose among constituents. Multiple studies of college and university presidents have found that academic leaders are able to accomplish comparable results if they use similar approaches (Bensimon, 1989; Birnbaum, 1988; Padilla, 2005).

Bill Bowen, former provost and president of Princeton University, provided an exceptional example of this type of academic leadership when he guided that institution through its transformation from a single-gender to a coeducational institution. According to Padilla (2005), Bowen was able to accomplish so much because of his ability to articulate and position any proposed change within the context of the university's established values. For example, he created a Priorities Committee of various stakeholders (faculty, staff, students, and administrators) to clarify the university's goals and set priorities to move forward (p. 205). The act of establishing such a committee demonstrated to the Princeton community that Bowen appreciated collegiality and academic excellence, two values that were widely shared by the Princeton academic community. Ultimately, his approach was interpreted by members of the Princeton community as visionary thinking, whereas he viewed it as simply creating a structure to encourage discourse within the university, which in turn produced better results (p. 215).

Another example of a leader demonstrating understanding of her institution's values and mission is Judith Rodin, former president of the University of Pennsylvania. An Ivy League research university, Penn had long ignored its surrounding neighborhood of West Philadelphia. According to

Maurrasse (2001), the horrible socioeconomic conditions of the neighbor-hood—including poor public education, deteriorating housing, rampant violence, and a lack of economic development—made university officials question the institution's relationship with and responsibility to the local community. By the 1990s Penn had established itself as one of the world's greatest research universities through its scientific research driven by federal funding. The importance of engagement with the local community, how-ever, was not an institutional priority and thus was never fully valued (p. 30).

Recognizing this disconnect, Rodin worked with the university commu-nity to create an "urban agenda" (Maurrasse, 2001, p. 31) for Penn, making that agenda one of the six top priorities for the institution. To build consen-sus among key constituents for this urban agenda, Rodin appointed Ira Har-kavy, a Penn graduate and respected university employee recognized as a national leader in the field of community engagement, to be the public face of this effort. She also reminded the academic community of Benjamin Franklin's original vision for Penn: for the university to serve the city of Philadelphia.

This call for a return to the original purpose of the university, coupled with a new interpretation of the part of Penn's mission that addressed the merging of theory and practice into teaching and research, helped stake-holders see that the university had a responsibility to its local community, and that by becoming more engaged, the institution would emerge stronger in the long run (Maurrasse, 2001). A decade later, Penn had estab-lished itself as a national leader in civic engagement and had enhanced its reputation as one of the world's leading research universities. In addition, West Philadelphia has become the focus of a good deal of Penn's research activities and outreach efforts, and the community and the university are stronger for it.

In the midst of creating this urban agenda, Rodin demonstrated her respect for the culture and mission of the University of Pennsylvania in two ways. First, she never suggested that Penn should reduce its emphasis on research to pursue an urban agenda. Instead, she recognized the importance of research and argued that Penn's research activities could be enhanced by focusing more resources on the local community. Second, she encouraged the support of internal constituents and community leaders by hiring some-one who was trusted by both groups to direct Penn's efforts. These actions demonstrated her understanding of Penn's mission and values while simulta-neously advancing a new agenda.

Using Symbols to Advance Institutional Objectives

Rodin and Bowen came to symbolize important advancements at their institutions because they understood that their actions spoke louder than their rhetoric. Examples of how academic leaders have used symbols to promote their work are important reminders of how powerful this approach can be in advancing institutional goals. Bill Friday, former president of the University of North Carolina system, declined pay raises later in his career because he believed the president of the system should not earn more than the governor of the state, as it would send the wrong message to North Carolinians about the university's priorities (Padilla, 2005).

In another example of symbolic action related to institutional finances, Gerald "Carty" Monette, former president of Turtle Mountain Community College in North Dakota, assumed the leadership of a college facing enormous challenges, including a student body that could not afford college tuition payments (Colby, Ehrlich, Beaumont, & Stephens, 2003). To help the college overcome its financial difficulties, Monette worked diligently to raise funds and served without an academic dean until the school had enough money to support the position (Colby et al.). This action was an important symbolic gesture because it demonstrated that his priority was to use the institution's limited resources to keep student costs low and enhance classroom instruction rather than hire more administrators.

Theodore Hesburgh, president emeritus of the University of Notre Dame, accepted the position of chair of the National Civil Rights Commission in the 1960s in the midst of his presidency at Notre Dame. During his tenure, he gave hundreds of speeches around the country to encourage support for civil rights legislation (Padilla, 2005). His actions symbolized the importance of inclusion and diversity at Notre Dame and across the nation.

The actions of an academic president can also serve as a negative symbol of an institution. In 2002 Mark Perkins, former president of Towson University, spent hundreds of thousands of dollars on renovations of a newly acquired presidential home and $25,000 on a medallion to symbolize the authority of the office of the president at official events. To the public these actions symbolized excess and an insatiable appetite to spend university money on items that served only his personal tastes and had nothing to do with his ability to perform his duties as president.

A president's harmful actions can also become a symbol of a problem within higher education more broadly. In 2005, for example, Benjamin Ladner came under national scrutiny when his personal expenses as president of American University were exposed and revealed a lavish lifestyle funded by the university. This scandal led to Ladner's dismissal by American's board, and he came to symbolize the abuse of power by leaders in higher education. His behavior led to changes in board policies at colleges and universities across the nation for better internal controls and greater oversight of university matters.

Even highly successful and talented presidents can become symbols of controversy in spite of the support of many at their institution. For example, in 2009 a group of over 100 college and university presidents joined a national movement called the Amethyst Initiative to call for a review of the national issue of underage drinking. The presidents hoped their action would open the debate on the range of options that could be pursued to address the epidemic of underage drinking on college and university campuses. Unfortunately, no real debate occurred, thanks to powerful organizations such as Mothers Against Drunk Driving, which argued that the presidents were out of line in suggesting that the minimum drinking age might be lowered.

The Amethyst Initiative quickly came to symbolize a movement to lower the drinking age rather than a national conversation about how to deal with a serious social issue. Those who supported the initiative were quickly besieged with negative messages from public interest groups, and pressure was placed on boards to make their presidents rescind their support of such a debate. In the end, no serious national discussion about the issue of underage drinking occurred, with the presidents backing away because of the negative publicity the initiative generated for their institutions and the pressure they received from various groups.

In 2010 E. Gordon Gee, president of Ohio State University and one of the most respected leaders in American higher education, publicly commented on the debate over the Bowl Championship Series (BCS) to determine the Division I national football champion. When the Boise State University and Texas Christian University (TCU) football teams, both from football conferences that did not automatically qualify for the BCS, were ranked in the top 10 nationally and had the potential to play for a national championship, Gee stated they should not be allowed to do so because their game schedules were weak compared to those of schools such as Ohio State. He even went so far as to describe the competition on the schedule of those two schools as the Little Sisters of the Poor.

When TCU won the Rose Bowl by beating the University of Wisconsin—the Big Ten champion, which had beaten Ohio State—some TCU boosters bought billboards throughout Ohio congratulating TCU and mocking Gee's quote. To those who wished to change the championship series, this episode came to symbolize what was wrong with the entire system and demonstrated that Gee was out of touch. To those who still believed Gee was right, one major bowl victory for TCU did not justify a wholesale change in the system.

These examples demonstrate that the actions of an individual or small group of presidents can become powerful symbols that unite people and can lead to significant consequences, positive and negative. In spite of the inherent risks associated with taking a stand on important national issues, many believe that college and university presidents are in a unique position to lead and should take on leadership roles through formal state and national higher education associations as well as commissions and task forces established by elected officials to deal with specific societal issues.

Hesburgh's role on the National Civil Rights Commission exemplifies the potential positive influence an academic president can have. It is important to note that many of the leaders we have mentioned have served in other important national roles. Most of the presidents mentioned in this chapter (especially Kerr, Gee, Bowen, Rodin, Friday, and Monette) used their position to advance important national and regional issues that affected their institutions and the country. Whether it was advocating for improvement of living conditions of Native Americans in North Dakota (Monette) or chairing ACE (Friday), these leaders used their positions on a broader stage to symbolize the positive role higher education can play in addressing important societal issues.

Shared Governance: The Creation of Democratic Partnerships

The idea that academic leaders can significantly influence the nature and course of an institution is as old as higher education itself. Unfortunately, much of what has been written about leaders who led successful change initiatives focused on the personal characteristics and traits of the leaders themselves. Scholarship has rarely approached these change efforts from the perspective that the leader and his or her followers collaborated to achieve organizational objectives. Some authors, however, do believe that leadership is best exercised when all parties share common values and goals. For example, in 1850 Ralph Waldo Emerson developed the idea that certain leaders are "representative; first of things, and secondly of ideas" (p. 7). He proposed that the best type of leader did not proceed until securing the consent of the followers through actions or words. Robert Coles (2000) had a slightly different way of framing this connection between leaders and followers. He believed that "leaders, by definition, have to come to terms with followers . . . whose deeds will confirm the reality of what has been sought as an ideal" (p. 194).

Coming to terms with those being led is a tough task for any leader, but in higher education it is a particularly challenging endeavor. Colleges and universities operate through a complex and often confusing system of governance and decision-making processes, commonly referred to as *shared governance*, which often is perplexing to people from outside the academy. The idea of shared governance is widely accepted in higher education, and the role of the president is critical to its success. Several authors have argued that academic leaders, especially presidents, need to be collegial in their approach to shared governance and must seek to maintain the delicate balance of authority between constituent groups (Birnbaum, 1988; Kerr, 1964; Mortimer & McConnell, 1978). Mortimer and Sathre (2007) expanded on this idea by suggesting that effective shared governance does not occur only between constituent groups. Instead, the president must also personally engage campus constituents to establish a collegial environment. This individual approach to creating a collegial atmosphere relates to the president's relationship to the governing board as well (Association of Governing Boards of Universities and Colleges [AGB], 2010).

Tierney and Minor (2003) found that over 90% of all four-year colleges and universities have some form of faculty governance that works within a broader framework of institutional decision making. What is often difficult for people unfamiliar with higher education's shared governance model to understand is that no two systems of faculty or institutional governance are exactly alike. On the surface, the vast majority of institutions follow generally accepted practices outlined by national bodies such as the American Association of University Professors, which helps define professional standards for faculty members, or the AGB, which shares best practices in board work. Such organizations bring some uniformity to governance across institutional boundaries, but just as every college and university has its own history and culture, each institution has its own unique decision-making processes. This diversity presents an interesting challenge to the academic president who is expected to mediate differences between myriad constituent groups while recognizing their individual sovereignty over certain decisions.

College and university presidents are expected to create democratic partnerships with all constituents, be collegial good listeners, and follow the unique governance traditions already established at their institutions, all the while remaining strategic in their thinking and bold in their decision making. Unfortunately, many decision-making processes and the role each constituent group plays in those processes are often poorly defined and appear contrary to democratic principles of governance. This ambiguity is especially prevalent surrounding issues that affect one constituent group but are not solely that constituent group's matters to decide, such as setting the cost for tuition.

At public or state-related institutions, setting tuition is often a complicated matter. Lacking the autonomy independent institutions have to set their own pricing, public colleges and universities are often restricted by state governments or coordinating boards on how much tuition they may charge. Presidents and chancellors of public institutions spend significant time dealing with elected officials on a wide range of issues, among which setting tuition often causes the most conflict.

The most successful public university leaders are often those who have built long-term relationships with government officials and have included them in the strategic planning and vision-setting processes of their institutions. These efforts are important because when elected officials feel public pressure to keep tuition costs down, if they do not understand the strategic direction or the value-added dimension of a public university, it is unlikely they will provide much support for tuition increases. Likewise, if a public university's leaders devise a strategic plan or set a direction that depends on specific funding levels from state and other sources without engaging state officials in that conversation, the legitimacy and feasibility of the entire process will be questioned on and off campus.

In the case of independent institutions, the amount of tuition revenue they collect has a direct impact on their ability to spend on different priorities, which in turn has consequences for institutional success. For example, if institution administrators desire to increase faculty salaries to become more competitive, increasing tuition may be the only mechanism to generate the necessary funds. Current and prospective students, however, may have difficulty affording to attend the institution if tuition increases and therefore may advocate for lower tuition or decide not to enroll at all. Lower enrollment would leave fewer dollars available to advance the strategic objective of competitive faculty salaries, even though more competitive salaries could attract and retain the very best faculty, thus improving student satisfaction and institutional prestige.

Most presidents of public and independent institutions quickly recognize the ambiguity inherent in the issue of tuition and understand that for shared governance to succeed, greater investment is needed up front about common goals and objectives before decisions about setting tuition costs can be finalized. Achieving such buy-in requires a governance system that respects the authority of each constituent group in the decision-making process as well as a leader with specific skills and competencies who can navigate such a complex structure and create a sense of harmony in an often chaotic environment.

Integral Leadership and Emotional Competency

In *The Leadership Imperative* (AGB, 2010), a group of distinguished scholars, trustees, and presidents proposed that "no person comes to personify an institution the way the president does" (p. vi). The report goes on to recommend that 21st-century higher education leaders must embrace a collaborative but decisive leadership style called integral leadership, which is supported by an institution's board and includes the faculty in pursuit of a shared and distinctive vision for the college or university.

The philosophy of integral leadership is that leaders need to have a broad worldview if they are to make decisions that are in the best interest of the institutions they serve. To acquire this broad perspective leaders are required to be collaborative yet resolute in their approach and willing to make appropriate changes in direction when the environment demands it. As the AGB (2010) report states,

> Integral leadership is where a president exerts a presence that is purposeful and consultative, deliberate yet decisive and capable of course corrections as new challenges emerge—aligns the president, faculty, and the board together in a well-functioning partnership purposefully devoted to a well-defined, broadly affirmed, institutional vision. (p. vii)

In other words, the practice of integral leadership calls for a special set of competencies in leaders that enable them to put aside their own personal agenda for the greater good of the organization.

According to AGB (2007), an institution's board of trustees is ultimately responsible for creating an environment where a president can exert such leadership. In its "Statement on Board Accountability" AGB reasserts that two of the major responsibilities for boards are to "approve and support the mission" and to "recruit, appoint, support and evaluate the chief executive officer" (p. 10). These tasks can be accomplished by working closely with the president and key constituents through an inclusive, evergreen planning process to articulate a clear vision for the institution. Once a vision is articulated and agreed upon, boards must encourage the president to be decisive while respecting institutional shared governance traditions. By doing this, boards can ensure a smooth transition for new academic presidents as they take on their responsibilities and assist experienced presidents in their effort to move an institution toward the stated vision of the future.

It is apparent that for an academic president to exercise integral leadership, he or she needs to possess a unique combination of professional experiences and expertise as well as an ongoing commitment to personal growth and development. To succeed in such a challenging role, academic presidents need to cultivate and develop certain leadership qualities that help them build consensus among diverse groups by creating an environment based on mutual respect and trust. This type of leadership quality is often referred to as emotional intelligence or emotional competence.

The idea that intelligence could be measured in different ways became formally recognized in the last quarter of the 20th century through the work of several authors who popularized the idea of emotional intelligence, which has been described as "the ability to monitor one's own and others' feelings and emotions, to discriminate among them and to use this information to guide one's thinking and actions" (Salovey & Mayer, 1990, p. 189).

One of the early writers on the subject was Howard Gardner. In his 1983 book, *Frames of Mind: The Theory of Multiple Intelligences*, he refuted the idea that a monolithic approach to intelligence, such as IQ, was the only way to view how smart or capable someone might be at handling different situations. Gardner proposed there was a wide range of intelligences and developed seven different prototypes. His groundbreaking work led to the discovery of a linkage between emotional skills or competencies that certain people possessed, such as being more self-aware, exhibiting empathy, and developing rapport with others, and the ability to accomplish personal and organizational goals.

In his 1995 book, *Emotional Intelligence: Why It Can Matter More Than IQ*, Goleman built on the ideas of Gardner and others and developed a framework and a method to measure someone's emotional intelligence. Goleman discovered that while IQ and technical skills were important "threshold capabilities" (p. 3), emotional intelligence was the most essential component of leadership. In one study he found that 90% of the difference between star performers and average performers was "attributable to emotional intelligence factors rather than cognitive abilities" (p. 3). Furthermore, Goleman found that emotional intelligence increases with maturity and, most importantly, it can be learned through dedication and concentrated effort such as working with a personal coach and by seeking feedback about one's own performance.

One of the nation's leading corporate executive coaches, Karol Wasylyshyn, has worked with senior executives from around the world and has drawn some conclusions about emotional intelligence based on her observations about their behaviors. A strong advocate for the cultivation of emotional competency skills, Wasylyshyn (2012) has found that leadership types fall on a continuum moving from remarkable to perilous to toxic. She believes that how a leader behaves at any point is influenced by the confluence of personal history and organizational factors (p. 8). The key difference in a leader who is remarkable versus one who is toxic is that a remarkable leader demonstrates strong emotional intelligence including attunement to others and adaptive functioning, adjusts better to change, and scores significantly higher on extraversion and conscientiousness domains (pp. 14–16).

Possessing and cultivating strong emotional competency skills are essential for an academic president to exercise integral leadership. The idea that leaders could be decisive and inclusive, putting their own personal needs aside so that institutional goals can be achieved, seems to be an improbable combination. Yet, several studies have found that this combination does exist in successful executives.

In his landmark study on why some corporations exceed expectations and move from good to great, Collins (2001) described the type of leadership necessary for organizations to achieve enduring success. He identified the executives of the highest-achieving corporations as level 5 executives, people who in his words are "a study in duality" (p. 22) characterized by personal humility and a strong will to succeed and do whatever had to be done to make a corporation great. Level 5 leaders were able to confront the reality of the situation at hand and successfully navigate challenges by focusing first on attracting a team of high performers and then imparting a sense of discipline to any change process. It is also important to note that in Collins's study, executives of great companies had a deep understanding of why they existed (a sense of mission) and were able to crystallize that focus through a carefully executed but simple plan (p. 95).

While there is not an adequate pipeline of qualified candidates to fill the demand for academic presidents in the next decade, there is a real need for boards, associations, nonprofit organizations, and individual colleges and universities to find ways to cultivate the next generation of academic leaders while continuing to support the successful presidents already in place. This can be accomplished through the integral leadership model proposed by AGB, but it will necessitate a different mind-set by institutional boards than simply filling one of the most demanding jobs in the world with a qualified candidate and letting the person go at it essentially alone, left to sink or swim. It will require an approach to institutional growth and renewal that recognizes the central importance of the academic president in any successful institution and take steps to train, nurture, and develop certain competencies in those individuals.

Developing and Retaining Academic Presidents

As we discussed earlier, the typical career path for an academic president is still most likely to start from an academic background, with some part of the individual's career dedicated to teaching and research. Just as in other professions, the skills necessary to be a successful teacher and scholar may not translate into the skill set needed by an academic president to flourish. The same is true for academic presidents who emerge from nontraditional career paths such as advancement, business, or student affairs. They may possess the knowledge and experience to understand very clearly one aspect of the academy but perhaps not grasp the complexity of the enterprise they will ultimately lead.

We recommend that colleges and universities seriously consider ways to develop future generations of academic leaders. We recommend that adoption of best practices to help new presidents get off to a good start and help experienced presidents maintain their enthusiasm and commitment to advancing the institutions they serve. One of the basic ways to accomplish these goals is to continue to support leadership development initiatives by identifying and cultivating individuals with leadership potential early in their careers and help them navigate the often confusing options they face for career advancement. Numerous programs for midlevel to senior-level individuals can help these professionals prepare for administrative roles and develop a support network that will help them throughout their career.

For example, ACE sponsors a fellows program for faculty members and administrators with leadership potential to spend a year working with a sitting college or university president and his or her management team at another institution. Obviously, this requires a great investment of time, money, and energy from the host institution, the mentor president, and the fellows themselves. The success rate of fellows eventually assuming senior-level positions is impressive (of the first 1,600 who went through the program, 1,000 became senior administrators, and 300 became CEOs of academic institutions), so it appears to be well worth the investment. Some presidents and boards may view this as a tremendous drain on the institution (loss of a talented colleague for a year) as well as the mentor president. However, most presidents who have had experience as a mentor find it a valuable way to reflect on their own leadership style and to promote their own institution.

While the ACE program has a proven track record of success, several other options are available for cultivating the next generation of higher education leadership. Some institutions have developed their own internships and leadership training opportunities for the faculty and staff, while others make it an annual practice to send colleagues with potential to other leadership development programs. These programs, lasting from a few days to several weeks, are now being offered at institutions such as Harvard University, Bryn Mawr College, and Pennsylvania State University, as well as by national organizations such as the Council of Independent Colleges and the American Association of State Colleges and Universities. Several similar programs and training opportunities also exist for newly appointed presidents and provosts who are in their first year on the job.

Once an academic president has been hired, it is incumbent upon the board of trustees to ensure that she or he has the support and resources to be successful. Too often presidents are selected and then left to their own devices to figure out the key players and to learn the culture and nature of the institution they have just agreed to lead. Boards can play a major role in supporting a new president by creating a transition team of key institutional constituents whose job is to do everything possible to introduce the president to other people who can influence his or her success, such as senior faculty and staff members, elected officials, benefactors, student leaders, and alumni.

The board should also have its own process for getting to know the president through formal meetings and casual gatherings. The most important thing a board can do, however, is be clear in its expectations of the new president. Ideally, within the first few months of a president's tenure, an opportunity should exist for board members and the president to discuss and reflect on the mission, values, and vision of the university, and establish a clear path going forward that is respectful of the established shared governance model.

Experienced presidents also need support and direction from the board as well as an opportunity for growth and renewal. As we have stated before, the demands of the presidency are many, and the fact that the average tenure of a president is about eight years speaks to the enormity of the responsibilities of the work and the toll it takes on individuals and their families. The issues academic presidents face in their first few years on the job may be very different from what they encounter years later. Board members of academic institutions that have successfully retained presidents seem to understand the changing nature of the academic presidency and have adjusted the way they support their leaders. For example, some have invested in executive coaches to help excellent presidents continue to grow and reflect on their leadership style and discover new ways to enhance their emotional competency skills. Many institutions have built in sabbaticals or extended vacations to allow presidents to stay current in their academic field, pursue personal interests, seek additional training, or simply take time to renew their energy.

In the end, boards are responsible for hiring, supporting, rewarding, and evaluating the president, and in some cases making the difficult decision that new leadership is necessary. To ensure the success of an academic president requires an engaged board that focuses on the mission, strategic direction, and achievement of an agreed-upon vision of the institution rather than on management issues best left to the administration. The best relationships between boards and presidents are ones that develop trusting, reciprocal, and democratic partnerships focused on the ultimate success of the institution they mutually serve.

One key part of developing a democratic partnership between the board and the president is the evaluation process. Once the board and the president have agreed on a set of objectives and the means of evaluating the president, then it is critically important that the executive committee of the board or some other appropriate board committee establish a formal annual review of the president's performance and share those results with the rest of the board.

According to AGB (2010), a board strengthens a presidency through regular feedback, and at a minimum the board should undertake an annual assessment of the president. Public and independent institutions differ in their requirements for reporting the board's assessment, but in either case, the evaluation should be fair and consistent with what is done for other employees, and the process should be transparent. After the president's performance is assessed and feedback given on strengthening individual and institutional performances, it is the board's responsibility to set a fair and competitive compensation package for the president, taking into consideration experience, success in the role, years of service, institutional norms, and national benchmarks. Once again, independent and public institutions differ in their public reporting responsibilities about executive compensation, but in either case the process for setting compensation should be fair, consistent with institutional values, and as transparent as possible. These practices are germane when dealing with new and experienced presidents.

The Future of the Academic Presidency

The idea that an academic president is or should ever become the personification of the mission and vision of the institution he or she serves is controversial and will continue to be debated for years to come. Some people believe there will be no more important role in the advancement of any college or university in the 21st century (and in fact the future of American higher education) than that of the academic president, while others believe the president will remain simply one of many important players in a complex system of shared governance. No matter where one stands in the debate, everyone can agree on a few things: The role of the president will continue to be demanding, changing, and critically important if shared governance is to work and the academy is to advance.

In the future the academic presidency will demand that the individuals who assume these roles possess strong emotional competency skills, an even temperament, appropriate experience, and expertise to handle the rigors of the work. The ability to create democratic partnerships and work in harmony with key constituents, especially the faculty, students, elected officials, alumni, and board members, will be essential if presidents are to succeed in the 21st century. The responsibility for developing the next generation of academic leaders should be a national priority, because the future of the academy and indeed our nation depends on it.

References

American Council on Education. (2007). *The American college president*. Washington, DC: Author.

Association of Governing Boards of Universities and Colleges. (2007). *AGB statement on board accountability*. Retrieved from http://agb.org/sites/agb.org/files/u3/AccountabilityStatement2007.pdf

Association of Governing Boards of Universities and Colleges. (2010). *The leadership imperative*. Washington, DC: Author.

Bensimon, E. M. (1989). The meaning of good presidential leadership: A frame analysis. *The Review of Higher Education, 12*(2), 421–431.

Bensimon, E. M., & Neumann, A. (1993). *Redesigning collegiate leadership: Teams and teamwork in higher education*. Baltimore, MD: Johns Hopkins University Press.

Birnbaum, R. (1988). *How colleges work: The cybernetics of academic organization and leadership*. San Francisco, CA: Jossey-Bass.

Birnbaum, R. (1999). Academic leadership at the millennium: Politics or porcelain? *Academe, 85*(3), 14–19.

Burns, J. M. (1978). *Leadership*. New York, NY: Harper & Row.

Cohen, M. D., & March, J. G. (1974). *Leadership and ambiguity: The American college president*. New York, NY: McGraw-Hill.

Colby, A., Ehrlich, T., Beaumont, E., & Stephens, J. (2003). *Educating citizens: Preparing America's undergraduates for lives of moral and civic responsibility*. San Francisco, CA: Jossey-Bass.

Coles, R. (2000). *Lives of moral leadership*. New York, NY: Random House.

Collins, J. (2001). *Good to great: Why some companies make the leap . . . and others don't*. New York, NY: HarperCollins.

Deal, T. E., & Kennedy, A. A. (2000). *Corporate cultures: The rites and rituals of corporate life*. Cambridge, MA: Perseus.

Dill, D. D. (1982). The management of academic culture: Notes on the management of meaning and social integration. *Higher Education, 11*(3), 303–320. doi:10.1007/BF00155621

Emerson, R. W. (1850). *Representative men: Seven lectures*. New York, NY: Hurst.

Gardner, H. (1983). *Frames of mind: The theory of multiple intelligences*. New York, NY: Basic Books.

Goleman, D. (1995). *Emotional intelligence: Why it can matter more than IQ*. New York, NY: Bantam.

Hartley, H. V., III, & Godin, E. E. (2010). *A study of chief academic officers of independent colleges and universities*. Retrieved from Council of Independent Colleges website: http://www.cic.edu/projects_services/infoservices/CICCAOSurvey.pdf

Ikenberry, S. O. (2010). The changing demands of presidential leadership. *Trusteeship, 18*(6). Retrieved from http://agb.org/sites/agb.org/files/u16/Ikenberry%20NovDec%202010_copyrighted.pdf

Kerr, C. (1963). *The uses of the university*. Cambridge, MA: Harvard University Press.

Maurrasse, D. J. (2001). *Beyond the campus: How colleges and universities form partnerships with their communities*. New York, NY: Routledge.

McLaughlin, J. B. (Ed.). (1996). *Leadership transitions: The new college president*. San Francisco, CA: Jossey-Bass.

Mortimer, K. P., & McConnell, T. R. (1978). *Sharing authority effectively: Participation, interaction, and discretion*. San Francisco, CA: Jossey-Bass.

Mortimer, K. P., & Sathre, C. O. (2007). *The art and politics of academic governance: Relations among boards, presidents, and faculty*. Westport, CT: Praeger.

Padilla, A. (2005). *Portraits in leadership: Six extraordinary university presidents*. Westport, CT: Praeger.

Pfeffer, J. (1977). The ambiguity of leadership. *Academy of Management Review, 12*(1), 104–112.

Rudolph, F. (1962). *The American college and university: A history*. New York, NY: Random House.

Salovey, P., & Mayer, J. D. (1990). Emotional intelligence. *Imagination, Cognition and Personality, 9*, 185–211.

Sinclair, U. (1923). *The goose-step: A study of American education*. Pasadena, CA: Author.

Tierney, W. G. (1989). Symbolism and presidential perceptions of leadership. *The Review of Higher Education, 12*(2), 153–166.

Tierney, W. G., & Minor, J. T. (2003). *Challenges for governance: A national report*. Los Angeles, CA: Center for Higher Education Policy Analysis.

Wasylyshyn, K. M. (2012), *Behind the executive door: Unexpected lessons for managing your boss and career*. New York, NY: Springer.

PART FOUR

THE ACADEMIC CORE

At most higher education institutions, upper-level administrators do not possess unilateral power to hire or fire faculty, initiate new or modify existing courses, determine the requirements for a degree, or admit or dismiss a student, among other activities. Rather, these responsibilities and other decision-making processes are shared among a college's or university's faculty, administration, and board of trustees. In fact, the relationship among boards, senior administrators, and faculty members resembles that of the federal and state governments in the United States. Each group has authority in certain areas of responsibility and has to collaborate with the other groups in the many issues that involve shared oversight. What makes academic governance even more difficult is that postsecondary institutions usually operate as organized anarchies in which organizational goals are unclear, decision-making procedures are uncertain, and participation in those procedures is fluid (Cohen, March, & Olson, 1972). The key elements of academic governance (academic administrators, faculty governance bodies, academic departments, and the faculty) are discussed in chapters 11, 12, and 13.

Chapter 11 reviews the evolution of academic governance; contains a discussion of many of the reasons for the frequent disconnect among boards of trustees, faculty members, and administrators; describes the positive and negative aspects of shared governance arrangements; and provides advice for boards, faculty members, and administrators to navigate and use academic governance structures effectively. The roles of an institution's chief academic officer, deans, and faculty senate are discussed to analyze their impact on the quest for shared governance and an interdisciplinary approach to the curriculum, research, and outreach.

In chapter 12 we present academic departments, which not only reflect the organization of knowledge but also serve as the pivotal units for delivery of an institution's core mission. Lattuca and Stark (2009) maintain that departments play the most important role in developing quality curricula. In addition, without cooperation from these units, an institution's interdisciplinary initiatives cannot be sustained. Leadership from a department chair or head is critical not only to the health of his or her department but to the college or university as a whole. A chair's leadership is essential for establishing a vision; planning strategically; allocating resources; and developing faculty potential in teaching, scholarship, research, and service. Chairs must hone their leadership, communication, and interpersonal skills to maintain a quality department and foster collaboration with other disciplines.

Chapter 13 focuses on the faculty. Gumport (1997) noted that higher education has traditionally been considered a "social institution" (p. 69) with responsibility for preparing youth for citizenship and service, as well as for advancing knowledge. Whether one views higher education as a social institution or as a business preparing a skilled workforce, the faculty is at the core of achieving its institution's mission. Rapid changes in technology, globalization, and demographic shifts have not only changed the nature of faculty work but affected the nature of faculty appointments. This chapter explores the changing demographic makeup of faculty, the nature of faculty work, changes in teaching and learning, and how these changes affect faculty development and the ways faculty teach.

References

Cohen, M. D., March, J. G., & Olson, J. P. (1972). A garbage can model of organizational choice. *Administrative Science Quarterly, 17(1)*, 1–25.

Gumport, P. J. (1997). Public universities as academic workplaces. *Deadalus, 126(4)*, 113–136.

Lattuca, L., & Stark, J. (2009). *Shaping the college curriculum: Academic plans in context* (2nd ed.). San Francisco, CA: Jossey-Bass.

II

GOVERNANCE OF THE
ACADEMIC CORE

Colleges and universities are typically bifurcated organizations (Blau, 1973), in that they have an academic structure to deliver education and an administrative structure that supports the academic structure. Indeed, over the past four decades the administrative structure has become quite expansive, with some institutions operating as cities within cities. Institutional governance is discussed in chapter 2; here we focus on governance of institutions' academic core.

The academic core is where the essential mission of a college or university is implemented and is typically overseen by a chief academic officer (CAO), known as a provost, a vice president for academic affairs, or an academic dean (at some smaller institutions). The CAO coordinates the efforts of his or her institution's academic units, such as schools, colleges, divisions, and academic departments, playing a pivotal role in ensuring that the institution and its academic units stay true to the institutional mission. In this way, the CAO is responsible for making certain the institution and its academic decisions are mission driven, which fulfills the first theme of this book.

This book's second theme is that an institution's adaptation to environmental change must be consistent with its core mission and values. The CAO, his or her academic deans, departmental leaders, and individual faculty members all contribute to this process, because such change needs to be reflected in curricular reform in degree programs and general undergraduate education requirements. In addition, as we have witnessed since the onset of the Great Recession in 2008, adaptations may include eliminating smaller programs that serve few students, aligning academic offerings with local workforce demands, and restructuring academic governance models (Bruce, 2012; Jacobs, 2012).

While environmental change may necessitate changes to degree programs, such adjustments should be made according to an institution's mission and not just in response to reduced funding or other challenges. Furthermore, such modifications should be made through an institution's democratic partnership mechanisms, the third theme of this book. An institution's academic governance system is crucial for maintaining this principle.

Academic governance processes engage an institution's faculty, departments, and academic administration in decision making that ultimately will be reviewed by the president and board of trustees. Shared governance, the predominant form of academic governance in higher education, exemplifies the concept of democratic partnership.

We begin this chapter with a discussion of shared governance. We then contrast this model with an emerging form of academic governance, the corporate model. We describe the roles of different parties within academic governance structures and the main responsibilities that fall to each of them. We conclude with issues that academic administrators should focus on to respond to a rapidly changing environment.

The Concept of Shared Governance

Within the bifurcated organizational structure of higher education, the concept of and process for governance and decision making in the academic core comes from a set of joint guidelines developed by the American Association of University Professors (AAUP, n.d.), the American Council on Education, and the Association of Governing Boards of Universities and Colleges. The *Statement on Government of Colleges and Universities* (AAUP, n.d.) delineated the roles of an institution's board of trustees, administration, and faculty in the decision making and governance of the academic core and established a partnership or collaborative relationship between these entities (Eckel, 2000), commonly known as the shared governance model.

At colleges and universities that practice shared governance, the board's role is to maintain the purposes of the institution's original charter and the institution's fiscal health. The president's role is to sustain current financial resources and generate new revenue sources. The role of the academic administrator is to coordinate and lead the institution's academic programs. The role of the faculty is to monitor existing academic programs and develop new curricula in response to environmental change. These roles are not discrete for any of the entities; rather, there is a great deal of overlap that necessitates collaboration.

The literature on shared governance usually focuses on institutional faculty governance committees, often called a faculty senate (Euben, 2003; Lee, 1991; Schoorman & Aucer-Hocevar, 2010). As Tierney and Minor (2003) noted, however, shared governance is more multifaceted than the structure and processes of a faculty senate (p. 5). To understand the complex structure and processes of shared governance, one needs to consider the ways an institution interacts with its environment, particularly in terms of curricular development and change. Faculty members interact directly with their environments, with the result that the curricula of many fields and disciplines have changed, and new interdisciplinary fields have emerged, particularly in the last two decades. As part of their academic governance structures, colleges and universities maintain processes for adding new courses and degree programs, but such changes emanate from faculty members' responses to environmental changes within their field or discipline. The governance and decision-making roles of departments and faculty are discussed in more detail in chapters 12 and 13.

An institution's shared governance system is also influenced by its type, size, history, and culture (Tierney & Minor, 2003). That being said, shared governance systems vary between institutions of the same Carnegie Classification and across all U.S. higher education institutions. Some generalizations, however, can be made. For example, large research, doctorate-granting, and comprehensive institutions have placed organizational units—schools or colleges—between the faculty governing body and the academic departments. Schools or colleges typically employ a governance structure for their academic programs and policies that interfaces with the institution's academic governance structure. In addition, larger institutions usually have a representative faculty senate that contains a designated number of representatives from each school or college.

In contrast, private liberal arts colleges, depending on the size of the faculty, may have a representative form of governance or a faculty governing body composed of all faculty members. At liberal arts institutions, faculty governing bodies typically have more control over curricular issues and academic decision making.

Academic governance is also important at community colleges. Lucey (2002), who served as president of several community colleges, discussed the importance of shared governance, and faculty involvement in curricular development in particular. She noted the negative consequences of faculty passivity when it comes to governance and the abdication of curricular decisions to administrators. She was particularly critical of outreach deans and faculty members who allow these deans to make decisions based on entrepreneurial priorities rather than on the quality and depth of the curriculum. She noted the responsibility that a community college has to its larger community as its most important customer:

> We realize that our customers must be the larger civic community, whose members have a right to expect delivery of an education that prepares students for an engaged life in a democracy—as well as one that offers them the opportunity to achieve a better life. To satisfy these customers, we should be willing to take the steps necessary to preserve such [faculty] engagement within our own college community. While continuing to support the goals of individuals, democracy's colleges also need to support democracy. (p. 31)

Lucey's observation about the need for faculty engagement to maintain strong academic governance is applicable to all colleges and universities that value democratic partnerships and want to be responsive to their environment.

Shared Governance Versus Corporate Governance

In the 1990s a number of higher education experts argued that colleges and universities of any size are no longer capable of responding to a rapidly changing environment (Association of Governing Boards of Universities and Colleges, 1996; Benjamin, Carroll, Jacobi, Krop, & Shires, 1993; Cole, 1994; Kennedy, 1993; Schuster, Smith, Corak, & Yamada, 1994). They maintain that traditional shared governance systems—namely, faculty senates—are unable to act on changing societal needs in a timely manner, particularly when compared with the burgeoning for-profit higher education sector. Consequently, they recommend that nonprofit higher education institutions make the transition from their traditional shared governance model to a corporate governance model in which decision making is concentrated at the presidential level. Their assumption is that such restructuring will allow institutions to respond more rapidly to changes in their environments.

Birnbaum (2004) connected the rising demand for corporate governance in higher education to the evolution of and the increase in for-profit institutions. He asserted that "governance is a means to an end" (p. 24), so academic governance should be structured to meet an institution's desired ends. In his analysis, Birnbaum characterized many for profits as entrepreneurial and labeled them as "market" institutions, while he described many non-profit colleges and universities as "academic" (p. 22) institutions. His main distinction between market and academic institutions was that market institutions' focus—that is, their end—is on producing individuals with the skills and abilities necessary to seek employment and perform effectively in their chosen occupation. On the other hand, academic institutions' end is the production of educated citizens who will contribute to society through the expansion of knowledge and understanding and involvement in a democratic society (p. 7). According to Birnbaum, market institutions' desired end requires them to embrace a corporate governance model, while academic institutions' desired end requires a shared governance system (p. 24). Birnbaum did not argue that one structure is better than the other, though. Instead, he asserted that contemporary society needs market and academic institutions with governance structures appropriate for their type to meet specific societal needs.

The focus of this book is on what Birnbaum (2004) would generally describe as academic institutions, most of which employ shared governance structures. Many shared governance systems involve faculty senates—the scapegoat for slow institutional decision making—but also involve many more parties and occur on many more levels than just senates. For example, at community colleges, liberal arts colleges, and research universities alike, individual faculty members interact with their specific disciplinary environments and respond to changes, which can be seen in the evolution of curricula, specific course content, and teaching methods. The corporate governance model may streamline some decision-making processes, but it also risks stifling faculty members' ability to respond to their disciplinary environments in a timely manner, debilitating decision making, and diminishing the development of an institution's social capital (i.e., individual faculty investment in institutional innovation and change). Moreover, rapid responses to change may not be the best approach for academic institutions, where deliberate and thorough analysis may lead to more effective long-term responses to environmental challenges.

At the heart of arguments for reform of institutional governance is the premise that academic institutions with shared governance are not capable of making difficult decisions in times of scarce financial resources. Another criticism is that faculty members do not willingly participate in academic governance and are reluctant to make hard decisions that involve their colleagues (Benjamin et al., 1993; Cole, 1994; Kennedy, 1993; Schuster et al., 1994). Scholarship and anecdotal evidence challenge these criticisms, however. In a comparative case study of four institutions, Eckel (2000) explored how these colleges and universities decided to cut programs in times of financial difficulty. All four institutions engaged their faculties, administrators, and in some cases, board members in their decision-making processes, through either their faculty senate as a whole, a standing committee of the senate, or an ad hoc committee appointed by the provost and containing members from the senate as well as other constituencies. These shared governance processes helped institutional leaders communicate the seriousness of the situation to the entire community, allowed interest groups to work constructively to address difficult issues, and provided a mechanism to correct misconceptions about and errors in the decision-making process (p. 31). Eckel found that faculty members were willing to participate actively in shared governance and could perform as effective and responsible contributors to the process (p. 32):

> When hard decisions needed to be made, faculty and administrators (and, in one case, the board) worked together to get the job done. The study challenges frequently articulated beliefs that faculty cannot and will not make hard decisions, are more concerned with preserving the status quo than with making institutionally beneficial decisions, and working to prolong rather than expedite campus decision-making. It additionally refutes the belief that more authority for administrators will lead to better institutional decision making. (p. 33)

Eckel's (2000) findings resemble those at Pennsylvania State University, where in 2010 the administration implemented a three-year budgeting process that required all departments—academic and administrative—to identify 10% budget reductions annually. These cuts were not intended to be applied equally across all units. Rather, they were designed to strengthen strong programs and eliminate weaker ones. The process, while difficult, provided faculty members and administrators with the opportunity to contribute to financial decision making and instilled in the faculty, staff, and students a new understanding of the challenging fiscal situation in which the university found itself. Ultimately, it created some understanding for the appropriateness of decisions made regarding distribution of resources.

These examples illustrate that shared governance can work. Moreover, they show that the system provided faculty members with some control over their destinies and the futures of their academic programs, based on the degree to which they respond to their changing environments. Shared governance allows institutions to adapt to environmental changes in ways that are consistent with their mission, goals, and values.

The Faculty Senate in Shared Governance

In a 2003 national report on academic governance in higher education, Tierney and Minor acknowledged that shared governance is a complex practice but focused their study on faculty governance structures. Specifically, they looked at faculty governance in research and doctorate-granting institutions and comprehensive universities, identifying three types of faculty governance and decision-making structures. First, they identified a "fully collaborative decision-making" model that corresponds to notions of collegiality, in which decisions are shared among the faculty and the administration. Second, they described a "consultative decision-making" model in which senior administrators and board members retain ultimate decision-making authority but seek faculty advice as part of their deliberations. Third, they observed a "distributive decision making" model that results in the delegation of decision making to the faculty, administrators, or the board according to each entity's assigned responsibilities. Their investigation found that 47% of institutions were "fully collaborative," 27% were "consultative," and 26% were "distributive" (Tierney & Minor, 2003, p. 9). Tierney and Minor noted that these models of faculty governance were one venue for faculty participation in decision making, but they also observed that there were other venues for faculty engagement, including academic departments, ad-hoc committees, school/college governance units, standing faculty administrative committees, systemwide governing units, and collective bargaining/union committees (p. 6).

Organizational theory can assist us in understanding the role and function of faculty senates. Birnbaum (1991) used theory to understand why faculty senates, as dysfunctional as they sometimes can be, have persisted over time. Citing Blau, Birnbaum suggested that faculty senates prevent the centralization of control of academic programs (p. 8). This decentralization gives faculty members the flexibility they need to respond in a timely way to the environmental changes that affect their disciplines and fields. When these changes begin to affect a number of fields or disciplines in the institution, the matter percolates to the senate for institutional resolution. This is an example of one of the "manifest functions" (p. 10) of the senate as a bureaucracy, a political system. The latent functions of the senate include its role as a symbol of faculty membership and participation, commitment to institutional and professional values, and authority over some institutional functions (p. 12). Another important latent function of senates is that they serve as a training ground for future academic leaders (Johnston, 2003). These manifest and latent functions serve to explain the persistence of faculty senates over time and their positive role within institutions of higher education that promote democratic partnerships.

The composition of senates varies. Some are composed of only tenured faculty members, whereas others are made up of all faculty members or a collaborative structure of faculty and administrators, staff, and students. The structure of a faculty senate is heavily influenced by institution type. For example, senates in larger institutions tend to be representative bodies with elected members from individual schools, colleges, or departments who serve two- to six-year terms. At smaller private institutions and some community colleges, faculty governance structures are made up of all tenured or full-time faculty members. As the number of contingent faculty members has grown, their role has become an issue for faculty governance. Some institutions include contingent faculty members in their governance structures, whereas others do not (see chapter 13, pp. 316–319).

The chair or presiding officer of a faculty senate is usually elected from the senate membership (typically a member of the faculty) and may also serve on the president's cabinet. In some cases, though, the CAO serves as the presiding officer of the senate. In either arrangement, the CAO works closely with the senate as part of his or her responsibility to oversee the academic governance of the institution (Tierney & Minor, 2003). Some senates contain an executive committee that sets the senate's agenda and works closely with the administration (Gilmour, 1991), while in some senates the executive committee contains administrators and faculty members.

The senate leadership should adopt an abbreviated and simplified form of *Robert's Rules of Order* (Robert, 2011) to keep meetings moving toward decision making.[1] As new members join the senate, they should participate in training to have a clear understanding of the institution's mission; the senate's constitution, bylaws, and organizational structure; the role of the faculty from departments through schools and colleges in the shared governance model of institutional decision making; the senate's relationship with the CAO; and the utility of *Robert's Rules* for making the senate an effective and timely decision-making body.

Senates' decision-making activities primarily affect the academic side of the institution. Issues that often fall to faculty senates include monitoring of curricula, such as ensuring of the integrity of existing degree programs, development of new courses and degree programs, authorization of changes to existing courses, and endorsement of the closing of existing programs; teaching evaluation processes and criteria; promotion and tenure and posttenure review processes; minimum requirements for associate's, baccalaureate, and graduate degree programs; president and CAO selection and periodic evaluations; faculty personnel policies; and sometimes strategic planning and budgeting (Tierney & Minor, 2003, p. 7). Most senates maintain subcommittees to monitor these matters, as well as to provide some oversight of cocurricular matters, such as student life, campus climate, and athletics. Subcommittees provide a venue for wider faculty involvement in academic governance because membership can be drawn from senate members as well as from representatives from the broader faculty. In all these activities, the senate plays a role in upholding the mission, goals, and values of its institution.

The CAO

A college or university CAO is responsible for overseeing the institution's academic mission. In today's colleges and universities the scope of the CAO's role has expanded to that of chief operating officer, meaning that he or she manages the internal functions of the institution, while the president's role has evolved into a concern for the institution's external relationships (Bright & Richards, 2001; Lambert, 2002). In higher education, a CAO is typically referred to as a vice president for academic affairs, vice chancellor for academic affairs, dean of academic affairs, or provost. In recent years, because of the broadened scope of responsibilities, institutions have also begun to use the title senior vice president and provost.

Little has been written about the function of the CAO, although a few works describe the scope and roles of this pivotal position (Atnip, 2009; Bright & Richards, 2001; Lambert, 2002; Martin & Samuels, 1997). The CAO has responsibility for all academic programs and academic support services such as the library, technology and computing centers, faculty personnel and development, admissions and enrollment management, teaching and learning, and the registrar's office (Atnip, p. 143). The CAO also is usually responsible for the largest portion of the institution's budget, plays a pivotal role in strategic planning, maintains oversight of the institution's physical facilities dedicated to academics, oversees the curriculum and complex personnel issues, and ensures that the institution upholds its mission and is responsive to environmental changes. In some smaller colleges the CAO is also responsible for oversight of research activities. The CAO must cultivate strong relationships and communication with the president and the board; the vice presidents of finance, administration, and student affairs; the deans of the colleges; and the faculty.

Lambert (2002) advocated for a strong CAO who not only is in charge of academic affairs but also serves as the chief operating officer, a designation that situates this office clearly as the second most powerful position in terms of authority and responsibility. This arrangement allows the president to focus on regional, state, and national public relations issues. The president and the CAO must share a similar understanding of their institution's mission, and their working relationship should include a joint long-term vision and close communication at all times.

For this working relationship to be successful, the president must give the CAO space to perform his or her role and responsibilities and not micromanage. In addition, the CAO and vice presidents for finance, administration, student affairs, and research and graduate programs should communicate regularly and develop a team approach to collaborate as members of the president's cabinet. These collaborative relationships will allow for a more coordinated effort in the institution's academic and support areas to promote the academic goals and values of the institution (Lambert, 2002, p. 426).

The deans of the colleges and the chair of the faculty senate (or a senate representative if the CAO is the chair of the senate) form the academic affairs leadership team that reports directly to the CAO, with the advice and consent of the faculty. These academic deans often serve at the pleasure of the CAO. The relationship between academic deans and the CAO is crucial to the CAO's ability to successfully guide the institution.

The institution's budget model is critical to the CAO's performance as well. At institutions where each college is financially independent with differential tuition and part of a loose federation of independent entities, the CAO is often weak and has difficulty moving the institution forward. Where the CAO has more control over the budgets of individual units, the CAO's leadership team can progress toward a common agenda and goals. In the latter arrangement, general education requirements can focus on liberal arts and sciences, and there will be less of a silo mentality across the colleges (although this mentality will linger), as well as a better understanding of the specific and unique needs of individual colleges (Lambert, 2002, p. 427). The reporting relationship between the CAO and the deans will vary based on how long individuals have served in their positions and the level of trust that has developed between them. Established deans may report to the CAO on a monthly basis but communicate urgent problems as needed, whereas new deans may meet with the CAO on a weekly or biweekly basis. The CAO must trust the deans to manage their own units and avoid micromanaging any of the colleges. When a dean repeatedly fails that trust, the CAO should discern whether it is time for a leadership change—a decision that is often made with faculty consultation.

The role of the CAO in faculty governance is important from a leadership and a developmental perspective. Just as the president develops a training program for the board of trustees, the CAO should work with the senate leadership to develop a training program for members of the senate. Such a program will enhance the effectiveness of the senate in decision making and benefit the institution. We recommend that the CAO meet with the senate leadership on a regular basis to plan the agenda for regular faculty meetings and cultivate a sense of trust. He or she should educate the senate leadership on the changing environment and issues faced by the institution. The CAO should also attend regular senate meetings and be open to attending subcommittee meetings where information is needed to provide advice, counsel, and forward legislation to the senate. The CAO should solicit planning and budgeting suggestions from the senate on an annual basis. The senate should be provided with appropriate data and institutional research that will facilitate its ability to make recommendations (Lambert, 2000, p. 429). The strength of the senate leadership may wax and wane over the years, but the CAO cannot ignore the senate.

Academic Deans

An academic dean, who usually is responsible for an academic school or college, holds a midlevel academic leadership position that serves as a bridge between the faculty and the CAO. Literature that focuses on the role of the dean includes, for example, Bolton (2000), Bright and Richards (2001), Chen (2009), and Leaming (2002). Not only do deans need to cultivate relationships with the faculty and provide leadership development to department chairs, but they must also pay attention to managing up in terms of their relationship to their CAO. Colleges or schools are complex units made up of a number of disciplines or fields.

Bright and Richards (2001) compare being the dean to working a crossword puzzle. The dean's work is defined by constraints that are not the administrator's creation; there are defined boundaries that will affect any solution, and academics like to keep things complex and interrelated (p. 6). They noted,

> Our work as academics is a kind of semantic and logical game, and this inevitably carries over into the way we talk. Academics take a frequently

maddening pleasure in ambiguity, wit, and other forms of verbal play. As a result, discussions of new ideas, suggestions—and even strongly stated requests—sometimes seem more like a trail of bread crumbs than a well-formed loaf of bread to chew on! (p. 7)

Bright and Richards said there are three types of deans: the corporate dean, who sees the enterprise as a business first and an intellectual beehive second; the faculty-citizen dean, who is a respected senior scholar and holds the position for a short time; and the accidental-tourist dean, who rises through the ranks of academic administration to upper-level administrative responsibilities.

A dean needs to cultivate a number of skills. He or she needs to be an advocate to the CAO for the departments and disciplines in his or her unit. Advocacy should not be blind, however, and the dean needs to understand and confront areas of weakness when improvement is needed. In collaboration with faculty members and academic administrators in the college, the dean needs to embrace a vision for the college and communicate that vision articulately to faculty, students, alumni, benefactors, administrators, and staff. The dean should possess the skills to evaluate the performance of academic administrators and staff, and in an honest but caring way identify strengths and areas for improvement. Tough love and a collaborative approach to improvement are essential in dealing with personnel, as are knowing how to develop and cultivate the leadership skills of department heads and avoiding micromanagement. Having said that, a dean also must have the strength to replace someone when it becomes obvious that the person cannot perform the job effectively. Successful deans also demonstrate budget management and planning skills and cultivate donors to build the endowment of the college and the institution.

In the midst of all these concerns, deans must be mindful of the idiosyncratic nature of academic departments. In a college of liberal arts or a college of arts and sciences, a diversity of disciplines and fields of study coexist, from the humanities to the social sciences to the hard sciences. These colleges are much more difficult to lead than a college of engineering, for example, in which disciplines and fields are more closely related. Regardless of the way schools and colleges are structured in an institution, each discipline or field in the college interacts with different external environments, which creates the idiosyncratic nature of each college or school.

No matter a school's or college's focus, academic departments are idiosyncratic because of the nature of the disciplines or fields of study they house.

Some departments may be a combination of several disciplines or fields. Each of these fields or disciplines could have its own graduate degree programs and environment it relates to. Grasping the distinctive nature of each department is particularly important in a time of fiscal constraint, because deans may look across their college for ways to streamline resources, and what they may see as a way to operate more efficiently may not work because of departmental idiosyncrasies. For example, some departments may employ one graduate officer to oversee their single master's and doctoral programs, while other departments may employ multiple officers to handle different types of graduate programs. To conserve resources, a dean may decide that every department needs only one graduate officer, even though some departments' diverse graduate programs require unique recruitment, admissions, certification, and credentialing processes. While on the surface such a restructuring may appear more efficient, it may not be the most effective way to maintain strong degree programs: The complexity of the job may actually harm the integrity of the individual programs.

One key way to understand academic departments' idiosyncrasies is to maintain strong relations and communication with department heads. An advisory body of department heads, unit directors, and associate or assistant deans can assist the dean in understanding issues and intended and unintended consequences of solutions under consideration. College-level faculty governance bodies are also useful resources for deans. In most cases, a proportion of the faculty is elected from each department, and several faculty members serve in at-large positions. Such a structure provides the dean with a venue to bring pressing issues and changes to the faculty for review. It also provides the college's faculty senate representatives with a place to bring back issues to their colleagues for input. In times of rapid change, college-level faculty governance bodies can be especially helpful in facilitating necessary change.

Responsibilities of Academic Leaders

Academic leaders must focus on a number of areas to ensure their institution continues to be mission driven while adapting to environmental change through democratic partnerships. First, in this age of rapid expansion of knowledge and technology, academic leaders must evaluate, coordinate, and plan curricular adaptation and change to ensure their institution's offerings remain relevant. Second, changes in research policy and practice require leaders to remain current on institutional research policy issues, as well as to develop strategies to encourage faculty research and scholarship activities consistent with their institution's mission. Third, the complex problems society faces require cross-disciplinary solutions, so leaders must identify ways to promote collaboration across academic units.

Curriculum Coordination and Planning

Work on curriculum planning by Lattuca and Stark (2009) has provided academic leaders with a reconceptualization of the process. Specifically, they describe curriculum as an "academic plan" (p. 4) that takes into account the sociocultural context in which teaching and learning occur. The academic plan model for curriculum design also considers factors internal to the institution, including its history, culture, and mission. At the department level, the backgrounds and agendas of faculty members and the nature of students influence the development of the academic plan. Lattuca and Stark identified the following elements of an academic plan:

1. Purposes: to provide knowledge, skills, and attitudes to be learned
2. Content: subject matter selected to convey specific knowledge and skills
3. Sequencing: an arrangement of subject matter and experience intended to lead to specific outcomes of learners
4. Learners: how the plan will address a specific group of learners
5. Instructional processes: the instructional activities by which learning may be achieved
6. Resources: the materials and settings to be used in the learning process
7. Evaluation: the strategies used to determine whether decisions about the elements of the academic plan are optimal
8. Adjustment: enhancements to the plan based on experience and evaluation. (pp. 4–5)

Crucial to the plan is the feedback loop that provides assessment and evaluation of the curricular responses to environmental change.

The academic plan model is useful for the evaluation and adaptation of undergraduate general education curricula and academic programs and courses at the associate's, bachelor's, and graduate degree levels, especially as they need to adapt to an ever changing environment. Lattuca and Stark (2009) provided detailed strategies to use this model to implement curriculum plans at the degree, program, and course levels. The model is particularly useful for undergraduate-level curricula that cover general education requirements and disciplinary majors. It can be an evaluation tool to achieve the optimization of student learning and the creation of engaged citizens in society. (For an in-depth discussion of the undergraduate curriculum, see chapter 14, pp. 354–360.)

Governance and Research Policy

In response to historical abuses of human and animal research subjects, colleges and universities whose faculty members engage in research are required to comply with research standards defined by the federal government. Because of the complexity of these regulations, most institutions employ staff members who are dedicated to the development and monitoring of such on-campus research. Academic administrators and faculty leaders should also be involved in the development of research policies and the implementation of federal regulations and guidelines for good research practice.

Designating specific members of the CAO's staff to coordinate their institution's research initiatives will facilitate compliance and stimulate faculty and student research initiatives, such as research on teaching, assessment, and learning outcomes, as well as applied and basic research. The focus of a college's or university's research agenda will hinge significantly on the institution's mission, and as the research office staff develops internal incentives to promote research projects and the acquisition of private and federal funding resources, it should ensure these efforts are consistent with the institutional mission.

Institutions with a research mission should develop incentive programs to assist faculty research agendas. Such programs assist the faculty in developing a concept or an idea into a competitive proposal ready for submission to a funding agency. Significant institutional funding—amounts will vary, with higher levels in the hard sciences—should be made available to faculty members to build their capacity to apply for external research sponsorship. These funds should be distributed through an internal review process that allows a faculty committee to issue awards based on the merit or promise of the research proposal.

An institution's research office staff should also provide information on available funding opportunities and assist the faculty in search of relevant funding sources. The office should develop policies governing budget development, course buyouts, and the indirect cost or overhead rates to be built into project budgets. Upon the award of a grant or contract, policies need to be developed for the adequate administration and oversight of all externally funded projects. In larger universities, many of these functions will be distributed to the colleges or schools, but there should be overarching institutional polices governing these subunits' operations.

The U.S. Department of Health and Human Services Office for Human Research Protections website provides a wealth of information on federal regulations and requirements for human subjects research (see www.hhs .gov/ohrp/). Periodically, faculty members and students who conduct research involving human participants must complete tutorials and tests to confirm they understand the protections given to human subjects involved in a research project.[2]

Laws governing the use of animals in research projects exist on the state, federal, and international levels. A resource for these regulations is the National Association for Biomedical Research (2011), which provides guidance from Health and Human Services, the Department of Agriculture, the Animal Welfare Act, the Office of Laboratory Animal Welfare, the Public Health Service Act, the Food and Drug Administration Good Laboratory Practices for Nonclinical Studies, and federal interagency policies that outline practices for use of animals in research and clinical practice.

Developing Interdisciplinary Collaboration

Nurturing collaboration across disciplines and fields in teaching, research, and service is an essential function of academic leaders in the 21st century. As Kezar and Lester (2009) noted,

> A variety of external organizations and sectors are encouraging higher education to become more collaborative in its approach to teaching and research, including accreditors, foundations, business and industry, and government agencies such as National Institutes of Health and National Science Foundation. (p. 4)

Indeed, there is a growing body of literature on fostering collaboration (Austin & Baldwin, 1991; Kezar, Hirsch, & Burack, 2001; Senge, 2000, 2006). The emphasis on collaboration in teaching, research, and service emanates from the complex nature of problems facing society. Diseases such as AIDS and cancer involve not only biomedical issues but also lifestyle, behavioral, economic, and environmental issues that affect prevention and cure. The challenges of poverty, war, and environmental degradation must be approached from a cross-disciplinary perspective involving history, economics, political science, sociology, education, and the hard sciences, which together enhance opportunities for the development of viable solutions to improve the human condition. Colleges and universities seeking to advance knowledge and engage with society must promote collaboration in ways consistent with their missions.

Academic administrators can use their institution's governance structure to change their organization in ways that will foster and promote collaboration in teaching research, and service. To make collaboration part of an institution's mission, Kezar and Lester (2009) argued that one must understand the organization's structural barriers to collaboration (p. 21). One barrier to collaboration is structural: Disciplines and fields are organized in departments or units in colleges or schools. These loosely coupled units have a great deal of autonomy, with each discipline interacting with its specific environment. This arrangement creates a silo effect that is hard to break down. Another barrier concerns college and university reward structures such as promotion and tenure. These systems are designed to maintain disciplinary integrity, but they result in faculty members' inclination to act as lone researchers who work as individuals, and not in teams.

Administrative structures also create barriers in that they are hierarchical, with divisions such as academic affairs, student affairs, and support services all reporting upward and with little lateral communication. Responsibility-centered management, a new strategy adopted by many institutions to bring about fiscal health by setting standards to measure unit profitability and requiring all units to be profitable, places renewed emphasis on units as silos and creates another barrier to working across units (Kezar & Lester, 2009, p. 33). Under responsibility-centered management, the governance structure is also designed as a hierarchy with authority centralized at the institution level. Ultimately, the academic silo effect and administrative hierarchies create minimal interactions laterally in the faculty and the administration. These barriers are further exacerbated by the general gulf that has developed between the faculty and the administration at some institutions. The question becomes how to overcome these barriers to become a collaborative institution.

To bring about institutional change that promotes lateral communication and collaboration in teaching, research, and service, Kezar and Lester (2009) proposed using an adapted version of the Mohrman, Cohen, and Mohrman (1995) model for business corporations. The model advocated changes in six organizational areas. The first area is adaptation of the mission to promote collaboration in teaching, research, and service. The second context is the translation of the new mission into the specific work of the institution in terms of teaching, curriculum, research, and service. The third area involves the identification of the integrating and centralizing structures that need to be put in place to change the way members of the institution communicate, work across boundaries, and break down barriers. The fourth issue concerns institution members changing goal-setting strategies, planning, management, and decision-making processes to promote collaboration. The fifth area involves the ways reward structures should be changed and collaborative research, teaching, and service incentivized. The sixth and final matter concerns the developmental programs that are required to develop collaboration among the faculty and administrators. Changes in these six areas depend on institutional context and may be manifested in very different ways in specific colleges and universities.

Conclusion

The themes of this book—being mission driven, adapting to environmental change, and embracing democratic partnerships—are essential to academic leadership, administration, and governance. Shared governance is key to the success of colleges and universities in performing as effective organizations meeting societal needs of the 21st century, because these structures provide higher education institutions with the checks and balances necessary to inform the academic decisions that fall to the faculty, academic administrators, the CAO, and ultimately the president and the board of trustees. Academic programs operationalize an institution's mission and require careful consideration to be given to curriculum development and degree integrity. Promoting collaboration in teaching, research, and service will make colleges and universities relevant institutions meeting societal needs in the 21st century.

Notes

1. For more information on *Robert's Rules*, see Susskind, McKearan, and Thomas-Larmer (1999).

2. See www.hhs.gov/ohrp/humansubjects/guidance/45cfr46.html for the federal regulations governing the use of human subjects in research.

References

American Association of University Professors. (n.d.). *Statement on government of colleges and universities*. Retrieved from http://www.aaup.org/AAUP/pubsres/pol icydocs/contents/governancestatement.htm

Association of Governing Boards of Universities and Colleges. (1996). *Renewing the academic presidency: Stronger leadership for tougher times.* Washington, DC: Author.

Atnip, G. W. (2009). Role of the chief academic officer. In S. Chen (Ed.), *Academic administration: A quest for better management and leadership in higher education* (pp. 39–51). New York, NY: Nova Science.

Austin, A., & Baldwin, R. G. (1991). *Faculty collaboration: Enhancing the quality of scholarship and teaching.* Washington, DC: George Washington University.

Benjamin, R., Carroll, S., Jacobi, M., Krop, C., & Shires, M. (1993). *The redesign of governance in higher education.* Santa Monica, CA: RAND.

Birnbaum, R. (Ed.). (1991). *Faculty in governance: The role of senates and joint committees in academic decision making.* San Francisco, CA: Jossey-Bass.

Birnbaum, R. (2004). The end of shared governance: Looking ahead or looking back. In W. G. Tierney & V. M. Lechuga (Eds.), *Restructuring shared governance in higher education* (pp. 5–18). doi:10.1002/he.152

Blau, P. M. (1973). *The organization of academic work.* New York, NY: Wiley.

Bolton, A. (2000). *Managing the academic unit.* Philadelphia, PA: Open University Press.

Bright, D. F., & Richards, M. P. (2001). *The academic deanship: Individual careers.* San Francisco, CA: Jossey-Bass.

Bruce, D. B. (2012). The impact of the 2008 Great Recession on college and university contributions to state and regional economic growth. In J. E. Lane & D. B. Johnstone (Eds.), *Colleges and universities as economic drivers: Measuring and building success* (pp. 277–293). Albany, NY: SUNY Press.

Chen, S. (2009). Administration of academic units and shared governance. In S. Chen (Ed.), *Academic administration: A quest for better management and leadership in higher education* (pp. 83–104). New York, NY: Nova Science.

Cole, J. R. (1994). *Balancing act: Dilemmas of choice facing research universities.* Baltimore, MD: Johns Hopkins University Press.

Eckel, P. D. (2000). The role of shared governance in institutional hard decisions: Enabler or antagonist? *The Review of Higher Education, 24*(1), 15–39. doi:10.1353/rhe.2000.0022

Euben, D. R. (2003). *Some legal aspects of collegial governance.* Retrieved from http://www.aaup.org/AAUP/issues/governance/legal/topics/legal-govern.htm

Gilmour, J. E., Jr. (1991). Participative governance bodies in higher education: Report of a national study. In R. Birnbaum (Ed.), *Faculty in governance: The role of senates and joint committees in academic decision making* (pp. 27–40). San Francisco, CA: Jossey-Bass.

Jacobs, J. (2012). The essential role of community colleges in rebuilding the nation's communities and economies. In J. E. Lane & D. B. Johnstone (Eds.), *Colleges and universities as economic drivers: Measuring and building success.* Albany, NY: SUNY Press.

Johnston, S. W. (2003). Faculty governance and effective academic administrative leadership. In S. L. Hoppe & B. W. Speck (Eds.), *Identifying and preparing academic leaders* (pp. 57–63). San Francisco, CA: Jossey-Bass. doi:10.1002/he.130

Kennedy, D. (1993). Making choices in the research university. *Daedalus, 122*(4), 127–152.

Kezar, A., Hirsch, D., & Burack, K. (Eds.). (2001). *Understanding the role of academic and student affairs collaboration in creating a successful learning environment.* San Francisco, CA: Jossey-Bass.

Kezar, A., & Lester, J. (2009). *Organizing higher education for collaboration: A guide for campus leaders.* San Francisco, CA: Jossey-Bass.

Lambert, L. M. (2002). Chief academic officers. In R. M. Diamond (Ed.), *Field guide to academic leadership* (pp. 425–435). San Francisco, CA: Jossey-Bass.

Lattuca, L., & Stark, J. (2009). *Shaping the college curriculum: Academic plans in context* (2nd ed.). San Francisco, CA: Jossey-Bass.

Leaming, D. R. (2002). Academic deans. In R. M. Diamond (Ed.), *Field guide to academic leadership* (pp. 437–450). San Francisco, CA: Jossey-Bass.

Lee, B. (1991). Campus leaders and campus senates. In R. Birnbaum (Ed.), *Faculty governance: The role of senates and joint committees in academic decision making* (pp. 41–62). San Francisco, CA: Jossey-Bass.

Lucey, C. (2002). Civic engagement, shared governance and community colleges. *Academe, 88*(4), 27–31. doi:10.2307/40252185

Martin, J., & Samuels, J. E. (1997). *First among equals: The role of the chief academic officer.* Baltimore, MD: Johns Hopkins University Press.

Mohrman, S., Cohen, S., & Mohrman, A. (1995). *Designing team based organizations.* San Francisco, CA: Jossey-Bass.

National Association for Biomedical Research. (2011). *Animal law section: Overview of existing system.* Retrieved from http://www.nabranimallaw.org/Research_Animal_Protection/Overview_of_Existing_System/

Robert, H. (2011). *Robert's rules of order* (11th ed.). Philadephia, PA: Da Capo Press.

Schoorman, D., & Acker-Hocevar, M. (2010). Viewing faculty governance within a social justice framework: Struggles and possibilities for democratic decision making in higher education. *Equity & Excellence in Education, 43*(3), 310–325. doi:10.1080/10665684.2010.494493

Schuster, J. H., Smith, D. G., Corak, K. A., & Yamada, M. M. (1994). *Strategic governance: How to make big decisions better.* Washington, DC: American Council on Education/Oryx Press.

Senge, P. M. (2000). The academy as learning community: Contradiction in terms or realizable future. In A. F. Lucus (Ed.), *Leading academic change* (pp. 275–300). San Francisco, CA: Jossey-Bass.

Senge, P. M. (2006). *The fifth discipline: The art and practice of learning organizations.* New York, NY: Doubleday.

Susskind, L., McKearan, S., & Thomas-Larmer, J. (Eds.). (1999). *The consensus building handbook: A comprehensive guide to reaching agreement.* Thousand Oaks, CA: Sage.

Tierney, W. G., & Minor, J. T. (2003). *Challenges for governance: A national report.* Los Angeles, CA: University of Southern California.

12

ACADEMIC DEPARTMENTS AND
DEPARTMENTAL LEADERSHIP

Academic departments are the core units of colleges and universities, serving as the venues for the implementation of their institutions' academic missions (Chu, 2006; Lattuca & Stark, 2009; Lucas, 2000a; Seagren, Creswell, & Wheeler, 1993; Wolverton, Ackerman, & Holt, 2005). The work of academic departments exemplifies the three themes of this book—the need to base decisions on an institution's core mission and values, the need to adapt to environmental changes in ways that are consistent with the institutional mission, and the need to create and foster the democratic partnerships with various constituencies.

Faculty members play key roles in curriculum development, teaching, research, and service activities, all of which promote their institution's mission. Moreover, faculty members provide their departments and their institution with direct access to the external environment; in industrial organizations this type of contact is limited to certain units. Faculty members' interactions with their disciplinary counterparts elsewhere provide them with information about changes in the environment they may use to adapt their courses, research, and service. Finally, academic departments are the base unit of democratic partnerships in higher education. Individually, departments are expected to function in a democratic manner, and institutionally, departments provide the bulk of the membership in all levels of governance of the academic core. In this chapter, we discuss the nature of academic departments, the role of department leaders, faculty development, and the academic work of departments.[1]

The Nature of Academic Departments

Academic departments began to mature into the units that we know today during the late 19th and early 20th centuries (Knight & Trowler, 2001).

290

There is great variation in terms of departmental cultures and structures, and these inconsistencies have led a number of observers to speak of the idiosyncratic nature of departments (Chu, 2006; Clark, 2007).

Departmental diversity has many sources. In institutions, for example, distinctions often exist because of different disciplinary traditions based on the structure of knowledge. Biglan (1973a, 1973b) developed a taxonomy to elaborate on the knowledge structures perpetuated by various disciplines and fields, which provides a framework for understanding differences in departmental cultures and structures. Biglan employed a three-way matrix to describe the structure of knowledge, dividing knowledge into hard and soft disciplines. Within these categories, he identified pure and applied fields. He also differentiated in the hard and soft disciplines between life sciences and nonlife sciences.[2]

Biglan's (1973a, 1973b) taxonomy is useful, but further specializations within disciplines and fields also affect how the members of academic departments behave. These traditions influence the ways faculty members are educated, their ways of knowing and seeking truth, their professional standards, and the environment of their field or discipline, all of which influence the structure and functions of their academic departments. (For more on Biglan's model, see chapter 13, p. 313.)

Despite similarities in the training and perspective of scholars in particular fields, great variation remains across departments within the same discipline, particularly in terms of culture and structure. For example, the history of individual departments and the makeup of their faculties contribute to their idiosyncratic nature. In addition, institution type can affect departmental organization and culture. Specifically, smaller colleges and community colleges may consolidate related disciplines or fields into single departments according to the number of faculty members employed in specific areas. These combinations create unique departments within and across institutions.

Institutionwide policies and standards should be balanced against academic departments' need to adapt to the changing requirements of their particular environments. Academic leaders can enhance their understanding of academic departments by conceptualizing them as systems, as well as by taking time to understand their individual cultures and climates.

Departments as Systems

Birnbaum (1988) asserted that postsecondary institutions can be best understood in their structure, decision making, politics, and relation to their environment through the lens of systems theory.[3] Moreover, academic departments, which are situated at their institutions' boundaries with the broader environment, can be analyzed with systems theory (p. 30).

One view discussed in the literature is that academic departments are closed systems since their work is performed in classrooms and labs in their institutions. The more appropriate view is that departments are open systems composed of faculty members who serve a bridging function between their institutions and the environment. Chu (2006), for example, noted that academic departments interact through their faculty members with disciplinary and professional groups; external accrediting bodies; funding agencies; the local community; representatives of the local, state, and national economies in which graduates will eventually work; and students, parents, alumni, and the media (p. 5). Just as Austin (1994) talked about the cultural systems that have an impact on the faculty (see chapter 13, pp. 311–312), some environmental systems have an impact on departments. These systems include the professional, economic, research, service, and institutional environments, and departments' interactions with them across institutional boundaries, resulting in the flow of influence from departments to their environments and vice versa.

The professional environment includes professional and disciplinary associations that influence the curriculum, faculty research, and the employment of program graduates. Many professional or disciplinary associations perform an accreditation function to ensure that academic programs meet minimum expectations. These associations also set standards for research, including the scholarship of teaching and the scholarship that is written to expand knowledge. Some of these associations have also established standards for eligibility and practice in the particular discipline.

The economic environment at the local, state, and national levels is another environment that affects academic departments. For example, the employability of a department's graduates will affect the department's reputation and current and future student enrollment. As technology changes the way work is performed in different sectors of the economy, departments must adapt their curricula to address those changes.

The research environment also affects academic departments. Federal and state agencies and private foundations heavily influence research agendas by designating areas in which they fund basic and applied research and community engagement projects. This relationship is reciprocal, however, as faculty research and scholarship interests also inform funding agencies' and foundations' priorities.

Academic departments also have reciprocal relationships with their institutional environments. For example, while promotion and tenure standards are set at the institutional level, a department has significant input into how those standards are applied within its specific unit. In addition, while general education and baccalaureate degree standards may be set at the institutional level, departments influence the requirements for individual majors. Moreover, on the graduate level, control over degree requirements is more strongly centered in departments or specific degree programs.

Departmental Culture and Climate

Effective administration and leadership requires an understanding of departmental culture and climate. How open has the faculty been in discussing controversial issues? How involved has the faculty been in decision making in the department? Does a leadership clique run the department? Is there a class system that clearly demarcates junior and senior faculty members? Are gender and diversity issues dividing the faculty? Are culture wars splitting the faculty into various camps? Responses to such questions will provide insight into the culture and climate of an academic department. Ideally, the members of an academic department should be able to develop and maintain a collegial environment in which all are advancing a shared vision and mission. Perpetuating such a culture does not mean there will never be conflict. In fact, conflict when dealt with openly fosters collegiality and a healthy climate. Departments that engage in these practices make strong contributions to their institution.

A department's climate characterizes the interpersonal relationships among faculty members. To encourage positive interactions and climate, department chairs can employ a model of shared governance in which they serve as facilitator in conjunction with faculty colleagues to resolve controversial issues (Christie, 2007; Fisher, 2007; Gmelch, 1995). The climate is more likely to be a wholesome environment when conflict is placed on the table and openly discussed and a decision is made afterward. Experience tells us that conflict is best resolved by taking a majority rule vote after a period of open discussion. Typically after a vote, winners and losers walk away accepting the outcome and continuing a healthy professional relationship. In contrast, unresolved conflict creates an unhealthy environment in which parties connive and foster dissent to the detriment of departmental well-being. Transforming a department that seems to thrive on conflict and controversy to a more collegial atmosphere takes time and persistence by its leader. Presenting controversial topics incrementally and constructively will gradually change the climate to one of collaboration and cooperation.

The Role of the Department Chair and Leadership

An extensive body of literature exists concerning the role of the department chair or head in higher education leadership (Brown & Dan, 2002; Gmelch, 1991, 1995, 2004; Gmelch & Burns, 1993, 1994; Gmelch & Miskin, 1995; Knight & Trowler, 2001; Leaming, 2007; Lucas, 2000b; Wheeler et al., 2008).

Department Chairs and Department Heads

The use of the titles department chair and department head is potentially confusing. Some literature defines a department chair as one who is elected by the department faculty, while a department head is appointed by a dean after consultation with the department faculty. The election of a department chair may be for a multiyear term (of two to five years) or for a single-year term, after which he or she will step down. Appointed department heads usually serve three- to five-year terms with the option of one or two renewals.

Lucas (2000b) noted that rotating faculty members through the chair position significantly weakens the chair's ability to lead the department effectively. Since elected chairs are beholden to their faculty colleagues, they tend to have less influence than an appointed chair, whose authority comes from the dean. Elected chairs must also worry about what might happen when they return to the faculty. For example, if an outgoing chair made unpopular decisions, the chair's successor could retaliate. In addition, if an associate professor were to serve as an elected chair, any future promotion application may be negatively affected by colleagues who did not approve of the professor's performance as chair. The literature (Gmelch, 2004; Lucas, 2000b; Lumpkin, 2004) suggests that an appointed head with a strong relationship with the dean is in a better position to lead a department and strengthen and improve its teaching, research, and service activities.

Gmelch (2004) described the difficult position of a department head or chair in relation to the college or university. Specifically, a department head or chair serves the administration and the faculty:

> The academic core of teaching and research operates freely and independently in a loosely-coupled system, whereas the managerial core maintains

the mechanistic qualities of a tightly coupled organization. The department chair is at the heart of this tension between these two systems and
suffers from conflict inherent in the position. (p. 200)

On the one hand, the faculty expects the department chair to be its advocate
with the administration. On the other hand, the administration expects the
department chair to represent its interests to the faculty.

The Department Chair's Role

A useful way to contend with this ambiguity and effectively perform the role
of department chair is to approach situations in terms of Bolman and Deal's
(2008) concept of organizational frames. They identified four frames department chairs can use to understand their role and the role of their department
within the institution. The structural frame considers the academic structure
of the institution, how decisions are made, and where the department chair
fits in that structure. The political frame addresses where the department
and its chair fit in political processes in the institution, as well as where the
chair fits in the politics and culture of the department. The human resource
frame deals with developing an understanding of interpersonal relationships
within the organization; hiring processes; investment of time, effort, and
resources; and how to encourage quality work and professional development.
The cultural frame situates issues and problems in the context of the history
and culture of the institution and the department to make sense of the
perceptions of stakeholders. Lumpkin (2004) added a fifth frame, the personal frame, which is a department chair's understanding of his or her personal strengths and weaknesses and when to rely on the strengths of other
members of the department. Gmelch (2004) noted that new department
chairs tend to focus on the structural and human resource frames. As they
grow and develop in the position, however, they start to use the political and
symbolic frames (p. 71). Building on Lumpkin's idea of the personal frame,
department chairs should play to their individual strengths and draw on
colleagues whose strengths mitigate their weaknesses. Using all these frames
will assist department chairs in understanding their role as a leader and an
administrator.

A number of specific department chair roles are creating a culture of
adaptation and change, developing a shared vision and mission, embracing
conflict toward problem resolution, developing an academic and intellectual
community, fostering growth and professional development, and developing
evaluation processes and strategic plans. Each of these roles is discussed next.

Creating a culture of adaptation and change. Much has been written about departments and adaptation to change (Cheldelin, 2000; Lucas, 2000a, 2000b, 2000c). The department chair plays a pivotal role as a change agent and must be aware of colleagues' potential resistance to change. Usually the roots of opposition involve issues of power and control and feelings of vulnerability. By creating an environment in which all department members participate in setting goals and developing change strategies, resistance to change will be diminished, although it will never go away entirely (Cheldelin).

The adaptive leadership model (Heifitz, 1994) requires department chairs to take a proactive role in change processes through six steps. First, a chair must identify the challenge the department faces. Second, the chair needs to identify the key issues and communicate them clearly to department faculty and staff. Third, the chair must frame and prioritize the areas in which change is required. Fourth, he or she needs to secure faculty ownership of the problem-solving process. Fifth, the chair must manage any emerging conflicts and maintain focus on the problem. Sixth, it is the chair's task to create a safe place where disparate perspectives can be aired openly and without negative repercussions (Coakley & Randall, 2006). In addition to addressing issues of immediate concern, the adaptive leadership model can work in conjunction with environmental scanning to allow a department to be on the cutting edge of a rapidly changing environment.

Developing a shared vision and mission. The need for a chair or head to nurture a shared departmental vision and mission has been emphasized in the literature (Leaming, 2007; Lucas, 2000b). When there is no shared vision in a department, its faculty members tend to act individualistically and in ways that may or may not be in concert with their departmental colleagues. For example, when Robert Hendrickson, one of the authors of this book, became chair of a department housing three fields, each of which offered separate degree programs, there was no shared vision in the department as a whole, and one of the programs lacked a program vision or direction. Faculty members in that program acted as autonomous units and moved in different directions, and no collaboration existed across the department's degree programs.

To address this lack of unity, he began a dialogue with the faculty to develop a vision and goals for the department compatible with the vision and goals of each degree program and consistent with the institution's vision and mission. Out of those discussions a vision emerged for the department that had a profound effect on the degree programs, curriculum, and faculty work. Faculty members no longer operated as independent entrepreneurs and began to collaborate within and across programs in their teaching and their research activities. The development of a set of four courses required for students in all three graduate degree programs is an example of how a shared vision led to collaboration. A committee of faculty members from the three programs monitored the content of each of the courses, and faculty members team-taught the courses.

Embracing conflict toward problem resolution. The issue of conflict has already been discussed in some detail. Most important, we have addressed the necessity of bringing issues to the table for discussion and resolution because ignoring conflict exacerbates problems and allows them to persist. Gmelch (1995) noted there are three types of conflict—institutional, interpersonal, and positional—and argued that successful department chairs need to recognize the nature and cause of conflict (p. 35). While one needs to be aware of institutional conflict, it may be outside a chair's purview to resolve, so he or she must discern ways to work around such challenges. Positional conflict deals with the department chair's struggles with being caught between the administration and the faculty, with obligations to respond to the needs of both constituencies. Interpersonal conflict could occur between faculty members in the department or between the department chair and individual faculty members.

Bissell (2003) wrote about "handling conflict with difficult faculty." He categorized difficult faculty members into several types:

- The "bully" shouts or uses threats and intimidation to get what he or she wants.
- The "complainer" sees himself or herself as a victim and cannot solve problems because of the perceived behavior of others.
- The "procrastinator" chooses to ignore problems.
- The "guerilla fighter" uses sarcasm and criticism to make others feel incompetent or inadequate for raising an issue.
- The "expert" does not listen to others' arguments and uses knowledge to support his or her arguments and show that he or she has all the answers.
- The "icicle" freezes up at the first sign of conflict and has no opinion about the issue under discussion. (pp. 199–120)

These difficult faculty types continually complain, and others find them difficult to be around. They overemphasize problems and are horrible problem solvers. As a result of these weaknesses, they consume a significant portion of a department chair's time.

While department chairs may never change difficult faculty members, strategies exist to assist them in confronting—not rewarding—their behavior. Bissell (2003) identified a number of steps to resolve challenging situations: discern the emotional climate and calm the situation; identify the problem and remain focused on it; resist assigning blame; avoid name calling; develop and evaluate alternative solutions, and then select one; spell out procedural issues; and evaluate the solution's success. Throughout such a process, straight talk and careful listening, including reading between the lines, are important. The chair should avoid conflict triangles by not becoming the third person in a conflict between two faculty members. In addition, control of body language is important so that one's words, not one's body, communicate one's position on an issue. Department chairs need to be aware of their own personalities, mannerisms, and emotions so they will be in control of them rather than be controlled by problem faculty members.

Developing an academic and intellectual community. To cultivate the intellectual life of a department, a chair must encourage faculty and student acceptance to assume responsibility for a healthy intellectual climate. While a chair may need to initiate the first few events such as guest lectures and presentations by faculty and students of current research and findings, eventually the initiative for these sessions will come from faculty and students. One way to begin this tradition is to highlight the scholarly work of faculty members in the department. Another way is to invite faculty members from other departments with similar research interests to present their research and scholarship, which will also encourage collaboration across departments. Such gatherings can also highlight outstanding student research.

Fostering growth and professional development. Encouraging an academic and intellectual community in a department is connected to nurturing professional development among faculty members. Rapid changes in technology have dramatically affected the ways faculty teach. The development of more interactive technology, for example, has greatly enhanced the delivery of online courses and degree programs. As technology continues to evolve, one can only imagine the effects these changes will have on the delivery of higher education in the coming decades. As Bates (2000) noted, there is a need for professional development to assist the faculty in employing these technological developments as effective teaching and learning tools. Department chairs and faculty members collectively should develop strategies that capitalize on technology to enhance their work. Faculty members in a department whose scholarship focuses on teaching and learning in their discipline or field should be consulted in the creation of these professional development strategies.

Developing Evaluation Processes and Strategic Plans. While other sections of this book address strategic planning and evaluation (see, for example, chapter 15, pp. 376–387), it is worth emphasizing the importance of these practices at the department level, as well as the role of the department chair in these processes. Wergin and Swingen (2000) described an "ideal approach" to planning and assessment:

> The ideal approach would be to evaluate academic departments and other academic units in ways that are not too costly or time-consuming, that respect the diversity of disciplinary missions and cultures, that promote departmental self-reflection, all while rewarding collective accomplishments appropriate to larger school and institutional missions. (p. 1)

While such activities as program review, outcomes assessment, specialized accreditation, financial accounting, and internal quality control are often the responsibility of units beyond individual academic departments, chairs should initiate these evaluations and planning processes in their departments when appropriate.

Department Faculty

The faculty in a department converts the institutional mission and vision into programs and activities such as teaching and learning, research and scholarship, and service and community engagement (Leaming, 2003; Lucas, 2000b). One way to achieve a collegial departmental culture is to establish solid employment practices that foster trust and a sense of fairness among the faculty. In this section, we draw on the literature and personal experience to discuss such employment practices, including processes for recruitment and hiring of new faculty members, fair and honest annual reviews of faculty performance, application of transparent and consistent promotion and tenure criteria, and a constructive posttenure review process.

Recruiting and Hiring

Hiring new faculty members is one of the most important tasks of an academic department. While the current economic situation may mean that occasions for hiring are rare, the imminent retirement of baby boomer faculty members will result in significant changes in the makeup of departments' faculty. Their exodus will provide a tremendous opportunity for departments to embrace changes in their disciplines and society more broadly, as well as to move in strategic directions. Capitalizing on this opportunity will require department chairs to embrace hiring strategies that serve their departments and institutions.

Leaming (2007) has provided excellent advice on how to orchestrate successful recruitment and hiring of new faculty members. To begin, the chair and faculty members should identify the disciplinary specializations that are inadequately covered in their department, taking into account any shifts in their discipline's knowledge base or changes in the larger environment. This process will help the department develop a specific position description and the specific criteria used to screen applicants. It will also help, in a time of scarce resources, to justify the need to fill the vacated position.

The selection of the search committee is a critical step in the success of any hiring process. The committee chair and members should be able to navigate between their department's various philosophical and ideological camps by adhering to the agreed-upon job description and selection criteria. The institution's affirmative action policies should be considered in the selection of committee membership and in the selection of candidates. Moreover, recruitment of candidates is more than just advertising in the appropriate trade journals and newspapers. That is, faculty members need to be proactive, actively contacting good prospects and encouraging them to apply. Using Leaming's (2007, p. 251) recommendations as a guide, we have developed an expanded checklist for departmental leaders and committee members to follow as they recruit new colleagues:

1. Develop a job description that is consistent with the department's and institution's mission and promotes diverse ideologies and research interests within the field or discipline.
2. Appoint search committee members who will not try to clone themselves but rather seek a rich pool of candidates with strong teaching, research, and service experiences that will contribute to the department's mission.
3. Task the committee with embracing the institution's diversity objectives and conducting a fair and honest search for the best-qualified candidate who meets diversity objectives and predetermined academic and professional criteria.
4. Develop a mechanism for applicants who are not under consideration to be notified of their status as soon as possible during the

  search, and ensure that all applicants are personally notified by letter of the search's outcome.

5. Voice-over-Internet services (e.g., Skype) may be a good way to screen applicants prior to deciding which candidates should be brought to campus.
6. Campus visits should be a well-organized opportunity for the department to showcase its programs and activities, as well as a chance for candidates to highlight what they would contribute to the department and the institution.

Indeed, the department chair should remind faculty members that a job interview is a reciprocal situation (Leaming, 2007, p. 248). Not only are the faculty, the department, and the institution looking at the candidate as a potential colleague and employee, the candidate is considering the departmental and institutional contexts to determine whether they offer an environment in which the candidate would want to spend all or part of his or her professional career. It is important to be open about conditions at the institution, but it is appropriate to accentuate the positive aspects of working there and living in the community. A careful, transparent hiring process should lead to the recruitment of positive and enthusiastic additions to the department, which in turn should avoid future problems.

Annual Reviews

High-quality departments contribute to high-quality colleges and universities. The annual evaluation of faculty is an important step in the promotion of a strong, vibrant department that delivers quality teaching, research, and service (Chu, 2006; Leaming, 2003; Lucas, 2000b). Many institutions have instituted annual reviews to respond to societal demands for accountability and as a way to monitor and encourage quality performance and faculty development. Annual reviews are most effective when they are directly linked to salary increases or merit pay (Leaming, 2007, p. 284). Those who perform well should receive a salary increase reflective of their good work, while those performing below expected levels should receive no merit increase until they improve their performance.

  Annual review criteria should be developed by the chair and the faculty together. Measures should be consistent with the mission and values of the department, as well as with the specific disciplines or fields in the department. Criteria may also vary according to institution type. For example, the measures used in a small, private liberal arts institution with a strong teaching mission may focus on student and peer review of teaching and the assessment of learning outcomes. In the area of research and scholarship, measures may focus on the scholarship of teaching in the field and applied research and engagement activities in the community and the region. Regardless of a department's discipline or an institution's mission, however, review processes and criteria should be enforced consistently across the department.

A standardized format for annual reviews will allow for a fair assessment of the strongest through the weakest faculty members in a program, identification of strategies to address weaknesses, and the ability to assign workloads to accentuate faculty strengths.[4] Prior to their annual reviews, faculty members should create a report of their activities during the previous year and a list of goals for the upcoming year. The format of the report should be standard across the department, with department-required and self-reported data provided by the faculty member to measure the effectiveness of teaching and advising, research and scholarship, and service and outreach.

One of the most challenging aspects of performing annual reviews is working with underperforming colleagues. While department leaders may shy away from frank evaluations of weaker faculty members, the problems these colleagues present will not disappear without constructive intervention and salary increases linked to performance. Addressing a faculty member's shortcomings in performance of teaching, research, or service roles in a thoughtful manner may have a long-term positive effect on the faculty member in question, particularly in terms of potential promotion, tenure, or faculty development issues. In addition, it should also have a favorable impact on the department climate more broadly.

A department chair who ignores problems with faculty performance sends the message that he or she does not care about the faculty member's behavior, which will ultimately damage the chair's relationship with this faculty member (and potentially with the rest of the department, as colleagues may resent the chair's lack of intervention in the situation). In the process of directly addressing faculty weaknesses in the context of the annual review, the chair can employ the "we" concept. That is, the chair and the faculty member in question can identify ways in which "we" can work together to address problems and implement strategies to improve performance. In the end, however, for interventions with weak faculty members to be successful, the faculty member must be willing to appraise his or her performance honestly and engage in the work necessary to improve performance.

Promotion and Tenure

Promotion and tenure considerations begin at the department level and are based on peer faculty's evaluation of whether a probationary faculty member is eligible to be promoted to associate professor or receive tenure (a contract without term). Academic departments must develop promotion and tenure processes consistent with their institution's processes and criteria, but they must also tailor their standards to the needs of the specific disciplines or fields housed in the department.

Historically, teaching and advising have been the most difficult areas to assess, with performance typically based on students' teacher evaluations and faculty members' classroom observations. More recently the assessment of learning outcomes has been incorporated into the evaluation of teaching, which holds promise to improve our ability to assess teaching effectiveness (Lattuca & Stark, 2009).

The challenges of measuring teaching effectiveness have resulted in an excessive focus on research and scholarship at many institutions, including some whose primary mission is undergraduate education. Instead of emulating the research and scholarship criteria used by doctoral/research universities (as designated by the Carnegie Basic Classifications), colleges and universities whose primary mission is undergraduate teaching, and whose faculty members are expected to teach six to eight courses in an academic year, need to ensure that their research and scholarship expectations appropriately reflect their mission. Their focus ought to be on criteria such as the scholarship of teaching, applied research, and community engagement (Chu, 2006; Knight & Trowler, 2001; Leaming, 2003, 2007; Lucas, 2000b).

In terms of the development of specific promotion and tenure criteria, Diamond (2000) highlighted the following points for consideration in crafting departmental policy:

- It should clearly articulate the criteria that will be used to determine the quality of a faculty member's work, providing the candidate and faculty review committee with a clear indication of not only the review process but also the documentation required.
- It is the ideal vehicle for describing the mission and priorities of your department and how they relate to the mission and priorities of the institution. In the best of worlds this statement would be the basis on which you, your unit, and your faculty would be judged.
- It is the ideal vehicle for describing to others what scholarly, professional, and creative work is in your unit and discipline. One of the major

challenges you will face as chair is communicating to those in other fields this aspect of the work done in your department.

- It can play an important role in communicating to potential and new faculty the priorities of the unit and institution. It can reduce problems associated with new faculty expecting one thing and finding another— thus increasing the potential for long-term personal growth and productivity. (p. 96)

Diamond emphasized the value of engaging the entire department in the development of promotion and tenure standards, as wide participation will create a shared vision and priorities among department members.

A chair should play a significant leadership role in promotion and tenure considerations at the department level. Hiring probationary faculty members is an expensive process and should be viewed as an investment in the development of departmental programs. The department chair should work closely with probationary faculty members to ensure they have every opportunity to successfully navigate the promotion and tenure process. For example, probationary faculty members should be assigned teaching loads that include chances to teach upper-level undergraduate courses (and graduate courses, if offered). In addition, a mentoring program should be developed to assist new assistant professors to hone their teaching, research, and service skills. Periodically throughout the year, the chair should meet collectively or individually with assistant professors to assess their progress and provide assistance as needed. Annual reviews also provide probationary faculty members with an accurate assessment of their progress toward tenure and a context in which to develop strategies to assist them as they move toward tenure review. This combination of consultation, advice, and mentoring from the department chair and other faculty members in the department is very effective in reducing stress and resulting in strong professional growth and the development of probationary faculty.

Posttenure Review

The practice of posttenure review developed in the 1980s as part of states' implementation of accountability measures for their public institutions and higher education systems. About 40% of private institutions have also instituted this type of review. Licata and Morreale (2002) define *posttenure review* as "the systematic evaluation of tenured faculty performance and the establishment of future goals to stimulate professional growth and development" (p. 3). Usually posttenure reviews coincide with annual reviews and occur every five or seven years. Some institutions, such as Texas A&M University, use a substandard evaluation during an annual review to trigger a posttenure review (Licata, 2000, p. 113). Licata (2000) suggested several fundamental objectives that should be incorporated into a posttenure review:

1. Comprehensive assessment of performance utilizing multiple sources of evidence and reflective self-reporting
2. Significant involvement of peers in review and opportunity for collective departmental perspectives
3. Establishment of professional goals and consideration of career direction
4. Provision of meaningful feedback and opportunity for improvement, if necessary (p. 111)

At Pennsylvania State University, a posttenure review is a compilation of the last five annual reviews and an articulation of goals for the next five years. The compilation of the annual reviews is compared with the last posttenure review goal statement. While not a panacea, if used correctly the posttenure review process can be helpful in keeping faculty members who have lost enthusiasm or are nearing the end of their career engaged and motivated in their work. The "we" strategy discussed on p. 302 can also serve as an effective tool for department chairs in the posttenure review process.

Fostering the Academic Work of the Department

Monitoring and improving the quality of a department's academic work are significant and shared responsibilities of the department's chair and its faculty. Through the chair's leadership, the faculty can embrace planning and assessment strategies that include curricular development and adaptation to environmental change, improvement in teaching strategies that capitalize on technological innovation, assessment of learning outcomes, and fostering of research and scholarship (Corey, 2007; Knight & Trowler, 2001; Lucas, 2000b; Sommer, 2008; Wergin & Swingen, 2000).

Curriculum development, teaching strategies, and assessment of learning are inextricably linked to departmental goals and should not be approached as separate processes. Gardiner (2000) discussed curriculum development and adaptation to a changing environment and their links to curriculum assessment, changing teaching strategies, and assessment of learning outcomes. This process includes the assessment of the effectiveness of the curriculum in developing disciplinary or field knowledge and skills, as well as values that are consistent with department and institutional goals that prepare graduates for effective citizenship in society.

This assessment includes the development of standards of performance such as "criterion-referenced evaluations," "value-added assessment," and assessment of individual course learning outcomes (Gardiner, 2000, p. 176). Wergin and Swingen (2000) built on this idea, suggesting that accountability issues drive the need for assessment. They argued that there ought to be institutional coordination of assessment, but that departments should be allowed to adapt institutional guidelines to their specific needs—a practice that will yield variation across departments in terms of "how and what" is assessed (Wergin & Swingen, 2000, p. 11). The department chair and faculty should assume shared responsibility for developing a quality educational program that adapts to environment change and develops the knowledge and skills of their students. (See chapter 15 for a discussion of learning outcomes and assessment strategies.)

Another aspect of faculty work is to foster research and scholarship. This practice is linked to curriculum and teaching assessment. Some research and scholarship, for example, should include studies that will improve pedagogy using technological advances and other innovative teaching tools. Research and scholarship should fit with and reflect the mission and goals of the institution and the department.

One way to encourage research activity—if it is indeed in line with institutional and departmental missions—is for the chair to distribute resources based on faculty research productivity or potential for productivity. Distributing resources equally across all faculty members dilutes resources and will frustrate and create deterrents for productive faculty members. If faculty members desire to pursue external funding sources, it might be helpful to conduct workshops in which faculty members with grant experience educate their colleagues in the craft of pursuing grants. In addition, it might be useful to provide travel funding to enable faculty members to meet with project officers at funding agencies of interest. These investments can be very effective in bringing external funds to departments to help meet their teaching, research, and service objectives.

Conclusion

Academic departments are the primary units that implement a college's or university's mission and goals. Moreover, they are the main venues for higher education institutions to adapt to environmental change and perpetuate shared governance. College and university leaders need to understand the idiosyncratic nature of departments and develop policies and processes that provide sufficient flexibility for implementation of the institution's objectives across diverse academic units. In an academic department, the chair is in a unique leadership position, situated between the administration and the faculty, each of which has very different demands and expectations. To be an effective leader, a chair must understand the environments, cultures, personalities, and traditions that influence his or her department or academic unit.

Leaders who contend successfully with conflict can develop a collegial department that can progress toward a shared vision. The head must play a unique role in developing this shared vision among department faculty. In addition, the chair must lead the faculty in the assessment of work performance, curricular development, ongoing assessment of teaching and learning outcomes, and the promotion of research and service. Departments that are stable and moving toward a shared vision enhance the quality of their institution and make significant contributions toward the achievement of their institution's mission and goals.

Notes

1. As we speak about department leaders, we use the term *department chair* throughout unless we are contrasting specific differences between a chair's role and that of a *department head*.

2. Examples of hard, pure life sciences include biology, biochemistry, and physiology; examples of hard, applied life disciplines include agriculture, medicine, and pharmacy. Examples of hard, pure nonlife fields include mathematics, physics, and chemistry; hard, applied nonlife fields include engineering, telecommunications, and computer science. Among the soft disciplines, examples of pure life disciplines include psychology, sociology, and political science, while examples of pure nonlife disciplines include economics, history, and philosophy. Examples of soft, applied life disciplines include art, education, and management; examples of soft, applied nonlife disciplines include finance, accounting, and law.

3. Open systems theory describes the relationship and response between an organization (in this case, an academic department) and its internal and external environments. See chapter 2, pp. 27–28 for a discussion of this theory.

4. See Leaming (2007, pp. 284–308) for examples of methods and forms to gather information on faculty members' performance in teaching and advising, research and scholarship, and service and outreach.

References

Austin, A. E. (1994). Understanding and assessing faculty cultures and climates. *New Directions for Institutional Research, 1994*(84), 47–63. doi:10.1002/ir.37019948406

Bates, A. W. (2000). Giving faculty ownership of technological change in the department. In A. F. Lucas (Ed.), *Leading academic change: Essential roles for department chairs* (pp. 215–245). San Francisco, CA: Jossey-Bass.

Biglan, A. (1973a). The characteristics of subject matter in different academic areas. *Journal of Applied Psychology, 57*, 195–203. doi:10.1037/h0034701

Biglan, A. (1973b). Relationships between subject matter characteristics and structure and output of university departments. *Journal of Applied Psychology, 57*(3), 204–213. doi:10.1037/h0034699

Birnbaum, R. (1988). *How colleges work: The cybernetics of academic organizations.* San Francisco, CA: Jossey-Bass.

Bissell, B. (2003). Handling conflict with difficult faculty. In D. R. Leaming (Ed.), *Managing people: A guide for department heads and deans* (pp. 119–138). Bolton, MA: Anker.

Bolman, L. G., & Deal, T. E. (2008). *Reframing organizations: Artistry, choice and leadership.* (4th ed.). San Francisco, CA: Jossey-Bass.

Brown, F. W., & Dan, M. (2002). Herding academic cats: Faculty reactions to transformational and contingent reward leadership by department chairs. *Journal of Leadership Studies, 8*(3), 79–93. doi:10.1177/107179190200800307

Cheldelin, S. I. (2000). Handling resistance to change. In A. F. Lucas (Ed.), *Leading academic change: Essential roles for department chairs* (pp. 55–73). San Francisco, CA: Jossey-Bass.

Christie, V. (2007). Deciding who is in charge. *Department Chair, 18*(2), 15–17. doi:10.1002/dch.20020

Chu, D. (2006). *The department chair primer: Leading and managing academic departments.* Bolton, MA: Anker.

Clark, T. M. (2007). Merging departments—practical lessons in leadership: Thoughts from a chair's journal. *Department Chair, 18*(1), 10–13. doi:10.1002/dch.20005

Coakley, L., & Randall, L. M. (2006). Orchestrating change at the departmental level: Applying the process of adaptive leadership. *Academic Leadership, 4*(2). Retrieved from http://www.academicleadership.org/80/orchestrating_change_at_the_departmental_level/

Corey, K. A. (2007). From the other side of the desk. *Department Chair, 18*(1), 25–26.

Diamond, R. M. (2000). The department statement on promotion and tenure: A key to successful leadership. In A. F. Lucas (Ed.), *Leading academic change: Essential roles for department chairs* (pp. 95–107). San Francisco, CA: Jossey-Bass.

Fisher, M. L. (2007). Engaging faculty: Departmental shared governance that works. *Department Chair, 18*(1), 21–23. doi:10.1002/dch.20009

Gardiner, L. F. (2000). Monitoring and improving educational quality in academic departments. In A. F. Lucas (Ed.), *Leading academic change: Essential roles for department chairs* (pp. 165–194). San Francisco, CA: Jossey-Bass.

Gmelch, W. H. (1991, April). *Paying the price for academic leadership: Department chair tradeoffs*. Paper presented at the annual meeting of the American Educational Research Association, Chicago, IL.

Gmelch, W. H. (1995). Department chairs under siege: Resolving the web of conflict. *New Directions in Higher Education, 96*(1), 35–42. doi:10.1002/he.3691 9959207

Gmelch, W. H. (2004). The department chair's balancing acts. *New Directions in Higher Education, 126*(3), 69–84. doi:10.1002/he.149

Gmelch, W. H., & Burns, J. S. (1993). The cost of academic leadership: Department chair stress. *Innovative Higher Education, 17*(4), 259–270. doi:10.1007/BF 00917050

Gmelch, W. H., & Burns, J. S. (1994). Sources of stress for academic department chairpersons. *Journal of Educational Administration, 32*(1), 79–95.

Gmelch, W. H., & Miskin, V. D. (1995). *Chairing an academic department*. Thousand Oaks, CA: Sage.

Heifitz, R. (1994). *Leadership without easy answers*. Cambridge, MA: Belknap Press.

Knight, P. T., & Trowler, P. R. (2001). *Departmental leadership in higher education*. Buckingham, UK: Society for Research into Higher Education and Open University Press.

Lattuca, L., & Stark, J. (2009). *Shaping the college curriculum: Academic plans in context* (2nd ed.). San Francisco, CA: Jossey-Bass.

Leaming, D. R. (2003). *Managing people: A guide for department chairs and deans*. Bolton, MA: Anker.

Leaming, D. R. (2007). *Academic leadership: A practical guide to chairing the department* (2nd ed.). Bolton, MA: Anker.

Licata, C. M. (2000). Post-tenure review. In A. F. Lucas (Ed.), *Leading academic change: Essential roles for department chairs* (pp. 107–137). San Francisco, CA: Jossey-Bass.

Licata, C. M., & Morreale, J. C. (2002). *Post-tenure faculty review and renewal: Experienced voices*. Merrifield, VA: American Association for Higher Education.

Lucas, A. F. (2000a). A collaborative model for leading academic change. In A. F. Lucas (Ed.), *Leading academic change: Essential roles for department chairs* (pp. 33–54). San Francisco, CA: Jossey-Bass.

Lucas, A. F. (Ed.). (2000b). *Leading academic change: Essential roles for department chairs*. San Francisco, CA: Jossey-Bass.

Lucas, A. F. (2000c). A teamwork approach to change in academic departments. In A. F. Lucas (Ed.), *Leading academic change: Essential roles for department chairs* (pp. 7–32). San Francisco, CA: Jossey-Bass.

Lumpkin, A. (2004). Enhancing the effectiveness of department chairs. *Journal of Physical Education, Recreation & Dance, 75*(9), 44–48.

Seagren, A. T., Creswell, J. W., & Wheeler, D. W. (1993). *The department chair: New roles, responsibilities, and challenges* (ASHE-ERIC Higher Education Report). Washington, DC: George Washington University.

Sommer, R. (2008). Models of departmental leadership. *The Department Chair*, *18*(3), 5–6.

Wergin, J. F., & Swingen, J. N. (2000). *Departmental assessment: How some campuses are effectively evaluating the collective work of faculty*. Washington, DC: American Association for Higher Education.

Wheeler, D., Seagren, A., Becker, L., Kinley, E., Mlinek, D., & Robson, K. (2008). *The academic chair's handbook*. San Francisco, CA: Jossey-Bass.

Wolverton, M., Ackerman, R., & Holt, S. (2005). Preparing for leadership: What academic department chairs need to know. *Journal of Higher Education Policy and Management*, *27*(2), 227–238. doi:10.1080/13600800500120126

13

THE FACULTY

The faculty at a college or university plays an essential role in fulfilling the institution's mission of the advancement of knowledge and education of citizens. While an institution's mission is based in part on its environmental niche within society, its faculty is responsible for the translation of the mission into academic programs and activities. In its execution of this responsibility, the faculty puts into practice the three guiding principles of this book: being mission driven, practicing environmental adaptability in alignment with that mission, and perpetuating democratic partnerships. These three themes inform this chapter's discussion of cultural influences on faculty work, the faculty's institutional role, the nature of faculty work, emerging changes to the role, employment issues, and professional development of the faculty.

Cultural Influences on Faculty Work

Just as higher education institutions, colleges and schools, and academic departments are influenced by a variety of environments, faculty members operate in a number of cultural environments that significantly influence their work. Austin (1994) identified five of these cultures: the culture of the academic profession, the culture of the academy as an organization, the culture of the discipline, the culture of the institution type, and the culture of a particular department.

According to Austin (1994), the culture of the academic profession is a value system that is universal to all academics. It mandates that academics pursue truth, advance knowledge, and promote learning (p. 48). The culture of the academy as an organization differentiates academic institutions from other organizations through norms of collegiality and autonomy and notions of governance, decision making, and the distribution of authority and influence (p. 49), which are keys to the concept of shared governance discussed at length in chapter 11. The culture of the discipline influences a faculty member's identity and values system. This values system is established during graduate school (Austin, 2002) and is reinforced and perpetuated by disciplinary professional associations. Allegiance to disciplinary culture, embraced through graduate education, can be a barrier to faculty members' fulfillment of the mission of the institution that employs them.

The culture of institutional type also influences faculty work. Austin (1994) described the effect of this culture in this way:

> The employing institution affects the responsibility, opportunities and rewards available to faculty. In particular, the type of institution in which a faculty member is employed affects his or her relationship to the discipline and its culture, how the new faculty member is socialized, what work is viewed as important and what standards of excellence are used. (p. 50)

Specifically, Austin (1994) suggested that faculty members at research universities, comprehensive institutions, and liberal arts colleges tend to identify more strongly with their disciplines, while community college faculty members relate more closely to their institutions (p. 49). Failure to compromise between disciplinary and institutional cultures can lead to employer-employee conflicts and may affect the institution's ability to execute its mission.

Just as specific institution types perpetuate particular cultures, Austin (1994) identified the culture of a particular department, each with a unique set of values and norms. Departmental culture is in part defined by the other cultures in which faculty members operate, and it varies across academic departments in a school or college. These differences may be accounted for based on variations in the cultures of fields, disciplines, and subdisciplines, but they also emanate from each department's unique history, membership, and leadership.

The Faculty's Institutional Role

The faculty role is typically conceptualized as tripartite: teaching, research, and service. However, a fourth faculty role springs from professors' teaching, research, and service activities. Faculty members work at the boundary of their institution and its external environment, meaning they serve as boundary spanners.

Faculty members' teaching role includes classroom instruction, one-on-one work with students, and student advising. All these activities are intended to facilitate students' knowledge acquisition. What is actually taught is influenced by the culture of the discipline and the needs of the external environment where graduates will ultimately live and work. Faculty members' research activities also bring them into contact with the external environment. Whether they practice basic research for advancement of knowledge and theory or applied research to connect theory to practice, faculty members' scholarly inquiry—and the process of sharing its results through publication—is a means of engagement with the environment. Faculty members also interact with the environment through their service activities, which include involvement in institutional governance and professional and disciplinary associations, as well as engagement with the local community and broader society.

Some researchers who have studied faculty roles have found them to be mutually exclusive and fragmented (Jordon, 1994; Massey & Zemsky, 1994), while other researchers have identified significant integration among teaching, research, and in some cases service (Clark, B. R., 1987; Colbeck, 1998, 2002; Layzell, 1996). In the practice of all three roles, however, faculty members practice their fourth role of creating a bridge between their institutions and their external environments.

The conceptualization of faculty roles varies across academic disciplines. Biglan (1973) developed a classification scheme that categorizes differentiation of roles according to the theoretical frames or paradigms in different disciplines. This model can help our understanding of the effects that disciplinary culture has on the role of the faculty and the nature of faculty work. According to Biglan, there are two main categories of disciplines: high paradigm (disciplines organized by clearly articulated theories, namely, the hard sciences) and low paradigm (disciplines organized around perceptions and understandings, such as the arts, humanities, and social sciences). In high-paradigm disciplines, knowledge is cumulative, theoretical frameworks are highly structured, and there are clear boundaries between disciplines. At these boundaries where two or more disciplines overlap, new interdisciplinary fields have developed (e.g., biotechnology, bioengineering, astrophysics). In this paradigm, the nature of faculty work is clearly defined through rigid structuring of curricula and standardization of research methodologies. In contrast, in low-paradigm disciplines, a general understanding exists that there are multiple ways of knowing, which causes these fields' boundaries to be fluid, curricula to be more flexible, and research methodologies to be more diverse. This lack of consensus results in more role ambiguity for faculty. (Biglan's classification scheme was discussed in chapter 12, p. 291 and note 2 on p. 307.)

Beyond disciplinary traditions, institutional mission influences the definition of faculty roles and the balance among teaching, research, and service activities. For example, at research universities, while teaching has taken on more importance in the faculty reward structure, research remains the coin of the realm. Research universities' change in emphasis toward teaching is the result of public pressure as the cost of higher education has escalated. The public demands students have more contact in the classroom with tenured faculty instead of graduate assistants and instructors. In addition, since the Kellogg Commission on the Future of State and Land-Grant Universities' (1999) report emerged, community outreach has taken on more importance at research universities. Still, at research universities in which the faculty-reward structure continues to emphasize research and external funding, faculty teaching loads are smaller, particularly in hard-paradigm disciplines.

In contrast, at institutions whose mission focuses on undergraduate teaching and learning (e.g., community colleges, baccalaureate institutions, and private liberal arts colleges), the faculty role includes all three traditional components—teaching, research, and service—although greater emphasis is placed on teaching and engagement. In these contexts, faculty research tends to include the scholarship of discovery, but much research activity is directly related to teaching and learning (Palmer, 2002). As Fairweather (1996, 2005) has shown, however, many teaching-oriented institutions' reward structures try to mirror those of research universities, ignoring their own missions to pursue the prestige associated with research productivity.

As faculty members navigate their teaching, research, and service roles, they are also functioning as boundary spanners in and beyond their institutions. Some faculty members span internal boundaries by bridging disciplines, centers, and academic units to foster collaboration and interdisciplinarity. Others participate in civic engagement activities that provide opportunities to interact directly with community, state, and federal entities as well as professional and disciplinary associations. These boundary-spanning functions provide faculty members with a certain level of autonomy within their institution, especially if they receive external funding for community action work or applied or theoretical research.

The Nature of Faculty Work

Conventional wisdom suggests that faculty work is a cushy job that involves spending a few hours teaching in the classroom and some time holding office hours, while the professors spend the rest of their time free to do as they please. However, the reality could not be more different for most faculty members. Faculty work is a balancing act among the roles of teaching, research, and service. As mentioned previously, faculty members place greater emphasis on their different roles depending on their institution's mission and type. Typically, however, faculty members spend 50 hours per week on their work (Schuster & Finkelstein, 2006).

All faculty members with teaching responsibilities spend time on course preparation and delivery (O'Meara, Terosky, & Neumann, 2009). For example, to ensure that course offerings remain current in the field, professors should develop new course syllabi and revise existing course syllabi prior to the semester when the classes will be offered. Course development should capitalize on lessons learned from previous teaching experiences, including the use of such tools as course websites. Faculty members should make themselves available to meet with their students outside the classroom, exchange e-mails as appropriate, and participate in online discussions. In addition, they should share with colleagues what is working well and seek input where improvements might be needed. Ultimately, the time faculty members spend on each course will depend somewhat on their prior experience with teaching the course (such as how often they have taught it previously) and the level of the course (i.e., introductory, advanced, or graduate level), but all these tasks indicate that, in reality, effective teaching practices consume a significant portion of a faculty member's time. In addition, beyond course preparation, faculty members' teaching role includes student advising and mentoring responsibilities, which can continue even after students graduate.

As we have already discussed, research responsibilities vary by institution type and by discipline (O'Meara et al., 2009). For example, faculty members in hard-paradigm disciplines at a research university are expected to support a laboratory, graduate assistants, and postdoctoral researchers. Although there is an expectation of funded research in soft-paradigm disciplines, there is greater emphasis on the publication of books, book chapters, and articles in refereed journals. At comprehensive colleges and liberal arts colleges that have not reformed their rewards structures, faculty members are expected to have an extensive research agenda despite the high teaching load typical of these institutions. Pressure for prestige, reputation, and national rankings drives these expectations.

At comprehensive colleges and liberal arts colleges whose administrators understand their teaching mission and have reformed their rewards structure to reflect this focus, faculty research agendas tend to involve keeping current in disciplines and fields and focusing on the scholarship of teaching and the development of textbooks for college-level courses (Rice, 2002). In fact, Palmer (2002) found that tenured faculty in community colleges were in many cases involved in the scholarship of teaching and textbook authorship.

Faculty members' service or engagement role varies somewhat by institutional type but can be divided into institutional, disciplinary, and community activities. At all institutions, faculty members are involved in the governance of their institution, including making decisions surrounding hiring and determination of rank. Most faculty members participate in their national or regional disciplinary associations, serving as officers or committee chairs or members and participating in conferences. The faculty's service role continues to evolve, and civic engagement has become an important aspect of the service mission of many institutions (Berberet, 2002). (For more information on civic engagement, see chapter 7.)

The Changing Nature of the Faculty Position

Lately, U.S. higher education has witnessed a shift in faculty employment practices, with more contingent (part-time and full-time fixed-term) faculty members being hired in colleges and universities. This hiring strategy has affected faculty demographics, which have also changed significantly because faculty members have become more diverse on the basis of race and gender. The consequences of an aging professoriate and looming retirements will have a profound impact on the makeup of U.S. colleges' and universities' faculties in the future.

Contingent Versus Tenure-Track Faculty

For the past couple of decades, higher education institutions have been moving toward a greater reliance on contingent, part-time, and fixed-term full-time contract faculty. This practice is said to give institutions the ability to adapt to environmental, programmatic, and technological changes, as well as societal needs and demands (American Federation of Teachers [AFT], 2009). Specifically, institutions have moved to a contingent faculty model to gain flexibility in staffing and adaptability in academic programs, as well as to reduce costs. Schuster and Finkelstein (2006) reported that in 2003 the number of non-tenure-track positions increased to 58.6%, and the number of tenured and tenure-track positions declined to 41.4% for all faculty in U.S. higher education institutions. The AFT (2009) explored the growth of contingent faculty and the decline of tenure-track faculty in U.S. higher education and indicated that tenure-track faculty positions in all higher education institutions had declined to 27.3% of all faculty, although total faculty appointments increased by 31.8%.

The AFT (2009) report indicated that the distribution of contingent versus tenure-track faculty varies across institution types. Public community colleges, for example, rely heavily on contingent faculty (over 80% of the faculty), with 13.5% of faculty members hired on fixed-term full-time contracts and 68.6% hired on part-time contracts—meaning that the tenure-track faculty makes up only 17.5% of the faculty at these institutions. Public and private comprehensive institutions are hiring more contingent faculty members. Fixed-term full-time faculty has increased to 10.9% at public comprehensives while increasing to 17.2% at private comprehensive institutions. Part-time faculty members at public comprehensive institutions make up 43.9% of the total faculty and 52.2% of all faculty at private comprehensive institutions. This change in types of faculty appointments has reduced the percentage of tenured and tenure-track faculty members to 39% at the public comprehensives and 29% at the private comprehensives. However, public and private research universities have seen only a slight decline in full-time tenured and tenure-track faculty and a small increase in the percentage of part-time faculty to 15.8% at public institutions and 31.3% at private institutions. Other studies have found similar changes in faculty hiring patterns (Ehrenberg & Zhang, 2005a, 2005b; Schuster & Finkelstein, 2006).[1]

The demographics, career aspirations, and job satisfaction of contingent faculty members are not widely understood. Overall, however, contingent faculty members have been found to be consistently high performers (Gappa, 2000, p. 78). According to a study by Gappa, 64% of part-time faculty members held full-time jobs elsewhere, with 45% employed at several different institutions in the same region (p. 79). Gappa and Leslie (1993) developed a classification system that sheds light on who these part-time faculty members are. It classified part-time faculty as "professional specialists or experts" (employed in business or industry), "career enders" (retired or in transition to retirement), and "aspiring academics" (pursuing a faculty career). Leslie and Gappa (2002) found that only 16% of the part-time faculty population consisted of aspiring academics, and these individuals were concentrated in fine arts and the humanities and taught at several institutions simultaneously (p. 79). In this study, Leslie and Gappa reported that a majority of contingent faculty members (85%) expressed satisfaction with their academic positions. Fixed-term, full-time contingent faculty members were more involved in academic governance and had greater access to professional development programs than part-time faculty. Hired because of their strong teaching skills, 75% reported being satisfied with their workload, job security, and salary, but they expressed some dissatisfaction with the overall status of contingent faculty in their institutions (p. 84).

Moreover, Leslie and Gappa (2002) found that

> part-timers in community colleges look more like full-time faculty than is sometimes assumed. Their interests, attitudes, and motivations are relatively similar. They are experienced, stable professionals who find satisfaction in teaching. Contrary to popular images, only small fractions of part-timers are eagerly seeking full-time positions and subsisting on starvation wages while holding multiple part-time jobs—the prevalent stereotype so often profiled in the popular media. (p. 65)

Part-timers have been recognized for their teaching, but they tend to lack comfort in expressing their opinions, and they receive less institutional support than their full-time colleagues. Institutions should invest in these faculty members as a long-term asset by integrating them more effectively into the academic processes of the institution rather than isolating them as a "replaceable part" (Leslie & Gappa, 2002, p. 66).

Hiring more contingent faculty members may make an institution more adaptable, but it may negatively affect fulfillment of its teaching mission as well. In a study of a state system of public higher education, Jaeger and Eagan (2010) found that the use of high concentrations of contingent faculty in first-year students' courses reduced retention rates to the second year of college at doctoral-extensive, master's, and baccalaureate institutions. While the proportion of courses taught by graduate students at master's and baccalaureate institutions increased a first-year student's propensity to drop out, full-time contract faculty also had a negative impact on retention. Jaeger and Eagan identified an exception to these trends at doctoral-intensive institutions, where employment of part-time faculty positively influenced student retention (p. 22). In contrast to part-time faculty's treatment at master's and baccalaureate institutions, they noted that at these doctoral institutions, part-time faculty members were more frequently viewed as an important asset for student retention, given more institutional support, and included in faculty orientation programs (p. 23).

Similarly, Ehrenberg and Zhang (2005b) found that increases in part-time faculty reduced graduation rates at some institutional types. While noting questions about the reliability of the institutional data used in the study, the authors said that when making staffing decisions, institutions must weigh the negative aspects of reduced graduation rates against the savings accrued by hiring contingent faculty. They calculated that institutions saved on average $6,596 per salary annually by replacing an assistant professor with a full-time contingent faculty member (p. 657).

Increasing dependence on contingent faculty may also have implications for the faculty's research role. In a study of the impact of faculty employment patterns on research and development (R&D) expenditures, Zhang and Ehrenberg (2010) found that a 1% increase in the number of full-time faculty resulted in a .2% increase in R&D expenditures, while a 1% increase in the proportion of full-time contingent faculty as a share of the total full-time faculty resulted in a .6% decrease in R&D expenditures. However, increasing contingent faculty while holding full-time faculty constant resulted in a .44% increase in R&D expenditures. (Increasing the number of graduate students—many of whom teach undergraduate courses—also increased R&D expenditures.)

As these studies have shown, faculty staffing decisions have direct effects on an institution's ability to achieve its mission and educational outcomes. To ease negative consequences for undergraduate education, institutions may want to concentrate part-time faculty members in upper-division courses and graduate programs. When full-time contingent faculty teach first- and second-year students, they should be included in curriculum development and faculty governance activities and be fully oriented to all the learning resources available to students. Out of class, contingent faculty members should be encouraged and rewarded for engaging with students since research has suggested that such contacts positively affect persistence (Pascarella & Terenzini, 2005). These practices will allow an institution to remain true to its mission while addressing its need to be adaptable in a rapidly changing environment.

Faculty Demographics

Since the 1960s the demographic makeup of faculty members at U.S. institutions of higher education has become much more diverse in terms of gender, race, and ethnicity. In particular, since the 1970s colleges and universities have increased the percentage of female faculty members and African American and Hispanic faculty members (Schuster & Finkelstein, 2006). These changes occurred in response to the Civil Rights Act of 1964 but also because of national and state policies to promote affirmative action in employment in and admission to higher education institutions. Bowen and Bok's (1998) study gave credence to the assumed benefits of affirmative action policies, reporting that student and faculty diversity enhances learning.

In terms of changes in the gender distribution of faculty members since the 1960s, Schuster and Finkelstein (2006) found that the percentage of female faculty had grown from 17.3% of the total faculty in U.S. colleges and universities to 35.9% in 1998 (p. 50). Wilson (2010) reported that as of 2005–2006, women in all U.S. higher education institutions held 39% of all full-time faculty positions and 48% of the part-time positions. Of tenured and tenure-track faculty members who are women, just 24% held full professor positions in 2006—a percentage that had declined from 29.2% in 1998 (Wilson). Women are concentrated at the instructor, assistant professor, and associate professor levels of faculty employment (p. 50). The concentration of women in the lower faculty ranks, along with instances of pay disparities, suggests that gender discrimination remains an issue in faculty employment. Such data are cited in legal cases to provide evidence of inequity and the existence of a glass ceiling for women in higher education.

In a different interpretation of the concentration of female faculty members in lower ranks, Hargens and Long (2002) suggested that this concentration is less about discrimination and more about the demographic (age) makeup of the faculty. While they acknowledged that although the percentage of female PhDs and the percentage of new female faculty hires were increasing, both trends were having little positive impact on the percentage of female faculty members in the senior level of their profession. Hargens and Long postulated, however, that as retirements increase in the next 10 to 15 years the number of women in senior faculty positions should increase dramatically.

The National Center for Education Statistics (NCES, 2011) reported that in 2003 female faculty members constituted 42.2% of all teaching faculty, but according to the data they tended to be employed at certain institution types. For example, women made up 48.2% of the faculty at public two-year colleges and 40% of the faculty at private four-year colleges and public four-year colleges. At research and doctorate-granting institutions, women made up just 28% and 33% of the faculty (Schuster & Finkelstein,

2006, p. 52). Female faculty members are also concentrated in some disciplines. For example, women hold 67% of the positions in education, 62% in health sciences, 45% in communications, and 48% in law and social service. The number of female faculty is lower in engineering (10%), agriculture and natural resources (22%), and business administration (30%; NCES, 2011).

The racial and ethnic makeup of faculties has also become more diverse over the last five decades. For example, Schuster and Finkelstein (2006) reported that the percentage of non-White full-time faculty members increased from 3.8% in 1969 to 20% in 1998 (p. 54). Using 2007 data, the "Almanac of Higher Education" (2010) reported that the U.S. higher education faculty was 75% White, 8% Black, 4% Hispanic, 6% Asian, and 3% non-U.S. foreign. As these figures indicate, there is still a need for more diversification in the faculty based on race and ethnicity. Diversification of faculty by race and gender is more pronounced in the humanities and social sciences than in the hard sciences (Schuster & Finkelstein, 2006, p. 54). Institutions should be in a better position to address barriers to diversification of faculty as positions open up when baby boomers begin to retire.

Faculty Retirements

The graying of the faculty is a phenomenon that will have a significant impact on higher education in the next 12 to 20 years. Schuster and Finkelstein (2006) reported that in 1998, 51.2% of the faculty was under 50 years of age, 35.6% was between 50 and 59, and 16.1% was 60 years old or over (p. 59). While the economic downturn has caused some older faculty members to delay their exit from the academy, the next 10 to 15 years will see an onslaught of faculty retirements from the 49.8% of faculty members who were 50 years and older in 1998. Their retirement should have a significant and positive effect on gender, racial, and ethnic diversity in faculties.

While at first, given the difficult economic times, institutions may eliminate some retirees' positions, in time they will have to replace them to maintain academic programs, advance knowledge, and educate citizens. The main question is whether colleges and universities will opt to replace tenured faculty members with contingent faculty members, or whether institutions will choose to recruit entry-level, tenure-track faculty candidates. Our three principles of mission, adaptability, and democratic partnerships should drive institutions' decision-making processes as they develop strategies for the composition of their faculties.

Faculty Employment Issues

As is the case with most organizations, colleges and universities must contend with staff issues. In this section, we address concerns specifically related to the employment of faculty members. With the retirement of substantial numbers of senior faculty members looming, higher education institutions should develop plans for the recruitment and hiring of new faculty members. As institutions replace faculty members, they must address diversity issues in ways that are consistent with laws prohibiting discrimination. In addition, administrators of institutions should identify ways to protect faculty members' academic freedom—an important concept in the advancement of knowledge. They also should consider how faculty members can engage in academic governance as a democratic partner with administrators and board members.

A Faculty Employment Plan

In the wake of the economic downturn of 2008, institutions began to downsize their faculties and staffs using attrition through retirement and resignations. While the crash of 2008 caused some faculty members to delay retirement, in the next decade retirements are expected to increase (American Council on Education, 2010). Institutions should not leave staffing decisions to fate. Rather, administrators should develop and define faculty hiring strategies for the next 10 to 15 years. Such strategic planning should be completed in light of the institution's mission and if done properly will positively affect its academic programs.

In a study commissioned by the Teachers Insurance and Annuity Association to investigate the changing demographics of higher education faculty, R. L. Clark (2004) made the following recommendation:

> A faculty-planning model should be based on demographic models of population growth and employment records of individual institutions. Using the planning model, academic administrators would be able to observe the changing age structure of their faculty, expected turnover rates and retirement rates, and the need for new faculty. The model will also be able to address the changing composition of the faculty between full-time tenure track faculty and other types of faculty appointments. (p. 10)

Such a plan should take into account the themes of this book: institutional mission, adaptability to environmental change, and democratic partnerships. The plan should account for the faculty positions needed to deliver quality programs, including the ratio of contingent to tenured and tenure-track faculty members and their hiring rank. In addition, no plan should ignore the quest for diversity within the faculty. With half of faculties expected to retire in the next decade, now is an excellent time for colleges and universities to plan for new faculty hires that will allow them to adapt to environmental changes in ways that are consistent with their mission and values. Here are some questions that should be posed in developing a faculty staffing plan:

- Based on institutional mission, what should be the ratio of tenure or tenure-track faculty to contingent faculty (fixed-term, full-time, and part-time faculty)?
- If hiring tenured faculty, what should be the rank of a faculty member to maintain the quality and reputation of the degree program?
- Can quality of academic programs be maintained where we only employ contingent faculty to deliver those programs?
- Will what we know about the relationship between faculty staffing patterns and student learning be used in developing the plan?

Discrimination in Employment

Just as colleges and universities must consider affirmative action issues as they develop new faculty positions in the coming decade and beyond, administrators must also be attentive to these concerns with current faculty members. A number of federal laws inform these matters, including Title VII of the Civil Rights Act of 1964 (as amended by the Equal Employment Opportunity Act of 1972), Title VI of the Civil Rights Act of 1964, the Equal Pay Act of 1963, the Age Discrimination in Employment Act of 1967, the Rehabilitation Act of 1973 (amended by the Americans With Disabilities Act of 1990), and Title IX of the Education Amendments of 1972. The foci of each of these affirmative action and antidiscrimination laws are discussed in chapter 6, but here we emphasize the need to be mindful of these laws in hiring, salary, promotion, and tenure decisions, and in nonrenewal, layoff, and termination for cause actions.

In faculty employment decisions, institutions must uphold the relevant federal laws and any state statutes that mirror or expand upon federal laws. Today most institutions maintain affirmative action policy statements that prohibit discrimination on the basis of race, gender, national origin, sexual orientation, and veteran's status, meeting or exceeding federal and state employment obligations. Discrimination against individuals with physical handicaps is treated somewhat differently in that a person with a physical disability must be otherwise qualified to perform the requirements of the position.

Academic Freedom and the First Amendment

Academic freedom as a concept was established by the American Association of University Professors (AAUP) around the turn of the 20th century, although it originated in the German university traditions of *Lehrfreiheit* (freedom to pursue truth) and *Lernfreiheit* (freedom to learn). The purpose of these freedoms was to protect faculty members from religious, political, and societal interference in the pursuit of truth, wherever that might lead (Toma, 2011, p. 95). The *1940 Statement of Principles on Academic Freedom and Tenure* (AAUP, n.d.) institutionalized the standards used to define academic freedom today. The statement identified the following freedoms:

1. The freedom to research issues to advance truth and to publish results without institutional retribution;
2. The freedom of teachers in the classroom to present knowledge and discuss matters pertaining to the subject matter of the class, but not to include unrelated controversial subject matter; and
3. The freedom to speak or write publicly as concerned citizens, without institutional retribution, although in public pronouncements faculty members should use only their academic titles when speaking within their area of technical expertise.

Traditionally, only tenure-track and tenured faculty are protected by academic freedom, and in some cases only tenured faculty enjoy this protection. Tenure is defined as a contract without term, but it is not a job for life, and the contract can be terminated for cause as long as due process is observed (see chapter 6, pp. 152–153).

The AAUP considers academic freedom to be a First Amendment right. Based on U.S. Supreme Court cases such as *Minnesota State Board for Community Colleges v. Knight* (1984) and *Waters v. Churchill* (1994), Hendrickson (1999) has maintained that while faculty members have rights under the U.S. Constitution, including free speech rights under the First Amendment, academic freedom is a contractual right granted by an institution (p. 82).[2] DelFattore (2011), based on the Supreme Court's decision in *Garcetti v. Ceballos* (2006), has also argued that academic freedom becomes a profession standard guaranteed by the institution through a contract.

All public employees are protected by First Amendment speech rights when discussing matters of public concern (*Garcetti v. Ceballos*, 2006; *Jeffries v. Harleston*, 1994; *Waters v. Churchill*, 1994). These matters include the quality of education, health, and safety that affect the public. Faculty pronouncements about matters of employee concern—such as teaching assignments, class schedules, and expectations of time in the office—are not covered by the First Amendment. While matters of employee concern may not be covered by the First Amendment, they may be covered by academic freedom guidelines, depending on the content of the speech. Such matters could include course content or pedagogical strategies.

These academic freedoms and First Amendment rights are fundamental values that go to the core of higher education's concept of democratic partnerships. Academic freedom is not, however, academic license. For example, the curriculum of an academic program—that is, course sequences and course content—should be determined by the collective faculty of that program. Academic freedom does not give individual faculty members the right to teach whatever they want whenever they want. It is, however, the prerogative of individual faculty members to determine how and with which resources (i.e., readings, problems, and case studies) to deliver the content. Issues surrounding how course content is taught are a matter of employee concern and are not covered by the First Amendment, although they are certainly covered by academic freedom.

As institutions hire more contingent faculty members, questions are emerging concerning academic freedom and First Amendment protections, and administrators of institutions need to rethink their academic freedom policies. Gappa, Austin, and Tice (2007) have argued that institutions need to expand their academic freedom policy to cover contingent and tenured and tenure-track faculty members alike. Specifically, they have asserted that contingent and pretenure faculty members should receive explanations of adverse personnel actions, such as decisions not to renew contracts. Such decisions should be based on written peer evaluations of performance using consistent appropriate evaluation criteria; renewals of contingent faculty members' contracts should be based on programmatic needs; grievance procedures should follow the tenets of fundamental fairness and due process commonly used in discrimination cases. Finally, decisions should be reviewed by an impartial body according to academic freedom policies, and review committee members should be protected from retribution resulting from their findings (p. 236). Developing an academic freedom policy that protects all faculty members is consistent with higher education's core mission and reflects adaptability to change in the institutional environment and dedication to fostering democratic partnerships.

Faculty Governance

Some research on the effects of increases in contingent faculty has indicated that concurrent declines in learning outcomes may be the result of isolation of contingent faculty members from academic governance in their institutions (Jaeger & Eagan, 2010; Leslie & Gappa, 2002). Involving contingent faculty members in academic governance including curriculum development provides them with a better understanding of institutional mission and curricular design. Contingent faculty members can serve students more effectively when they know how the courses they teach fit into general education and the undergraduate major. By bringing these faculty members into the academic governance and culture of the institution, they will become active contributing members instead of being kept on the sidelines as second-class citizens. (See chapter 11 for a more in-depth discussion of academic governance.)

Faculty Reward Structures

Designing an evaluation and reward structure for faculty that reflects the mission and goals of the institution is important in maintaining a strong and vibrant faculty. A number of evaluation processes important to faculty growth and development include annual reviews, promotion and tenure, and posttenure reviews.

Annual reviews and merit pay. While the process of annual evaluations of faculty performance and the award of merit pay is discussed in chapter 12, p. 301, it is relevant to discuss faculty work and productivity criteria briefly here. Diamond and colleagues have studied these issues since the 1990s (Diamond, 1993, 1995, 1999, 2002a, 2002b, 2002c; Diamond & Adam, 1993, 2004). A key recommendation that has emerged from their scholarship is that institutions need to ensure that criteria for annual reviews and rewards are consistent with their mission and their promotion and tenure process. What faculty members reported to Diamond (2002c), however, is that their institutions' rhetoric does not reflect what is actually rewarded, nor are personnel reward policies consistent with their institutions' stated mission. In addition, they found that applied research, teaching, course and curriculum design, and community service do not receive much in the way of rewards or recognition (Diamond, 2002c, p. 31). Beyond connecting to the institutional mission, Diamond and his colleagues have also argued that reward structures need to be discipline specific so they will more accurately reflect the realities of faculty work.

Promotion and tenure. Scholars have asserted there is no longer a need for contracts without term, commonly known as tenure, because it stifles institutional adaptability (Breneman, 1997; Chait, 1997). Others have suggested that while the inability to adapt was one of the main arguments for eliminating tenure, the transition to a mix of tenured and tenure-track and contingent faculty has provided institutions with more flexibility to adapt to change (Allen, 2000; Finkin, 1998). Tenure advocates also argue that while contingent faculty members are protected by academic freedom at many institutions, they lack the job security of tenured faculty members. Moreover, they lack the freedom to set their own research agendas and pursue truth wherever it leads, free from intimidation and threats.

While this debate will continue, we propose that institutions need to maintain a ratio of different types of faculty positions based on their mission. This ratio will vary by institutional type and geographic location, but a cadre of tenure and tenure-track faculty should be maintained at all institutions. While the promotion and tenure process is discussed in chapter 12, current trends in faculty evaluation, promotion, and tenure are considered here (see, for example, Green, 2008; Huber, 2002; Shapiro, 2006).

In his 1990 book on the professoriate, Boyer proposed revisions to the criteria used to evaluate faculty performance in awarding promotion and tenure. Specifically, he advocated for diversification of the criteria to move away from a primary focus on research and publication productivity, a secondary concern for teaching, and a tertiary interest in service. Instead, Boyer recommended that promotion and tenure criteria include balanced consideration of the four areas of scholarship: discovery, teaching, integration (interdisciplinarity), and application (engagement). Moreover, Boyer maintained that faculty members' productivity should be based on four mandates: doing original research, staying current in their fields, maintaining high standards of performance in teaching and discovery, and improving assessment tools of faculty performance (p. 27).

A number of scholars have subsequently studied the impact of Boyer's (1990) recommendations on faculty reward criteria in higher education institutions (Braskamp, 1994; Braxton, Luckey, & Holland, 2002; Diamond &

Adam, 1993). More recently O'Meara (2005) surveyed a national sample of college and university chief academic officers (CAOs) to determine whether their faculty reward structures had changed in light of Boyer's proposals. The findings of O'Meara's study were that 68% of CAOs indicated that changes had been made to their institutional mission and policies and faculty evaluation criteria, and that they developed incentive grants, established policies for flexibility in workloads, and expanded the definition of scholarship (p. 488). Since O'Meara's findings came from CAOs' responses to a survey, we lack specific information about the scope of change at their institutions, but the study certainly indicates that some reform is taking place in U.S. higher education.

The most prominent reform in promotion and tenure has involved the tenure clock. Traditionally, a probationary faculty member (pretenured, tenure-track faculty member) has six years to be awarded tenure. During that period, the faculty member would be evaluated annually and given some indication of his or her progress toward the award of tenure. In recent years, many institutions have established a process to stop the tenure clock so that young women on the tenure track can have children. Even with such policies in place, however, research shows that female probationary faculty of childbearing age avoid having children because of concern that it could jeopardize their chances of being awarded tenure (Bellas & Toutkoushian, 1999; Finkel, 1994; Harper, Baldwin, Gansneder, & Chronister, 2001; Johnsrud & Des Jarlais, 1994).

Any institutional reform that changes the faculty evaluation and reward structure for promotion and tenure should be based on the institution's mission and the work its faculty members actually perform. Too often changes in faculty reward structures have sought to mirror those of major research universities—a trend that contributes to the phenomenon of "mission creep" (Lane, 2005). For example, institutions whose primary mission is baccalaureate education should resist the temptation to adopt research universities' traditional standards for research and publication. Calabrese and Roberts (2004) noted that the quest to publish or perish forces faculty members to prepare articles for publication that are often inconsequential and are submitted to achieve the designated number of publications required for tenure and not to contribute to the advancement of knowledge. Indeed, it is incomprehensible how an institution that requires its professors to teach six to eight courses per academic year can also expect its faculty members to produce research and publications of a quality comparable to that of faculty members at research universities where they may teach two to four courses each year. Rather, an institution with an undergraduate teaching mission should make teaching and the scholarship of teaching the top criteria for faculty evaluation and awards.

To avoid the trap of mission creep and the negative ramifications it can have for institutions and their faculty members' work, Diamond (2002c) has outlined the following principles for determining faculty reward criteria:

- Individual academic units can be given the responsibility of determining *if* a specific activity falls within the work of the discipline and the priorities of the institution, school, college, and department.
- The criteria that are used can be clear, easy to understand, and consistent across all disciplines, thus reducing problems for administrators, committees, and the faculty members being reviewed.
- The system is fair and the criteria are clearly understood, with no one discipline or group of disciplines determining what scholarship should be for another discipline or group of disciplines.
- The process is cost-effective, in that faculty members up for review know what is required of them and faculty members serving on review committees can focus their attention on the quality of the product and process rather than on whether or not the activity should be considered scholarly. (p. 77)

Using these principles, colleges and universities can develop faculty reward structures that are consistent with their mission and more accurately reflect faculty work and institutional expectations for faculty performance.

Posttenure review. With the rising cost of higher education and increasing calls for accountability in colleges and universities, tenure has been targeted as an expensive and enigmatic practice, particularly at public higher education institutions. As the critique of tenure stiffened, institutions began to adopt posttenure review processes as a way to address the public's concern about the value and performance of tenured faculty members.

As is the case with other evaluation and reward systems, posttenure review criteria and objectives must be a realistic representation of an institution's mission. Posttenure reviews usually take place every five to seven years after a faculty member receives tenure. They can be either formative or summative, and they can require faculty peer review or be the sole responsibility of the department chair. Formative and summative reviews require presentation of an updated curriculum vitae; compilation of prior annual reviews;

evidence of student and peer evaluations of teaching; evidence of publications, research, and creative work; and a letter of evaluation from the chair of the primary academic unit (Alstete, 2000). A summative review typically includes a professional development plan that addresses any performance weaknesses identified during the review, while in a formative review a faculty development strategy would be voluntary. In the formative review process, however, the faculty member usually develops a five-year plan to define his or her future areas of productivity, growth, and improvement (Alstete; Licata & Morreale, 2002). These plans are revisited during subsequent reviews.

Licata and Morreale (2002) have investigated the consequences of implementing posttenure review processes at higher education institutions. They explored how posttenure reviews can enhance the importance of good teaching, define tenured faculty work and expectations, and redefine the types of appointments and work expectations for some senior faculty. Out of these enhancements should come continual improvement and the elimination of deadweight, development of individual faculty members as good academic citizens, and reinforcement of the institution's values and mission (Licata & Morreale).

Faculty Development

In line with calls for posttenure review, the professional growth and development of faculty members has become a pressing issue in the past several decades. Gappa et al. (2007) and O'Meara et al. (2009) have discussed the need to approach faculty growth and development individually, taking into account the faculty member's career stage and other issues specific to that person. For example, the needs of midcareer faculty members differ greatly from those of new faculty members (Austin, 2002; Baldwin, Dezure, Shaw, & Moretto, 2008; Gappa et al. 2007). Zahorski (2002) advocates a holistic approach to faculty development to achieve this individualization, including a variety of programs such as a resource center, mentoring and orientation programs, minigrants, sabbaticals, funding for annual conference attendance and participation, topical workshops, faculty exchange programs, newsletters, faculty development networks, phased retirement, awards programs, and individual counseling for faculty members.

Faculty and Civic Engagement

Expectations for faculty members to engage in development activities come from several sources, including rising calls for colleges and universities to be civically engaged. The old stereotype of solitary faculty members holed up in the ivory tower to engage in their individual research agendas is rapidly disappearing, particularly at institutions where the primary mission is teaching and civic engagement but also in some disciplinary units at research universities (O'Meara et al., 2009). Faculty members may need assistance, though, to learn how to participate in civic activities effectively.

In thinking about ways to foster faculty development and academic growth O'Meara et al. (2009) suggested the following:

> Identify ways to foster, in faculty, the desire and will to craft themselves as teachers, researchers, and partners in service and community engagement who have actively chosen—and continue actively to choose—the academic career as a way to lead their lives. (p. 19)

Enhancing Teaching and Learning Through Technology

Rapid changes in technology, computers, the Internet, and gaming are revolutionizing teaching and learning (Dede, 2004). Dede has written about changes in the learning style of the members of the Internet generation, who frequently are more independent learners, intellectually open-minded, innovative, curious, and self-reliant (p. 4). Other generational age groups are adopting this learning style as well. New technologies have resulted in the development of new media tools, such as groupware for virtual collaboration, asynchronous threaded discussion, multiuser virtual environments, video-conferencing, and mobile wireless devices, all of which have changed teaching and learning (p. 5).

As we discuss in chapter 14, numerous theories of learning have been developed over time. Dede (2004) distinguished among the behaviorist theory of learning, or presentational instruction; the cognitive theory of learning, with tutorials and guided learning by doing; and the situational theory of learning, which uses mentoring and apprenticeships in communities of practice (p. 12). Dede asserted that new technologies are having the most impact in these situational contexts. Technological innovations are allowing the creation of new types of student-faculty learning communities that are changing significantly the ways professors and students learn and grow.

Others have also written about these issues, advocating that faculty members should acquire skills and knowledge about teaching and learning in online and distance education environments (Howell, Saba, Lindsay, & Williams, 2004), while still others have argued that faculty members and graduate students can learn how to use new and evolving technologies by working collaboratively to design online courses and capitalize on the knowledge and skills of the Internet generation (Koehler, Mishra, Hershey, & Peruski, 2004).

Conclusion

The faculty is a college's or university's key to the promotion of the three themes of this book: being mission driven, adapting to the environment, and practicing democratic partnerships. To understand how faculty members fulfill their roles in their institutions, one needs to understand the different cultures professors operate in as they seek to fulfill their four roles of teaching, research, service, and boundary spanning.

The nature of faculty appointments is changing, as contingent faculty members now constitute the majority of the professoriate. The role of contingent faculty in institutional culture and governance has become a critical issue that will affect student learning outcomes. Demands for accountability, expectations for diversity, and the anticipated retirement of over half of the current faculty in the next decade are forcing institutions to be more adaptable to their environment and to develop faculty staffing plans for the future.

Meanwhile, an institution's faculty reward structure must be consistent with its mission. Faculty development programs need to assist professors in their civic work as well as in the classroom, where emerging technologies provide opportunities to improve teaching and learning. An individualized approach to faculty development should focus on the continuing acquisition of knowledge and skills that promote growth.

Notes

1. Private liberal arts colleges are not typically included in these studies because they are not hiring contingent faculty members to the extent that research and comprehensive institutions are.

2. For a discussion of the link between academic freedom and the First Amendment see Van Alstyne (2011).

References

Age Discrimination in Employment Act, 29 U.S.C. § 621 et seq. (1967).

Allen, H. L. (2000). Tenure: Why faculty, and the nation, need it. *NEA Higher Education Journal, 16,* 75–88.

Almanac of Higher Education. (2010). [Special issue]. *Chronicle of Education, 57*(1).

Alstete, J. W. (2000). Post-tenure faculty development: Building a system of faculty improvement and appreciation. *ASHE-ERIC Higher Education Report, 24*(4).

American Association of University Professors (n.d.). *1940 statement on principles of academic freedom and tenure.* Retrieved from http://www.aaup.org/AAUP/pub sres/policydocs/contents/1940statement.htm

American Council on Education. (2010). *Review of retirement literature.* Retrieved from http://www.acenet.edu/AM/Template.cfm?Section=faculty_career_flexibil it&Template=/CM/ContentDisplay.cfm&ContentID=41757

American Federation of Teachers. (2009). *American academic: The state of higher education workforce 1997 to 2007.* Retrieved from http://www.aft.org/pdfs/high ered/aa_highedworkforce0209.pdf

Americans With Disabilities Act, 42 U.S.C. § 12101 et seq. (1990).

Austin, A. E. (1994). Understanding and assessing faculty cultures and climates. *New Directions for Institutional Research, 1994*(84), 47–63. doi:10.1002/ir.37019948406

Austin, A. E. (2002). Preparing the next generation of faculty: Graduate school as socialization to the academic career. *The Journal of Higher Education, 73*(1), 94–122. doi:10.1353/jhe.2002.0001

Baldwin, R., Dezure, D., Shaw, A., & Moretto, K. (2008). Mapping the terrain of mid-career faculty at a research university: Implications for faculty and academic leaders. *Change: The Magazine of Higher Learning, 40*(5), 46–55. doi:10.3200/CHNG.40.5.46-55

Bellas, M. L., & Toutkoushian, R. K. (1999). Faculty time allocations and research productivity: Gender, race, and family effects. *The Review of Higher Education, 22*(4), 367–390.

Berberet, J. (2002). Nurturing an ethos of community engagement. *New Directions for Teaching and Learning, 90,* 91–100. doi:10.1002/tl.59

Biglan, A. (1973). The characteristics of subject matter in different academic areas. *Journal of Applied Psychology, 57,* 195–203. doi:10.1037/h0034699

Bowen, W. G., & Bok, D. (1998). *The shape of the river: Long-term consequences of considering race in college and university admissions.* Princeton, NJ: Princeton University Press.

Boyer, E. (1990). *Scholarship reconsidered: Priorities of the professoriate.* Princeton, NJ: Carnegie Foundation for the Advancement of Teaching.

Braskamp, L. (1994). *Assessing faculty work: Enhancing individual and institutional performance.* San Francisco, CA: Jossey-Bass.

Braxton, J., Luckey, W., & Holland, P. (2002). *Institutionalizing a broader view of scholarship through Boyer's Four Domains* (ASHE-ERIC Higher Education Report No. 29). San Francisco, CA: Jossey-Bass.

Breneman, D. (1997). *Alternatives to tenure for the next generation of academics* (Faculty Career and Employment for the 21st Century Working Paper No. 14). Washington, DC: American Association for Higher Education.

Calabrese, R. L., & Roberts, B. (2004). Self-interest and scholarly publication: The dilemma of researchers, reviewers, and editors. *International Journal of Educational Management, 18*(6), 335–341.

Chait, R. (1997, February 7). Thawing the cold war over tenure: Why academe needs more employment options. *The Chronicle of Higher Education, 43*(22), B4.

Civil Rights Restoration Act, U.S. P.L. 100-259 (1987).

Clark, B. R. (1987). *The academic life: Small worlds, different worlds.* Princeton, NJ: Carnegie Foundation for the Advancement of Teaching.

Clark, R. L. (2004). *Changing faculty demographics and the need for new policies.* Paper presented at the TIAA-CREF Institute Conference, New York, NY.

Colbeck, C. L. (1998). Merging in a seamless blend: How faculty integrate teaching and research. *The Journal of Higher Education, 69*(6), 647–671. doi:10.2307/2649212

Colbeck, C. L. (2002). Integration: Evaluating faculty work as a whole. *New Directions for Institutional Research, 114,* 43–52. doi:10.1002/ir.45

Dede, C. (2004). Planning for neomillennial learning styles. *Educause Quarterly, 28*(1), 7–12.

DelFattore, J. (2011). Defending academic freedom in the age of Garcetti. *Academe Online, 97*(1). Retrieved from http://www.aaup.org/AAUP/pubsres/academe/2011/JF/Feat/delf.htm

Diamond, R. M. (1993). Changing priorities and the faculty reward system. In R. M. Diamond (Ed.), *Recognizing faculty work: Reward systems for the year 2000* (pp. 5–12). San Francisco, CA: Jossey-Bass. doi:10.1002/he.36919938103

Diamond, R. M. (1995). *Preparing for promotion and tenure review: A faculty guide.* Bolton, MA: Anker.

Diamond, R. M. (1999). *Aligning faculty rewards with institutional mission: Statements, policies & guidelines.* Bolton, MA: Anker.

Diamond, R. M. (2002a). Curricula and courses: Administrative issues. In R. M. Diamond (Ed.), *Field guide to academic leadership* (pp. 135–156). San Francisco, CA: Jossey-Bass.

Diamond, R. M. (2002b). Defining scholarship for the twenty-first century. *New Directions for Teaching and Learning, 2002*(90), 73–79. doi:10.1002/tl.57

Diamond, R. M. (2002c). The mission-driven faculty reward system. In R. M. Diamond (Ed.), *Field guide to academic leadership* (pp. 271–291). San Francisco, CA: Jossey-Bass.

Diamond, R. M., & Adam, B. E. (Eds.). (1993). *Recognizing faculty work: Reward systems for the year 2000.* San Francisco, CA: Jossey-Bass.

Diamond, R. M., & Adam, B. E. (2004). Balancing institutional, disciplinary and faculty priorities with public and social needs: Defining scholarship for the 21st century. *Arts and Humanities in Higher Education, 3*(1), 29–40. doi:10.1177/1474022040396243

Ehrenberg, R. G., & Zhang, L. (2005a). The changing nature of faculty employment. In R. L. Clark & J. Ma (Eds.), *Recruitment, retention and retirement in higher education: Building and managing the faculty of the future* (pp. 32–52). Northampton, MA: Edward Elgar.

Ehrenberg, R. G., & Zhang, L. (2005b). Do tenured and tenure-track faculty matter? *Journal of Human Resources, 40*(3), 647–659.

Equal Employment Opportunity Act of 1972, 42 U.S.C.a. 2000e et seq.

Equal Pay Act, 29 U.S.C. 206(d) et seq. (1963).

Fairweather, J. S. (1996). *Faculty work and public trust: Restoring the value of teaching and public service in America.* Needham Heights, MA: Allyn & Bacon.

Fairweather, J. S. (2005). Beyond the rhetoric: Trends in the relative value of teaching and research in faculty salaries. *The Journal of Higher Education, 76*(4), 401–422. doi:10.1353/jhe.2005.0027

Finkel, S. K. (1994). Childbirth, tenure, and promotion for women faculty. *The Review of Higher Education, 17*(3), 259–270.

Finkin, M. W. (1998). Tenure and the entrepreneurial academy: A reply. *Sociological Perspectives, 41*(4), 729–746. doi:10.2307/40252281

Gappa, J. M. (2000). The new faculty majority: Somewhat satisfied but not eligible for tenure. *New Directions for Institutional Research, 105*, 77–86. doi:10.1002/ir.10507

Gappa, J. M., Austin, A. E., & Tice, A. G. (2007). *Rethinking faculty work: Higher education's strategic imperative.* San Francisco, CA: Wiley.

Gappa, J. M., & Leslie, D. W. (1993). *The invisible faculty.* San Francisco, CA: Jossey-Bass.

Garcetti v. Ceballos, 547 U.S. 410 (2006).

Green, R. (2008). Tenure and promotion decisions: The relative importance of teaching, scholarship, and service. *Journal of Social Work Education, 44*(2), 117–127. doi:10.5175/JSWE.2008.200700003

Hargens, L., & Long, J. (2002). Demographic inertia and women's representation among faculty in higher education. *The Journal of Higher Education, 73*(4), 494–518. doi:10.1353/jhe.2002.0037

Harper, E. P., Baldwin, R. G., Gansneder, B. G., & Chronister, J. L. (2001). Full-time women faculty off the tenure track: Profile and practice. *The Review of Higher Education, 24*(3), 237–258. doi:10.1353/rhe.2001.0003

Hendrickson, R. M. (1999). *The colleges, their constituencies and the courts* (2nd ed.). Dayton, OH: Education Law Association.

Howell, S. L., Saba, F., Lindsay, N. K., & Williams, P. B. (2004). Seven strategies for enabling faculty success in distance education. *The Internet and Higher Education, 7*(1), 33–49. doi:10.1016/j.iheduc.2003.11.005

Huber, M. T. (2002). Faculty evaluation and the development of academic careers. *New Directions for Institutional Research, 114*, 73–83. doi: 10.1002/ir.48

Jaeger, A. J., & Eagan, M. K. (2010). Examining retention and contingent faculty use in a state system of public higher education. *Educational Policy, 20*(10), 1–31. doi:10.1177/0895904810361723

Jeffries v. Harleston, 516 U.S. 862 (1994).

Johnsrud, L. K., & Des Jarlais, C. D. (1994). Barriers to tenure for women and minorities: The case of a university's faculty. *The Review of Higher Education, 17*(4), 335–353. doi:10.1080/0729436940130101

Jordon, S. M. (1994). What we have learned about faculty workload: The best evidence. In J. F. Wergan (Ed.), *Analyzing faculty workload* (pp. 15–24). San Francisco, CA: Jossey-Bass.

Kellogg Commission on the Future of State and Land-Grant Universities. (1999). *Returning to our roots: The engaged institution* (3rd report). Retrieved from http://www.aplu.org/NetCommunity/Document.Doc?id=183

Koehler, M. J., Mishra, P., Hershey, K., & Peruski, L. (2004). With a little help from your students: A new model for faculty development and online course design. *Journal of Technology and Teacher Education, 12*(1), 25–31.

Lane, J. E. (2005, November). *Politics of mission creep: A framework for understanding the phenomena.* Paper presented at the annual meeting of the Association for the Study of Higher Education, Philadelphia, PA.

Layzell, D. T. (1996). Faculty workload and productivity: Recurrent issues with new imperatives. *The Review of Higher Education, 19*(3), 267–282.

Leslie, D. W., & Gappa, J. M. (2002). Part-time faculty: Competent and committed. *New Directions for Community Colleges, 118*, 59–67. doi:10.1002/cc.64

Licata, C. M., & Morreale, J. C. (2002). *Post-tenure faculty review and renewal: Experienced voices.* Washington, DC: American Association for Higher Education.

Massey, W. F., & Zemsky, R. (1994). Faculty discretionary time: Departments and the "academic ratchet." *The Journal of Higher Education, 65*, 1–22.

Minnesota State Board for Community Colleges v. Knight, 465 U.S. 271 (1984).

National Center for Education Statistics. (2011). Career/technical education (CTE) statistics. Table P59. Retrieved from http://nces.ed.gov/surveys/ctes/tables/P59.asp

O'Meara, K. A. (2005). Encouraging multiple forms of scholarship in faculty reward systems: Does it make a difference? *Research in Higher Education, 46*(5), 479–510. doi:10.1007/s11162-005-3362-6

O'Meara, K. A., Terosky, A. T., & Neumann, A. (2009). Faculty careers and work lives: Professional growth perspectives. *ASHE Higher Education Report, 34*(3).

Palmer, J. C. (2002). Disciplinary variation in the work of full-time faculty members. *New Directions for Community Colleges, 2002*(118), 9–19. doi:10.1002/cc.59

Pascarella, E., & Terenzini, P. (2005). *How college affects students: A third decade of research* (Vol. 2). San Francisco, CA: Jossey-Bass.

Rice, R. E. (2002). Beyond scholarship reconsidered: Toward an enlarged vision of the scholarly work of faculty members. *New Directions for Teaching and Learning, 90*, 7–17. doi:10.1002/tl.51

Rehabilitation Act, 29 U.S.C. 701 et seq. (1973).

Schuster, J. H., & Finkelstein, M. J. (2006). *The American faculty: The restructuring of academic work and careers*. Baltimore, MD: Johns Hopkins University Press.

Shapiro, H. N. (2006). Promotion & tenure & the scholarship of teaching & learning. *Change: The Magazine of Higher Learning, 38*(2), 39–43.

Title IX of the Education Amendments, 20 U.S.C. 1681(a) (1972).

Title VI of the Civil Rights Act, 42 U.S.C. 2000d to 2000d-7 (1964).

Title VII of the Civil Rights Act, 42 U.S.C. 2000I et seq. (1964).

Toma, J. D. (2011). *Managing the entrepreneurial university: Legal issues and commercial realities*. New York, NY: Routledge.

Van Alstyne, W. (2011). Academic freedom and the first amendment in the Supreme Court of the United States: An unhurried historical review. *Law and Contemporary Problems, 53*(3), 79–154.

Waters v. Churchill, 511 U.S. 661 (1994).

Wilson, R. (2010). AAUP report blames colleges for gender inequity among professors. *The Chronicle of Higher Education, 53*(11), A11.

Zahorski, K. J. (2002). Nurturing scholarship through holistic faculty development: A synergistic approach. *New Directions for Teaching and Learning, 2002*(90), 29–37. doi:10.1002/tl.53

Zhang, L., & Ehrenberg, R. G. (2010). Faculty employment and R&D expenditures at research universities. *Economics of Education Review, 29*(3), 329–337. doi:10.1016/j.econedurev.2009.10.006

PART FIVE

IMPLEMENTATION OF THE ACADEMIC MISSION

The implementation of a college's or university's core academic mission requires the development and adaptation of undergraduate and graduate curricula, which are processes that necessitate an understanding of student development theory and of how students learn in the classroom and through cocurricular experiences. As a curriculum represents an institution's core academic mission, its design is essential for enhancing learning outcomes as well as for an institution's financial management, strategic planning, and assessment.

Chapter 14 explores how colleges and universities can employ student development theory to develop academic programs and cocurricular learning experiences. In particular, it focuses on the undergraduate curriculum in terms of general education requirements and major academic programs. Beyond classroom-based teaching and learning opportunities, the chapter addresses the role of the cocurriculum in student learning—an area that present research suggests augments learning and retention. To ensure that the curriculum and cocurriculum are parts of a coherent whole, we recommend approaching them through Lattuca and Stark's (2009) academic plan model. To enhance the student experience, academic leaders must collaborate with their institution's faculty and student affairs staff to develop effective curricular and cocurricular experiences.

Part of academic leaders' role in this process is to develop a cycle of strategic planning, budgeting, and assessment that advances the mission of the institution while adhering to the democratic traditions of the academy, which is the topic of chapter 15. Planning, budgeting, and assessment transcend a simple understanding of the budget process and how to maximize the impact of precious resources. Successful colleges and universities in the

21st century connect strategic planning, budgeting, and assessment to strengthening their academic mission. A significant aspect of this process is rigorous institutional research. Moreover, accountability requirements of the federal and state governments, accrediting bodies, and the public necessitate that academic leaders understand and use assessment techniques effectively, particularly in terms of how they relate to student learning outcomes.

Reference

Lattuca, L., & Stark, J. (2009). *Shaping the college curriculum*. San Francisco, CA: Jossey-Bass.

14

THE STUDENT EXPERIENCE

An extraordinary amount of research and writing has been dedicated to understanding how the curricular and cocurricular experiences of college students affect their intellectual, moral, social, and attitudinal development. Since the college student is often at the core of the work of academic leaders, it is important for faculty members and administrators to understand the characteristics of the students they are dealing with and the myriad ways collegiate experiences affect student development. This chapter explores how students change by attending college. It provides a general overview of the topic of student development and the transformation that occurs from the point of matriculation to graduation and beyond. This type of growth, along with academic achievement, is often discussed in the literature under the umbrella of student outcomes. Since a college education is intended as a developmental process, we examine the nature of that development and the role the curriculum and cocurriculum play.

Over the past several decades, the student body has become increasingly heterogeneous in terms of age, gender, ethnicity, religious association, and sexual identity. As such, it is not possible to provide one description of the modern college student. For this reason, we begin the chapter with a broad description of the composition of today's college students in the United States. The resulting diversity of individuals enriches the college experience, but it also makes it difficult to describe all the ways students are affected by that experience. Moreover, readers should be aware that the ways that new learning opportunities such as online and hybrid learning modalities affect college student development have not been fully explored by researchers. Therefore, much of the research included in this chapter is based on the more traditional four-year undergraduate student experience.

We begin with a discussion of the cultural, demographic, and experiential diversity of college students; a brief history of student development as a field of study; and an overview of various theories of student development and their relationship to the curriculum and the cocurriculum. We then offer a brief synthesis of the major themes that have emerged from decades of research on the impact of college on students in an effort to answer the fundamental question: Is college truly beneficial and worth the time, effort, and expense?

College Students in the 21st Century

Students attending college in the United States come from a wide variety of economic and social backgrounds. According to the National Center for Education Statistics (2011), more than 20 million students were enrolled in undergraduate and graduate degree-granting programs in 2009. Most of them were women (57%), attended full-time, and were over the age of 25 (62%). They were predominantly non-Hispanic White (62.3%), with White enrollments at nonprofit four-year institutions reaching nearly 70%; Whites held a small majority at for-profit institutions. Black students were the largest minority group in the U.S. student body, constituting 14% of all college students, although they represented more than a quarter (27%) of all enrollments at for-profit institutions. Nearly 20% of all college students were Hispanic, Asian/Pacific Islander, or American Indian/Alaskan Native.

If we look at national survey data of the 2011 class of first-time full-time students, a more varied picture emerges (Pryor, DeAngelo, Blake, Hurtado, & Tran, 2011). Seventy percent were White (non-Hispanic), while the percentage of Black/African American students was 12%; Asian students, 9.8%; and Mexican American/Chicano students, 7%. About half of the respondents self-reported being politically "middle-of-the-road" (p. 6), with a vast majority agreeing with such statements as "abortion should be legal," "global warming should be a federal priority," "a national health care plan is needed to cover everybody's medical costs," and "the chief benefit of a college education is that it increases one's earning power." Most respondents participated in social networks at least three hours every week, but fewer than half spent more than one hour a week reading for pleasure. Despite the economic downturn, they reported a fairly rosy financial picture. More than half (51%) reported that their parents earned at least $75,000 per year, and only 11.9% believed that being able to pay for their college education would be a major problem for them.

One of the challenges with trying to describe the 21st-century college student is that no one summary can paint a holistic picture. The data provided here offer snapshots and averages, but few college campuses represent or reflect these standard compositions. Many institutions are more or less diverse, or have student bodies that are more or less conservative. What is important for academic leaders to keep in mind is that the modern student body is likely to be different from the one they were a part of during their own collegiate experience.

The magnitude of these changes is illustrated by the work of Arnett (2000), which suggested that not just the average college student has been changing. Rather, the very stages of life that humans experience have been evolving in the last two decades. While representing a broader evolution, Arnett's observations have particular relevance for college administrators. Traditionally, the three stages of life have been understood to be childhood; adolescence, usually encompassing ages 13–18; and adulthood, which one often enters around the age of 18. Arnett, however, suggested there is a fourth life stage that could be called *emerging adulthood*. This stage may be increasingly common among young twentysomethings, particularly those who do not have children, do not live in their own house, are not involved in a significant long-term personal relationship, or do not make a sufficient income to be fully independent. Individuals who fall into this life stage, many of whom are college students or recent college graduates, tend to grapple with numerous challenges, including a tendency to move frequently and be unsettled in their career and relationships. In their late 20s career goals become more focused and they began to settle into more lasting relationships (Arnett, 2000, p. 471).

Not all students fit in this category, however. An increasing number of individuals, including veterans of the prolonged wars in Iraq and Afghanistan, are returning to school later in life. They may be married, have children, have a mortgage, or be supporting elderly parents. These individuals often perceive themselves as being in a very different stage of life from other students, need different types of support from their institution, and have different expectations for faculty and administrators. They tend to be more focused and goal driven, seeking to balance their course demands with their other responsibilities, resulting in little time for cocurricular experiences.

The composition of the college student population in the United States is incredibly complex. Academic leaders need to keep in mind that this complexity results in having to address a wide variety of developmental challenges and expectations. The notion of a new life stage, emerging adulthood, suggests different developmental needs for students than those of adolescents or young adults and involves a significant portion of students enrolled in higher education. We need to understand at which life stage students are regardless of whether they are adult learners, veterans, or pursuing a second career. Where students are in their various life stages helps to define their development needs and learning expectations in pursuit of higher education. The remainder of this chapter delves more deeply into issues of how the collegiate context affects the development of students.

The Purpose of Education

Conventional wisdom perpetuates the belief that the path to the American dream must pass through some level of higher education attainment. Census data lend credence to this belief, as individual indicators of economic success, such as earning potential and socioeconomic advancement, directly correlate to the amount of one's higher education. For example, Baum, Ma, and Payea (2010) reported that in 2008 the median income of full-time workers 25 and older with a high school degree was $33,800, while for comparable holders of associate's degrees the median income was $42,000, and for bachelor's degree holders it was $55,700 (p. 11). These findings suggest that a college education clearly enhances annual income. Apart from the improved economic prospects that often come from attending or completing college, it is commonly accepted that higher education confers upon individuals a variety of personal and social benefits that vastly enhance their quality of life and that of their family (Carnevale & Rose, 2012).

Although enormous individual and societal advantages are to be gained from higher education, the United States is witnessing a stagnation in the percentage of U.S. citizens with a college degree. For more than four decades, the proportion of the U.S. population with a two-year or four-year degree has remained constant at about 39% according to the Organisation for Economic Cooperation and Development (OECD, 2011). While the United States ranks first among industrialized nations in the number of adults ages 55–64 with a college degree, that ranking drops to 16th for those ages 25–34 (OECD). Meanwhile, a debate about the purpose, utility, and relative worth of a college education is growing in the United States and is gaining momentum for several reasons. A fragile economic environment precipitated by the Great Recession of 2008 and ever rising college costs are making higher education unaffordable for many. Moreover, the weak economy is raising questions about the relative value of a college education when job prospects upon graduation are contracting. The residential and degree requirements of today's traditional higher education institutions are also being questioned as students seek quicker options to complete degrees and access higher learning through more convenient—and untested—online modalities offered by emerging for-profit and traditional nonprofit institutions.

As a result of these trends, colleges and universities are experiencing heightened scrutiny of the measurable benefits to individual students. Essentially, the subject of student development centers on the purpose of college and its role in the broader society. Decades ago, Knefelkamp, Widick, and Parker (1978) posed four questions that helped frame the discussion concerning the theoretical knowledge base student development should be viewed from, and these questions remain relevant today.

1. Who is the college student in developmental terms?
2. How does development occur?
3. How does the college environment influence student development?
4. Toward what ends should development in college be directed?

Of course, multiple answers to each question are likely, but the questions help us focus on the important factors for considering issues of student development. As we discussed earlier, there is no one archetype of the contemporary college student, and the perceived purposes of education may vary based on an individual's situation and perspective. For example, the purpose of college may be viewed as purely utilitarian, or it may represent a mechanism for advancing human culture and intellectual values that have distinguished humankind throughout history. Increasingly, these opposing views are being debated as economic pressures raise questions over access, affordability, and the worth of the individual and societal benefits provided through higher education.

Murray (2008) highlighted this rising debate over the value of higher education in a controversial essay that reflected our society's growing disenchantment with the benefits of a college education. He argued that with the exception of engineering and some of the sciences, a "bachelor's degree tells an employer nothing except that the applicant has a certain amount of intellectual ability and perseverance" (p. 17). He proposed that the traditional bachelor's degree be replaced with a certification process in which students complete a rigorous course of study in a specific discipline. Murray's opinion centered on the belief that the primary role of higher education should be preparation for a specific job or career. As utilitarian as this perspective may be, one should also ask whether preparation for employment is the *only* reason one should seek learning beyond high school. It is this vocational education view that prompted Presidents George W. Bush and Barack Obama to propose federal programs to enhance associate's degree programs at community colleges (U.S. Department of Labor, 2005; White House, 2012). What other purposes exist for higher education, and what outcomes can and should be expected from the experience of attending college?

Menand (2011) explored the different purposes of higher education, including the various personal and social benefits associated with a college degree. He noted that in popular culture there are generally three theories why people go to college. Theory 1 states that education is meritocratic, a social stratifier that effectively sorts individuals based on their willingness and ability to demonstrate a range of competencies: "Society needs a mechanism for sorting out its more intelligent members from its less intelligent ones" (para. 6). Theory 2, the democratic approach, holds that education provides an enlightened citizenry reflective of the skills, attributes, and characteristics that distinguish humankind at its best: "College exposes future citizens to material that enlightens and empowers them, whatever careers they end up choosing" (para. 8). Theory 3 asserts that higher education should be vocationally oriented, specifically designed to train and equip the student with skills relevant to a job: Since "advanced economies demand specialized knowledge and skills, and since high school is aimed at the general learner, college is where people can be taught what they need in order to enter a vocation" (para. 33). Behind these three distinct theories rest fundamental questions on what constitutes higher education and what students should learn from it. Further questions exist regarding the cognitive and affective outcomes shown to result from acquiring a higher education, and whether those outcomes have proven beneficial and worthy of the time and expense of obtaining them.

Keller (2008) projected that U.S. higher education would be forced to transform itself and redefine its purposes in response to the knowledge economy. Specifically, he predicted that colleges and universities will have to reorient instruction from faculty-prescribed curricula to market-defined skills. A decade earlier, Gibbons (1998) predicted Keller's call for change:

> During the past twenty years, a new paradigm of the function of higher education in society has gradually emerged. Gone, it seems, is the high-mindedness of a von Humboldt or a Newman, with its pursuit of knowledge for its own sake. In their places has been put a view of higher education in which universities are meant to serve society, primarily by

supporting the economy and promoting the quality of life of its citizens. While it is true that universities still retain their role as the "conscience of society," the critical function of universities has been displaced in favour of a more pragmatic role in terms of the provision of qualified manpower and the production of knowledge. . . . The new paradigm is bringing in its train a new culture of accountability. . . . In all countries, developed or developing, the culture of accountability is going to become more and more firmly established . . . [and] relevance will be judged primarily in terms of outputs.

Perhaps it is on the topic of student development that this book's three central themes—a commitment to institutional mission, an ability to adapt to environmental change, and the creation and fostering of democratic partnerships—have the greatest significance. All we do as educators is directed toward achieving specific student outcomes, and these outcomes differ according to a host of variables that are institutionally and environmentally generated. For institutions that aspire to improve undergraduate instruction, understanding student development for all types of students is a prerequisite. "The question of how development occurs is of particular interest to educators, since understanding the process of development provides a way of understanding the steps or issues that may be involved in helping students achieve a given desired educational outcome" (King, 1994, p. 417). This chapter offers an introductory understanding of student development and the various outcomes it generates.

Historical Considerations

Education has long been a core component of U.S. society. Shortly after landing in Massachusetts, the Puritans founded Harvard College in 1636. Their primary motives focused on creating learned leaders for the community and their churches as well as ensuring that the cultural and intellectual traditions established by the Puritans in Europe were perpetuated in the New World. Centered in a culture unified by Protestant orthodoxy and situated in the hamlet of Cambridge, Harvard began as a community's effort to elevate learning and humanism as an intellectual expression of humanity's commitment to God.[1] Character development within the moral code of the church was particularly important. For the early colonists, education was intended as an instrument of societal and cultural preservation.

While various settlements established their own colleges with the hope of having the educational experience reflect their cultural heritage (e.g., Yale

College was founded by Congregationalists who settled Connecticut, and the College of William and Mary was heavily influenced by the Anglican church), the organizational models were remarkably similar. Hofstadter (1955) argued there were three common distinguishing features of early American higher education that differed significantly from earlier European models: private denominational sponsorship, an absence of professional faculties in separate and distinct disciplines, and lay governance where non-resident governors rather than teachers decided policy and institutional direction (p. 114). These characteristics perpetuated the practice of approaching educational purpose and student learning from a religiously partisan perspective, since the earliest colleges functioned as agents of their faith traditions, established to promote sectarian ideals of what society should be. The overt notion that colleges and their curricula existed for the sole purpose of individual student transformation was simply not considered in this context. Rather, colleges were viewed as sectarian instruments of societal, rather than personal, change.

This bias began to erode in the early 1800s with the eventual demise of the doctrinal moralism that characterized the early colonial colleges, and it was further weakened in the latter 19th century with the rise of the university and the attendant emergence of disciplines, especially in the sciences. This development led to the broadening of the knowledge base and the need to provide greater choice in curricular offerings, which contributed substantially to a more student-centered focus than had been evident in earlier centuries.

According to Strange (1994), as the behavioral sciences emerged in the late 19th and early 20th centuries, interest grew in the study of "thought, emotions and capacities" (p. 399) in a measurable fashion, and later the measurement of aptitude was added as new behavioral measurement instruments were devised. As attention to these areas expanded, concern for the holistic growth of the student began to appear, prompting questions about how the entire collegiate experience was contributing to students' cognitive and affective growth.

Generally, however, it was only in the past 50 years that student development became a formal area of study resulting in a new and vibrant profession. This new field became firmly entrenched in the culture and administration of higher education during the upheavals of the 1960s, as higher education faced enormous curricular and social challenges resulting from student demands for greater equality. Called student development or student affairs, this field was appropriately defined by Miller and Prince

(1976) as "the application of human development concepts in postsecondary settings so that everyone involved can master increasingly complex developmental tasks, achieve self-direction, and become interdependent" (p. 3).

Student development involves the study of change. It bears repeating that student development is of central importance to higher education because only through the knowledge and understanding of how students learn and develop as humans can institutions of higher learning create and operate academic environments that yield the type and degree of individual transformation desired. A college or university typically describes in its mission statement the type of change desired or the purpose of the education provided. Current accreditation practices, discussed in chapter 8, focus on ensuring that the articulated mission of an institution is being achieved in the outcomes of its students. Colleges and universities are increasingly required by accrediting and governing agencies to continually assess their academic programs and educational environment to defend empirically the fulfillment of their mission.

The study of student development is highly challenging because of the plethora of variables surrounding individual differences among students themselves. Innate and formative factors, coupled with infinite differences in the personal, family, environmental, and social experiences of students, render virtually useless any broad, concrete application of theoretical constructs that may provide guides to understanding this complex subject. Although each student brings to college a unique set of personal traits and backgrounds, the role of higher education is not to mold them all in similar fashion. As Bowen (1977) stated, higher education provides

> opportunities to which individual students will respond in different ways according to their talents, interests, and aspirations. College is intended to give its students a chance to work out their destiny in an environment that encourages certain ranges of outcomes, rather than specific preprogrammed outcomes. (p. 432)

The administrative foundation that supports these opportunities is based on the philosophical and practical considerations described next as we examine a selection of the theories and experiences upon which the concept of student development is based. We should note that as there is no one type of student, there is no single theory of student development that can guide all administrative decisions. Students develop at different rates and in different ways, and students attend college at all different life stages. Moreover, many theorists now believe that culture, ethnic identity, and sexual orientation also affect the developmental patterns of individuals (Pascarella & Terenzini, 2005). However, basic concepts can be derived from the corpus of these theories that can aid academic leaders in addressing issues relevant to student development.

Theories of Student Development

Despite a significant volume of literature devoted to the subject over the last half century, student development as a concept remains fluid, lacking a universal definition. The absence of agreement on a definition is largely attributable to the challenges inherent in understanding and empirically demonstrating how human development occurs. Summarizing this point, King (1994) noted that student development refers to the growth and change that occurs in a student as a result of a specific combination of cognitive and affective stimuli. Since cognitive, social, environmental, and personal attributes vary so widely and affect individuals so differently, the concept of *student development* cannot be easily defined. As King stated, "There is no one set of theories or theoretical assumptions that constitute THE student development knowledge base. In light of such inconsistencies, it is not surprising that the term means so many things" (p. 413).

It is beyond the scope of this introduction to the subject to enumerate the scores of theories and models of student development that exist in the literature. However, a number of useful summaries of this body of literature have been offered over the years, which we highlight here.

In synthesizing earlier theories of student development, Cross (1976) identified three broad approaches to the field. The humanistic approach views individual growth and change as conditional, based on the nature of the environment one is exposed to. Borrowing from the work of Abraham Maslow and Carl Rogers, humanists value efforts toward the creation of learning conditions that will lead to self-discovery. Personal growth is organic and natural. In contrast, according to the developmental approach, individual change is the result of passing through a series of hierarchical developmental stages. Employing personality theory and the work of theorists such as Jean Piaget and Erik Erikson, the developmental approach asserts that growth is a structured process, and education is the mechanism through which much of that process occurs. The multidimensional approach understands growth as different cognitive and affective dimensions that operate independently of one another. Fluid and pluralistic, this approach views growth and change as a function of developing individual competencies in a broad range of measures such as ego and emotional, ethical, moral, interpersonal, as well as intellectual development. Despite the diversity in these approaches, Cross asserted that all three schools would likely concur on these propositions:

> 1) Development is a lifelong process occurring in sequences and spurts rather than in linear or regular progression. 2) Development involves the total being, integrating cognitive and affective learning. 3) Development involves active internal direction rather than "adjustment" to culturally determined criteria. 4) Development is stimulated when the individual interacts with an appropriately challenging environment. 5) The phenomena of developmental growth can be submitted to scientific study. 6) Educational programs and interventions can be designed to make an impact on the rate, level, and direction of development. (p. 167)

In their landmark examination of the impact of college on students, Pascarella and Terenzini (2005) grouped the predominant theories and models of student development into two realms approximating the themes outlined by Cross (1976). They characterized the first group of theories as developmental or student-centered models, focusing on the intrapersonal changes that occur as part of human growth. The developmental perspective centers on theories of personality and psychological growth, including the formation of identity, the nature and process of change and how individuals ultimately derive meaning and understanding, typological factors that distinguish individuals from one another, and the role environment plays in effecting change within a specific individual (pp. 19–50). The second group of theories focuses on environmental factors and college impact, including how one's surroundings, and other individuals one comes into contact with, contribute to the change process. This set of theories and models includes such factors as the type of higher education institution one attends, the values and norms of the organization and its players, socioeconomic status, race, ethnicity, and age or level of maturity, among other variables. According to Pascarella and Terenzini (2005),

> The primary difference between the two families of theories lies in the relative degree of attention they give to *what* changes in college students versus *how* these changes come about. Whereas student-centered developmental models concentrate on the nature or content of student change, college impact models focus on the sources of change. (p. 19)

Evans, Forney, Guido, Patton, and Renn (2010) attributed college and university leaders' heightened attention to student developmental theories starting in the late 1960s to the expansion of higher education opportunities and the rise of student unrest. The individual, societal, and environmental challenges of that era stimulated a desire to understand students better, which resulted in the psychological and sociological communities' production of a plethora of new theoretical constructs relating to student development. These ideas borrowed heavily from existing theories of human development that emerged from studies conducted earlier in the 20th century on vocational training, as well as later studies on more individualistic and behavioral measures, resulting in a new focus in higher education "to address students' multidimensional needs rather than focusing exclusively on vocational preparation" (p. 8).

From their analysis, Evans et al. (2010) suggested that student development can be viewed through two types of models, both of which effectively link theory and practice: process models and procedural models. Subscribing to the belief that human change results from a linear progression through successive developmental stages, process models are theoretically based and call for the curricular structuring of the academic experience to support those human developmental steps toward a defined outcome. Procedural models, on the other hand, are more experientially based and prescribe specific interventions during a student's college career to effect change toward the desired learning outcome. Regardless of the conceptual framework one chooses to use to approach student development, learning and change should be a function of deliberate articulation of desired outcomes and the programmatic offerings that will best achieve them.

Using the four framing questions posed by Knefelkamp et al. (1978) at the beginning of this chapter, Strange (1994) suggested 14 propositions, each supported by developmental theories, to serve as the basis for future research and improved student developmental practices. These propositions provide a useful, if unproven, matrix for viewing the fluid and complex subject of student development:

Question 1: Who is the college student in developmental terms?

- Students differ in age-related developmental tasks that offer important agendas for "teachable moments" in their lives.
- Students differ in how they construct and interpret their experiences, and such differences offer important guides for structuring their education.

- Students differ in the styles with which they approach and resolve challenges of learning, growth and development, and such differences are important for understanding how and why students function in characteristic manners.
- Students differ in the resolution of tasks of individuation according to their gender, culture-ethnicity, and sexual orientation; such differences offer important contexts for understanding the challenges students face in their search for personal identity.

Question 2: How does development occur?

- Development occurs as individuals reach points of readiness and respond to timely and appropriate learning experiences.
- Development occurs as individuals respond to novel situations and tasks that challenge their current level or capacity.
- Development occurs as individuals evaluate a learning task to be sufficiently challenging to warrant change and sufficiently supportive to risk an unknown result.
- Development proceeds through qualitative and cyclical changes of increasing complexity.
- Development occurs as an interactive and dynamic process between persons and their environments.

Question 3: How does the college environment influence student development?

- Educational environments restrict and enable individuals by the form and function of their natural and synthetic physical characteristics.
- Educational environments exert a conforming influence through the collective, dominant characteristics of those who inhabit them.
- Educational environments, as purposeful and goal directed settings, enable or restrict behavior by how they are organized.
- The effects of educational environments are a function of how members perceive and evaluate them.

Question 4: Toward what ends should development in college be directed?

- Educational systems are embedded in various contexts of select values and assumptions that shape their expectations, processes, and outcomes. (pp. 402–410)

These propositions are supported through existing student development theories and are intended only as a framework for examining the issue of institutional outcomes. The key point is that the programs, policies, and practices at colleges and universities as they relate to student development must be grounded in a theoretical and practical understanding of how students learn, mature, and grow so that the institution is able to create specifically defined learning experiences that will yield desired developmental outcomes.

Student Development and the Curriculum

The college curriculum represents the formal mechanism that can shape student outcomes. The content of an institution's curriculum is a formal statement by its faculty, administration, and board of trustees of its educational values. Particularly important to this discussion is which academic content is viewed by the institution as central to what the student should know. Such content is generally considered part of a student's general education. Most general education requirements include some combination of courses that focus on writing, mathematics, science, social science, and the arts. The idea is to provide students with an advanced general knowledge of a range of topics and develop their critical thinking skills before they focus more deeply on a specific academic major.

It is a common misconception, however, that all colleges and universities provide the same type of general education. In fact, the type and focus of classes, the extent to which classes relate to each other (e.g., through clustering, coteaching, or living-learning communities), and the philosophy of the general education program can all vary markedly. For example, associate's degree programs tend to include fewer and more professionally oriented classes than their four-year counterparts because of their shorter time frame and more vocational orientation. Some baccalaureate institutions may require all students to take the same courses as a way of encouraging a common student experience, while large research institutions will often offer dozens of different courses students can choose from.

We begin by looking at general education, often referred to as the core curriculum, after which we turn to the cocurricular experiences of students. We then discuss the importance of creating an academic plan as a blueprint for the education each institution wishes to impart to its students.

General Education

Debate over the role of general education, that is, the prescribed curricular offerings thought to be essential to producing a learned graduate, has persisted throughout the history of U.S. higher education. As noted earlier, with the expansion of knowledge and the rise of student choice in selecting courses that occurred in the late 19th and early 20th centuries, proponents of the traditional general curriculum warned of the dilution of education in the hands of student choice and the more flexible curricular requirements that permitted it. Ardent defenders of general education argued for its reassertion as the central purpose of higher education based upon the first two of four philosophical themes identified by Levine (1979). The first theme was perennialism, whereby a general education provides universal truths that are perennial or everlasting and therefore serve as a foundation for the learned person. The second was essentialism, whose argument was that general education should be based upon a prescribed or essential body of knowledge. Redefinitions of general education emerged later in the post–Civil War period as universities developed concurrently with advances in the sciences. The two new philosophical themes to emerge were progressivism, which viewed general education as a preparation for one's life and was problem oriented rather than subject oriented, and reconstructionism, which held that general education should be progressive in applying life's experiences to changing or reconstructing society. To this day, these four philosophical themes continue to echo throughout the debate on the essential role of higher education in our society.

We noted earlier in this chapter that the curriculum has evolved substantially since the early 17th century in a manner that has reflected the values and societal developments of each successive century and generation of learners. One of the most prominent statements in defense of the idea of a common curriculum came from what is commonly referred to as the Yale Report of 1828 (Committee of the Corporation and the Academical Faculty, 1828), which acknowledged that the college curriculum "may, from time to time be made with advantage, to meet the varying demands of the community, to accommodate the course of instruction to the rapid advance of the country, in population, refinement, and opulence" (p. 5). However, in responding to increasing demands for moving the college curriculum toward a more vocational orientation, the report's authors emphasized:

> The two great points to be gained in intellectual culture, are the *discipline* and the *furniture* of the mind; expanding its powers, and storing it with knowledge. The former of these is, perhaps, the more important of the two. A commanding object, therefore, in a collegiate course, should be, to call into daily and vigorous exercise the faculties of the student. Those branches of study should be prescribed, and those modes of instruction

adopted, which are best calculated to teach the art of fixing the attention, directing the train of thought, analyzing a subject proposed for investigation; following, with accurate discrimination, the course of argument; balancing nicely the evidence presented to the judgment; awakening, elevating, and controlling the imagination; arranging, with skill, the treasures which memory gathers; rousing and guiding the powers of genius. All this is not to be effected by a light and hasty course of study; by reading a few books, hearing a few lectures, and spending some months at a literary institution. (p. 7)

The concept of a general education reflected a value to impart a uniform and broad knowledge base, which included such topics as the study of religious doctrine, an understanding of the world, knowledge of the classics and the foundations of human culture, a common understanding of the democratic principles society was based on, and other broad subjects, all of which together rendered a comprehensive understanding and appreciation of the competencies and capacities of humankind. This broad knowledge base and exposure to a variety of topics rooted in the humanities, arts, religion, culture, and science "liberated" the mind from parochialism and came to be referred to as the liberal arts. Against this backdrop emerged the broadening of disciplinary specialties and an expanded knowledge base in the late 19th century at institutions such as Johns Hopkins and Harvard, giving rise to free electives that provided students with latitude in determining which of the general education courses they could ultimately choose (Thelin, 2011).

Having to broaden what constituted general education effectively acknowledged the advancement of knowledge that was under way and the inevitability that not all subjects previously valued as central to higher learning could be accommodated in a student's limited academic schedule. By offering students choices in their general education program, they began to define which subjects were of personal interest or importance. This shift continued throughout the 20th century as new and more specialized fields and academic disciplines grew, rendering an even greater choice within the overall curriculum. This process culminated with the introduction of free electives that also served as general education requirements for graduation. The history of general education, therefore, involved three distinct phases of development—core requirements, distribution requirements, and free electives—which corresponded roughly with the growth of knowledge and the introduction of choice over the centuries.

The advent of student choice and broad elective offerings in the general education component of the curriculum yielded disagreement in the academic community over the relative value of general education's content.

This debate continues and is manifested in the vast array of curricula among colleges and universities and their interpretation of how, or even if, general education requirements should be offered. Individual colleges and universities periodically review and change their curricula, adjusting to changing perceptions of the relative educational or market value of given educational content. Levine (1979) noted a variety of concerns and criticisms about general education including:

- It is a good idea in theory, but it fails in practice.
- It is unpopular with students.
- The student clientele of U.S. colleges and universities is too heterogeneous to permit common general education programs.
- It is of little economic value to the student who is forced to study it.
- General education courses are weak in educational and philosophical integrity.
- General education is poorly timed (i.e., more appropriate to older adults). (pp. 21–26)

Such criticisms remain strong today and reflect changing values on what student learning outcomes should be. This issue is especially important for colleges and universities that place a special value on the liberal arts, focusing on certain core competencies and skills often minimized or absent from curricula that focus primarily or exclusively on vocational or career preparation. Efforts led by the Association of American Colleges and Universities (2008) to elevate the importance of the liberal arts in U.S. society have resulted in the identification and promotion of four essential learning outcomes: knowledge of human cultures and the physical and natural world, including the humanities and social, natural, and physical sciences; intellectual and practical skills that promote critical and creative thinking, strong written and oral communication, and teamwork and problem solving, among other skills; personal and social responsibility, such as civic knowledge and engagement, ethical reasoning, and the establishment of foundations and skills for lifelong learning; and integrative learning, which involves a synthesis and advanced accomplishment across general and specialized studies.

Juxtaposed against such efforts to reaffirm the value of a liberal arts education is the increasing attention being given to the mission of community colleges. These important institutions contribute substantially to furthering educational access to broader segments of society by virtue of their lower costs and more vocational focus. Another important aspect of many community colleges is the transfer function they provide (Lane, 2003). For some students, community colleges help prepare them for more advanced study at four-year institutions. In addition, community colleges have become increasingly used as a less expensive way for students to complete some of the course work for their baccalaureate requirements. There is also a reverse transfer phenomenon in which students who complete a baccalaureate degree then enroll in community college programs to obtain or update their technical skills (Townsend & Dever, 1999). Finally, such institutions contribute to the economic development of their regions, and especially in these challenging economic times it is apparent why the value of community colleges is being highlighted by President Barack Obama and other political leaders (U.S. Department of Labor, 2005; White House, 2012).

Liberal arts colleges' active defense of general education and a more broadly defined approach to education provide a counterbalance to a rising sense in the wider society and government that the principal role of higher education is to secure future employment, an increasingly loud mantra for students and parents who seek a more definitive return on investment for the ever more costly privilege of attending college. While no one would dispute the role that higher education plays in preparing individuals to be productive members of society in a variety of capacities, Bowen (1977) envisioned a future in which higher education could successfully integrate liberal and vocational values:

> The overriding purpose of higher education would change from that of preparing people to fill particular slots in the economy and of adding to the GNP to that of helping them to achieve personal fulfillment and of building a civilization compatible with the nature of human beings and the limitations of the environment. Vocational education would continue to be an essential function, but it would be combined in symbiotic relationship with liberal education. (p. 459)

That our society is still debating the nexus between liberal education and vocationalism reminds us of the challenges inherent in understanding and achieving the outcomes we seek when attempting to address more broadly the complex subject of student development.

The debate over what is to be included in a college's or university's curriculum will be forever with us as the definition of student development remains elusive. What is important, however, is that leaders of each institution must decide for themselves what outcomes their school seeks for its students given the organization's mission, and what should be contained in its curriculum in order to achieve them. In other words, institution administrators must be thoughtful in creating their academic offerings. Such thoughtfulness requires a blueprint for achieving prescribed outcomes for their students, a subject we now turn to.

The Academic Plan

Just as a budget represents a college's or university's managerial statement of its organizational priorities, a curriculum represents an institution's academic value statement. An institution's mission is best defined by the academic offerings developed and delivered by its faculty, supported by the cocurricular experiences provided by faculty and others in the professional staff. Lattuca and Stark (2009) conceptualized the curriculum as an "academic plan":

> The intention of any academic plan is to foster students' academic development, and a plan, therefore, should be designed with a given group of students and learning objectives in mind. This focus compels course and program planners to put students' educational needs, rather than subject matter, first. The term "plan" communicates in familiar terms the kind of informal development process recognized by a broad range of faculty members across academic fields. (p. 4)

The importance of faculty consensus and cooperation in devising an appropriate academic plan for a specific learning environment cannot be overstated. This process is complicated, however, because (as we have seen earlier) multiple theories of learning exist, as do multiple definitions of learning. Lattuca and Stark (2009) identified three broad traditions of learning—behavioral, cognitive, and sociocultural (pp. 154–157). Behaviorists define *learning* as that which can be observed and measured. Here, learning is indicated by a change in one's behavior. The cognitive approach to learning posits that learning is a function of acquisition and understanding of knowledge, irrespective of any behavioral change that can be observed as a result of gaining that knowledge. While behaviorists understand learning to be a response to environmental stimuli, those who subscribe to the cognitive approach focus on the internal processing of information and the development of memory. "Whereas behavioral theorists see the environment as shaping behavior, cognitive theorists view the individual as the locus of control in learning" (p. 155). The sociocultural perspective combines the first two perspectives in some ways; it recognizes the role of environment in shaping understanding as well as the importance of internal processing of that information into some form of understanding. However, the sociocultural tradition emphasizes the social context and interactional relationships that provide perspective and, thus, understanding.

Though many faculty members believe their role is to develop the cognitive (intellectual) abilities of students, they often neglect the importance of those aspects of learning that affect their students' attitudinal, personal, or vocational development. Lattuca and Stark (2009) warn, however, "Separating intellectual outcomes from others . . . is both artificial and counterproductive because intellectual development is inextricably linked to students' emotions and attitudes, that is, their affective development" (p. 153). Furthermore, a universally embraced definition of what constitutes human intelligence does not exist in the literature. Some have defined it as a combination of many capabilities, as noted in chapter 10, in reference to Gardner's (1983) theory of multiple intelligences. "One important conclusion drawn from research on intelligence is that, as behaviors become more contextualized, measures of general intelligence become less useful for predicting and explaining achievement" (Lattuca & Stark, 2009, p. 160). Learning strategies, therefore, should differ according to the circumstances in which learning takes place. Consequently, the academic plan must be tailored specifically to the environment where it will be applied and the outcomes it seeks. This theme was advanced over 40 years ago when Chickering (1969) noted that "differences in institutional objectives and internal consistency, size, curriculum, teaching and evaluation, residences, faculty and administration, friends and student culture make a difference to student development" (p. 157). The contextual variables of student development remain as true today as they have for generations.

Yet, for all students, one's ability to graduate is inexorably linked to one's determination to complete the requirements for a degree, which brings us to the all-important subject of student persistence.

Student Development and Persistence

One of the more pressing issues many institutions are now dealing with is how to retain their students after they have matriculated. In fact, since the 1980s, student persistence has been a topic of intense discussion and debate among academic leaders. The topic has lately garnered interest from policy makers increasingly concerned about issues of student debt and success, and the first-to-second-year retention rate is a factor used by *U.S.News & World Report*'s annual rankings of America's best colleges. However, the percentage of students who graduate from a four-year college within five years has remained around 50% for the past two decades, and the percentage of first-year students who return for their second year has decreased from 74.5% in 1988 to 72.3% in 2008 (American College Testing, 2008). Thus, despite decades of administrative attention, there has been very little impact on student persistence.

This lack of impact, though, is not because of a lack of knowledge. Student persistence is probably one of the most well-studied topics in higher education research. The early work of scholars such as Spady (1970), Tinto (1975, 1987), and Terenzini and Pascarella (1980) spurred the interest of an army of researchers. These scholars have identified a wide range of student background characteristics, precollege experiences, student behaviors, campus activities, and institutional policies, programs, and practices that can affect student outcomes (Kuh, Kinzie, Buckley, Bridges, & Hayek, 2006).

In reviewing the expansive literature on persistence, Reason (2009) devised a conceptual model that highlights the factors that may affect persistence at two-year and four-year institutions. In his model, Reason argued that a student's decision to persist or not is influenced by a combination of personal characteristics (e.g., traits; academic preparation; and the student's academic motivation, self-discipline, and self-confidence), organizational factors (e.g., institutional size, type, and selectivity), and individual student experiences in and outside the classroom (e.g., faculty interactions, engagement in student activities, and employment). Based on these factors, Reason argued:

> To fully and effectively address student persistence, any intervention must consider the local organizational context and the local student peer environment. Individual student's [*sic*] decisions about whether to persist are made within, and influenced by, these two proximal contexts. It seems clear that no effective interventions can be devised without consideration of them (p. 678).

While academic leaders cannot control all the factors that influence a student's decision to stay in school, certain programs have proven to have a positive influence in this regard. First, one of the most significant factors influencing student persistence is interaction with faculty members. Astin (1993) and Astin and Kent (1983) found that when students have meaningful interactions with faculty outside the classroom (e.g., working on research projects, assisting with a lecture, being a guest in the faculty member's house) there is a positive correlation with students' intellectual and social development in college. Some scholars have gone further in arguing that small classes and the use of full-time faculty members in teaching first-year-experience courses are important factors in students' persisting to the second year (Crissman Ishler & Upcraft, 2005). Second, orientation programs have been found to be an effective way to integrate students into the collegiate experience, an important factor for increasing student persistence (Braxton, McKinney, & Reynolds, 2006; Hossler, 2006). Third, early warning systems designed to identify potentially at-risk students, namely those with high numbers of Ds and Fs and withdrawals, and provide them with targeted additional academic support are an important intervention for keeping students from dropping out (Beck & Davidson, 2001; Reisberg, 1999).

However, there is often a large gap between knowing what factors affect student persistence and adapting the academic environment to influence students positively in this regard. A report from the College Board (2009) observed that despite the large number of studies on issues affecting persistence, no analysis has been made of the extent to which colleges and universities actually adapted to improve student persistence. The report, which summarized the first national study of how institutions are trying to address this issue, concluded with two primary observations. First, institutions were investing resources in such things as early warning systems to identify at-risk students, requiring students to meet with faculty advisers, and hiring retention activity coordinators. However, the allocated resources were minimal and often did not meet the needs of the students. For example, staff members responsible for retention efforts spent, on average, less than one third of their time on retention-related activities, and very few institutions actively encouraged faculty participation in advising first-year students. Second, there is a need for more empirical, institution-based information about efforts regarding persistence. Rarely are institutions actively engaged in tracking student persistence rates or the effects of different activities intended to encourage persistence. The report's author argued that for institutions to improve, they need to establish benchmarks to compare their results.

Because of the long-standing and growing interest in student persistence, academic leaders need to be aware of some of the ways student characteristics and institutional factors affect a student's decision to stay in college. Moreover, effective leaders should try to align their policies and practices to bolster student persistence. Faculty members, in their teaching and advising capacities, also play an important role in guiding students through the educational process, including redirecting students into more appropriate majors when interest or academic success in a chosen field of study diminishes. In addition, as Pascarella and Terenzini (2005) pointed out, student involvement in college life outside the classroom through such activities as athletics, clubs, student government, and other cocurricular opportunities can contribute substantially to measures of student satisfaction and, ultimately, their persistence to graduation. We now turn to a discussion of the importance of the cocurriculum.

Student Development and the Cocurriculum

The organizational structure of most colleges and universities assigns responsibility for the cognitive (intellectual) component of learning to academic leaders and the faculty and assigns the affective (behavioral) component to student affairs professionals. While the classroom-based academic process has been assumed to require expertise and understanding in such matters as curriculum, pedagogy, and assessment, the out-of-class experiential learning process has been understood to entail expertise in the affective realms of counseling, psychology, and human development. Cross (1976) viewed this dualistic approach to the higher education learning experience critically:

> At best, this division of labor represents an administrative convenience; at worst, it depicts an erroneous and even dangerous conception of education in which values and attitudes are considered affective education—as though human values were devoid of intellectual analysis—while the study of physics is considered cognitive education—as though the development of humane and compassionate use of scientific knowledge were irrelevant to its possessor. (p. 140)

Calls for greater integration of both developmental realms have been raised throughout the history of higher education, but to this day an underlying tension remains on our campuses between these perspectives.

As mentioned earlier, the curriculum of any college or university should be approached as an academic plan (Lattuca & Stark, 2009) developed by the institution's faculty to provide intellectual content designed to achieve predefined knowledge and skills outcomes. If we are truly to integrate the cognitive with the affective, however, the desired outcomes cannot be shaped exclusively by those charged with providing classroom experiences. Rather, they must be informed by the sociocultural dimension that corresponds to the behavioral and psychosocial growth that helps to shape students' total learning experience. Such learning is most effectively influenced by deliberately prescribed and optional experiences found in an institution's cocurricular programs. The nature and number of these cocurricular offerings vary considerably depending on the type of institution that offers them, as institutions that are nonresidential or primarily serve adult and working populations may have educational missions that tailor cocurricular activities to the needs of adults with significant life responsibilities and limitations on time.

We define the *cocurriculum* as a set of required and elective noncredit student experiences provided apart from, or in conjunction with, for-credit academic offerings for the purpose of producing specific student developmental outcomes. Such experiences can range from mandatory (e.g., first-year student orientation programs) to elective (e.g., intercollegiate sports, Greek life, student government, clubs, residence life, civic engagement). Cocurricular programs exist at institutions that serve traditional four-year undergraduate students as well as at community colleges. The greatest difference, however, rests in the *relative* investment made by these institutions in reflecting the overall importance such offerings hold for the institution's mission and the needs of its students. What encompasses the cocurriculum and how it is organized and supported is a significant determinant of the specific experiences of students during their college years. Nearly as much as academic offerings, the cocurriculum helps shape the environment and character of an institution and will serve an important role in the attraction, retention, and ultimately the development of its students.

Deliberately shaping the student experience involves not only campus programs but community activities as well. Efforts to instill a sense of civic and community responsibility in students contribute substantially to overall student growth when those activities introduce students to experiences that augment the learning occurring in the classroom while helping them apply classroom material to real-world situations. Linking student learning to community service also fosters town-gown relationships and a spirit of cooperation between the institution and the community that transcends the academic benefits. For these reasons, community engagement has become an important component of the curriculum and cocurriculum at so many institutions. (See chapter 7 for a full discussion.)

The literature on the effect cocurricular activities have on student development is replete with studies that establish their positive effect in producing individual change, but Pascarella and Terenzini (2005) noted that research studies on the impact of college on the cognitive aspects of individual change exceed those pertaining to the more affective realms of personal development: "The evidence supporting the net impact of postsecondary education on learning and cognition, moral reasoning, and career and economic returns is more extensive and consistent than the evidence concerning changes in attitudes, values, and psychosocial characteristics" (p. 579). This inconsistency in the literature suggests the challenges inherent in measuring individual change in the affective domains as a direct result of the experiences gained through attending college.

As Astin (1977) noted, assessing how students change because of their college experience is a highly complex undertaking, first requiring the identification of the relevant outcome variables and then determining how those outcomes are affected by college attendance (p. 11). The multitude of intervening variables—based on differences between and among students according to their backgrounds, levels of intelligence, values, predispositions, work ethic and so forth, not to mention the differences of each educational environment in which learning and personal growth occurs—makes the task of establishing causality difficult. This challenge accounts for the great diversity of research methodologies and constructs employed in student development scholarship. Moreover, it accounts for the limitations of much student development research whose findings often cannot be extrapolated to broader populations because of the enormous diversity of student experiences. Rather, interested people serving higher education must rely on those few ambitious and gifted scholars who sift through the mountain of empirical evidence accumulated on the broad subject of student development to synthesize the findings into either specific conclusions about the net effect of college or broad but defensible generalizations that appear to confirm that such direct impacts do occur.

Discussions of the cocurriculum tend to be biased toward the residential collegiate experience since the bulk of opportunities for student engagement are greater there than in nonresidential institutions. Research on the effect that living on campus has on student outcomes has demonstrated that living at college versus remaining at home increases artistic interest, liberalism, self-esteem, hedonistic tendencies, academic persistence, and higher achievement in extracurricular areas, but it reduces religiousness. Most notable of these findings is that resident students are more likely than their nonresident peers to express higher levels of satisfaction with their educational experience and have higher academic success (Astin, 1977, p. 220). In fact, Pascarella and

Terenzini (2005) concluded, based on a synthesis of research on intracollege effects on student development, that "living on campus was the single most consistent . . . determinant of the impact of college" (p. 603). Such findings hold enormous implications for the future of higher education as pedagogy and communications increasingly employ technology, especially in those academic settings where educational content is delivered exclusively online, and experiential opportunities for direct, personal, face-to-face, ongoing interaction between students and faculty or among student peers is either waning or nonexistent.

How the educational experience is structured determines the manner in which student growth occurs, and educational experiences are idiosyncratic to the mission and environment of each institution. College administrators are sensitive to the issue of "fit" between student and their institution, and research (see Pascarella & Terenzini, 2005) supports the assertion that most students will seek out those colleges that most closely reflect their interests, skills, and values. In similar fashion and as mentioned earlier, institutions will attempt to recruit those students whose personal and academic profiles most closely mirror the institution's educational values. According to Feldman and Newcomb (1976), college selection often involves a process of accentuation—matching and mirroring values and characteristics held by the student. Within these homogeneous settings, however, lie opportunities for growth and elucidation, a departure from the normative experiences of the individual. The paradox is that while it is important to have a good fit between institution and student, the goal is to bring about individual change and growth. Apart from the academic content a student is exposed to in the process of meeting degree requirements, structuring the cocurriculum effectively can bring about significant change. If one were to closely examine college and university budgets, it would illuminate the priorities and values institutions place in shaping the entire collegiate experience to meet a set of specified student outcomes in their academic and nonacademic offerings.

The College Experience and Student Change

We began this chapter with evidence that the percentage of the U.S. population completing a four-year college degree is significantly declining relative to the percentage completing such a degree in other major industrialized nations. Moreover, we are witnessing rising skepticism on the overall benefits of obtaining a higher education, especially in light of the growing costs to obtain a college degree. Valid arguments support the position that higher education is losing some credibility as a sure pathway to the American dream. Some even adopt a cynical view that higher education is merely a partitioning tool of the social elite to perpetuate the status quo rather than change society for the better:

> College is nothing more than an elaborate and expensive mechanism for employers to identify the people who were smarter and harder workers and had all the social advantages in the first place, and those people then get the higher paying jobs. Now that it's illegal to discriminate in employment by race, ethnicity, gender, religion, or sexual orientation, judging people by where and how much they went to school is just about the only acceptable form of prejudice left. (Kamenetz, 2010, p. 35)

Though critics of today's higher education enterprise have ample reason to judge its structure and process harshly because of its adherence to traditional cultures and practices and reluctance to adapt to new economic and pedagogical realities, the body of evidence surrounding how the college experience develops and changes students is consistent and unambiguous: The undergraduate experience changes one in significant ways that would not have occurred had one not attended college. Numerous successive and important works by Chickering (1969), Feldman and Newcomb (1969), Astin (1977), Bowen (1977), and Pascarella and Terenzini (1991, 2005), among others, have explored this subject in detail, and a broad review of their conclusions is unequivocal in asserting the developmental value the college experience can give an individual on a variety of cognitive and affective measures.

Two particularly important points emerge, however, when one examines the evidence surrounding this important and comprehensive body of literature. First, there is the nature of change itself. The normal process of human maturation will naturally produce individual change on a variety of measures apart from those experiences gained while enrolled in college. Any study of this complex subject, therefore, needs to control for intervening and normative variables so that the definitive effects of the cognitive or affective inputs resulting from the college experience itself will emerge. Second, the research constructs employed in many studies from which variables of student development have been measured must account for the enormous individual, environmental, and institutional variations that exist among the students studied, their personal backgrounds, the experiences they undergo, and the types and missions of the institutions they attend. Given these challenges, we must rely on conclusions that, although grounded in sound methodological practices, can be synthesized and viewed holistically in generalized summaries.

Another challenge of student development research is an apparent bias in the types of institutions from which the authors of many studies draw their conclusions. Traditional four-year institutions (regardless of size) dominated the earliest studies of student change, only to be augmented with two-year institutions in later decades as the role and importance of the community college has grown. Today, studies on the effects of college between institutional types can now be broadly analyzed because of the richness of data that has been obtained over the past 30 years. The more recent rise of proprietary institutions and the subsequent growth of new online modalities have not yet realized that depth of richness, though scientific and assessment efforts to understand how such experiences affect student development and outcomes are emerging.

Conclusion

Throughout this book, we discuss the importance of being mission driven, adaptive to environmental changes, and grounded on solid partnerships among stakeholders. These themes are particularly relevant when considering the student experience. It is widely acknowledged that the experiences of college students, inside and outside the classroom, contribute to their social, moral, and cognitive development. However, the actual experience of individual students will vary markedly among institutions, influenced by a combination of history, traditions, and mission. This last factor is probably the most important as academic leaders should be careful to ensure that the opportunities for students, in and out of the classroom, reflect the mission of the institution. However, academic leaders also need to be diligent in ensuring that previous decisions and legacies help, not hinder, the student experience. Therefore, they need to be able to adapt the college experience to changing demographics and the latest research on factors that influence student success.

We do not believe that all institutions should provide the same college experience—quite the contrary. The diversity of campus cultures is a strength of the U.S. higher education system. However, it is important to ensure that particular characteristics of any college experience support the success of students, particularly in light of the changing demographics of the students many institutions now serve. Finally, academic leaders should look for ways to become partners with students to support the college experience. Students can be an important source of information about the health and vitality of a college community and should be considered as one of the key stakeholders when developing partnerships.

In this overview of student development we are limited in our ability to discuss the vast findings of decades of research on the subject, so we highlight findings from the latest and most comprehensive review on this subject by Pascarella and Terenzini (2005). We have selected a few conclusions that may hold the greatest interest to students and professionals new to higher education administration or to laypeople serving in volunteer governance roles, the target audiences for this book. Commentary on certain findings is also offered when such findings support or refute accepted wisdom in the higher education community.

First, the notion of "four critical years" (Astin, 1977) is an apt description of the college experience, since research confirms that college produces measurable gains in cognitive and intellectual skills along with a wide array of change in affective dimensions such as moral, psychosocial, attitudinal, and values. College also yields positive changes in self-esteem and academic and social self-concept. Cognitive dimensions of student growth such as learning, career, and skills acquisition yielded more robust findings than affective changes such as attitudes and values.

Second, the impact of college lasts far beyond the college years themselves and contributes substantially to people's lives and the lives of their significant others, including their children's quality of life. This finding confirms the wise adage once conveyed from a parent to a child when the college-educated parent said, "The most important thing that separates you from poverty is my education." These findings are also confirmed in U.S. Census data. The median economic and social benefits to college graduates far outweigh those of individuals who do not possess postsecondary degrees. Evidence is also strong that those with a higher education tend to have healthier lifestyles and live longer.

Third, where one attends college has less of a net impact than the net effect of not attending college. According to Pascarella and Terenzini (2005), "The great majority of postsecondary institutions appear to have surprisingly similar net impacts on student growth, although the 'start' and 'end' points for students differ across different institutions" (p. 590). This finding is noteworthy for it debunks the myth that one necessarily benefits more from attending a more selective institution. Rather, "little consistent evidence suggested that college selectivity, prestige, or educational resources had any important net impact in such areas as learning, cognitive and intellectual development, the majority of psychosocial changes, the development of principled moral reasoning, or shifts in attitudes and values" (p. 593). Especially for those who may subscribe to academic elitist notions that institutional ranking is the only true arbiter of quality, these findings should prove revealing.

Fourth, institutional context has a substantial effect on student change. Academic environments with a scholarly emphasis stimulate learning growth. Such an emphasis can be found at any institutional type, not just at highly selective institutions. Also, a wide range of cognitive and affective growth occurs in environments that foster close student-faculty ties. The level of student learning is directly correlated to the nature of the classroom instruction, including the teaching skills of the instructor and the manner in which course material is structured and delivered.

Fifth, college impact is significantly determined by the level of involvement by the student in curricular and cocurricular activities. It is axiomatic that what one puts into his or her academic experience will contribute substantially to what one gets out of the experience.

Sixth, service-learning programs, covered in chapter 7, have been shown to have positive and lasting effects in helping students clarify their values and identities, improve their self-esteem, and enhance their sense of volunteerism and social justice during their lives beyond graduation.

In short, the value of college is irrefutable in positively affecting individual development and change. But is it worth it? In finding an answer to that question today, one can reflect on the thoughts of Bowen (1977) when he said:

> One may argue that whatever is being spent on higher education is a measure of its worth. Just as we might say that the nation's output of automobiles is worth what people individually and collectively are willing to pay for them, so one could argue that higher education is worth whatever people are willing to pay for it. That is to say, the total expenditure on higher education would not have been made unless the students and their families, the citizenry, the philanthropic donors collectively thought the returns justified the outlays. (p. 438)

As this chapter has demonstrated, those fortunate enough to gain access and admission to higher education will be making a personal investment that will reap lifelong dividends.

Note

1. A liberal arts education in Harvard's early years differs from the modern concept. According to Morison (1936), in a Harvard education at that time, "one can discern three elements: the 'Seven Liberal Arts' and 'Three Philosophies' as studied in the medieval universities; and the reading of *bonae litterae* or classical belles-lettres; and the study of the 'learned tongues'" (p. 29).

References

American College Testing. (2008). *2008 Retention/completion summary tables*. Retrieved from http://www.act.org/research/policymakers/pdf/retain_trends.pdf

Arnett, J. J. (2000). Emerging adulthood: A theory of development from late teens through the twenties. *American Psychologist, 55*, 469–480.

Association of American Colleges and Universities. (2008). *College learning for the new global century*. Retrieved from http://www.aacu.org/advocacy/leap/docu ments/GlobalCentury_ExecSum_final.pdf

Astin, A. W. (1977). *Four critical years: Effects of college on beliefs, attitudes, and knowledge*. San Francisco, CA: Jossey-Bass.

Astin, A. W. (1993). *What matters in college? Four critical years revisited*. San Francisco, CA: Jossey-Bass.

Astin, H., & Kent, L. (1983). Gender roles in transition: Research and policy implications for higher education. *The Journal of Higher Education, 54*(3), 309–324.

Baum, S., Ma, J., & Payea, K. (2010). *Education pays 2010: The benefits of higher education for individuals and society*. Retrieved from http://trends.collegeboard .org/downloads/Education_Pays_2010.pdf

Beck, H. P., & Davidson, W. D. (2001). Establishing an early warning system: Predicting low grades in college students from survey of academic orientations scores. *Research in Higher Education, 42*(6), 709–723.

Bowen, H. R. (1977). *Investment in learning*. San Francisco, CA: Jossey-Bass.

Braxton, J. M., McKinney, J., & Reynolds, P. (2006). Cataloging institutional efforts to understand and reduce college student departure. In E. P. St. John & M. Wilkerson (Eds.), *Reframing persistence research to improve academic success* (pp. 25–32). San Francisco, CA: Jossey-Bass.

Carnevale, A. P., & Rose, S. (2012). The convergence of postsecondary education and the labor market. In J. E. Lane & D. B. Johnstone (Eds.), *Colleges and universities as economic drivers*. Albany, NY: SUNY Press.

Chickering, A. (1969). *Education and identity*. San Francisco, CA: Jossey-Bass.

College Board. (2009). *How colleges organize themselves to increase student persistence: Four-year institutions*. Retrieved from http://professionals.collegeboard.com/prof download/college-retention.pdf

Committee of the Corporation and the Academical Faculty. (1828). *Reports on the course of instruction*. New Haven, CT: Hezekiah Howe.

Crissman Ishler, J. L., & Upcraft, M. L. (2004). The keys to first-year student persistence. In M. L. Upcraft, J. N. Gardner, & B. O. Barefoot (Eds.), *Challenging and supporting the first-year student: A handbook for improving the first year of college* (pp. 27–46). San Francisco, CA: Jossey-Bass.

Cross, K. (1976). *Accent on learning.* San Francisco, CA: Jossey-Bass.

Evans, N., Forney, D., Guido, F., Patton, L., & Renn, K. (2010). *Student development in college.* San Francisco, CA: Jossey-Bass.

Feldman, K., & Newcomb, T. (1969). *The impact of college on students.* San Francisco, CA: Jossey-Bass.

Gardner, H. (1983). *Frames of mind: The theory of multiple intelligences.* New York, NY: Basic Books.

Gibbons, M. (1998). *Higher education relevance in the twenty-first century.* Paper presented at the UNESCO World Conference on Higher Education, Paris, France.

Hofstadter, R. (1955). *Academic freedom in the age of the college.* New York, NY: Columbia University Press.

Hossler, D. (2006). Managing student retention: Is the glass half full, half empty, or simply empty? *College and University, 81*(2), 11–14.

Kamenetz, A. (2010). *DIY U: Edupunks, edupreneurs and the coming transformation of higher education.* White River Junction, VT: Chelsea Green.

Keller, G. (2008). *Higher education and the new society.* Baltimore, MD: Johns Hopkins University Press.

King, P. M. (1994). Theories of college student development: Sequences and consequences. *Journal of College Student Development, 35,* 413–421.

Knefelkamp, L., Widick, C., & Parker, C. A. (Eds.). (1978). *Applying new developmental findings.* San Francisco, CA: Jossey-Bass.

Kuh, G. D., Kinzie, J., Buckley, J. A., Bridges, B. K., & Hayek, J. C. (2006). *What matters to student success: A review of the literature.* Washington, DC: National Postsecondary Education Cooperative.

Lane, J. E. (2003). Studying community colleges and their students: Context and research issues. In M. C. Brown & J. E. Lane (Eds.), *Studying diverse students and institutions: Challenges and considerations* (pp. 51–68). San Francisco, CA: Jossey-Bass.

Lattuca, L., & Stark, J. (2009). *Shaping the college curriculum.* San Francisco, CA: Jossey-Bass.

Levine, A. (1979). *Handbook on undergraduate curriculum.* San Francisco, CA: Jossey-Bass.

Menand, L. (2011, June 6). Live and learn: Why we have college. *New Yorker.* Retrieved from http://www.newyorker.com/arts/critics/atlarge/2011/06/06/110606crat_atlarge_menand

Miller, T., & Prince, J. (1976). *The future of student affairs: A guide to student development for tomorrow's higher education.* San Francisco, CA: Jossey-Bass.

Morison, S. E. (1936). *Three centuries of Harvard: 1636–1936.* Cambridge, MA: Belknap Press.

Murray, C. (2008, August 13). For most people, college is a waste of time. *Wall Street Journal*, p. 17.

National Center for Education Statistics. (2011). *Digest of education statistics, 2010* (NCES 2011-015). Washington, DC: U.S. Department of Education.

Organisation for Economic Cooperation and Development. (2011). *Education at a glance: OECD indicators*. Retrieved from http://www.oecd.org/dataoecd/61/47/48630200.pdf

Pascarella, E., & Terenzini, P. (1991). *How college affects students: Findings and insights from twenty years of research*. San Francisco, CA: Jossey-Bass.

Pascarella, E., & Terenzini, P. (2005). *How college affects students: A third decade of research* (Vol. 2). San Francisco, CA: Jossey-Bass.

Pryor, J. H., DeAngelo, L., Blake, L. P., Hurtado, S., & Tran, S. (2011). *The American freshman: National norms fall 2011*. Retrieved from http://www.heri.ucla.edu/PDFs/pubs/TFS/Norms/Monographs/TheAmericanFreshman2011.pdf

Reason, R. (2009). An examination of persistence research through the lens of a comprehensive conceptual framework. *Journal of College Student Development, 50,* 659–682.

Reisberg, L. (1999). Colleges struggle to keep would-be dropouts enrolled. *The Chronicle of Higher Education, 46*(7), A54–A56.

Spady, W. G. (1970). Dropouts from higher education: An interdisciplinary review and synthesis. *Interchange, 1*(1), 64–85.

Strange, C. S. (1994). Student development: The evolution and status of an essential idea. *Journal of College Student Development, 35*(6), 587–598.

Terenzini, P. T., & Pascarella, E. T. (1980). Student/faculty relationships and freshman year educational outcomes: A further investigation. *Journal of College Student Personnel, 21*(6), 521–528.

Thelin, J. (2011). *A history of American higher education* (2nd ed.). Baltimore, MD: Johns Hopkins University Press.

Tinto, V. (1975). Dropout from higher education: A theoretical synthesis of recent research. *Review of Educational Research, 45,* 89–125.

Tinto, V. (1987). *Leaving college: Rethinking the causes and cures of student attrition*. Chicago, IL: University of Chicago Press.

Townsend, B. K., & Dever, J. T. (1999). What do we know about reverse transfer students? *New Directions for Community Colleges, 106,* 5–14. doi:10.1002/cc.10601

U.S. Department of Labor. (2005). *The president's community-based job training grants*. Retrieved from http://www.doleta.gov/business/pdf/community-based_job_training_grants.pdf

White House. (2012). *Building American skills through community colleges*. Retrieved from http://www.whitehouse.gov/issues/education/higher-education/building-american-skills-through-community-colleges

15

PLANNING, ASSESSMENT, AND BUDGETING

ormer U.S. president Dwight D. Eisenhower once stated, "I have always found that plans are useless, but planning is indispensable." In this observation, Eisenhower seems to have been suggesting that the act of planning is more useful than the plan that emerges from the process, and that any organization that seeks to maximize its potential should keep this advice in mind. Too often, people believe that the end result of planning is a written plan or another final document that clearly outlines an organization's future, whether it is a corporation seeking an advantage in the marketplace or a university seeking to fulfill its mission. A more meaningful way to think about the end result of planning is that it is a living document that necessitates continuing to scan, monitor, and act on ever-changing variables in the environment. This notion, that a continuous loop of assessment and feedback is part of a robust strategic planning process, is the best possible way to ensure that an institution is fulfilling its mission, making decisions based on its values, and being inclusive in its decision-making processes.

This continuous loop of strategic planning, environmental scanning, and change management can be traced to ancient military campaigns and the leaders who waged them. In fact, the word *strategic* comes from the Greek words for *army* and *leading*. Leading an army into battle requires significant planning and ongoing assessment of the situation. Leaders must first understand the assets and liabilities of their own organization and attempt to discover as much as they can in advance about their enemies' strengths and weaknesses. It is also important to understand other variables such as the topography of the land where the battle will take place; the condition of the troops; and, if possible, other factors such as weather conditions, supply lines, and the abilities of leaders in the field. Once a battle commences, any number of factors can influence the outcome, and history has shown that in most cases, the leaders who have been able to make adjustments in the middle of a battle often prevail, while those who stubbornly stick to their original plans are defeated.

The idea of preparing for a battle or war campaign is just one metaphor for strategic planning, but no matter what organization is involved, continuous assessment from the field about what is happening outside the organization and the ability to adjust to that information most often will decide the fate of an institution. The same is true for colleges and universities: Planning is useful and necessary, but the process of continuously assessing what is going on and adjusting plans accordingly is what really has the greatest potential to advance the institution.

National Priorities and Higher Education's Response

Post–World War II U.S. higher education functioned in a time of tremendous growth and expansion of resources. Changing demographics, growing national ambitions, and the vision of a better future for the United States drove the incredible growth in U.S. higher education from 1944 until the middle of the 1980s.

One of the major motivations for the passage of the Servicemen's Readjustment Act of 1944 (better known as the GI Bill) was the United States' recognition of the challenge of assimilating into the workforce all the soldiers coming home from World War II and the need for time to accommodate them when they returned. This adjustment process led to incredible growth in enrollments at colleges and universities across the country, which institutions often responded to by expanding their missions and capacities to serve larger populations of students. The post–World War II baby boom forecasted that the demand for higher education would continue, and individual institutions and state systems of higher education developed plans for the anticipated growth.

As the Cold War emerged, U.S. higher education was also asked to respond to other urgent issues. For example, when the Soviet Union launched the world's first satellite, Sputnik, in 1957, the U.S. response was to find new ways to prepare the next generation of citizens to be more competitive, especially in scientific fields. Among the strategies adopted by the U.S. government was the National Defense Education Act of 1958, which created federally subsidized loans for college students to finance their education as well as more funding for graduate fellowships and research.

The need to accommodate returning veterans, rapid growth in the number of college-age students, and new funding sources for education created a different paradigm for the leaders of U.S. colleges and universities. Prior to World War II, public resources for higher education were limited, and only a small percentage of the adult population attended college. Consequently, academic leaders were accustomed to incremental growth in enrollments and cautious expansion of academic offerings. They could not only afford but were encouraged to be gatekeepers who limited the luxury of a college education to a privileged minority. However, the postwar era was a time of relative abundance and increased demand that required academic leaders to respond to national priorities, build new facilities, and attract the best possible talent to teach students and conduct research.

Planning during a time of growth brings about its own set of demands and stresses on institutions of higher learning. During the postwar era a number of factors remained constant and facilitated planning: Government spending on education and research increased, national high school graduation rates grew, and demand for a college education rose dramatically. Given this relative steady state, or at least steady trajectory of growth, higher education leaders could plan accordingly.

In contrast, the 21st century has emerged as an era of numerous challenges, including increasing competition for shrinking state and federal education and research resources, an aging faculty population, and dropping high school graduation rates. Therefore, the competition for resources, faculty, and students has never been greater. During this time of scarcity and heightened competition, government officials, accrediting bodies, and the general public have begun to demand more accountability about how public dollars are being used and how institutions measure success. In this environment, institutions of higher learning need to leverage and optimize their limited resources, and those leaders who establish continuous processes of strategic planning, assessment, and institutional renewal will be better positioned for the future.

The Growing Need for Strategic Planning and Accountability

By the 1980s U.S. higher education faced a crisis. With increasing global competition, reduced government support, and tough economic times, colleges and universities were being asked to do more with less. During this period, the expectation for higher education to be more accountable for institutional results became paramount. One response to this demand was a push for colleges and universities to adopt established business practices such as strategic planning and zero-based budgeting, as well as to become more attuned to the needs of the workforce and research needs of U.S. businesses in an effort to boost the economy. There was also growing pressure for the creation of new accrediting bodies, including some that would be government sponsored, to impel higher education to meet these demands. These forces led existing accrediting organizations to introduce new accountability metrics and resulted in an expansion in measures by governing boards and state and federal agencies to hold higher education more accountable.

In his book *Academic Strategy: The Management Revolution in American Higher Education*, George Keller (1983) extolled the virtues of strategic planning and introduced a new generation of higher education leaders to the power of this idea. He proposed that "design was better than drift" (p. 118), and that it was time for U.S. colleges and universities to recognize that, while they had special traditions and different cultures, they were not immune to the influences of the external environment. During the troubling economic times of the early 1980s, Keller asserted, institutions needed to "pick up management's new tools and use them" (p. 118).

Keller (1983) went further to suggest that colleges and universities had to prepare for an uncertain future, be aggressive in their competitive strategies, be more nimble, and position themselves to take advantage of opportunities that came their way (p. 116). His basic premise was that U.S. higher education would benefit from greater planning, assessment, and environmental scanning, and that strategic planning methods would eventually become the sine qua non of higher education management, being accepted by educational leaders at all levels from boards of trustees and state governing organizations to presidents. However, the special culture and traditions of higher education—such as shared governance, academic freedom, and tenure—made the adoption of what were viewed as business practices sometimes difficult to implement. Over time, by engaging faculty in an inclusive process to create the best possible learning environment and assess its outcomes, colleges and universities have developed their own tools to navigate difficult times while answering increased calls for accountability.

It should not have been surprising that faculty and others in the academy would be unreceptive to new management techniques and practices. Faculty members and administrators resisted adoption of business practices in higher education for years (Birnbaum, 1988; Cohen & March, 1974). Most colleges and universities existed for decades, if not centuries, without adopting what are now considered standard business management practices. An incremental, conservative approach to change had worked well in the past, and higher education leaders widely believed these outside pressures would subside so they could return to their old ways. By the end of the first decade of the 21st century, however, most administrators and faculty members had accepted that the need to be accountable for institutional and student learning outcomes as well as other societal measurements was here to stay.

Academic leaders in the 21st century must recognize it is preferable to leverage their deep knowledge of their institution's mission and culture to plan strategically, develop their own assessment metrics, and be held responsible for those outcomes than for some external organization to impose more standardized and often artificial measurements of success across the board. This realization goes well beyond a simple understanding of the budget process and how to maximize the impact of precious resources. Rather, it involves the linkage among strategic planning, budgeting, and assessment and the recognition that this relationship is critical to strengthening and executing the academic mission of the institution.

A Sense of Purpose and a Deliberate Process

If a successful college or university is truly driven by a clear sense of purpose and a core set of values, an institution's strategic vision should answer basic questions such as what it will do—and, equally important, what it will not do—with its resources to accomplish its mission (Montgomery, 2008, p. 35). This principle applies not only to academic institutions but to all successful organizations. Montgomery averred that all organizations need to learn to change and adapt over time while fully recognizing the "fluid nature of competition" (p. 33). Holding too firmly to a particular strategy for realizing its mission may not be in the best interest of an organization in the long run. Rather, an "organic conception of strategy" (p. 37) should be sought. In other words, organizations might develop strategies that provide them with a competitive advantage, but no single strategy is likely to provide an organization with a distinctive advantage forever. The preferable goal is to ensure that an organization can add value over time, a goal that requires continuous scanning of the environment and making small and large adjustments to adapt to changes inside and outside the organization.

Collins (2001) found in his study of corporations that made the leap from good to great that there was no single "miracle moment" (p. 169) when these companies were transformed. Likewise, there was no real sense within the organizations that they were in the midst of radical change. Rather, he found in great companies a "quiet, deliberate process" (p. 169) of determining what steps needed to be taken to create a desirable future. This fluidity indicated that great organizations are always in the process of becoming better and maintain the discipline necessary to pay attention to what is happening around them, never fully resting on their accomplishments.

Collins (2001) also asserted that an organization's core values or fundamental reasons for being should drive its decisions, and when adapting to changes in the environment, all organizations need to preserve their core ideology (p. 198). In a monograph he wrote in 2005 about nonprofit organizations in the social sector, Collins stated, "Greatness, it turns out, is largely a matter of conscious choice, and discipline" (p. 31). Changing practices or strategies and setting ambitious goals are good methods for any organization when they are done deliberately, but Collins (2001, 2005) and Montgomery (2008) seem to suggest what distinguishes great organizations (for profit and nonprofit) is that, in the midst of such practices, their core sense of purpose remains constant.

Whether an organization is an international corporation or a small liberal arts college, the need to develop and maintain a robust planning process is paramount. All colleges and universities are required by regional and professional accrediting bodies to demonstrate that their mission is appropriate for an institution of higher learning and that they are living out that mission in meaningful ways. For example, the Middle States Commission on Higher Education (MSCHE, 2006) requires that an institution's mission "clearly define its purpose" and "indicates who the institution serves and what it intends to accomplish" (p. 1). Moreover, Middle States asks institutions to document ongoing assessment activities that lead to organizational renewal and demonstrate educational effectiveness. The Southern Association of Colleges and Schools Commission on Colleges (2010) requires every college or university in its membership to create a quality enhancement plan and demonstrate that all stakeholders are involved in the process of developing the plan. Key to the quality enhancement process is the identification of assessment measures and evidence of self-renewal.

Accrediting bodies are not the only organizations that require colleges and universities to provide a clear statement of purpose and produce evidence that appropriate assessment mechanisms are in place. Corporations, foundations, state governing boards, and federal agencies all require documentation and accountability for the resources they provide colleges and universities. With myriad demands for demonstrating a sense of purpose and establishing processes to assess institutional and student learning outcomes, institutions of higher education must develop deliberate planning and assessment processes involving all their major stakeholders. For most colleges and universities, however, the question remains regarding which processes will work best in light of their unique histories, missions, and cultures.

Developing an Appropriate Planning Model

Despite assumptions to the contrary, strategic planning and documentation of outcomes in their basic forms have been around for centuries. Even in the time of the colonial colleges, institutional leaders developed strategies to attract more resources and demonstrate they were good stewards of the funding they received. Lately, colleges and universities have established more formal processes to plan and document results, especially in anticipation of regional accreditation visits (usually every 5 to 10 years). Until the last quarter of the 20th century, few institutions had robust and continuous processes for planning and assessment, although regional accrediting bodies' and government agencies' expectations for accountability necessitated institutionalization of such processes by the first decade of the 21st century.

A key element of planning and assessment is serious thought on the part of academic leaders about the mission of their institution and what it means to fulfill it. Therefore, every college and university that embarks on a planning process should start by ensuring that its mission statement is appropriate to the institution and the institutional outcomes can be tied directly to that mission. For example, officials of a regional comprehensive state university with a reputation for undergraduate teaching must carefully consider how vigorously the institution will pursue graduate degree programs and faculty research.

While institutions may certainly expand their focus or core mission, it is challenging to do so. The process of affirming or expanding an institutional mission should not be taken lightly, and in the tradition of democratic participation in decision making in higher education, changes in mission require input from all affected stakeholders. Many colleges and universities have successfully navigated these conversations by developing a discernment process in which representatives from various constituencies gather to discuss and reflect on the mission of the institution and its relevance in moving forward.

For some institutions this process may require only a few meetings in which key stakeholders (e.g., board members, faculty members, administrators, alumni, and students) discuss the core values inherent in the mission and decide how best to chart a future course. For others (especially those with a larger or more complicated set of stakeholders), this discernment process may be more elaborate. For example, a state teachers college that wants to expand its mission to become more research focused may require greater input from elected state officials. A religiously affiliated institution that seeks to move in a more secular direction may require input from its sponsoring religious organization, or a single-sex college leaning toward educating men and women may need to collect input from graduates and benefactors before moving forward.

Regardless of institutional type, this process should model the best practices of shared governance if academic leaders want it to be supported as it progresses. In the end, leaders, particularly board members and the president, must either affirm the current mission or decide to change it to reflect an agreed-upon set of new or revised core values. Once the mission has been affirmed by the board, a continuous planning process can begin in earnest.

Widener University provides an example of engaging key stakeholders in a discussion about institutional mission. In 2003 Widener held a "visioning" summit on its main campus, which included board members, faculty members, administrators, students, community members, alumni, benefactors, and local elected officials to discuss what should be included in the university's mission and vision statements (Harris, 2011). The summit was one component of a two-year process to incorporate key constituents' feedback regarding the university's core values into a long-term plan that would chart the university's direction for the next decade. Based on the planning process and feedback from the summit, Widener's leaders developed a new mission statement that was later vetted by the entire university community and approved by the Widener board of trustees.

There are numerous ways for colleges and universities to plan for the future and collect evidence that they are achieving their mission. Chaffee (1985), for example, identified three models (linear, adaptive, and interpretive) as inherent in the vast literature about strategic planning (p. 431). First, the linear model of strategic planning identifies a sequence of events an organization will undertake to achieve a particular set of goals and objectives. According to Chaffee, this model requires an organization to be "tightly coupled" (p. 432) with a top-down approach to planning and a strong belief in leaders' control. In this approach, an organization may forecast future outcomes in the external environment, but the most important outcome is the accomplishment of the stated organizational goals. One of the drawbacks with this approach is that it does not take into consideration changes in the external environment during the implementation of the plan that may alter the success of achieving the stated goal.

Second, in the adaptive model of planning, organizational leaders view the external environment as ever-changing and recognize the need to constantly assess internal and external factors that may influence the outcome of a stated goal (Chaffee, 1985, p. 433). In an adaptive approach, organizational goals represent "a co-alignment of the organization with its environment" and a need for the organization to "change with" that environment (p. 434).

Third, the interpretive model assumes that reality is not objective and is interpreted differently by myriad players both internal and external to the organization (Chaffee, 1985, p. 436). Instead of dealing with the environment as something the organization can control or change with, the interpretive approach requires the organization's leaders to purposefully shape the attitudes of stakeholders toward the organization and its dealings with the outside world (p. 436).

Most successful college and university planning efforts incorporate elements of all three approaches. Certainly there needs to be some discipline in the approach and a clear sense of direction that will help people inside and outside an institution understand its desired outcomes and how it plans to achieve those goals. Leaders of successful organizations also realize, however, that the environment is neither static nor always malleable to the will of the institution. Moreover, changes in direction in response to environmental factors are frequently necessary. It is also important to understand that organizational leaders can and should play a significant role in interpreting the environment and conveying its meaning to the key institutional constituents (Chaffee, 1985, p. 437).

Much has been written about the best way to involve stakeholders in strategic planning and help them make sense of these processes. The options for planning are as diverse as the shared governance models across the country. Trainer (2004) identified what he called the top 10 planning tools for higher education, including more familiar approaches such as conducting SWOT (strengths, weaknesses, opportunities, and threats) analyses, TOWS (turning opportunities and weaknesses into strengths), and using SMART (specific, measurable, achievable, results oriented, and time bound) language for goals as well as less well-known approaches. For some institutions a specific, structured approach may work best, whereas for others a hybrid of several different approaches might be better.

If a college or university has not previously engaged in a comprehensive planning and assessment process, there are several key elements its leaders may wish to include when developing their own procedure. Morrison, Renfro, and Boucher (1984) described the strategic planning process as a merger between scanning the external environment and long-range planning and identified six critical stages: "environmental scanning, evaluation of issues, forecasting, goal setting, implementation and monitoring" (p. 5).

Although all planning processes are unique to the institution that employs them, most include the basic elements of scanning the internal and external environments, scenario planning, charting a course of action, implementing specific strategies, assessing desired outcomes, and continuously providing feedback for future decision making. In addition, a formal monitoring process is important to ensure that feedback is timely and that the correct data are being collected and used. This type of monitoring is often controlled by internal processes specifically designed to examine institutional effectiveness and student learning outcomes.

Whatever process an institution develops, the need to create a planning and assessment culture within a college or university is crucial. For this culture to succeed, appropriate resources must be allocated to the institutional entities that will be responsible for it. Several researchers have discovered that one of the key reasons a planning effort fails is the lack of dedicated resources and organizational structures to support it (Keller, 1983; Taylor & Schmidtlein, 1996).

No matter which specific process an institution selects, the best option for most colleges and universities is one that is highly inclusive, fits the institution's culture, provides the necessary evidence of achievement of outcomes, and is sustainable over time. In other words, the planning process should fit the current governance structure while minimizing undue or cumbersome requirements for implementation. For example, many institutions have found ways to incorporate planning and assessment directly into the work of existing administrative and faculty committees, and boards of trustees have restructured their meetings to focus more on accountability measurements, including assessing their own performance. There is also evidence to suggest that for an organizational planning effort to be sustainable over time, departmental and individual staff goals and performance evaluations need to be tied directly to the institution's strategic plan (Sullivan & Richardson, 2011).

Pennsylvania State University developed an annual planning model in 1983 that is still in use today. Two years after reorganizing its campus college system in 1999, Penn State enhanced its annual planning model by creating what it described as an integrated planning model for the entire university to "improve alignment, reduce redundancy and streamline processes" (Sandmeyer, Dooris, & Barlock, 2004, p. 91). This new integrated approach required more coordination across the Penn State system and necessitated university-wide coordination of data collection and assessment of that information. This process has helped the individual campuses in the Penn State system to use their resources more effectively as well as determine more quickly the financial ramifications of the decisions their administrators make. One of the reasons this approach has worked has been that Penn State did not scrap its long-term approach to planning. Rather, it worked within its established process to develop improved data collection methods and provide evidence that the university's goals and objectives were being met.

Another positive example of incorporating existing practices into a more comprehensive approach to institutional renewal was the process used by David Ward when he became chancellor of the University of Wisconsin, Madison in 1993. Ward, who had previously served as provost, helped create a planning document to meet the requirements set forth in the North Central Association reaccreditation process in 1989. That document, *Future Directions*, laid the foundation for future planning and was so successful in its implementation that it remained the basis for the next round of accreditation in 1999 (Paris, 2004). Instead of creating an entirely new planning model, Ward institutionalized the process used in the accreditation cycle so that there was little duplication of effort going forward. He saw the need to "infuse the plan throughout the organization" by making it part of the "routine of academic life" (p. 124). This stability was accomplished by identifying key people to champion priorities identified in the plan, requiring deans and administrators to report annual progress based on these priorities, and always basing university decisions on those priorities, even in the face of budget reductions (Paris).

Developing a Culture of Evidence: The Value of Assessment

What has emerged in the 21st century is the need to continuously plan and assess specific outcomes by developing what the Educational Testing Service has labeled "a culture of evidence" (Millett, Payne, Dwyer, Stickler, & Alexiou, 2007). The idea that an institution needs to create a culture of evidence is based on the premise that continuous cycles of assessing outcomes, analyzing data, and acting on that information will improve student learning and hold institutions more accountable for the outcomes they seek to achieve through their stated mission.

Collecting data and using it to inform the decision-making process of a college or university is at the heart of creating a culture of evidence. This type of assessment usually falls into two broad categories typically found in all accreditation processes: institutional assessment and student learning outcomes assessment (MSCHE, 2006). Institutional assessment asks a college or university to demonstrate it is carrying out its stated mission and goals, while student learning outcomes assessment is concerned with the competencies, knowledge, and skills individual students possess at certain critical junctures during their time in college (MSCHE, 2006, pp. x–xi). What is important to understand about these two elements is that no institution ever finishes assessing either aspect. What truly matters is a continuous improvement cycle in which data are perpetually collected; decisions to act on that data are made; and the process of scanning, planning, and implementing is reinitiated.

Unfortunately, too few colleges and universities have developed a culture of evidence that enhances student learning, leads to better teaching, and improves the functioning of departments across the institution. Most view assessment, particularly student learning outcomes assessment, as a requirement they must comply with when their department or university is seeking some form of accreditation or undergoing a review by another outside entity. This idea, that assessment is useful only to satisfy the needs of organizations and agencies outside the academy, has led to what Wergin (2003) described as an "outside-in" focus or "compliance mentality" with regard to assessment (p. 37). This attitude can inhibit the development of a deeper dialogue about what it means to reflect on student learning data and act on institutional findings to improve teaching and learning.

Two examples of institutions that have successfully developed a culture of evidence and a continuous improvement approach to student learning are Alverno College and the U.S. Air Force Academy (USAFA). Both institutions have devised ways to incorporate assessment of student learning outcomes into a meaningful dialogue about how their students need to be prepared for the future.

Alverno College, a Roman Catholic college for women located in Milwaukee, Wisconsin, has been a leader for decades in identifying specific learning outcomes for its students, assessing those outcomes, and making changes based on the data it has collected. This approach, called *abilities-based education*, has established Alverno as a model for assessing student learning and providing clear evidence that students are achieving desired outcomes. Although Alverno developed this reputation many years ago, it still receives recognition because of the continuous improvement process the college has integrated into the fabric of the institution. For example, whether an individual is asked to serve on the board of trustees or is hired to serve as a faculty member, he or she is introduced to this process. Several support mechanisms are in place to ensure that faculty members can successfully define appropriate student learning outcomes for their courses as well as strategies for assessing student success and that board members understand how these assessment measures are related to the mission and goals of the institution.

Since the inception of the USAFA, its curriculum has functioned based on the idea that a broad liberal education, coupled with professional training in specific disciplines such as engineering, important for every student. Over the first 50 years of its existence, the USAFA followed the pattern of most universities, focusing conversations about outcomes on the accumulation of credits toward a degree. In 1993, however, the conversation changed when the dean of the faculty introduced "educational outcomes" (Enger, Jones, & Born, 2010, p. 17) for liberal and professional studies, which was followed by the development of comparable outcomes for other aspects of cadet training.

In 2006 a team of faculty members from the USAFA attended a summer workshop sponsored by the Association of American Colleges and Universities, and using data they collected about USAFA graduates and their educational experiences, they decided to revamp their curriculum and develop a set of measurable core competencies for each cadet (Enger et al., 2010). Since the development of these competencies, the USAFA has been engaged in an ongoing process to determine the most effective practices regarding student learning outcomes, and mechanisms have been developed to ensure a continuous conversation about the competencies air force officers will need in the future. This example exemplifies how an ongoing conversation about student learning can bring about meaningful change in an institution. It is also important to note that the air force approach takes into account that the skills and competencies needed to be an air force officer are ever-changing, and therefore, the learning outcomes at the USAFA will need ongoing monitoring and adjustment.

The most frequent question asked about assessment concerns whose responsibility it is at a particular institution. The Association of Governing Boards of Universities and Colleges (AGB) (2011) statement on board responsibility asserted that fiscal accountability is not the sole responsibility of a board of trustees; rather, it is also tasked with assessment of academic quality. Unfortunately, as prepared as most board members are to assess the financial health of an organization, they often feel ill equipped to assess the quality of the educational and cocurricular experiences their institutions provide to students.

To help trustees feel more confident in their ability to understand and track academic progress, many institutions have developed dashboards or metrics, similar to those they use for fiscal concerns, for assessing academic matters. These metrics can include data on retention and graduation rates, students' passage rates on state or national professional licensing examinations, or comparative data on student learning outcomes or student community engagement as measured by national surveys such as the National Survey of Student Engagement. Once again, an institution's mission, its stated learning objectives, and its vision for the future will have an impact on which assessment tools are most appropriate for that institution.

Boards, however, must avoid dictating what should be taught in a specific course or classroom. Instead, their role is to determine how academic quality is to be measured and by whom. In an article published by the AGB, Allen (2007) makes the case that trustees might consider certain approaches to assessing educational outcomes such as asking faculty members to articulate clearly how certain learning goals are indicative of their institution's mission as well as how any collected data or evidence will be used to improve students' experiences.

Developing a culture of evidence and demonstrating outcomes can help an institution in myriad ways. For example, Allen and Durant (2009) documented how their work in bringing strategic planning, assessment, accreditation, and fund-raising into a seamless process informed their institution's fund-raising goals and improved the university's ability to attract resources during tough economic times. In addition, Saltmarsh and Gelmon's (2006) work on engaged departments suggests that academic departments that are able to demonstrate evidence that they are accomplishing learning outcomes in various engagement activities should be most effective in attracting resources.

Linking Planning and Assessment to Budgeting

In this book we have made the case that the creation of an institutional vision through a comprehensive planning process, coupled with the development of measurable outcomes to assess progress, can have a tremendous impact on the future of a college or university. As important as these steps are to the success of an institution of higher education, any long-term plan requires a realistic budgeting process that considers the institution's financial viability and the resources necessary to accomplish its stated goals.

Colleges and universities have prepared annual budgets since the founding of the colonial colleges. The act of projecting what it will cost to provide high-quality educational offerings and appropriate auxiliary programs to attract and retain students is part of every institution's annual plan of action. In recent years, the focus has shifted from a simple calculation of annual revenues and expenditures to more sophisticated long-term forecasting that requires accurate data collection and an ongoing environmental scanning process. These exercises can help an institution calculate more accurately what resources it will need over the long term to fulfill its mission.

One approach that has gained momentum at colleges and universities in recent years has been scenario planning, which includes a 360-degree scan of an institution's internal and external environments and focuses on any signals that may forecast a trend that could affect the institution negatively or positively. The data and information collected during any environmental scanning exercise are used to create a set of scenarios of how a trend may play out in the long term, discerning its impact—with a special focus on financial impact—at the macro- and microlevels. Morrison and Wilson (1997) described scenarios as "stories of possible futures that the institution might encounter" (p. 7). Some of the issues in a scenario could include economic, environmental, political, social, or technological elements.

In its simplest form, scenario planning has always been part of the annual budgeting process at colleges and universities. All institutions plan the next year's budget by considering components such as projected enrollment, endowment returns, and predicted fund-raising success. True scenario planning goes a step further by projecting, over a longer period of time, such elements as the long-term demand for academic programs, state and federal funding, and potential changes to philanthropic trends (depending on economic prosperity or decline). Other scenarios might include more global issues such as environmental disasters or the impact of social media on breaking down barriers between cultures.

Given all of these possible outcomes, many institutions have developed processes for multiple constituencies to provide feedback about the likelihood of certain scenarios occurring as well as possible ways the college or university might respond, in light of its mission and vision for the future. The inclusion of diverse stakeholders provides different perspectives and can serve as an opportunity to educate people on how certain events can affect the organization and its financial health.

Once a course is charted, scenarios have been analyzed, and the costs of reaching desired outcomes have been determined, an institution should project a budget of three to five years, including a detailed annual budget. Determining what should be included in these budgets is one of the most important elements of successful planning and is often the determining factor on whether an organization achieves its goals in the long run.

Much has been written over the years about the failure of planning initiatives because of a lack of funding or an institution's inability to reallocate resources to support priorities identified in the strategic plan. In his analysis of great companies, Collins (2001) found that those organizations had the discipline to "stop doing" (p. 140) through what he described as unique budgeting processes. To stop doing something means that a company chooses to move in a completely new strategic direction, and to fund that effort, its leaders may decide to drop an existing business line completely. Of course, higher education, with its shared governance tradition and often limited agility for eliminating a department or program, needs to incorporate a more democratic process to implement a new strategic vision.

One process that has worked for many institutions is an annual budgeting and planning summit involving the administration, faculty, and staff, who determine the priorities for the following year as well as longer-term funding for initiatives identified in the strategic plan. A particular benefit of this approach is that if stakeholders are meaningfully involved in their institution's visioning and planning processes, it is more likely that a proposal to reallocate resources from one area to fund new priorities will be supported by a majority of constituents.

Conclusion

Regardless of the strategy used by an institution to plan for and gain consensus on budget priorities, if a college or university lacks the discipline to require that every new budgetary request demonstrate how it advances the institutional mission and strategic goals, it is unlikely that its strategic plan will be successful in the long run. Moreover, although planning is essential, if an institution's results are not funded, future efforts to gain support for strategic planning are doomed to fail. Successful boards, presidents, and academic leaders in the 21st century must understand that all three elements—

planning, assessment, and budgeting—are inextricably bound and that institutional health and prosperity, not to mention accreditation, are all by-products of that union.

References

Allen, J. (2007). Ask the right questions about student assessment. *Trusteeship, 15*(3), 14–18.

Allen, J., & Durant, L. S. (2009). Better together: Widener University marries academic assessment and the reaccreditation process to strengthen its fund raising. *Currents, 35*(7), 44–45.

Association of Governing Boards of Universities and Colleges. (2011). *AGB statement on board responsibility for the oversight of educational quality*. Retrieved from http://agb.org/sites/agb.org/files/u3/AGB_Boards_and_Ed_Quality.pdf

Birnbaum, R. (1988). *How colleges work: The cybernetics of academic organization and leadership*. San Francisco, CA: Jossey-Bass.

Chaffee, E. E. (1985). Three models of strategy. *Academy of Management Review, 10*(1), 89–98.

Cohen, M. D., & March, J. G. (1974). *Leadership and ambiguity: The American college president*. New York, NY: McGraw-Hill.

Collins, J. (2001). *Good to great: Why some companies make the leap . . . and others don't*. New York, NY: HarperCollins.

Collins, J. (2005). *Good to great and the social sectors: A monograph to accompany good to great*. Boulder, CO: HarperCollins.

Enger, R. C., Jones, S. K., & Born, D. H. (2010). Commitment to liberal education at the United States Air Force Academy. *Liberal Education, 96*(2), 14–21.

Harris, J. T. (2011). How Widener developed a culture of civic engagement and fulfilled its promise as a leading metropolitan university. In M. W. Ledoux, S. C. Wilhite, & P. Silver (Eds.), *Civic engagement and service learning in a metropolitan university: Multiple approaches and perspectives* (pp. 1–12). New York, NY: Nova Science.

Keller, G. (1983). *Academic strategy: The management revolution in American higher education*. Baltimore, MD: Johns Hopkins University Press.

Middle States Commission on Higher Education. (2006). *Characteristics of excellence in higher education: Eligibility requirements and standards for accreditation*. Retrieved from http://www.msche.org/publications/CHX06060320124919.pdf

Millett, C. M., Payne, D. G., Dwyer, C. A., Stickler, L. M., & Alexiou, J. J. (2007). *A culture of evidence: An evidence-centered approach to accountability for student learning outcomes*. Retrieved from Educational Testing Service website: http://www.ets.org/Media/Education_Topics/pdf/COEIII_report.pdf

Montgomery, C. A. (2008). Putting leadership back into strategy. *Harvard Business Review, 86*(1), 54–60.

Morrison, J. L., Renfro, W. L., & Boucher, W. I. (1984). *Futures research and the strategic planning process: Implications for higher education* (ASHE-ERIC Higher Education Research Report No. 9). Retrieved from HORIZON website: http://horizon.unc.edu/projects/seminars/futuresresearch/

Morrison, J. L., & Wilson, I. (1997). Analyzing environments and developing scenarios in uncertain times. In M. W. Peterson, D. D. Dill, L. Mets, & Associates (Eds.), *Planning and management for a changing environment: A handbook on redesigning postsecondary institutions.* San Francisco, CA: Jossey-Bass. Retrieved from HORIZON website: http://horizon.unc.edu/courses/papers/JBChapter.html

National Defense Education Act of 1958 (P.L. 85-864, 72 Stat. 1580).

Paris, K. A. (2004). Moving the strategic plan off the shelf and into action at the University of Wisconsin–Madison. *Successful Strategic Planning: New Directions for Institutional Research, 123,* 121–128.

Saltmarsh, J., & Gelmon, S. (2006). Characteristics of an engaged department: Design and assessment. In K. Kecskes (Ed.), *Engaging departments: Moving faculty culture from private to public, individual to collective focus for the common good* (pp. 27–44). Bolton, MA: Anker.

Sandmeyer, L. E., Dooris, M. J., & Barlock, R. W. (2004). Integrated planning for enrollment, facilities, budget and staffing: Penn State University. *Successful Strategic Planning: New Directions for Institutional Research, 123,* 89–96.

Servicemen's Readjustment Act of 1944 (P.L. 78-346, 58 Stat. 284m).

Southern Association of Colleges and Schools Commission on Colleges. (2010). *The principles of accreditation: Foundations for quality enhancement.* Retrieved from http://www.sacscoc.org/pdf/2010principlesofacreditation.pdf

Sullivan, T. M., & Richardson, E. C. (2011). Living the plan: Strategic planning aligned with practice and assessment. *Journal of Continuing Higher Education, 59*(1), 2–9. doi:10.1080/07377363.2011.544975

Taylor, A. L., & Schmidtlein, F. A. (1996). *Issues posed by graduate research universities' change environment and their planning responses: Final technical report on National Science Foundation project: Strategic planning's role in establishing university research policies and plans* (Project No. RST9320680). Washington, DC: National Science Foundation Project.

Trainer, J. F. (2004). Models and tools for strategic planning. *Successful Strategic Planning: New Directions for Institutional Research, 123,* 129–138.

Wergin, J. F. (2003). *Departments that work: Building and sustaining cultures of excellence in academic programs.* Boston, MA: Anker.

ABOUT THE AUTHORS

Robert M. Hendrickson is professor of education in higher education and senior scientist and interim director of the Center for the Study of Higher Education at Penn State. His research and teaching interests include legal issues, organizational theory, administration and governance, and faculty employment issues. He has published a number of articles, monographs, and books. From 2001 to 2007 he served as associate dean for graduate programs, research, and faculty development in the College of Education. During his tenure as associate dean, six graduate programs were ranked in the top 10 in the *U.S.News & World Report* rankings, and research awards grew from $4 million in 2001 to $18 million in 2007. His prior positions include head of the Department of Education Policy Studies for eight years and professor in charge of the Higher Education Program for nine years. Hendrickson has directed a number of doctoral dissertations, several of which have won outstanding dissertation awards. His former students serve in faculty or administrative positions in the United States and foreign countries and several are presidents of colleges and universities.

Jason E. Lane is director of education policy studies at the Nelson A. Rockefeller Institute of Government, the public policy think tank of the State University of New York. He is also an associate professor of educational administration and policy studies and a senior researcher with the Institute for Global Education Policy Studies at the University at Albany, SUNY, where he codirects the Cross-Border Education Research Team. His research interests include government planning and policy, economic development, organizational leadership, and the role of higher education in international relations. Recently these interests have focused on investigating the organizational tensions associated with the cross-border provision of higher education, particularly the development of multinational universities. Lane has written more than 30 articles, book chapters, and policy reports and published five books, including *Organization and Governance in Higher Education*, with M. C. Brown and Eboni Zamani-Gallaher (San Francisco, CA: Pearson, 2010); *Multinational Colleges and Universities*, with Kevin Kinser

(San Francisco, CA: Jossey-Bass, 2011); and *Colleges and Universities as Economic Drivers*, with D. Bruce Johnstone (Albany, NY: SUNY Press, 2012). He is a consultant to educational, governmental, and nongovernmental organizations domestically and in Asia, Europe, South America, and the Middle East. He serves on the board of the Comparative and International Education Society and the Council for International Higher Education and is the publisher of globalhighered.org, a clearinghouse of scholarship and news about the movement of educational institutions across international borders.

James T. Harris III is president and professor of education at Widener University. Under his leadership, Widener has been recognized by *The Chronicle of Higher Education* as a "Best College to Work For," and *Newsweek* ranked Widener in the top 10 nationally for community service. Prior to his appointment at Widener, Harris served as president of Defiance College. Harris has served on the national boards of Campus Compact, the National Collegiate Athletic Association, the National Association of Independent Colleges and Universities, the Coalition of Urban and Metropolitan Universities, and the Council for Advancement and Support of Education. He has earned numerous awards, including being named as one of the top 50 character-building presidents in America by the Templeton Foundation, and the Chief Executive Leadership Award from the Council for Advancement and Support of Education. Harris has published over 20 academic articles and book chapters and has been a faculty member in the Harvard University Management Development Program for over a decade. He earned degrees from the University of Toledo, Edinboro University of Pennsylvania, and Pennsylvania State University.

Richard H. Dorman is the 14th president of Westminster College in Pennsylvania, a coeducational national liberal arts institution that has been ranked first in the nation by Forbes.com as the "Best College for Women in Science, Technology, Engineering, and Math." He has served in various senior administrative capacities, including vice president for institutional advancement at Otterbein University and assistant vice president at the University of Louisville, where he oversaw all development operations for the Health Sciences Center. Prior to that, Dorman was associate executive director for alumni relations at the Penn State Alumni Association. During his tenure, the association received the Council for Advancement and Support of Education Grand Gold Medal as the best alumni association in America for an unprecedented three successive years. His research has centered on role conflict and role ambiguity of lay governing boards, and he has served as a frequent speaker and consultant on institutional governance and alumni affairs. He holds a bachelor's of music degree from Susquehanna University, and a master's degree in counselor education in student personnel services and a doctorate in higher education administration, both from Penn State.

Stanley O. Ikenberry, author of the foreword, served as president of the University of Illinois from 1979 through 1996. From 1996 through 2001 he led the American Council on Education. From 2001 to 2010 he was a professor of higher education at the University of Illinois. In 2010 he served as Interim President of the University of Illinois. He has served as Chairman of the Board of Trustees of the Carnegie Foundation for the Advancement of Teaching and as a member of the boards of the National Association of State Universities and Land Grant Colleges, the Association of American Universities, and The American Council on Education. Dr. Ikenberry is currently a senior scientist and professor of higher education in the Center for the Study of Higher Education at Penn State University and a principal investigator for the National Institute for Learning Outcomes Assessment (NILOA).

INDEX